MAGILL'S
SURVEY
OF
AMERICAN
LITERATURE

MAGILL'S SURVEY OF AMERICAN LITERATURE

Volume 7

Ai–Levertov

Edited by
FRANK N. MAGILL

Marshall Cavendish Corporation
New York • London • Toronto • Sydney • Singapore

Published By
Marshall Cavendish Corporation
2415 Jerusalem Avenue
P.O. Box 587
North Bellmore, New York 11710
United States of America

∞ The paper used in these volumes conforms to the American
National Standard for Permanence of Paper for Printed Library
Materials, Z39.48-1984.

Library of Congress Cataloging-in-Publication Data
Magill's survey of American literature. Supplement / edited by Frank
N. Magill.
     p. cm.
Includes bibliographical references and index.
    1. American literature—Dictionaries. 2. American literature—
Bio-bibliography. 3. Authors, American—Biography—Diction-
aries. I. Magill, Frank Northen, 1907
PS21.M34   1994 Suppl.
810.9'0003—dc20
[B]
ISBN 1-85435-734-4 (set)   94-25192
ISBN 1-85435-732-8 (volume 1)   CIP

PUBLISHER'S NOTE

The six volumes of *Magill's Survey of American Literature* (1991) explored the lives and works of 190 of America's most important writers. This two-volume supplement updates and extends the original series' coverage by examining the careers of seventy-six contemporary or hitherto neglected writers who have had—and, in many cases, are still having—a substantial effect on the evolution of American literature.

As in the original series, the works covered here are drawn from a wide range of genres, including long and short fiction, poetry, drama, and nonfiction. The increasing prominence of ethnic voices in American literature is reflected by articles on such writers as Rolando Hinojosa, Garrett Hongo, and August Wilson. Important developments in women's literature are treated in essays on such authors as Maya Angelou, Barbara Kingsolver, and Wendy Wasserstein. Discussion of such best-selling writers as Tom Clancy and Scott Turow reflects the state of American popular fiction. Essays on such past writers as Gertrude Stein, Chester Himes, and Jean Toomer help to give a more complete picture of America's literary history.

Each article begins with ready-reference information that presents the date and place of the author's birth (and death, if applicable). A separate boxed section then briefly encapsulates the writer's literary significance. The main text of the article begins with "Biography," a chronological account of the author's life. An "Analysis" section follows and discusses the writer's styles, themes, and literary characteristics; this section can be read independently as an overview of the author's work. Following the analysis are separate sections on individual works by the author. Each section is introduced by a boxed section of information presenting the date of first publication (and, for dramatic works, first production) and a capsule description of the work. Each essay concludes with a brief "Summary" section and a bibliography that directs the reader to books and articles for further study. An illustration of the author under discussion accompanies each article.

A complete alphabetical list of authors profiled in the set appears at the end of volume 7. As in the original series, the final volume contains an Author Index and a Title Index that reference the contents of the entire set. Two new indexes, a Cultural Index and an Index of Women Writers, respond to recent trends in literary studies by conveniently listing authors according to background and gender.

We would like to thank the many academicians and other writers who contributed to this supplement. A list of their names and affiliations appears at the beginning of volume 7.

Photograph Credits

AP/Wide World Photos: *Paula Gunn Allen, Rudolfo A. Anaya, Maya Angelou, Kay Boyle, Gwendolyn Brooks, Tom Clancy, Rita Dove, Mona Van Duyn, Charles Fuller, Ernest J. Gaines, Susan Glaspell, Michael S. Harper, Oscar Hijuelos, Chester Himes, Charles Johnson, Barbara Kingsolver, Jerzy Kosinski, David Leavitt, Elmore Leonard, Terry McMillan, Paule Marshall, W. S. Merwin, Muriel Rukeyser, Anne*

Sexton, Jean Stafford, William Stafford, Wallace Stegner, Gertrude Stein, William Styron, Amy Tan, Luis Miguel Valdez, Wendy Wasserstein, Lanford Wilson, August Wilson. University of Houston: *Rolando Hinojosa.* Jerry Bauer: *Mark Helprin.* The Beinecke Rare Book and Manuscript Library, Yale University: *Jean Toomer.* Miriam Berkley: *Stanley Elkin.* Cleveland Public Library: *Charles Waddell Chesnutt.* John Cofer: *Judith Ortiz Cofer.* Gabriel Amadeus Cooney: *May Sarton.* Nancy Crampton: *James Wright.* The Department of State: *Nella Larsen.* Sigrid Estrada: *Jamaica Kincaid.* James Gudeman: *Adrienne Kennedy.* Rubén Guzmán: *Sandra Cisneros.* James Hamilton: *Richard Ford.* Marc Hefty: *James Welch.* Ellen Foscue Johnson: *Garrett Hongo.* Rendered by Kimberly L. Dawson Kurnizki: *Ai, Thomas Berger, Guy Davenport, William Gass, John Guare, Robert Hayden, Stanley Kunitz, Frank O'Hara, Ann Petry, Jay Wright.* Ann Resor Laughlin: *George Oppen.* M. L. Martinelli: *Gary Soto.* Stephen Mortensen: *Jane Smiley.* Dagmar Schullz: *Audre Lorde.* L. Schwartzwald: *Denise Levertov.* Peter Serling: *Walter Mosley.* Skrebneski: *Scott Turow.* Nancy Wong: *Frank Chin.*

CONTRIBUTORS

Michael Adams
Fairleigh Dickinson University

Thomas P. Adler
Purdue University

Gerhard Brand
Independent Scholar

John Brehm
Independent Scholar

Balance Chow
San Jose State University

Mary Virginia Davis
California State University, Sacramento

Bill Delaney
Independent Scholar

Ted William Dreier
Portland State University

James Feast
*Baruch College of the City University
   of New York*

John W. Fiero
University of Southwestern Louisiana

Ann D. Garbett
Averett College

Jill B. Gidmark
University of Minnesota

Marc Goldstein
New York State Department of Social Services

Daniel L. Guillory
Millikin University

Natalie Harper
Simon's Rock of Bard College

Terry Heller
Coe College

Joseph W. Hinton
Portland State University

Rebecca Stingley Hinton
Indiana University, East

W. Kenneth Holditch
University of New Orleans

Steven G. Kellman
University of Texas, San Antonio

Marilyn Kongslie
Independent Scholar

Eugene Larson
Pierce College

Leon Lewis
Appalachian State University

Paul R. Lilly, Jr.
State University of New York at Oneonta

James Livingston
Northern Michigan University

Janet Lorenz
Independent Scholar

Janet McCann
Texas A & M University

Joanne McCarthy
Tacoma Community College

Patrick Meanor
State University of New York at Oneonta

Philip Metcalfe
Independent Scholar

Kathleen Mills
Independent Scholar

Robert A. Morace
Daemen College

William Nelles
Northwestern State University of Louisiana

Lisa Paddock
Independent Scholar

Tom Petitjean
University of Southwestern Louisiana

Rosemary M. Canfield Reisman
Troy State University

Carl Rollyson
*Baruch College of the City University
of New York*

Paul Rosefeldt
Delgado Community College

Susan Rusinko
Bloomsburg University

Barbara Kitt Seidman
Linfield College

R. Baird Shuman
University of Illinois at Urbana-Champaign

Marjorie Smelstor
The University of Wisconsin-Eau Claire

Ira Smolensky
Monmouth College

Katherine Socha
Independent Scholar

Louise M. Stone
Bloomsburg University

Gerald H. Strauss
Bloomsburg University

James Sullivan
California State University, Los Angeles

Terry Theodore
University of North Carolina at Wilmington

James M. Welsh
Salisbury State University

Michael Witkoski
Independent Scholar

Robert E. Yahnke
University of Minnesota

CONTENTS

MAGILL'S
SURVEY
OF
AMERICAN
LITERATURE

AI

Born: Albany, Texas
October 21, 1947

Principal Literary Achievement
Ai uses disturbing, often violent imagery to explore the darker aspects of human nature.

Biography
The poet now known as Ai was born Florence Anthony in Albany, Texas, on October 21, 1947. Her mother was sixteen at the time, and married, but Ai was born out of wedlock. She did not know who her father was until she was twenty-six.

Ai's ancestry was a mixture of Choctaw, Caucasian, Japanese, and Filipino. Although Florence clearly looked black, as did her mother, she found it difficult in early life to identify with any particular ethnic group. She was born at her grandparents' house after her mother's husband had found out about his wife's affair and had beaten his wife in retribution.

Florence was sent to an "integrated" Catholic school in Albany that was in fact largely black; there, she was taunted by her schoolmates (she has remembered being called a "nigger-jap," among other things). She therefore rejected her obvious ethnic background and adopted the name of Ai, the Japanese word for love. Her first academic degree, a bachelor's degree from the University of Arizona awarded in 1969, was in Oriental Studies.

In 1971, Ai earned a master's degree in creative writing from the University of California; about that time, she began writing poetry under her adopted name. Along the way, she worked at a variety of jobs, including modeling and teaching.

Ai's strange beginnings and her rage at having no ethnic "home" are clearly reflected in her poetry. As part of no particular ethnic group, she shunned established ways of viewing the world, and her anger and her sense of homelessness permeated her work.

When her first collection of poetry, *Cruelty*, was published in 1973, Ai met with a variety of critical responses. She received Guggenheim and Radcliffe Fellowships in 1975 and a Massachusetts Arts and Humanities Fellowship in 1976. These honors proved that she was a poet to be taken seriously, but there were negative reactions as well.

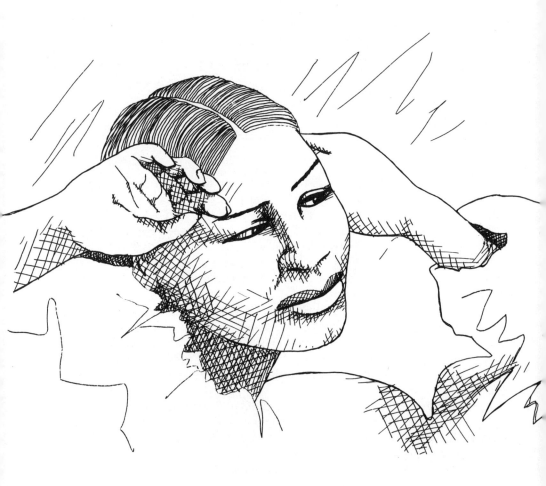

Ai's poetry was far from gentle. She wrote of graphic violence, rape, child molestation, and murder, and her work was condemned by many critics as pornographic. When *Killing Floor* (1979) was named the 1978 Lamont Poetry Selection by the Academy of American Poets, Ai had to be taken more seriously, even by those who had disparaged her in the past. Still, there was continued objection to her graphic depictions of sex and violence.

Ai has been lauded by many but has also been criticized for her forthright manners. She has been loudly attacked by feminists for her graphic descriptions of rape and violence against women. She has been applauded as a speaker for minority groups, but she has also been attacked for her refusal to identify herself with any particular group.

In response, Ai has declared, "I was forced to be loyal to myself as a multiracial person or be immersed in the black struggle for identity with which I had little in common. Except a desire to be accepted as I was."

Ai's poetry, her life, even her chosen name have made it quite clear which road she has taken. She has chosen the Japanese culture as her own, but she has clearly shown through her works that she can identify with the human race in general, and especially the darker aspects of the human soul.

The publication of *Sin* (1986), *Fate* (1991), and *Greed* (1993) have added to Ai's reputation. She has continued to write poetry, and she has continued to comment on her life and work in interviews and prose articles. Far from being a voice of black or feminist literature, Ai has continued to be her own person, not tied to any ethnic or racial group but, rather, identifying with the most intense aspects of humanity in general.

Analysis

The first observation one cannot help making about Ai's poetry is that she uses a straightforward narrative style to describe the most horrible people and events. Almost all of her works are first-person narratives in which she assumes the voices of a variety of people—men and women, adults and children, murderers and victims. Her characters come from many times and places, but they all have one thing in common: They are experiencing, in various ways, the darkest parts of human nature.

Ai's first published collection, *Cruelty* (1973), is essentially a series of one-page monologues told from the points of view of a variety of anonymous people. A short poem called "Abortion," told from a father's point of view, expresses his anger that his wife or lover (it is not clear whether this is a married couple) has killed "his son." "The Hitchhiker" is the story of a man who hitches a ride and then kills the woman who has picked him up. There is even a monologue told from the point of view of a child beater.

What all these people share is violence. Ai's world is not a pretty one. People kill and die, rape and murder. They do not pick flowers or look at sunsets.

In *Killing Floor* (1979), Ai continued in this direction. These poems are generally much longer and are more varied in style. There are dialogues between characters and even a few prose poems, written in the same narrative style but in paragraph form, rather than broken into lines as poetry usually is. Moreover, in *Killing Floor*, the characters do not exist in isolation as they did in the first collection. They are placed within their environment, and in some cases within historical settings.

Some of the narrators, in fact, are historical figures, including actress Marilyn Monroe and Ira Hayes, a Native American World War II hero who died broke and drunk after the war. Other poems are written from the point of view of people who are not named but who are archetypes of the most horrid sorts.

The poem "Jericho" is told from the point of view of a fifteen-year-old girl in bed with an older man who feeds her candy and who has already gotten her pregnant. "The Mortician's Twelve-Year-Old Son" is the story of a boy who makes love to a corpse. "Almost Grown" is a prose poem about a boy visiting a prostitute for the first time.

It is interesting to note that in this collection, sixteen of the twenty-four narrators are men. The poet here is clearly identifying with all humanity, or at least with the darker side of all human souls.

These first two collections of poetry have much in common. Death, violence, and sex are of paramount importance. Children appear often in both collections, but they are never happy boys and girls. The unifying factor in both books is misery, but there is also something else, something astounding, at work here. Readers identify with these characters. Horror, including horror poetry, has long been a popular genre of writing. Ai's poetry is completely different, however, with respect to the points of view taken.

Readers are drawn inside the minds of rapists, child molesters, murderers, and victims of violent death, perspectives that are rarely seen in literature. This is not to say that Ai's readers are sympathetic to these monsters; her readers do not feel compassion for the rapist, do not come to think that it is a good idea to have sex with a corpse. Her readers do, however, understand how these people feel, and this is Ai's greatest strength.

In *Sin*, Ai goes one step further in her attempt to encompass all humanity. The book makes strong political and religious statements in addition to the sorts of statements the poet had previously been making about human nature in general. Many of the figures here are well known; as usual, though, they are seen from a new perspective.

"Two Brothers," the poem that opens the book, is told from the points of view of John and Robert Kennedy. The poem is about death, not surprisingly, but it is also about immortality. These two characters are already dead, after all, and they are not speaking as if they were alive. Indeed, they discuss their deaths. Yet the poem ends with a suggestion that death is not final: "Give 'em a miracle. Give 'em Hollywood. Give 'em Saint Jack." There is a suggestion that, ultimately, God is responsible for all that has occurred, that the human players involved are secondary.

"The Prisoner" takes a similar tone. This poem is told from the point of view of an anonymous prisoner who is regularly tortured; his jailer refers to himself as "Our Father." "The Testimony of J. Robert Oppenheimer: A Fiction" is an imagined confession by the man generally considered the "father of the atomic bomb" after he has seen the bomb's effects. He is horrified at what has happened, horrified that people now have a godlike control over the very fabric of the universe.

Ai has changed the face of American poetry by her forthright, often horrific renderings of some of the grimmer aspects of reality. She has been extolled as a great poet and reviled as a writer of pornography. Ai can identify with so many types of people because she has such a strange and varied history herself and has never really identified with any one ethnic or racial group. She can deal with pain and anger so well because she has been hurt and she is angry.

Perhaps Ai's poetic point of view is best summed up in her note to *Fate*: "Fate is about eroticism, politics, religion, and show business as tragicomedy, performed by men and women banished to the bare stage of their obsessions." This can be said to be true of all of her works. Ai's poems are indeed about people laid bare, and her poetic style attests this. There is no embellishment, no flowery speech, no use of complex metaphors. She is simply telling people about the deepest and darkest parts of themselves.

THE KID

First published: 1976
Type of work: Poem

A young boy describes his murderous acts and his state of mind.

"The Kid" is perhaps the most disturbing of Ai's poems. Told in the first person, this is the story of a boy of fourteen who is far from ordinary.

The poem begins in a fairly straightforward way. The boy clearly lives on a farm; he is busy whacking the tires on the family's truck with an iron rod. His father calls to him "to help hitch the team," and then his mother calls him. He tosses a rock at the kitchen window, but he is unsuccessful in making his point in such a tame manner.

In the second stanza, this boy has given up whacking tires, and he splits his father's skull open with the iron rod; when his mother comes running, he bludgeons her as well. He then proceeds to abandon the rod for a gun and starts shooting, first killing horses and then his little sister.

The short poem is, however, more than a mere picture of bloody violence. It is the boy's attitude that gives this poem its power:

> Yeah. I'm Jack, Hogarth's son.
> I'm nimble, I'm quick.
> . . . .
> I'm fourteen. I'm a wind from nowhere.
> I can break your heart.

There is no attempt by some outsider to justify the boy's acts. The reader is not told about overly stern parents, about a "disturbed" child, or any such situation. Yet, obviously, something is wrong.

After the boy has killed his family, he puts on his father's best clothes, packs his sister's doll and his mother's nightgown in a suitcase, and heads for the highway. It is as if, by taking his family's belongings and symbolically identifying with his father, he has somehow justified his actions.

The most terrifying aspect of the poem is that the reader is compelled to identify with the boy and, in some strange way, to feel sorry for him. Modern culture tends to assume that a boy of fourteen who murders has somehow been mistreated by society.

The point is that even a child can be a monster, and perhaps the way in which children are viewed is a large part of the problem. As the poem opens, there is a tendency to picture a cute, innocent-looking boy who is merely being hassled by his parents and annoyed by his sister while he is trying to play. The fact that this play turns to grisly murder hardly changes that opinion. Readers can hardly excuse the boy's acts, but they wish they could, somehow.

THE GOOD SHEPHERD: ATLANTA, 1981

First published: 1986
Type of work: Poem

"The Good Shepherd: Atlanta, 1981" is a dramatic monologue by a mass murderer of children.

"The Good Shepherd: Atlanta, 1981" was inspired by the case of Wayne Williams, who made headlines by committing a series of murders of black children in and around Atlanta from 1979 to 1981. The poem begins with a graphic description of the murderer pushing a child's body over an embankment. He identifies with the boy and imagines himself within the dead body: "I watch it roll/ and feel I'm rolling with it." He speaks of "the little lamb/ I killed tonight," and then he goes and has some hot cocoa. The murderer then describes washing out the blood that stains his bathroom. He cleans and cleans, then finishes his hot chocolate.

Once again, the reader can understand how this man is thinking. He is clearly pleased by his actions: He is "a good shepherd," seducing little boys to their deaths. Yet there is more involved here; the killer opens a book on mythology and remarks,

> Saturn, it says, devours his children.
> Yes, it's true, I know it.
> An ordinary man, though, a man like me
> eats and is full.
> Only God is never satisfied.

This is a rather strange religious statement. Saturn, a god of Roman mythology, killed and ate all of his children except for Jupiter, who escaped and later killed his father, thus becoming king of the gods.

It is clear that the murderer is identifying himself with divinity. As a god, he has the right to dispose of his subjects and feels no particular guilt in doing so.

The poet's basic idea is that, ultimately, God is responsible for everything and that humans are merely pawns in a great game. These sometimes destroy other pawns, but it really does not matter, because God is never quite satisfied.

Sin is full of such ideas, but this is an unusually powerful presentation. It is difficult to feel sympathy for a mass murderer, but it is also difficult not to see his way of looking at the situation. Even a man who kills young children has a point of view worth considering.

Lastly, there is a sense of satisfaction once the children are murdered and the mess is cleaned up: "Only God is never satisfied," the killer says. Does this mean that the murderer is somehow more merciful, or more just, than God? This is a question left open by the poem.

EVE'S STORY

First published: 1990
Type of work: Poem

A sixteen-year-old girl recounts her experiences with a fraudulent evangelist.

"Eve's Story" is a clear statement about established religion and its most evangelistic proponents. The poem is told from the viewpoint of a sixteen-year-old girl who leaves home after her father strangles a deformed kitten; she winds up in an evangelist's tent.

The girl is quickly seduced by the evangelist. She becomes his servant, even helping him to procure prostitutes. When he becomes increasingly successful, the girl is edged out of his inner circle by more photogenic women: "We had gone video,/ but I wasn't in them./ I did not fit his image anymore./ Cheryl did, with her blue contacts, blonde hair,/ and silicone implants." The girl avenges herself by filming the evangelist engaged in a lurid sex act and exposing him as a hypocrite; his followers desert him, and blonde, blue-eyed Cheryl becomes a talk-show celebrity. Yet the speaker stays with the fallen preacher, explaining, "So now we live like any other/ retired couple in Sarasota."

Ai is commenting not merely upon the preacher himself but also upon the religious system that has produced him and people like him:

> Of a sudden, I realize
> this is how Eve must have done it.
> The snake and God were only props
> she discarded when she left Adam
> writhing on the ground.

Unlike most of Ai's narrators, this girl inspires real compassion and real pity. She is clearly a victim of other people's actions. The actual blame is still hard to place. Is it the preacher himself who is to blame? Is it the religion he espouses? Or, in the final analysis, is it God who is to blame? If sex is original sin, and also one of the most pleasant actions a human being can experience, does this mean that it is sinful to have fun?

As always in Ai's work, the reader is not told very much about the girl in question, whether, for example, she is black or white, Christian, Jewish, or atheist. She is simply presented as having been victimized by a religious system and a man who embodies it. The reader is also confused about how much blame to lay on the evangelist; perhaps he, too, should be considered a victim.

Summary

Ai's poetry is forthright and pulls no punches. Her characters are murderers, child molesters, rapists, and prostitutes, types of people most readers do not like to think about and most writers do not address. Life is not necessarily pretty, and Ai shows the ugliest parts of it. While readers might not like to admit that the people Ai talks about exist, her work makes them impossible to ignore.

Bibliography

Ai. "On Being One-Half Japanese, One-Eighth Choctaw, One-Quarter Black, and One-Sixteenth Irish." *Ms.* 6 (May, 1978): 58.

Cramer, Steven. Review of *Fate*, by Ai. *Poetry* 159 (November, 1991): 108-111.

Monaghan, Pat. Review of *Fate*, by Ai. *Booklist* 87 (January 1, 1991): 902.

Ostriker, Alicia. Review of *Sin*, by Ai. *Poetry* 144 (January, 1987): 231-237.

Seidman, Hugh. Review of *Killing Floor*, by Ai. *The New York Times Book Review*, July 8, 1979, 14.

Marc Goldstein

PAULA GUNN ALLEN

Born: Cubero, New Mexico
October 24, 1939

Principal Literary Achievement
A storyteller, poet, and essayist, Allen advocates awareness of tribal cultures as integral to a balanced, harmonious understanding of Native American literatures.

Biography

Paula Gunn Allen was born in Cubero, New Mexico, in 1939, to Elias Lee Francis, a Lebanese American who had once been lieutenant-governor of New Mexico, and Ethel Gunn Francis, a Laguna Sioux-Scottish woman of the Keres Indians, an intensely gynecocratic-centered culture. Allen's multiethnic (or "breed") origins are not unusual in the Laguna Pueblo, which consists of a multitude of cultural worlds uniting through mutual desire into a reciprocal tribal whole.

Allen was born in the seventh year of a thirty-year drought and in the first year of the area's uranium mining. She remembers blocking windows and doors to keep out dust, which at times was so thick that it was difficult to see across a room. Equally vivid are her memories of her stone-walled home, surrounded by white flowers and safely nestled in a hollow, where she would read and listen to her sister play classical music on the family's upright piano. Both her parents were also musicians, and Allen learned early in life to recognize and value the distinctive rhythms of both music and language in the cultures that nurtured her.

The road by their house fascinated Allen. In one direction, it ran to a city; in another, it ran to a mountain. Yet it also remained there, in her homeland. This road is dominant in Allen's life and in her writing. Allen sees herself as standing at a crossroad, valuing the mountain (sacred wilderness) more highly than the city (civilization) and measuring civilization in terms of the mountain.

The bicultural alienation that haunts Allen appears to have begun when she was sent to an Albuquerque convent school, where she was taught that all humans are innately hopeless, guilt-ridden sinners and that Indians are worthless savages. In "Easter Sunday: Recollection," Allen describes herself on Good Friday "waiting for the earth to tear itself apart and swallow me,/ to reveal my murderous intent" and believing "cold wind and dust and snow sure signs of my guilt,/ the murderous

compulsion of those I loved/ god-killers condemned to grief." These teachings are in direct contradiction to the nonpunitive, life-affirming teachings of her mother and her tribal culture, yet they were pronounced as truth by purportedly holy women, convent nuns, and reinforced with punishments. Consequently, Allen as a young girl was unable to reconcile the dichotomies, hated school, and withdrew as quickly as possible into reading, with a strong preference for popular literature rather than the classics.

Nevertheless, her Laguna culture values learning, and Allen persevered. After attending Colorado Women's College, she received her B.A. in English in 1966 and her M.F.A. in Creative Writing in 1968 from the University of Oregon. While working on her master's degree, Allen felt so fragmented, dissociated, and alone that she experienced a suicidal despair. Her Laguna mother's teachings to nurture all the living and to avoid self-indulgent negativity because it sickens the earth did not alleviate her depression. Allen's poems in *The Blind Lion: Poems* (1974) come from this dark journey.

Allen credits the arrival of a Santee Sioux friend and the publication of N. Scott Momaday's *House Made of Dawn* (1968) with restoring her sense of tribal community. "Land sickness" is a state of grief over not being with the land where one's heart is. To the Native American, experiences are related to and defined by the places in which they occur. *House Made of Dawn* helped Allen to restore her groundedness in the earth, as well as her sense of humor. As she explains, any kind of humor, even gallows humor, is integral to life. Momaday's book demonstrated to her that she was not crazy; but, even if she were, at least she was no longer alone.

Although Allen wanted to continue in English for her doctorate, no program was available for her to concentrate in Native American literature; therefore, she specialized in Native American literature under the University of New Mexico's American Studies program and received her Ph.D. in 1975. Allen's postdoctoral awards include a 1978 National Endowment of the Arts Creative Writing Fellowship, a 1980-1981 University of California at Berkeley fellowship in Native American Studies, and a 1984-1985 Ford Foundation research grant. *Spider Woman's Granddaughters: Traditional Tales and Contemporary Writing by Native American Women* (1989), edited by Allen under the Ford Foundation grant, won a 1990 American Book Award.

Analysis

Native Americans honor all existence as sacred. They do not set up arbitrary barriers between spirit and matter, human and other-than-human. Instead, they perceive the universe as living, dynamic, and fluid, with each being (such as trees, rocks, animals, water, and humans) contributing its own awareness to the integrated and constantly reforming continuance of the whole. In all of her writings, Paula Gunn Allen is an "environmental advocate" who reveals the consequences of harmonious and disharmonious relations with the universe. In "Los Angeles, 1980," Allen describes the "vitamin-drenched consciousness" of the city-dwellers: "The death people do not know/ what they create, or how they hide/ from the consequences of their dreams."

To Allen, the female force is "about balance and mutual respect and reciprocal obligation." Reality involves a vigilant awareness of, and caring for, self, others, and place, because all realities coexist in the cycle of life. Time itself is fluid, and spirit is the creative force. The journeymaker who walks in balance recognizes the essential beauty of the universe and explores each experience for its fundamental, communal truth. In *Grandmothers of the Light: A Medicine Woman's Sourcebook* (1991), Allen teaches a spiritual discipline through twenty-one stories of tribal tradition and sacred power.

Allen was taught that her mind is irrevocably hers, an aspect of her reality that no one else can ever possess. To a people who have survived a genocidal colonization and who are still hostages facing nonexistence on their own land, this is a crucial message. Allen sees Native American literature as a means of "taking control of the image making again," of choosing ritual right action to reestablish an earth-connectedness and to abandon the illusory path of powerlessness. "Hoop Dancer," in *Shadow Country* (1982), is an unforgettable, synaesthetic experience in poetry of these principles.

Native American literature and Western literature are fundamentally different. Approaching Native American literature metaphysically, psychically open to all of its levels of reality, rather than didactically superimposing an external critical or cultural context, is essential. As a teacher, an essayist, and an editor, Paula Gunn Allen has contributed with distinction to integrating Native American literature into Western awareness as well as to providing the appropriate contexts through which the literature can best be understood. She is the editor of, and contributor to, *Studies in American Indian Literature: Critical Essays and Course Designs* (1983), a definitive text published by the Modern Language Association.

Rather than emphasizing an individual in crisis, Native American literature focuses upon tribal continuity and the nature of the individual's connection to it, with the purpose of enhancing the fulfillment of both. Self-expression for its own sake would be considered invasive, self-indulgent negativity. Therefore, if an individual is isolated, the isolation is examined in terms of how the individual and the cosmos can be reconnected.

The Native American universe is integrated, rather than divisive: Great Mystery (God) does not sit apart in judgment from the elements of the universe but lives within all in reciprocity. Place is never incidental; instead, place is crucial to the significance of an action. All planes of existence are recognized as "real." Time is cyclical and coexistent. The treatment of time provides important contextual clues as to the consciousness with which the work can most appropriately be approached. Finally, Native American literature is life-affirming rather than death-preoccupied.

As a professor of English at the University of California at Los Angeles, Paula Gunn Allen lives in both the Native American and the Western worlds. Her writing, however, is profoundly Native American. In describing her life, she does not speak of a straight-line journey from one event to another but of an energy flow along a path that resembles a Mobius strip.

Six books of poetry attest the reality that Allen's journey has not been without turbulence: *The Blind Lion, Coyote's Daylight Trip* (1978), *A Cannon Between My Knees* (1981), *Star Child* (1981), *Shadow Country,* and *Skins and Bones: Poems 1979-87* (1988). Each shares her search for balance and groundedness: from the mountains to the cities, through idealism and despair, to survival, affirmation, and healing transformation.

Self-alienation, often a consequence of bicultural or multicultural experience, is a recurrent theme in Allen's work. An individual displaced by ancestry is highly susceptible to psychic deterioration from the absence of both internal and communal grounding. In addition, Allen focuses upon the scarring effects of a patriarchal colonialism forced upon gynecocratic tribal cultures. The debilitation of land sickness, the powerlessness of nonexistence for tribal women, and the imposition of an alien dualistic, materialistic culture brought searing disharmony and imbalance to the Native American world.

Myth, ritual action, and oral tradition are the healing foundations of the Native American universe. All three are visionary and real. Allen reinforces their curative, sacred powers with rhythm and sound repetition to create shifts in consciousness that open awareness. The Western use of symbolism is unrecognized in Native American literature; if all existence is sacred, then a river can be a river and stand for itself in its sacredness.

As a desert person, Allen has a special affinity for the mountains, water, and dawn. Her use of shadows is strikingly intense: "shadow too stricken to flow/ dream in your silent shadow/ celebrate." Shadows are places of interdimensional exploration. They are opportunities for earth-connectedness and mutual creation. From the thought-image to the word-action creates the reality. Allen's only novel, *The Woman Who Owned the Shadows* (1983), exemplifies each of these characteristics as it follows the walking path of a half-breed woman to intrapsychic centeredness.

Allen's style has become less obscure over the years; the author attributes this transformation to her long-held belief that after the age of forty, a woman has the power of enhanced clarity. The reality that she no longer holds as deep an emotional investment in avoiding being misunderstood, a condition she had once equated with death, has also contributed to the evolution of her style.

MAY IT BE BEAUTIFUL ALL AROUND

First published: 1991
Type of work: Short story

Two Navajo sisters are taught healing ceremonies by a group of supernatural beings.

"May It Be Beautiful All Around," in *Grandmothers of the Light,* is one of eight stories in which Allen demonstrates the role of ritual magic in the interplay between humans and supernaturals. Allen has stated that "the essential nature of the cosmos is female intelligences," and she has created the word "cosmogyny" to represent this enduring and transformative gynocentric cosmos.

Navajo chantways are intricate healing ceremonies based upon the knowledge that reintegration with the inviolate inner forces of the land and the natural elements restores a diseased individual into balance with the sacred order. The chantways can last from two to nine days and can involve fifteen or more trained practitioners. Although many chantway rituals are shared, each chantway belongs to a specific healing group and contains its own songs, stories, herbal medicines, prayers, and curative processes.

In "May It Be Beautiful All Around," Older Sister and Younger Sister have been pledged to two strong but old warriors whom they do not love. During a raid, the two sisters are separated from their family. Although they are afraid, they ignore tribal knowledge to consider the possibility that they might not have to fulfill their uncle's pledge to marry the old warriors, Bear Man and Snake Man.

As the women search the mountains for their family, two handsome young men appear and offer their help. Because the hour is late, the four decide to take shelter until daybreak in nearby ruins, where Older Sister and Younger Sister are each joined by a virile warrior for the night. In the morning, despite omens that all may not be as it seems, Younger Sister follows her young warrior to a rock that opens at his four knocks (four being the most sacred of numbers) onto another land.

The warrior leaves her at his home to help his mother with her tasks. For the next four days, she is given a different chore each day. Although the tasks are simple ones, she fails every time through inattention, impatience, and undisciplined behavior. Each time, her mother-in-law responds with serene patience. On the fifth day, her warrior-husband offers to teach her a ceremony that she can take to her people.

This time, Younger Sister works diligently to learn every movement and every sound of the ceremony. After four days of right action, she is successful. Her husband, now old and bent, leads her home. As she and her family talk, Younger Sister learns that she has been gone for months, not days. She is rejoined by Older Sister, who has been with Bear Man's mother all these months, and the two women return with their knowledge to their people. After the sisters have taught their ceremonies to their brothers, they rejoin their supernatural husbands, and "because of their continuing thought the ceremonies continue to have the power to heal."

DEAR WORLD

First published: 1984
Type of work: Poem

Bicultural self-alienation is represented by the poet's half-breed mother, who has contracted lupus.

"Dear World" is an agonizing eulogy for the living and the dead who have experienced the internal isolation of non-belonging. Undercurrents of rage and grief score the poem's essence. In her foreword to Jane Caputi's *Gossips, Gorgons, and Crones: The Fates of the Earth* (1993), Paula Gunn Allen explained the context of the poem, which concerns illnesses and death.

Allen once worked for the New Mexico Cancer Control Project, which dismissed discussion of such issues as radiation poisoning and toxic waste in favor of a more publically acceptable antismoking campaign. Yet in 1976, Allen claimed, her home was using water in which "the level of lethal radiation-associated toxins" was life-threatening. Allen's mother contracted not only lupus and diverticulitis but also lung and heart diseases. Furthermore, Allen questioned whether her mother died of the diseases or the treatments of radiation and chemical therapy. Experiencing the poem with this knowledge adds an ironic dimension to the title "Dear World."

In the poem's first stanza, Allen presents her mother's point of view. Her mother sees lupus as a "self-attack"; she says that the disease is like calling the police when a mugger breaks into her home and then seeing the police attack the victim instead of the mugger. In the second and the third stanzas, Allen acknowledges the truth of her mother's perception before continuing in an ironic tone. Historical precedents, she writes, prove that Indians and Westerners cannot coexist harmoniously. Therefore, she sees it as logical that the different genetic compositions in her mother's blood— "it's conflicting stains"—would obliterate each other.

The concluding fourteen lines of "Dear World" employ graphic sensory images to detail the disease's progression until "the crucible and its contents vaporize." The sadness, the devastating powerlessness, of watching a mother dying in incurable pain is exacerbated for the poet by her mother's inability to breathe. Breath to breath is how sacred energy flows in the poet's universe, and even that, in the end, is denied.

Self-alienation, the poet concludes, is an internalized battle between seemingly irreconcilable facets of a single sacred existence. Often, self-alienation is accompanied by other-alienation and isolation. The process, Allen says, is progressive and all-devouring unless a healing connection is reestablished and the imbalance is corrected.

THE SACRED HOOP: RECOVERING THE FEMININE IN AMERICAN INDIAN TRADITIONS

First published: 1986
Type of work: Essays

Seventeen literary and feminist essays provide contexts from which to evaluate tribal traditions and the tribal roles of American Indian women.

The Sacred Hoop is a distinguished scholarly exposition of Native American traditions with an emphasis upon women-centered tribal life. In Native American tradition, the Sacred Hoop, or Medicine Wheel, is the all-encompassing circle of universal life. The Spider Woman is the central figure who thought the universe into being and who continues to weave her web of existence. The first section, "The Ways of Our Grandmothers," deals with her many aspects in tribal myth, tradition, and ritual. The genocidal impact through the centuries of patriarchal colonization upon the gynocracies is detailed. Allen also dispels several popular misinterpretations of Native American behavior toward women. The last essay in the section is a personal account of the author's experiences as a contemporary Keres Laguna woman.

Oral tradition has been an integral factor in tribal survival, and the second section of *The Sacred Hoop* is entitled "The Word Warriors." Both traditional and contemporary tribal literature is studied in terms of Native American culture; thought, structure, symbolism, style, ceremony, and authenticity are among the analytic considerations. Allen not only explicates the tribal perspective but also clarifies the problems inherent in approaching tribal literature from a Western bias.

The final section of *The Sacred Hoop,* "Pushing Up the Sky," concentrates upon contemporary American Indian women and the social issues (such as feminism, personal power, the female spiritual way, politics, lesbianism, and reformation of a gynocentric tribal structure) that affect them. "Pushing Up the Sky" is pro-female advocacy at its best. For women who lack a sense of continuity, community, self-esteem, or belonging, the essays in this section are healing words. For the self-alienated, *The Sacred Hoop* in its entirety offers the tools for survival.

Summary

Paula Gunn Allen is a powerful Native American author who writes with wisdom and passion. Her work has significantly increased both awareness of and understanding of American Indian literature.

Two of Allen's key strengths are her mastery of her subject matter and the care with which she expresses her ideas, whether in fiction, poetry, or criticism. Although her earlier writings are at times uneven and obscure, her later writings have an undeniable sharpness of vision. Her body of work is evocative, potent, and life-affirming.

Bibliography

Ballinger, Franchot, and Brian Swann. "A MELUS Interview: Paula Gunn Allen." *MELUS* 10 (Summer, 1983): 3-25.

Bruchac, Joseph. *Survival This Way: Interviews with Native American Poets.* Tucson: University of Arizona Press, 1987.

Cotelli, Laura, ed. *Winged Words: Native American Writers Speak.* Lincoln: University of Nebraska Press, 1990.

Hanson, Elizabeth I. *Forever There: Race and Gender in Contemporary Native American Fiction.* New York: Peter Lang, 1989.

Jahner, Elaine. "A Laddered Rain-Bearing Rug: The Poetry of Paula Gunn Allen." In *Women and Western American Literature,* edited by Helen Winter Stauffer and Susan J. Rosowski. Troy, N.Y.: Whitson Press, 1982.

Swann, Brian, and Arnold Krupat, eds. *I Tell You Now: Autobiographical Essays by Native American Writers.* Lincoln: University of Nebraska Press, 1987.

Kathleen Mills

RUDOLFO A. ANAYA

Born: Pastura, New Mexico
October 30, 1937

Principal Literary Achievement
Because of the critical and popular success of his 1972 novel *Bless Me, Ultima,* Anaya is considered one of the foremost contemporary Mexican American writers.

Biography

Rudolfo A. Anaya, son of Martin and Rafaelita Mares Anaya, was born October 30, 1937, in Pastura, a small farming village in the eastern part of New Mexico. As a young child, he suffered a spinal injury, but he still managed to attend school in the neighboring town of Santa Rosa and in Albuquerque. From 1956 to 1958, he attended the Browning Business School, and in 1963, he was graduated from the University of New Mexico with a B.A. in English.

From 1963 until 1970, Anaya taught in the Albuquerque public schools. During this time, he received his M.A. in English from the University of New Mexico (1968) and also his M.A. in guidance and counseling from the same university in 1972. In 1966, he married Patricia Lawless, another guidance counselor. In 1971, he left the public school system to become the director of counseling at the University of Albuquerque. He remained at this job two years.

His first novel, *Bless Me, Ultima,* was published in 1972. It tells the story of the relationship between Antonio, a young boy growing up in a small New Mexico village, and Ultima, his grandmother and spiritual guide, who helps him to understand his experiences. The book was a critical and commercial success and was translated into several foreign editions. *Bless Me, Ultima* received the Premio Quinto Sol Award, Anaya's first national recognition and a forerunner of later grants and fellowships. In 1974, he was appointed as an associate professor and in 1988 a full professor of English at the University of New Mexico.

His second novel, *Heart of Aztlán* (1976), was received much less enthusiastically. It portrays a year in the life of a Mexican family that moves from a small rural community to the barrio of Albuquerque. The family members respond very differently to the stresses of city life, and although Anaya uses some of the mystical, mythic elements of his earlier novel, the story relies heavily on traditional stereotypes.

His third novel, *Tortuga* (1979), won the Before Columbus Foundation American Book Award. The book tells the story of a sixteen-year-old boy's initiation into knowledge during his recovery from a nearly fatal accident. Using traditional mythic symbolism, *Tortuga* continues in the mystical vein of the previous two novels. Yet it was not well received by critics, who said the book had many of the same faults as *Heart of Atzlán.*

In addition to these three novels, which compose a trilogy, Anaya has written another novel, *The Legend of La Llorona* (1984). He also writes in many other forms. In 1982, his short-story collection *The Silence of the Llano* was published, and in 1985, his mock epic poem *The Adventures of Juan Chicaspatas.* Other of his stories, essays, reviews, and articles have been published in journals and anthologies. Anaya has also been an active editor and playwright.

Anaya received National Endowment for the Arts fellowships in 1979 and 1980 and a Kellogg Foundation fellowship in 1983. He has been honored by the New Mexico Governors' Public Service Award in 1978 and 1980 and the Award for Achievement in Chicano Literature in 1983 for his contribution to the state's native literature. He has been a guest lecturer at many universities, including Yale University, the University of Michigan, the University of California, and the University of Texas, while continuing to write and teach at the University of New Mexico in Albuquerque.

Analysis

With the 1972 publication of *Bless Me, Ultima,* Rudolfo Anaya became a popular writer and one of the most important voices in contemporary Chicano literature. In that novel, he succeeds in portraying the character of the Southwest's Mexican American people, with their myths, folklore, legends, and dreams. He also transcends these ethnic concerns so that the book appeals to many American readers. Because of this thematic universality, the novel has become widely read, and it appears in the curricula of many colleges and high schools.

Since the publication of *Bless Me, Ultima,* the first book in a trilogy, Anaya has published many other works. In all these, he uses similar subject matter: ancient myth, the Mexican American heritage, and the conflicts caused by Mexican American attempts to fit into mainstream American society. Though each work presents a different story, his themes remain consistent. His central theme is, in the words of critic Antonio Marquez, that "life is sacred and the love of life is the greatest human achievement." To find the spiritual fulfillment necessary to see life as sacred requires understanding the harmony of all the forces in the universe. It is the search for this oneness and harmony that lies at the heart of Anaya's work.

Each work in the trilogy illustrates Anaya's concern with the search for personal spiritual harmony. In *Bless Me, Ultima,* Antonio finds self-knowledge and insight as a result of his relationship with his spiritual guide, Ultima. She provides him with the stability he needs as he proceeds through life exploring intellectual and emotional situations. In *Heart of Aztlán,* a family searches for the answers posed by changes brought about by their move from a rural community to the barrio of Albuquerque. At the novel's end, the main character, Clemente, finds self-knowledge and begins to help other people who are not so fortunate. The last book in the trilogy, *Tortuga,* which Anaya patterned after a mythic journey, tells of a sixteen-year-old boy, Tortuga, who finds enlightenment during the desperately difficult time he spends recovering from a near-fatal accident.

To portray these themes, Anaya relies on mythopoetics, the art of mythmaking. He is able to fuse mythic poetic images with images from his own childhood and from the New Mexican landscape to connect the past and present so that the result is a completely new myth. Mythopoetics as an important element in understanding human nature is a belief Anaya shares with Carl Jung and other psychologists. In fact, Anaya's belief that all people share a collective memory of a time when there was more harmony in the universe is very similar to Jung's idea of the collective unconscious. Both Jung and Anaya have expressed the belief that people can make sense out of the fragmentation of the modern world through the use of certain archetypal symbols and images. Anaya works with many images and symbols: the turtle with its shell, representing alienation and a loss of faith, spiritual guides who lead the way to wisdom, and dreams that illuminate the past and foretell the future.

Dreams that reveal the collective unconscious and the path to self-knowledge appear frequently in Anaya's work. In *Bless Me, Ultima,* the boy Antonio gains wisdom from dreams that illustrate a tolerant attitude toward his father and from other dreams that help him to understand the troubled events of youth. In such short stories as "Iliana of the Pleasure Dreams," the dream symbolizes the harmony necessary for personal and spiritual fulfillment.

To integrate this material into his plots, Anaya frequently uses a favorite device, the epiphany, a moment when all things come together to reveal the truth. In *Heart of Aztlán*, the boy Clemente, in a moment of truth, can feel the rhythm of an ancient beat echoed in his own heartbeat. He can connect the dreams he has had with the reality around him. Doing this releases power into his life, and he can function because he understands. This synthesis of memory, dreams, and reality works best when the story is told in the first person, as in *Bless Me, Ultima.* Even though it sometimes appears that the book's narrator is not mature enough to have such insights, the epiphanies succeed, because the book is a flashback told from an adult perspective.

Though praised for his use of myth and his attention to the craft of writing, Anaya since *Bless Me, Ultima* has received fewer accolades. Some critics have argued that his mythmaking is too abstract and is inadequate to deal with the pressing social and political questions of the contemporary Mexican American. At the end of his stories and novels, the characters find enlightenment and personal harmony as the result of their long searches. No alienation, irony, or uncertainty appears. Anaya, however, defends his art with his own philosophy. He does not believe that the best writers deal directly with social and political issues, because such issues then become directives for art; rather, he believes that writers should deal with social consciousness indirectly, through myth. He defines a myth as a truth in the heart that people have had since the beginning of time. People need to get in tune with this truth by separating it from political concerns. Politics are indeed important, but they should be dealt with differently. Anaya's contribution is to invigorate Chicano writing; through his mytho-poetic art, using rich images and symbols to enhance his themes, he has accomplished this objective.

ILIANA OF THE PLEASURE DREAMS

First published: 1985
Type of work: Short story

A spiritual experience reconciles a young woman's dreams and reality and awakens her to the fullness of her life.

"Iliana of the Pleasure Dreams" is the last story in *Tierra: Contemporary Short Fiction of New Mexico* (1989), a book edited by Anaya that also contains stories by writers such as Tony Hillerman, Ed Chavez, and Patricia Clark Smith. The story illustrates Anaya's methods in his short works. In the preface, he tells about the *tierra*, the land, of New Mexico, which is "an ingredient which dictates the natural pace of the stories in this collection" and "nourishes our creativity." The story of a beautiful newly married young woman, Iliana, is set in a rural mountain valley. Anaya combines realistic details of the land with the details of Iliana's dream to tell an initiation story that ends with people in harmony with the earth and themselves.

One summer night, Iliana awakens from a dream in which she is running across a field of alfalfa toward a beautiful young man. The dream is very real, and she quietly moves toward the window to contemplate its meaning while looking at the night landscape. Anaya describes this scene so that the details of the breeze and the crickets in the landscape mesh with the dream. Iliana thinks of her early life with her strict religious aunts, her timidity with her shy, silent husband, and her uneasiness about the pleasure that was so real in her dream. She recalls her intention to confess her dream to the priest, but on the way to the church, trees seem to overwhelm her like the arms of men. The landscape is the connection between the dream life and the real world.

The next day, Iliana and her husband, Onofre, go to the church to see a miracle, the face of Christ, which reportedly has appeared on the wall. As the young couple drives to the church, Anaya again describes the earth and the landscape. Iliana is excited and surrenders herself to the mood of tense expectation. She smells the damp, rich earth and remembers the horse she used to ride.

Iliana goes with her aunts to pray, remembering the pleasure of her dream as she kneels. Anaya describes the images again. The smells of the mountains, the prayers of the women—all are entangled. As Iliana prays to see the image on the wall, her dream image appears, and she sees not Christ, but the man of her dreams. She is overwhelmed, and as she faints, she visualizes the rolling clouds, the red color of the earth, and the man.

When she awakes, it has grown cooler and darker, and Iliana wonders about what she saw, whether it was the devil tempting her or the answer to the dream. She cannot find Onofre right away and runs into a field of fragrant purple alfalfa, almost like her dream. This time, she sees the man in the field; it is her husband. Both confess that they did not see the face of Christ on the wall, but both have realized the meaning of their separate dreams. As they stand together, they speak of the dreams and the need to share them. They understand the meaning of dreams and go home, to new awakenings for each other and to their life connected to the land.

All through the story, the colors, shapes, and textures of the landscape blend into the texture of Iliana's life. The future relationship of the two young people will harmonize with that landscape, because the land nourishes the human spirit. By synthesizing the details of dream and reality, Anaya successfully communicates this creative energy throughout the story.

BLESS ME, ULTIMA

First published: 1972
Type of work: Novel

Helped by the spiritual guidance of his grandmother, a young Mexican American boy endures the struggles of growing up.

Bless Me, Ultima, the book that established Anaya as an important writer, is often considered his best work. The novel tells the story of three years in the life of Antonio Marez, a young Mexican American boy living in the small New Mexico farm village of Guadalupe around the time of World War II. During these years, Antonio experiences tragedies and struggles. He emerges as a more mature person because of his relationship with his grandmother and spiritual guide, Ultima.

In exploring this relationship, Anaya uses a large variety of interesting materials and techniques. He interweaves legendary and mythic details into realistic descriptions of the New Mexican landscape to create a rich picture of the lifestyle of the characters. He tells the story from the point of view of the narrator, the boy Antonio, but endows him with insights too mature for a young person, thus creating a multiple point of view for the events. Moreover, Anaya frequently incorporates dreams into the story. The plot consists of the struggles Anaya considers the important ones in life, those concerning loss of faith and family problems. It examines Anaya's favorite theme: that harmony and reconciliation are necessary for self-knowledge and spiritual fulfillment.

Antonio's parents welcome Ultima, a *curandera* (spiritual guide), into their family in the first chapter. This begins Antonio's awareness of the passage of time. He comments that the time of childhood seemed to stand still. In the middle of the chapter, Anaya uses the boy's dream to accentuate the element of time as well as to introduce the conflict between his mother's desire for a stable life and his father's desire to keep the old ways of the *vaquero*, the traditional Mexican life for a man.

It is Ultima who helps Antonio through the family struggle between these two philosophies, as well as through his problems with his three brothers and two sisters and through the other conflicts in the book. Antonio excels in school and socially; however, he has problems with his relationship to the church, because he cannot reconcile its spiritual teachings with the bureaucracy and artifice connected to it. He also experiences four deaths, including the drowning of a close friend. Through all these struggles, Ultima provides stability by satisfying Antonio's emotional and intellectual needs, thus enabling him to grow spiritually as well. The story ends with Ultima's death. The book describes only three years in Antonio's life, but at the end, he is a different person.

To add dimension to Antonio's character, Anaya frequently includes dreams made up of legendary and mythic materials. Dreams influence his outlook and conduct. For example, dreams in which battles of mythic proportion appear often lead into real arguments with his parents. A complex nightmare involving ancient rituals and symbols of horror enables him to understand the real events of a friend's murder. At the end, when events affirm Antonio's growth and development, the dreams become a quieting, healing experience, paralleling the influence of Ultima upon him.

Even though the boy is only eight years old at the novel's end, the process and themes Anaya deals with are universal. The structure of the narration, and the mingling of dream, legend, and reality make the work interesting. Anaya's vision of balance and wholeness and his ability to synthesize details from many sources to create myths make *Bless Me Ultima* an important work.

HEART OF AZTLÁN

First published: 1976
Type of work: Novel

Members of a Mexican American family react differently in confronting the problems they encounter when they move from a rural farming community to a barrio in a large city.

Heart of Aztlán is the second novel in a trilogy begun with *Bless Me, Ultima* and concluded with *Tortuga*. Each of the novels involves a seer, a spiritual guide to help the characters deal with the problems they face and to help structure the spiritual wholeness, peace, and harmony that bring them understanding of their identity and purpose. In *Heart of Aztlán*, this spiritual guide is Crispin, a blind poet who enters the life of the Chavez family as they encounter the hostile environment of the Albuquerque barrio.

The story takes place in 1950, when the family moves from the small rural community of Guadalupe to the barrio of the big city. There they encounter many problems, and each faces these differently. The family's eldest son manages to find work, but the youngest son becomes a drug addict and is eventually killed. The middle son, like his father, reveres the land they have left and cannot make the adjustment to new surroundings. Because his father becomes an alcoholic, the middle son must take over the leadership of the family. The women, who are portrayed stereotypically, face equal hardships. Two daughters become prostitutes, and the mother must take orders from her middle son. This is the family situation when Crispin enters.

His arrival brings changes, especially to the father, Clemente, who has not been able to cope with the technology, religion, or capitalism of the city. Crispin helps him to find the spiritual strength to see things clearly. Eventually, Clemente becomes a barrio leader. Anaya is working with social and political issues in this novel, and he leaves many parts of the story line confused as he makes a statement about the exploitation of human beings.

The end of the novel is intended to be uplifting but is, rather, confusing and unsatisfying. The people, along with Clemente, "shout without fear." Even though they are not afraid, they have not succeeded in achieving the spiritual wholeness suggested by the appearance of the seer Crispin. Anaya uses a mixture of dreams and symbols to suggest such events as the death of the youngest boy, Benjie, and their place in the universe. As a whole, however, these, too, do not fit together.

Anaya himself said that his novel was an experiment in combining elements from myth with socioeconomic themes from barrio life. The resulting novel covers too much too simplistically. Even though *Heart of Aztlán* gives a picture of conditions facing Mexican Americans in the 1950's, Anaya writes best when he deals with political themes indirectly.

Summary

Antonio Marquez, in his 1982 essay "The Achievement of Rudolfo A. Anaya," notes that "Anaya's work is at the vanguard that promises to liberate Chicano literature from the confines of 'ethnic' or 'regional' literature." Accomplishing this has made Rudolfo Anaya one of the most popular and acclaimed writers in contemporary Mexican American fiction.

Anaya's first work, *Bless Me, Ultima*, is still acknowledged as his best. Yet his vision, mythmaking, richly poetic images, and attention to the craft of the narrative characterize many of his other works, and the themes dealing with harmony and spiritual fulfillment continue to speak not only to a Chicano but also to a universal point of view.

Bibliography

Bruce-Novoa, Juan. *Chicano Authors: Inquiry by Interview*. Austin: University of Texas Press, 1980.

Cheuse, Alan. "The Voice of the Chicano: Letter from the Southwest." *The New York Times Book Review*, October 11, 1981, 15, 36-37.

Gonzales-Trujillo, Cesar, ed. *Rudolfo A. Anaya: Focus on Criticism*. La Jolla, Calif.: Lalo Press, 1990.

Gwynne, R. S. *Chicano Writers*. Vol. 82 in *Dictionary of Literary Biography*, edited by Matthew J. Bruccoli. Detroit: Gale Research, 1989.

Vassallo, Paul, ed. *The Magic of Words*. Albuquerque: University of New Mexico Press, 1982.

Louise M. Stone

MAYA ANGELOU

Born: St. Louis, Missouri
April 4, 1928

Principal Literary Achievement
Primarily known for her series of autobiographies, Angelou is also a poet, dancer, singer, actress, producer, director, and scriptwriter.

Biography
Born Marguerite Annie Johnson on April 4, 1928, Maya Angelou is the daughter of Vivian Baxter and Bailey Johnson. When her parents' marriage ended in divorce, she was sent to Stamps, Arkansas, to live with her paternal grandmother, Annie Henderson. Maya was three years old, and she was joined by her brother Bailey, who gave her the name Maya.

Angelou was graduated with top honors from the Lafayette County Training School in 1940 and was sent to the San Francisco Bay Area, where her mother had moved. Continuing her education at George Washington High School, she also attended evening classes at the California Labor School, where she had a scholarship to study drama and dance. Shortly after receiving her high school diploma, she bore a son, Guy Bailey Johnson. She began a career as a professional entertainer in the 1950's as a singer-dancer at the Purple Onion, a cabaret in California. She was invited to audition for a production of *Porgy and Bess* (1935) and did, in fact, receive a part in that George Gershwin musical, giving her the opportunity to travel widely with the cast in 1954 and 1955. In 1957, she appeared in the Off-Broadway play *Calypso Heatwave* and recorded "Miss Calypso" for Liberty Records.

Three years later, Angelou and her son moved to New York, where she joined the Harlem Writers Guild and collaborated to produce, direct, and star in *Cabaret for Freedom*, which raised funds for the Southern Christian Leadership Conference (SCLC). Upon the close of that show, she became Northern coordinator for the SCLC at the invitation of Martin Luther King, Jr., with whom she worked.

Inspired by King and other civil rights leaders, she decided to move to Africa, ostensibly so that her son could be educated in Ghana. While living there, she served as assistant administrator of the University of Ghana's School of Music and Drama and also worked for the Ghanaian Broadcasting Corporation and as a freelance writer for the *Ghanaian Times*.

In subsequent years, Angelou performed in various theater productions, adapted plays for the stage, and contributed to the performing arts in multiple ways. She performed in Jean Genet's *The Blacks* in 1960 (joining a cast of stars that included James Earl Jones and Cicely Tyson) and adapted Sophocles' *Ajax* for its 1974 premiere performance at the Mark Taper Forum in Los Angeles. She also wrote the screenplays *Georgia, Georgia* (1972) and *All Day Long* (1974). Her television appearances include playing the role of Kunta Kinte's grandmother in 1977's *Roots*, serving as a guest interviewer on *Assignment America*, and appearing in a special series on creativity hosted by Bill Moyers.

Her most important contributions, however, are her writings. In 1970, she began a series of autobiographies with her book *I Know Why the Caged Bird Sings*, which was followed by subsequent autobiographies and several volumes of poetry. In 1993, she became only the second poet to read at a presidential inauguration when she read her poem "On the Pulse of Morning" at President Bill Clinton's swearing-in ceremony.

Angelou is the recipient of more than four dozen honorary degrees and numerous literary awards, among them the North Carolina Award in Literature and a lifetime appointment as the Reynolds Professor of American Studies at Wake Forest University in Winston-Salem, North Carolina. Her other honors include an appointment by President Jimmy Carter to the Commission of the International Women's Year; her recognition by *Ladies' Home Journal* as Woman of the Year in communications in 1975; and her reception, in 1983, of the Matrix Award in the field of books from the Women in Communications.

Analysis

In an interview, Maya Angelou described her autobiographical style in the follow-ing way: "I've used, or tried to use, the form of the Black minister in storytelling so that each event I write about has a beginning, a middle, and an end. And I have tried to make the selections graduate so that each episode is a level, whether of narration or drama, well always dramatic, but a level of comprehension like a staircase." Angelou's autobiographies surely demonstrate this narrative and dramatic approach, and her poems also suggest the narrator and playwright at work.

Her five volumes of autobiography reveal a narrator's strong voice as well as a playwright's ability to set a stage, introduce characters, and portray the conflicts and tensions among those characters as they interact with one another and deal with their own internal conflicts and challenges. *I Know Why the Caged Bird Sings* was published in 1970 and has been followed by subsequent self-portraits, including *Gather Together in My Name* (1974), *Singin' and Swingin' and Gettin' Merry Like Christmas* (1976), *The Heart of a Woman* (1981), and *All God's Children Need Traveling Shoes* (1986). Each volume has the Angelou touch of storytelling and dramatic rendition, and each also has the incremental sense of movement toward Angelou's idea of "a level of comprehension like a staircase."

Additionally, the volumes deal with an important theme for Angelou: survival. *I Know Why the Caged Bird Sings*, for example, narrates the placement and displacement of the author as a Southern black girl, and demonstrates that her experiences of racial discrimination, rape, and numerous other victimizations did not destroy her; on the contrary, they emboldened and strengthened her, thus committing her to survival at all costs.

In her second volume of autobiography, *Gather Together in My Name*, the scene shifts, but the message remains the same: Young mother though she is, seventeen-year-old parent though she is, she must survive and triumph over the various discriminations, mostly racial, that she endures. In a book that has a beginning, middle, and end—a structure that Angelou claims exists in all of her autobiographies—the end is an especially poignant reminder of survival. Learning a lesson from a drug addict, Angelou proclaims: "I had walked the precipice and seen it all; and at the critical moment, one man's generosity pushed me safely away from the edge. . . . I had given a promise and found my innocence. I swore I'd never lose it again."

The following three autobiographies continue this emphasis upon survival—whether it is viewed through Angelou's experiences traveling with the *Porgy and Bess* production throughout Europe, the Middle East, and North Africa, as narrated in *Singin' and Swingin' and Gettin' Merry Like Christmas*; through her experiences in New York coordinating the Southern Christian Leadership Conference for Martin Luther King, Jr., as narrated in *The Heart of a Woman*; or through Angelou's quest to find her identity in Africa, as narrated in *All God's Children Need Traveling Shoes*. Seeking survival in all five volumes of autobiography, Angelou as narrator and playwright tells her stories and sets the stage for her dramatic productions.

While it might seem that Angelou's poetry departs from these narrative and dramatic impulses, since the five volumes are, after all, verse and not prose, the opposite is actually true. Like her autobiographical narratives and dramas, the poems also tell stories and present scenes from human dramas. Perhaps the best example of this appears in Angelou's fourth volume of poetry, a collection of songlike poems published in 1983 entitled *Shaker, Why Don't You Sing?* The poem "Caged Bird," an obvious echo of Angelou's best-known autobiography, *I Know Why the Caged Bird Sings*, narrates the story of a free bird and a caged bird, the latter singing a song of freedom and survival that is the same song sung by Angelou in all of her works. The caged bird's song is a protest, as are Angelou's autobiographies, and it is also a song of hope, still another characteristic of Angelou's self-portraits. Taken together, the ten volumes of prose and poetry are narrative dramas, portraits of a woman and her culture, songs of survival at all costs.

I KNOW WHY THE CAGED BIRD SINGS

First published: 1970
Type of work: Autobiography

In this self-portrait, Maya Angelou narrates her childhood in Stamps, Arkansas, and her adolescent years in California.

I Know Why the Caged Bird Sings, Angelou's first autobiography, is a story of a child becoming an adolescent, a story of a victim who comes to realize that all people are, to some extent, victims, and a story of survival. It is a lyrical narrative—almost a prose poem in some places—in which the autobiographer's voice is strong and musical, just as the title conjures up musical imagery.

Maya Angelou as a child is a displaced person, separated from her mother and father at the age of three and moved around almost as frequently as a chess piece. Her earliest memories are of Stamps, where she and her brother Bailey are reared by their grandmother, a woman of remarkable strength and limitless love for her grandchildren. This grandmother, known as Momma, provides security for Maya and Bailey and also offers a role model for the young girl, who is beginning to understand the role of victim to which black children—and especially black girls—are subjected.

Momma owns the general store in Stamps and is respected as a businesswoman, a citizen of the community, and an honest and straightforward person. She represents the qualities that will eventually define her granddaughter, and she demonstrates those qualities on a daily basis, most especially when dealing with members of the white community. In a significant incident, she reveals the ability to survive that her granddaughter will eventually develop herself. Three young white girls come to Momma's property to taunt Momma through various antics, including one of the rudest acts possible in the South of the 1930's: calling an adult by her first name. Throughout this series of insults, Momma does not react to the girls and, instead, stands on the porch, smiling and humming a hymn. While the granddaughter is outraged by this incident, wanting to confront the girls, the grandmother remains impervious and unwilling to demean herself by responding to her attackers—except when they leave, at which point she courteously bids them farewell, calling each by her first name preceded by "Miz." The young Angelou comes to realize that Momma had won the battle by rising above the pettiness and rudeness of her inferiors. She was superior, and she had survived. She had also taught her granddaughter a lesson for all time.

Most lessons, however, need to be learned and relearned, and so Angelou faces that uphill battle when, at the age of eight, she is displaced again, this time to be returned to her mother in St. Louis. Whereas Stamps represents security and orderliness, St. Louis symbolizes its opposites. The most dramatic example of this insecure, disorderly, frightening world is the rape of eight-year-old Maya by her mother's boyfriend, Mr. Freeman. Confused and terrified by this act and the subsequent murder of Freeman—a murder that the child mistakenly thinks she has caused—Angelou becomes a voluntary mute and lives in a world of silence for nearly five years. She is healed by Bertha Flowers, a woman in Stamps, to which Maya returns. Flowers extends friendship to the mute Maya, a friendship that beckons the young girl to leave her self-imposed silence and embrace a new world of words, poems, songs, and a journal that chronicles this new stage in her life.

Moving to Oakland and then San Francisco in 1941, at the age of thirteen, Maya rejoins her mother and deals with dislocation and displacement still again. At this point in her life, however, she is maturing and learning that the role of victim, while still a role to which she is assigned, is also a role played by others—blacks and whites. She learns that the human challenge is to deal with, protest against, and rise above the trap of being victimized and exploited. In the final scene of the novel, Maya Angelou is not merely a young woman coming to this realization for herself; she is a young mother who has just borne a son and who is therefore struggling to see how she can be responsible not only for herself but also for another. The book ends with this sense of mutual responsibility and mutual survival: Mother and child know why the caged bird sings, and they will sing their song together.

ALL GOD'S CHILDREN NEED TRAVELING SHOES

First published: 1986
Type of work: Autobiography

In her fifth autobiography, Angelou relates her pilgrimage to Ghana, where she seeks to understand her African roots.

All God's Children Need Traveling Shoes is about hopelessness. In the 1960's, Angelou travels to what she believes is the place of her African roots, hoping that this country will fill the vacuum she feels for home. She joins other black Americans also questing for identity and security, and, like most of them, Angelou discovers that the geographical search is a misleading one. The source of security, she comes to learn, is not in a place but within oneself.

Choosing to live in Ghana following the end of her marriage, Angelou hopes that she and her son will find a land freed of the racial bigotry she has faced wherever she has lived or traveled. Hopeful and idealistic, she sets herself up for disappointment and disillusion. During her three-year stay in Africa, she is not welcomed as she has expected to be; even more painful, she is frequently ignored by the very people with whom she thinks she shares roots, the Africans. As she tries to understand this new kind of pain and homelessness, she also struggles with the sense of having two selves, an American self and an African self.

A stunning example of this struggle occurs when the black American community in Ghana, together with some sympathetic Ghanaians, decides to support the August 27, 1963, March on Washington—the March led by Martin Luther King, Jr.—by leading a demonstration at the U.S. Embassy in Accra. The march does not have the impact its participants hope it will have because the demonstrators, including Angelou, are ambivalent about who they are, where they are, and where their quest for security is leading them. This ambivalence is dramatized when one of the marchers jeers a black soldier who is raising the American flag in front of the American embassy, prompting Angelou to reflect on the fact that the Stars and Stripes was the flag of the expatriates and, more important, their only flag.

This recognition of her divided self continues during the remainder of her stay in Africa, including during time she spends with Malcolm X. The volatile activist has a profound impact upon Angelou, who had met him two years earlier but who sees him and hears his words from her current context of an orphan looking for a home and looking for reasons to stay in that home. As she observes the various personalities Malcolm X exhibits—from big-brother adviser to spokesperson against oppression and for revolution—she reflects on his commitment to changing the status quo in America. As she leaves, she observes that Malcolm's presence had elevated the expatriates but that his departure left them with the same sense of displacement with which they had arrived in Africa.

Ultimately, Angelou is compelled to return to the United States. She leaves Africa, having become aware that home is not a geographical location but a psychological state. She leaves having learned that her survival depends upon finding herself within herself, wearing her traveling shoes, like all God's children.

ON THE PULSE OF MORNING

First published: 1993
Type of work: Poem

This poem speaks of the importance of human beings joining together, in hope, to create and greet the future.

"On the Pulse of Morning" was read at President Bill Clinton's swearing-in ceremony in January, 1993. Only the second poet to read at a presidential inauguration, Angelou has said this about her poem: "In all my work, what I try to say is that as human beings we are more alike than we are unalike." This piece celebrates that sense of similarity, connectedness, and human solidarity.

Beginning with the recognition that rocks, rivers, and trees have witnessed the arrival and departure of many generations, "On the Pulse of Morning" proceeds to have each of these witnesses speak to the future, beginning with the the Rock, which announces that people may stand upon its back but may not find security in its shadow. On the contrary, says the Rock, humans must face the future, their "distant destiny," boldly and directly.

The River sings a similar song, calling humans to its riverside, but only if they will forego the study of war. If human beings will come to the River, "clad in peace," this ageless body of water will sing the songs given to it by the Creator, songs of unity and songs of peace.

The Tree continues this hymn of peace and hope, reminding humankind that each person is a "descendant of some passed-on traveler" and that each "has been paid for." Pawnee, Apache, Turk, Swede, Eskimo, Ashanti—all are invited by the Tree to root themselves beside it. Thus united with Rock, River, and Tree, the poem announces, the human race can look toward a future of peace and connections and away from a past of brutality and discontinuity.

In the final stanza, this paean of praise is most lyrical:

> Here on the pulse of this new day
> You may have the grace to look up and out
> And into your sister's eyes, into
> Your brother's face, your country
> And say simply
> Very simply
> With hope
> Good morning.

Like Angelou's autobiographies and like her volumes of poetry, "On the Pulse of Morning" speaks of survival. Lyrical and inspirational, it calls human beings to have the imagination and courage to build up instead of tear down, and it echoes the titles of Angelou's other works, especially *I Know Why the Caged Bird Sings*. If all caged birds sing together, this poem asserts, then the human race will indeed survive.

Summary

Maya Angelou's many achievements in diverse fields testify to both the breadth of her talent, the strength of her character, and the power of her vision. As an actress, singer, activist, playwright, poet, and—especially—a compelling autobiographer, she has succeeded in communicating her remarkable experiences and perspective to an appreciative and ever-growing audience.

Bibliography

Angelou, Maya. *Conversations with Maya Angelou*. Edited by Jeffrey M. Elliot. Jackson: University Press of Mississippi, 1989.

Cordell, Shirley J. "The Black Woman: A Focus on 'Strength of Character' in *I Know Why the Caged Bird Sings*." *Virginia English Bulletin* 36 (Winter, 1986): 36-39.

Cudjoe, Selwyn R. "Maya Angelou and the Autobiographical Statement." In *Black*

Women Writers, 1950-1980: A Critical Evaluation, edited by Mari Evans. Garden City, N.Y.: Anchor Press/Doubleday, 1983.

Demetrakopoulos, Stephanie A. "The Metaphysics of Matrilinearism in Women's Autobiography: Studies of Mead's *Blackberry Winter*, Hellman's *Pentimento*, Angelou's *I Know Why the Caged Bird Sings*, and Kingston's *Woman Warrior*." In *Women's Autobiography: Essays in Criticism*, edited by Estelle C. Jelinek. Bloomington: Indiana University Press, 1980.

Kinnamon, Kenneth. "Call and Response: Intertextuality in Two Autobiographical Works of Richard Wright and Maya Angelou." In *Belief vs. Theory in Black American Literary Criticism*, edited by Joe Weixlmann and Chester J. Fontenot. Greenwood, Fla.: Penkevill Publishing, 1986.

McPherson, Dolly A. *Order Out of Chaos: The Autobiographical Works of Maya Angelou*. New York: Peter Lang, 1990.

Neubauer, Carol. "Maya Angelou: Self and a Song of Freedom in the Southern Tradition." In *Southern Women Writers: The New Generation*, edited by Tonnette Bond Inge. Tuscaloosa: University of Alabama Press, 1990.

Redmond, Eugene B. "Boldness of Language and Breadth: An Interview with Maya Angelou." *Black American Literature Forum* 22 (Summer, 1988): 156-157.

Saunders, James Robert. "Breaking Out of the Cage: The Autobiographical Writings of Maya Angelou." *The Hollins Critic* 28 (October, 1991): 1-11.

Tate, Claudia, ed. "Maya Angelou." In *Black Women Writers at Work*. New York: Continuum, 1983.

Marjorie Smelstor

THOMAS BERGER

Born: Cincinnati, Ohio
July 20, 1924

Principal Literary Achievement

Concerned more than perhaps any other American writer of his time with the control exerted over the individual by language, Berger has written novels exploring the banality and violence of existence.

Biography

Thomas Louis Berger was born in Cincinnati, Ohio, on July 20, 1924, the only child of Charles and Mildred Bubbe Berger. He grew up in the nearby suburb of Lockland, where his father was business manager of the local school system. Encouraged by both parents, especially his mother, young Berger read incessantly.

While in high school, he held jobs as hotel desk clerk and theater usher and worked in a branch of the Cincinnati Public Library. After briefly attending Miami University in Oxford, Ohio, and the University of Cincinnati, he enlisted in the Army in 1943. Berger served as a medic in England, France, and Germany, being stationed with the Occupation forces in Berlin following the end of World War II.

Berger was graduated with honors from the University of Cincinnati in 1948 and moved to New York City. He became a graduate student at Columbia University in 1950, took Lionel Trilling's famous course in modern American literature, and began a thesis on George Orwell but never finished. He also studied at Charles Glicksberg's writers' workshop at the New School for Social Research, at the same time as Jack Kerouac, William Styron, and Mario Puzo. Berger had decided to become a writer when he was sixteen, having been inspired by the urbane, erudite commentators on the radio program Information Please. At the New School workshop, he wrote a story a week for three months, beginning with melancholy, maudlin, simple stories in the manner of Ernest Hemingway before coming under the influence of William Faulkner. On June 12, 1950, he married Jeanne Redpath, an artist he had met at the New School.

During the late 1940's and early 1950's, Berger worked as a librarian at the Rand School of Social Science, as a staff member of *The New York Times Index*, and as a copy editor for *Popular Science Monthly*. In this period, he wrote reviews for *New Leader* and *Institute of Social Studies Bulletin* and published his first short story, the Hemingway-influenced "Dependency of Day and Night," in *Western Review* in 1952.

In 1954, the Bergers moved to Rockland County, New York, on the Hudson River so that he could devote more time to his writing while working as a freelance copy editor for publishing houses. After rejections from four publishers, Berger's first novel, *Crazy in Berlin*, was published in 1958. This novel and its sequel, *Reinhart in Love* (1962), sold a meager 4,500 copies. His third novel, *Little Big Man* (1964), sold 10,000 copies and won the Western Heritage Award and the Richard and Hinda Rosenthal Foundation Award, presented by the American Academy and Institute of Arts and Letters for a notable work of fiction not considered a commercial success. Berger began receiving more public attention with the release of the 1970 film version of *Little Big Man*, directed by Arthur Penn and starring Dustin Hoffman.

Sales of the film rights to several of his novels allowed the Bergers the freedom to move about while he has continued to practice his craft; they have lived in England, California, Maine, and New York. In addition, Berger has taught at the University of Kansas, Southampton College, Yale University, and the University of California at Davis.

Analysis

While his novels have been generally well received by reviewers, and while he is regarded by his colleagues as a writer's writer, Thomas Berger's overall critical reputation has suffered somewhat because of the difficulty of categorizing his work, which does not fit into any standard literary movement or school. Critics often misunderstand Berger's intentions or lazily lump him into a misleading category. Because of the humor, violence, and absurdity in most of his novels, he has sometimes been grouped with the black humorists, yet his fiction lacks the anger and delight in the grotesque associated with black humor. While there are strong satirical elements in his novels, Berger similarly rejects the label of satirist. He has little interest in overtly criticizing society; he is too pessimistic to believe it can change its ways.

Because several of his novels exploit the conventions of fictional genres, Berger has also been called a parodist—yet in these books, he is not making light of genres but lovingly paying homage to their conventions. *Little Big Man* is a Western; the futuristic *Regiment of Women* (1973) has science-fiction elements; *Who Is Teddy Villanova?* (1977) is a detective novel; *Arthur Rex* (1978) is an Arthurian romance; *Nowhere* (1985) resembles a spy thriller; *Being Invisible* (1987) is an antiutopian novel; and *Orrie's Story* (1990) retells the Orestes legend, updating Greek tragedy to small-town America at the end of World War II. In interviews, Berger has expressed his disgust at reviewers' labeling of these works as parodies. His goal has been, rather, to celebrate these genres by identifying and applauding their characteristic plots, protagonists, themes, and other devices.

Although Berger is also uncomfortable with being called a comic novelist, he is clearly a comic writer in the tradition of Charles Dickens (a major influence on his work), Mark Twain, and Franz Kafka. Lacking the moral fervor of the true satirist, Berger exposes his characters' foibles with compassion. He stands out from other American novelists of his time by writing about ordinary people with acceptance of their deficiencies and without condescension. Despite the almost complete absence of sentimentality in his fiction and despite his constant illustration of negative aspects of his characters' behavior, Berger displays an unusual tolerance for human weaknesses. Nevertheless, his characters are presented with strong irony. Their interpretations of the reality they encounter are never entirely accurate or reliable.

Resisting both idealism and despair, Berger is the least didactic of novelists. He apparently agrees with Dr. Otto Knebel in *Crazy in Berlin*, who says, "If you think I shall tell you what is right or wrong, my friend, you are mistaken. That is your own affair. I care only for practical matters." While his characters may believe in causes, they learn, often painfully, that such beliefs are not beneficial to their individuality, as with the devotion of the knights to the chivalric code in *Arthur Rex.*

Despite his claim that his fiction is not thematic, Berger's novels do say something about the problem of identity, the uncertainty of human relationships, the prevalance of violence in all societies, and the elusiveness of truth. Still, readers will best appreciate his work if they heed his warning to approach it "without the luggage of received ideas, *a priori* assumptions, sociopolitical axes to grind, or feeble moralities in search of support."

While a major subject in Berger's fiction is victimization, his characters are enslaved primarily by perceptions bounded by language. His books are about the characters' efforts to free themselves from someone else's definition of reality, a necessarily verbal definition. In *Killing Time* (1967), Berger shows how perceptions of violent crime are influenced by the language used to describe it, whether journalistic, legalistic (varying from police to lawyers), or sensationalistic, as in the tabloid press. *Killing Time*'s Joe Detweiler, a murderer, says, "The act is the truth, really. Everything else is language." By cutting himself off from language, Detweiler loses touch with reality.

Berger shows how language can be a weapon with varying degrees of effectiveness. In *Neighbors* (1980), Earl Keese foolishly attempts to protect himself from the assaults of his obnoxious neighbors, Harry and Ramona, with conventionally polite phrases and clichés. Rejecting the apparent advances of the seductive Ramona, Earl conducts a conversation through a keyhole: "If you'd act right for once, then maybe I could perform as a decent neighbor. My intent is good—in fact it has been since the first—but you and Harry have always succeeded in alienating me, I don't know why." Ramona replies, "Have you got gonorrhea or something?" After Earl expresses outrage at this suggestion and Ramona fails to respond, he modifies his position: "But maybe I didn't hear you correctly, so skip my criticism. I really would like to begin with a clean slate." Ramona unsettles this conventional man by saying the unexpected, and Earl's inherent decency, which is not being mocked, makes him think he may be the one in the wrong. Such failures to communicate are central to Berger's humor.

In *Who Is Teddy Villanova?*, detective Russel Wren constructs plausible theories to explain everything that transpires in the novel, only to have the theories finally explain nothing. Berger overturns the expectations of the typical reader of mysteries who expects logical explanations for everything by offering another set of explanations to offset those imagined by Wren. Berger illustrates how many human problems result from errors in communication and from confusion created by the inexact use of language, showing how, in a world of words, language determines the quality of experience.

CRAZY IN BERLIN

First published: 1958
Type of work: Novel

A naïve, somewhat idealistic young American soldier in post-World War II Berlin is initiated into the moral ambiguity and violence of life.

Crazy in Berlin, which opens on Carlo Reinhart's twenty-first birthday, is Berger's only remotely autobiographical novel, a coming-of-age tale in which his protagonist learns something about the complexities of the modern world. As an Army medic in Berlin following the end of World War II, Reinhart meets a wide variety of Americans, Germans, and Russians who introduce him to love, chaos, and madness. He spends much of the novel wandering from one lying or misinformed person to another as he acquires some sense of his identity.

The other characters include the idealistic Lieutenant Schild, a Jewish communist who leaks military secrets to the Russians; Lichenko, a Red Army deserter and would-be capitalist harbored temporarily by Schild; Bach, a giant, philosophical invalid who presents a case for anti-Semitism even though he hid his Jewish wife from the Nazis for four years; Dr. Otto Knebel, a former communist tortured and blinded in a Russian concentration camp who becomes a fascist after the fall of the Nazis; Schatzi, a former supporter of Adolf Hitler imprisoned in Auschwitz for his criminal activities and now a cynical Soviet agent. Then there are the three women in Reinhart's life: Lori, Bach's wife and Knebel's twin sister, who represents for Reinhart an unattainable romantic ideal; Trudschen, Lori's whorish, masochistic sixteen-year-old cousin, who appeals to Reinhart's irrational side; and Veronica Leary, a flirtatious, buxom Army nurse, who represents vulgar American normality.

After Schild, betrayed by Schatzi, is abducted by two communist agents, Reinhart attempts to rescue him. He kills one of the abductors, but Schild is murdered by the other. Reinhart, who receives a serious head wound, undergoes six months of therapy in a psychiatric ward. He obtains revenge for Schild by betraying the treacherous Schatzi.

Reinhart tells his psychiatrist that Schild was insane for believing in the King Arthur stories he read as a boy and that he is himself crazy for sharing Schild's romantic idealism. Reinhart senses that traditional values are without philosophical justification, yet he remains loyal to them in the name of decency and civilized behavior. Constantly musing on what it means to be Jewish, consumed by guilt over his German ancestry, aware of his potential for evil, Reinhart sees all sides to every argument and feels responsible for any injustice. He is on a seemingly endless quest to understand what cannot be understood.

Reinhart's often comic quest continues in *Reinhart in Love*, in which he returns to what passes for normality in America, finishes college, and marries a shrew; *Vital Parts* (1970), in which he has become a middle-aged failure at marriage, fatherhood, and business; and *Reinhart's Women* (1981), in which he keeps house for his daughter, a successful model, becomes a gourmet cook, and finally loses his grand expectations for himself, shedding his guilt and self-pity in the process. Reinhart has been called one of the most original heroes in American fiction because he embodies so many aspects of the American character in his journey through confusion and despair and because he maintains his integrity and humanity in an increasingly materialistic, nihilistic world. A good-hearted man in a corrupt society, he is a victim of his virtues.

LITTLE BIG MAN

First published: 1964
Type of work: Novel

A white man is adopted by Indians but eventually fits into neither white nor Indian societies.

Little Big Man is 111-year-old Jack Crabb's account of his life from 1852, when he is ten and most of his family is killed by drunken Indians, to 1876, when he becomes the only white survivor of the Battle of the Little Bighorn. During these twenty-four years, Jack is adopted first by Old Lodge Skins, chief of a small band of Northern Cheyenne, and later by the Reverend Mr. Pendrake and his beautiful, unfaithful young wife. Leaving the Pendrakes, Jack alternates between white and Indian societies, never fitting in comfortably with either. He longs for middle-class comforts, but circumstances and his restless nature block his success.

Jack is constantly being victimized. His white wife and child are stolen by Indians and later killed by the cavalry, as are his Cheyenne wife and their newborn son. Except for Old Lodge Skins, all Jack's Indian friends are killed—one, ironically, when he is unknowingly about to kill Jack. Jack is shot on four occasions, and only his roguish trickery saves him from being killed in a gunfight by Wild Bill Hickok. The novel builds to General George Armstrong Custer's fiasco at the Little Bighorn and to the death of Old Lodge Skins, who chooses to die when he recognizes that the destruction of the Indian way of life is inevitable. Despite Berger's presentation of the American West as violent, melodramatic, and absurd, *Little Big Man* has lighter moments stemming from a multitude of colorful characters and a plethora of coincidences recalling those in the novels of Dickens.

Always concerned with the differences between reality and the various ways it is perceived, Berger debunks the myth of the West. Legendary heroes are not that heroic: Kit Carson denies hard-luck Jack a handout, Wyatt Earp knocks him out for belching, and Hickok is tired, sad, and paranoid. Berger's Indians are hardly noble savages: Their camps stink, they eat dogs, and their women and children mutilate wounded enemies. The West is so beclouded by myth, however, that the truth can never be known. Even eyewitness accounts such as Jack's are untrustworthy because of the way matters are distorted to fit preconceptions and fulfill stereotypes.

Despite considerable evidence to the contrary, Berger's characters adhere to their romantic illusions. After their wagon train is attacked and members of her family are raped and murdered, Jack's sister Caroline follows the Cheyenne because she thinks they lust after her and because she wants to be an Indian princess. The savages dispel her misconceptions by failing to recognize that she is a woman. Years later, she reminds Jack of how the Indians "brutally stole" her "maidenhood." Since the truth is embarrassing, she has created her own myth.

Most important is *Little Big Man*'s presentation of Jack as the American innocent in search of his identity and the meaning of America. He is modern man trapped in a chaotic, often meaningless universe. The natural order of the Indian world is attractive but unrealistic when confronted by rampaging progress, but the more artificial order of the white world, in which all that can be aspired to is respectability, seems superficial. The only true order or meaning is that created by the individual, but he must recognize its limitations.

THE FEUD

First published: 1983
Type of work: Novel

In small-town America during the Depression, a series of misunderstandings result in a feud between two families.

The Feud is perhaps Berger's best example of what he has called "pure fiction"— relatively free of journalistic, sociological, and similar thematic concerns. The novel's deliberately complicated plot and large cast of characters serve primarily to support its stylistic concerns, which, more than anywhere else in Berger's work, center on the way in which people manipulate language to justify often outrageous behavior.

The dispute between these Depression-era families somewhere in middle America begins when Dolf Beeler goes to Bud Bullard's hardware store for paint remover and, when he refuses to dispose of his unlit cigar, gets into an argument with Junior Bullard (Bud's teenage son) and Reverton Kirby (Bud's cousin). When the store burns down that night, Dolf is blamed, and Bud, who has no insurance, attempts suicide and later has a breakdown. Events soon escalate; Dolf's car blows up, and Dolf bloodies the nose of kindly Walt Huff, Bud's brother-in-law, before having a heart attack. The endless series of disasters in this comedy of errors is complicated by a misguided love affair between Dolf's son and Bud's daughter, making the novel a blend of the legendary Hatfield-McCoy feud and William Shakespeare's *Romeo and Juliet* (1595).

As usual, Berger's characters are searching, blindly and ineptly, for freedom and self-respect and are hindered primarily by the foolish limitations they impose upon their perceptions of the world. The ironically named Rev considers himself a man of principles because of his faith in such beliefs as *"Worship the Lord, but never trust a preacher any farther than you can throw him."* *The Feud* is a catalog of such twisted clichés, which the characters employ as a way of ordering their chaotic universe. Berger does not condemn them but celebrates their faith in the American vernacular and the energy of their language: "Don't give me any lip, you runt. You want somepin t'eat, you just gimme your order." Berger also indulges himself occasionally by blending all of his linguistic devices into a frenzy, as when Rev comes upon Dolf's daughter Bernice engaged in sex with fireman Ernie Krum: "You think you can come up here where innocent women and children are living and corpulate like unto animals of the field, make a spectacle of yourself, hold up to mockery all the principles of God-fearing men, roll in slime and throw it in our face? I'd like to see you both kestrated."

Despite such excesses, Berger seems genuinely to like his foolish creations. They are always distinctive individuals, never types. The guardians of the Pulitzer Prize overruled their committee's selection of *The Feud* as the best work of fiction for 1983 probably because of their inability to understand the concept of pure fiction, because Berger's novel lacks the obvious thematic content expected of "serious" fiction. Yet in presenting the chaos created in part by language, Berger cannot escape such content, and he paints a loving tribute to contemporary paranoia.

Summary

Style and content are inseparable in Thomas Berger's distinctively American novels. His characters assert their identities through language. Speaking to his friend Reinhart in *Vital Parts*, Splendor Mainwaring, who defines himself in part by changing his name, says of his son, who also changes his name several times, "Raymond will say almost anything. He has discovered the technique of bold assertion, in which the content is almost irrelevant. He is American to the core: to *say* is to *be*. You and I make a distinction between rhetoric and reality." This distinction between reality and the way in which language is used to create or distort it is the essence of Berger's fictional world. He has said that he writes to amuse himself and looks for himself through the English language: "Language is tremendously important to me. It's a morality and a politics and a religion. I really believe that if you write well you're a 'good' man." Berger's novels deal uniquely and entertainingly with how language and morality are intertwined.

Bibliography

Cleary, Michael. "Finding the Center of the Earth: Satire, History, and Myth in *Little Big Man*." *Western American Literature* 15 (Fall, 1980): 195-211.

Hughes, Douglas. "The Schlemiel as Humanist: Thomas Berger's Carlo Reinhart." *Cithara* 15 (November, 1975): 3-21.

——————. "Thomas Berger's Elan." *Confrontation* 12 (Spring-Summer, 1976): 23-39.

Landon, Brooks. *Thomas Berger*. Boston: Twayne, 1989.

Lee, L. L. "American, Western, Picaresque: Thomas Berger's *Little Big Man*." *South Dakota Review* 4 (Summer, 1966): 35-42.

Madden, David. "Thomas Berger's Comic-Absurd Vision in *Who Is Teddy Villanova?*" *Armchair Detective* 14 (Winter, 1981): 37-43.

Pinsker, Sanford. "The World According to Carl Reinhart: Thomas Berger's Comic Vision." *Studies in American Humor* 2 (Fall, 1983): 101-110.

Ruud, Jay. "Thomas Berger's *Arthur Rex*: Galahad and Earthly Power." *Critique* 25 (Winter, 1984): 92-100.

Schickel, Richard. "Interviewing Thomas Berger." *The New York Times Book Review*, April 6, 1980, 1, 21-22.

Weales, Gerald. "Reinhart as Hero and Clown." *Hollins Critic* 20 (December, 1983): 1-12.

Michael Adams

KAY BOYLE

Born: St. Paul, Minnesota
February 19, 1902
Died: Mill Valley, California
December 27, 1992

Principal Literary Achievement

The author of novels, short stories, children's books, essays, and articles, Boyle received several major awards for her fiction.

Biography

Kay Boyle was born in St. Paul, Minnesota, on February 19, 1902, the daughter of Howard Peterson Boyle and Katherine Evans Boyle. Her father was a rather dim but well-intentioned figure in her life, while her paternal grandfather, Jesse Payton Boyle, was described by Kay as brilliant, reactionary, domineering, and destructive. Boyle's mother was active in the radical labor movement and other political causes, while her grandfather consistently criticized and opposed both mother and daughter. In Robert McAlmon's memoir, *Being Geniuses Together*, which Boyle revised and expanded in 1968, she credited her mother with being the dominant influence in her life. It was her mother who instilled in her daughter social, political, and artistic values that permeated Boyle's work.

Boyle's formal schooling was sketchy: a few terms at two private girls' schools, a short time at the Cincinnati Conservatory of Music, and two years at the Ohio Mechanics Institute in Cincinnati, Ohio, where the family had moved in 1916. Travel took the place of conventional education in Boyle's life; while still a girl she accompanied her family to Europe as well as to several cities in America. Indeed, travel became a constant factor in her life as she moved from one place to another; at various times, she lived in France, England, Austria, Germany, and Spain.

Before going off on her own, Boyle worked in her father's Cincinnati office for a short while, then moved to New York, where she found a job working on *Broom*, one of several avant-garde literary publications with which she was to become associated in America and Europe. The 1920's and 1930's were the era of the "little magazines," which promoted literary experimentation and innovation.

In June, 1922, Boyle married Robert Brault, a Frenchman, and the couple went to France in June, 1923, to spend the summer with Brault's family in St. Malo. Afterward,

they moved to Paris, Le Havre, and the village of Harfleur, where, in 1924, Boyle began her second novel (the manuscript of the first was lost in the mail). As was to be the case with almost all of her novels and much of her short fiction, Boyle drew heavily upon events and persons in her own life for her material. *Plagued by the Nightingale*, a novel published in 1931, grew out of the period that she and her husband spent with his family in St. Malo.

The marriage was shaky, and after meeting Ernest Walsh in 1925, Boyle became deeply involved with him and with his new magazine, *This Quarter*. Her early short fiction and poetry appeared in this review. Walsh died in October, 1926, and in March, 1927, Boyle gave birth to Walsh's daughter, Sharon. Briefly, she rejoined her husband, but the marriage came to an end in 1928.

Boyle was one of the many expatriate writers living and working in Paris in the period between the two world wars who came to be known as the "Lost Generation." Her work began to appear in a new magazine, *transition*, in which also appeared the work of such writers as James Joyce, Gertrude Stein, Hart Crane, and Archibald MacLeish. Her poems, stories, reviews, a translation, and the preliminary drafts of a novel, *Year Before Last* (1932), appeared in this review. Her first book, a collection of short stories, was published in 1929, followed by *Wedding Day and Other Stories* in 1930.

In the next ten years, Boyle's published work included six novels, three short-story collections, three translations, two ghostwritten volumes, a book of three short novels, a book for children, a collection of poems, and an anthology. During the same period, she won two O. Henry Awards for best short story of the year, and three of her stories appeared in the annual O. Henry anthologies. Forty of her stories were named in Edward O'Brien's annual collection of *Best American Short Stories*.

In 1931, Boyle married Laurence Vail, and the couple had three daughters. The Vails were divorced in 1943, after which she married Baron Joseph von Franckenstein and had two more children. The baron died in 1963.

In the years between 1942 and 1975, another eight Boyle novels appeared. Her short stories and short novels were published in ten collections. She also published five volumes of poetry and numerous translations, essays, articles, and other works of nonfiction.

Despite her prolific output, Boyle was not able to make enough money by her writing, and she supplemented her income by teaching. Although she had never been graduated from college, she taught writing at a girls' school in Connecticut and at San Francisco State College (later San Francisco State University). She lectured and served as writer-in-residence at several colleges and universities and was made a Fellow of Wesleyan University and the Radcliffe Institute of Independent Study. Boyle won two Guggenheim Fellowships, two honorary doctorates, a National Endowment for the Arts Fellowship for her "extraordinary contribution to American literature over a lifetime of creative work," and many other awards.

Following the example of her mother, Boyle was active in political causes all her life, in both Europe and America. Among the issues with which she was concerned were the rise of Nazism, the World War II defeat of France, the Resistance movement, the occupation of Germany, the Joseph McCarthy hearings, and the movement against the Vietnam War. An outspoken and passionate champion of the poor and oppressed and a strong spokesperson for the rights of individuals, Boyle reflected her concerns in her prose and poetry. Her personal life formed the substance of her fiction, and her political views permeated her work as well. For example, *Death of a Man* (1936) included material from her life in Austria, and her last novel, *The Underground Woman* (1975), concerns the experiences of a middle-aged woman who is arrested for taking part in an anti-Vietnam War demonstration, reflecting an experience that Boyle herself had undergone.

Because of her prodigious production over the years between 1931 and 1984, Boyle was recognized as a chronicler of the twentieth century, a popular author who occupied an indisputable place in the roster of important writers of her time. When she died in 1992, at the age of ninety, not all critics accorded her a place in the first rank of American writers, but it was universally acknowledged that she had made a worthy and valuable contribution to American literature.

Analysis

Kay Boyle's belief in the moral responsibility of the writer is clearly evident in everything that she wrote. Writing in *Story* in 1963, she expressed her conviction that a writer is "a moralist in the highest sense of the word" whose responsibility is "to speak briefly and clearly of the dignity and the integrity of individual man." The strongly autobiographical element in most of her work is also apparent. The theme running through all of her work is the absolute necessity of love and the many obstacles and failures that prevent its fulfillment, such as narrow-mindedness, social conventions, bigotry, misunderstandings, and the tragedies of ordinary lives caught in war and other insuperable obstacles. The assertion of her moral convictions and the dependence on personal experience for her narrative sources characterize Boyle's fiction, which is consistently concerned with the importance of love in its many guises, manifestations, and frustrations.

That Boyle's life was extraordinary cannot be denied; thus, her use of her own experiences is understandable. As Sandra Whipple Spanier pointed out in a study of Boyle's life and work, Boyle was "a fascinating woman who, in addition to writing over thirty books, had three husbands and six children and managed to be in the important places at the important times, participating actively in many of the major movements and events of our century. The effects of war—of defeat and occupation— were therefore prominent in her work." *Avalanche* (1944), her most popular novel, highlights the bravery of the French Resistance. *A Frenchman Must Die* (1946) also focuses on the Resistance as it describes how a former Resistance fighter brings to justice a French aristocrat who collaborated with the Nazis. Other novels deal with the problems faced by the French and Germans as they rebuild their war-ravaged countries. The short story "The White Horses of Vienna" also deals with the issue of the rise of Nazism in Austria. Other stories, such as those in *Life Being the Best and*

Other Stories (1988), concentrate on the search for love and meaning in individual lives. The novel *Monday Night* (1938) is an examination of two men on a quest for a prominent scientist whose false testimony has led to the conviction of several innocent men. In her last novel, *The Underground Woman*, Boyle capped her long career with an account of an event in her own life. The book tells of some women who were arrested and jailed for participating in a protest demonstration at an induction center during the Vietnam War. In her final fictional work, Boyle was thus true to the issues and ideals that had concerned her throughout her writing life.

Boyle received considerable attention and praise for her innovative and original style, especially in the early years, when she was a prominent member of the group of writers who in the 1920's and 1930's were rebelling against prevailing literary conventions. Boyle's style has been called poetic; it is intense, colored by strong images, trenchant metaphors, and telling details. Often, she writes in the stream-of-consciousness style that the modernists invented, expressing the thoughts and feelings of her characters through their own words, often in interior monologues, keeping herself as narrator in the background, even offstage.

One of the most notable of Boyle's literary characteristics is the way in which she tells her stories on two levels. The explicit events and descriptions are concerned with vividly drawn characters speaking in their own voices. She tends to use dialogue much more than narration. Beneath the surface, however, is the implied significance of what she is really writing about, the larger world stage on which individual lives are played out. Thus the focus, especially in her short stories, is highly concentrated—on, for example, a particular situation or an intense conversation that actually illustrates a larger theme, such as the human spirit in adversity or the disappointment of unfulfilled love. Boyle's tone is often rueful, even sad, revealing her compassion and concern for her characters.

Some critics have found Boyle melodramatic and self-conscious, her plots contrived, and her style affected. Her overriding aim, to transform society, has struck some as blatant and intrusive, and her emphasis on the necessity of love has been criticized as sentimental and overdrawn. Nevertheless, many other critics have admired her for the complexity and sensibility of her work and for the beauty and poignancy of her style. Certainly, the many awards and honors that she received indicate that Boyle deserved, and received, recognition as an important and distinguished writer.

ANSCHLUSS

First published: 1940
Type of work: Short story

A young American woman is deeply affected by the changes in Austria resulting from the unification of that country with Germany.

"Anschluss" was regarded by many readers as one of Boyle's best stories about the effects of the rise of Nazism before World War II. Boyle's so-called war stories never take place on the battlefield. Instead, she shows how individuals' lives are touched by the events leading up to and during the larger conflicts. The characters are usually civilians, but some are military personnel caught by Boyle's observant eye away from the war front.

The heroine of "Anschluss" is a young woman named Merrill who works in Paris as an assistant to a fashion editor. Twice a year, Merrill takes a trip to her favorite vacation place, the village of Brenau in the mountains of Austria. The time is the 1930's. Boyle draws a sharp contrast between the trivialities of Merrill's life in Paris and the desperate straits of her two Austrian friends, Fanni and her brother Toni. Because of worldwide Depression, the two young Austrians are struggling to survive in a place where there are only occasional small jobs and little money.

Merrill remembers meeting Fanni on her first visit two years ago, in 1936. Her brother Toni had been arrested for engaging in political activities deemed treasonous. On this night, Fanni is celebrating Toni's release from jail. His appearance at the guest house marks the beginning of Merrill's romance, in which she abandons herself to the casual, careless life of the young Austrians, who manage to enjoy themselves despite their poverty and the uncertainty of their future, "as if they all knew that something else was going to happen in a little while." Merrill tries to persuade Toni to return with her to Paris, but he refuses, saying that he belongs in his own country.

In 1938, the Anschluss (the uniting of Austria and Germany) takes place, and Merrill, returning to Brenau, expects that Toni is still rebelling and agitating. Yet the change that has taken place in the fortunes of Austria has changed Toni as well. He now has a real job, as director of the Austrian Youth Local. When Merrill goes to the lake where Toni is the sports organizer, she feels awkward and self-conscious in her two-piece bathing suit, as she is surrounded by large, plainly dressed Germans on vacation, the "invading cohorts," as Boyle calls them. Toni criticizes Merrill for looking like an actress in a musical comedy. Clearly, he has changed. His carefree manner has disappeared, and he speaks gratefully of the Germans, who respect the Austrians. He sees no irony in the fact that the Germans regard Austria as a vacation ground, just as the bitterly resented Americans and English had formerly done.

The next day, Merrill sees Toni for the last time. At the train station, he is on the platform with several other young people in uniform. She is on the train; through the window, she sees him step toward her as if to speak, but instead he clicks his heels together and lifts his hands in a salute. She cannot tell whether he is saying "Heil Hitler" or wishing her farewell.

It is characteristic of Boyle that she draws no morals in this story, nor does she point out the obvious concerning Fanni and Toni's acceptance of the Nazis. The bleak, simple ending is also typical of Boyle's style; having presented three appealing young characters and their situations in vivid, concise terms, she knows when to stop.

MONDAY NIGHT

First published: 1938
Type of work: Novel

Two men, searching for a famous toxicologist whose evidence has led to the convictions of several men, discover the shocking truth about him.

Monday Night, Boyle's sixth novel, is the only one that does not have an autobiographically-based American woman as its heroine.

Wilt, the main character of *Monday Night*, is an expatriate newspaperman who has lived in Paris for twenty years. He dreams of writing a great novel, if he can only find the right subject. A seedy, alcoholic, physically repulsive, single-minded middle-aged man, he believes that he has finally discovered the story that will enable him to realize his dream. He has been led to this conclusion by his chance meeting with Bernie, a young, naïve American doctor who has come to Paris to pay homage to the famous Monsieur Sylvestre, the toxicologist whose testimony has resulted in the conviction and imprisonment—and sometimes execution—of several men.

Wilt is captivated by Bernie's quest, but he is much less interested in helping the younger man fulfill his goal than he is in his own thoughts, fantasies, and thirsts. Bernie, bewildered and tired, cannot resist Wilt, who drags him from one bar to another looking for leads to the famous scientist. They find his house; he is not there, but a strange butler shows them around and obliquely reveals the truth about his employer. As they meet several people who know Sylvestre through various connections, Wilt begins to suspect that the man they are looking for is actually a criminal who has falsified his evidence in order to make up for his own failures in love and life.

Wilt becomes more and more excited, convinced that he now has the material to write the great novel of which he has dreamed. As the sinister and sordid story is revealed, Wilt is quite unconcerned about its effect on Bernie, who, after traveling all the way to Paris to express his admiration of his hero, has seen his ideals shattered.

At a train station, Wilt catches sight of Sylvestre alighting from a train. At the same time, Wilt sees a newspaper headline indicating that several murder cases involving Sylvestre's testimony have been reopened. Bernie has disappeared. It is clear that no one will ever know of Wilt's independent search and discovery.

This is not a pleasant story. Boyle seems to be saying that Wilt is doomed to failure, just as Bernie is fated for disappointment. Their quest was worthy, but they themselves were not able to meet the challenge. The fault lies not in their ideals but in their own weaknesses.

The larger political and social issues that concerned Boyle so urgently in her other fiction are not emphasized here; perhaps as a result, *Monday Night* is one of her most popular novels. It is also the one that Boyle said was her own favorite. It is not typical of Boyle's writing, but with its concentrated focus, its original characters, and its suspenseful plot, it is quite possibly not only her most popular but also her best novel.

THE UNDERGROUND WOMAN

First published: 1975
Type of work: Novel

A woman caught up in two of the major American issues of the 1960's reconciles the two roles that she has played in her life.

In *The Underground Woman*, Boyle's last novel, the author characteristically draws upon her own experiences for her basic framework. Like her heroine, Athena Gregory, Boyle was jailed for participating in a demonstration against the war in Vietnam; likewise, her daughter rejected her family and joined a religious cult; similarly, Boyle was a professor at a San Francisco university.

The book opens with Athena and fifteen other protestors in a patrol wagon on their way to jail because they blocked the entrance of an induction center. Slightly more than half the book is taken up with Athena's observations of the personalities and actions of three groups of women: her fellow demonstrators, the long-term prisoners, and those who work in the jail. Boyle describes in detail the routine of the monotonous days, the vile food, the various jobs the prisoners are given, and their ugly clothing. She learns about the oppression of black and Chicano women and is confirmed in her conviction that older people must share the responsibility of all Americans to fight for liberty and justice for everyone.

The second part of the book finds Athena returning home after her ten-day stay in jail. Again she experiences a kind of imprisonment, as her home has been taken over by members of the cult of Pete the Redeemer. Her daughter, Melanie, is not among them, and Athena feels sure that their promise of her return is false. With the help of a black neighbor, the cult people are forced out of her house. Melanie has been in Athena's mind throughout the book, but she never actually appears or takes any part in the action. As the book ends, Athena is once again in a patrol wagon, being taken off to jail for demonstrating against the draft. With her are some of the women with whom she had served before. Athena has made her choice; in silence, she prays for connection with reality as she and the other demonstrators reenter the jail.

All of her life, Athena has tried to play two roles. In one, she has tried to live up to the ideal represented by the name her father gave her, that of the Greek goddess of war and reason. She speaks of this role as "that ancient unreality." The other role is that of a woman who wants to participate in contemporary life, marrying young, having children, being involved in issues such as the war. She feels that she has always been two women, one visible and understandable and the other "functioning underground," bravely enduring and working out her conflicts and troubles alone.

In this final novel, Boyle once again expressed her lifelong commitment to the struggle for justice and freedom, "pleading for the exercise of conscience." Not long before her death, Boyle described herself as "a dangerous 'radical' cleverly disguised as a perfect lady." Clearly, Boyle saw herself as "an underground woman," and it was that self-awareness and dedication to her ideals that enabled her to produce her last novel at the age of seventy-three.

Summary

Among the women writers who were finding their voices and gaining increased recognition in the years between the two World Wars and afterwards, a time of great turmoil and upheaval, Kay Boyle earned a place as one who was true to her ideals and principles throughout her writing life. One of her most interesting and revealing books was *Being Geniuses Together, 1920-1930*, a memoir of the "Lost Generation" by her friend Robert McAlmon that she revised and greatly expanded in 1968. In this book, Boyle told of wanting to write of "the unseen world" of the poor and oppressed, which in her mind was too often ignored or belittled. She admitted that she had come to demand a great deal more of women, and even more of women writers. To her, "It was an actual pain in the heart when they failed to be what they themselves had given their word that they would seem to be." Whatever her faults and weaknesses as a writer might have been, no one ever questioned her integrity and dedication in a time when these qualities were maintained only with the greatest steadfastness.

Kay Boyle lived and wrote in challenging and interesting times. Her own life was a reflection of those qualities, and she did not hesitate to put her experiences and principles to use in the service of her craft, which was considerable.

Bibliography

Bell, Elizabeth S. *Kay Boyle: A Study of the Short Fiction*. New York: Twayne, 1992.

Porter, Katherine Anne. "Kay Boyle: Example to the Young." In *The Critic as Artist: Essays on Books, 1920-1970*, edited by Gilbert A. Harrison. New York: Liveright, 1972.

Spanier, Sandra Whipple. *Kay Boyle: Artist and Activist*. Carbondale: Southern Illinois University Press, 1986.

Wilson, Edmund. "Kay Boyle and the Saturday Evening Post." In *Classics and Commercials: A Literary Chronicle of the Forties*. New York: Farrar, Straus & Giroux, 1950.

Yalom, Marilyn. *Women Writers of the West Coast: Speaking of Their Lives and Careers*. Santa Barbara, Calif.: Capra Press, 1983.

Natalie Harper

GWENDOLYN BROOKS

Born: Topeka, Kansas
June 7, 1917

Principal Literary Achievement
Although she has published essays and a novel, Brooks is known primarily for her poetry, which realistically portrays African American life.

Biography

Gwendolyn Elizabeth Brooks was born June 7, 1917, the first child of David and Keziah Wims Brooks. Her birthplace, Topeka, Kansas, was the home of her maternal grandparents, but at the age of five weeks, she and her mother returned to the Brooks's residence in Chicago, the city in which Brooks would live for most of her life. Her brother Raymond was born in 1918.

David Brooks, a janitor, made only modest wages. His children's lack of material luxury, however, was offset by a warm home atmosphere that nurtured culture and creativity. David loved to sing, tell stories, and recite poems, while his wife enjoyed singing, playing the piano, and directing plays for young actors.

As a child, Brooks was encouraged to read and to dream. By the time she was seven, she was expressing her thoughts in two-line verses. This precocity prompted her mother to predict that her daughter would one day become "the lady Paul Laurence Dunbar." Brooks continued to write, producing at least one poem per day, mostly about nature and romantic love. At thirteen, she published her first poem, "Eventide," in *American Childhood*. Three years later, she became a weekly contributor to the *Chicago Defender*'s column "Lights and Shadows." By the age of twenty, she had had poems published in two anthologies.

Much of Brooks's inspiration came from James Weldon Johnson and Langston Hughes, two well-known African American poets to whom she had submitted several poems for criticism. Johnson concluded that she was indeed talented but needed to acquaint herself with more modern poets such as T. S. Eliot, Ezra Pound, and E. E. Cummings. Hughes also endorsed Brooks's ability and exhorted her to keep writing—especially about the things she knew.

After graduating from Wilson Junior College, Brooks worked briefly as a maid in a Chicago apartment building and as a secretary to one of its residents, a "spiritual adviser" who sold love potions. The building and its inhabitants would furnish the

subject matter for her poem "In the Mecca," published in 1964.

Frustrated by the inability to find more fulfilling work, Brooks started a mimeo-graphed newspaper that sold for five cents per copy. The paper, *News Review*, included stories about local events, discussions of cultural issues, brief biographies of success-ful blacks, and cartoons drawn by her brother.

In 1939, Brooks married Henry Lowington Blakely II, another aspiring poet. Their marriage produced two children, Henry Blakely III in 1940 and Nora in 1951. Henry supported the family through a variety of jobs, while Gwendolyn wrote poems and reviewed books (both novels and collections of poetry) for *Negro Digest, The New York Times*, and *The New York Herald Tribune*.

Brooks's reputation as a poet began with the publication of individual poems in magazines such as *The Crisis, Cross-Section, Twice a Year, Common Ground*, and *Negro Story*. In 1945, however, she produced a volume of poems entitled *A Street in Bronzeville*, published by Harper & Row. Four years later, she published *Annie Allen*, the work for which she won the 1950 Pulitzer Prize for poetry; she was the first black writer to win the award. Her other works include *The Bean Eaters (1960), Selected Poems* (1963), *In the Mecca* (1968), *Riot* (1969), *Family Pictures* (1970), *Aloneness* (1971), *Beckonings* (1975), *Primer for Blacks* (1980), *To Disembark* (1981), and *The Near-Johannesburg Boy* (1986), *Blacks* (1987), and *Gottschalk and the Grand Tarantelle* (1988). Brooks also wrote poems for children (*Bronzeville Boys and Girls*, 1956, and *The Tiger Who Wore White Gloves*, 1974) as well as several volumes of essays, including *Poets Who Are Negroes* (1950) and *They Call It Bronzeville* (1951). In 1953, she published a novel, *Maud Martha*.

Brooks received numerous awards for her writing and was named Poet Laureate of Illinois in 1968. Although she was reputed to be shy and introverted, she was eager to share her work and the art of writing poetry. She gave readings at many universities as well as in prisons and taverns. Moreover, she conducted a number of poetry workshops and organized writing contests in elementary and secondary schools, paying the prizes, which ranged from fifty to five hundred dollars, from her own pocket.

Despite her lack of a degree, Brooks taught courses in literature and writing at Chicago's Columbia College and Northeastern Illinois State College, the University of Wisconsin at Madison, and City College in New York. In 1969, however, health problems forced her to resign from teaching, and she devoted herself to the work she most loved: the production of poetry.

Analysis

Critics have called Brooks's poetry "elegant and earthy." While she portrays black life in Chicago in realistic detail, she blends realism with lyricism, giving her poems beauty as well as truth. For Brooks, realism for its own sake is not enough; beauty is the essential ingredient that enables a poem to move its audience.

Brooks's style is characterized by its diversity. She employs a variety of poetic forms, including the sonnet, the ballad, the blues, free verse, and blank verse, sometimes in combination. Her language is also varied. In "We Real Cool" (from *The Bean Eaters*), she writes in black English; in some works, such as "The Anniad" (the second part of *Annie Allen*), she uses language reminiscent of the Renaissance and Middle Ages; in still others, she creates compound words such as "whimper-whine," "heart-cup," "wonder-starred," and "oak-eyed," producing the flavor of Anglo-Saxon poetry. In all of her works, she strives for one central image and gropes painstakingly for the exact words to convey her message. In an interview with writer Brian Lanker, she cautioned that if a line entered a poet's mind too spontaneously, it probably was not original; quite likely, the poet had read it in the work of someone else.

Although Brooks's poems depict black life, her themes (at least in the works written prior to the mid-1960's) are universal. The characters are black Chicagoans, but their problems and experiences are shared by people of all races and in all localities. An example of Brooks's universality is seen in "Gay Chaps at the Bar" from *A Street in Bronzeville*. In this poem, the black and white soldiers fighting in World War II are united in a cause. They have common fears, common disillusions, and common concerns about the future—if they survive. Even though the soldiers' caskets are designated for black or white bodies, a corpse sometimes ends up in the "wrong" box, but, the poet asks, "Who really gave two figs?"

During the 1960's, Brooks gradually became more interested in black identity, her African heritage, and the need for unity among blacks in the struggle for equality. She had always advocated black solidarity but had also believed that achieving rapport with whites was the answer to racial inequality. Her poems of the 1940's and 1950's present blacks simply as people; in "Gay Chaps at the Bar," for example, she notes the surprise of the white soldiers when the blacks look and behave like ordinary men. Another poem stressing the humanity of blacks is "I Love Those Little Booths at Benvenuti's" in *Annie Allen*. Benvenuti's was a restaurant in the black section of Chicago; white diners frequented the establishment, however, in hopes of seeing the black patrons clown or eat in a comical manner. In the poem, the whites are disappointed when the blacks' table manners and general decorum are as "normal" as their own.

Near the end of the 1960's, Brooks changed her mind about the effectiveness of racial integration. Undoubtedly, she was influenced by the Civil Rights movement, the death of Martin Luther King, Jr., and a growing unity among young blacks. In an interview with Ida Lewis, a writer for *Essence* magazine, she admitted her belief that blacks should work together for equal rights, independent of white aid, rather than hope for understanding and help from whites. Although Brooks never expressed hatred of whites (as did some of the students in her poetry workshops), she commented in her 1972 autobiography *Report from Part One* that it is rare for blacks and whites to establish true rapport.

Nevertheless, Brooks's later views of the racial situation did not change her from a poet into a prophet or a preacher. In *Report from Part One*, she counters critics who accuse her of sacrificing lyricism for political activism. She maintains that she still regards poetry as an art and still writes lyrically of the things she sees about her. In her maturity, however, she notices phenomena she overlooked in her youth. Two poems reflecting Brooks's growing awareness of racial conditions are "The Ballad of Rudolph Reed" and "Riders to the Blood-Red Wrath," written both in the early to mid-1960's. Rudolph Reed is a black man who purchases a home in a white neighborhood only to be harassed and killed. "Riders to the Blood-Red Wrath" illustrates the pent-up anger of African Americans. Although he has learned to hold his tongue— as have most members of his race—the narrator of the poem implies that the era of black submission is coming to an end, for he concludes with the words, "We extend, begin."

Brooks's poetry reflects her attitude toward motherhood as well as racism. In her autobiography, she confides that she always wanted children. Not only did she desire offspring for their own sake, but she also wished to utilize the reproductive function of her body. Unlike some highly talented women, she did not view procreation and child rearing as impediments to art. For Brooks, motherhood represents wholeness in a woman's life. In "Sadie and Maud," a poem about two sisters from *A Street in Bronzeville*, Sadie, "one of the livingest chits," produces two children out of wedlock, to the disgrace of her family. Maud, the respectable sister, attends college. Yet it is Maud whose life is empty and who ends up living alone "like a thin brown mouse." "The Empty Woman" echoes the theme of futility in a life without children. The "empty woman" takes great interest in her nieces and nephews, but her life is unfulfilling, as she has no children of her own. In "Children of the Poor" (from *Annie Allen*), Brooks begins by saying, "People without children can be hard."

Brooks's poetry, then, presents the life she knows in stylistic beauty and also serves as the means of conveying her philosophies.

KITCHENETTE BUILDING

First published: 1945
Type of work: Poem

Brooks wonders whether dreams can germinate and survive amid the details of everyday life—especially in a small tenement apartment.

The efficiency apartment described in "Kitchenette Building," the first poem in *A Street in Bronzeville*, recalls the apartments Brooks and her husband shared prior to the early 1950's when they purchased a house. Bronzeville, so named by the *Chicago Defender*, was a black ghetto consisting of forty square blocks on the South Side of the city. With its cross-section of people and lifestyles, Bronzeville provided Brooks with a wealth of subject material.

Written in an irregular rhyme scheme that moves toward pentameter, "Kitchenette Building" bears stylistic traces of T. S. Eliot, Ezra Pound, and John Donne, while its message is reminiscent of that in Henry David Thoreau's *Walden, Or, Life in the*

Woods (1854), which Brooks had read and admired. Discussing the need for simplicity, Thoreau states that "our life is frittered away by detail." In a similar vein of thought, the narrator of the poem muses about whether dreams and aspirations can compete with the mundane details of life—onion fumes, fried potatoes, garbage rotting in the hall—especially in a cramped ghetto dwelling. She does not muse for long, however; another tenant has just vacated the communal bathroom, so she must scurry down the hall to use what is left of the hot water before someone else beats her to it. Practicality must supersede dreams.

The first line in "Kitchenette Building" suggests the wryness of Eliot: "We are things of dry hours and the involuntary plan/ Grayed in and gray." After this introduction, however, the poem moves into a lighter mood, as the narrator begins to wonder about dreams, which she describes as being violet and white. At age eleven, Brooks began writing her poems and reflections in notebooks; she noted that she associated colors with particular characteristics and images. These associations are found in some of her adult poetry. When the narrator says that she and her spouse are "gray," she means that they are gloomy, depressed with their surroundings. Violet, on the other hand, is a delicate shade of purple, which Brooks connects with art and beauty. In referring to the violet of dreams, she may also be thinking of the flower. Although its blossoms are fragile and short-lived, like many dreams, the violet is an independent, self-pollinating plant. Its independence suggests the individuality of dreams.

Brooks associates white with purity. In "Kitchenette Building," she may be wondering whether any dream can avoid becoming contaminated by the bustle and sordidness of a tenement apartment. In addition, "white" may refer to the white race, implying that only Caucasians have the time and opportunity to dream of the future.

Obviously, Brooks herself was able to dream and write in her small apartments, but her ability stemmed from her upbringing and innate talent. In the poem, she seems to be asking whether most people living in such places can nurture an aspiration amid the petty details of daily life.

THE CHILDREN OF THE POOR

First published: 1949
Type of work: Poem

A mother gives advice—her only gift—to the orphans of war.

"The Children of the Poor" is contained in the third part of *Annie Allen*. Partly autobiographical, *Annie Allen* consists of three sections: "Notes from the Childhood and Girlhood;" "The Anniad," a poem of forty-three stanzas, in which the central character, Annie, attains personhood; and "The Womanhood," in which Annie reaches maturity. In general, *Annie Allen* requires more concentrated reading than *A Street in*

Bronzeville, as Brooks makes more obscure implications regarding human nature and uses more complex language marked by symbolism, figures of speech, twists of diction, and unusual combinations of words.

In "The Children of the Poor," Brooks looks at the ravages of World War II from a mother's standpoint. To her, the most vulnerable survivors were the children left fatherless, especially those whose widowed or abandoned mothers were economically impoverished. The poem consists of five sonnets in the Shakespearean and Petrarchan styles, each sonnet examining a different aspect of life from a maternal view.

In the first sonnet, Brooks describes the nature of motherhood by combining positive and negative images. For example, children's "softness" makes a "trap" and a "curse" for their mothers. Nevertheless, youngsters provide "sugar" for the "malocclusions" of the love that produced them. Motherhood is confining, yet fulfilling.

In the next sonnet, Annie declares the need to give her children something that will lend shape and meaning to their lives. Lacking material resources, she concludes that her gift will be a few lessons in coping with the world.

Sonnet three proceeds to examine the issue of religion. Having come from a Christian home, Annie retains a core of faith along with a degree of skepticism. Therefore, she advises her children to hold their faith in "jellied," or pliable rules; to "resemble graves," that they might bury doctrines that do not conform to their personal beliefs; and to become "metaphysical mules," stubbornly refusing to accept church teachings without first scrutinizing them. At the same time, she tells them that should their faith falter, she will be there to rebuild it, even if rebuilding involves reinterpreting scripture or blinding the eyes of her young to disturbing doctrines.

In the following sonnet, Annie sets priorities: Although esthetics are important, politics must come first. That is, if her children are to be productive, they must first attain a strong sense of self as well as a sense of the dignity of the black race.

In the final sonnet, Annie ponders whether her children will achieve justice for themselves and their race or will succumb to "the universality of death." Ironically, Brooks presents dying in a positive light. By referring to death as completion and the grave as "familiar ground," she may be implying that for the poor, death is a release from the hardships of life and the only thing poor children really have to look forward to.

THE LOVERS OF THE POOR

First published: 1960
Type of work: Poem

Two women from the Betterment League visit a tenement apartment and are overwhelmed by what they see.

"The Lovers of the Poor" is one of thirty-five poems in *The Bean Eaters*, a collection that moves beyond the descriptive and autobiographical to show Brooks's growing social awareness. A satire on people with neither respect not genuine charity, the work was inspired by a visit Brooks received from two wealthy white women who wanted to see how the black winner of the Pulitzer Prize looked. In Brooks's words, they behaved "rather sniffingly." The women barge into Brooks's apartment, apparently without warning, and silently criticize, while their hostess copes with the usual business of the day. The women feel it their duty to step outside their affluent environment and help the less fortunate, but they are totally unprepared for the raw, teeming poverty that they encounter.

Brooks uses several devices to help the audience perceive the women's true attitude toward the poor. First, she employs sensual images that repel the visitors, such as the stenches of garbage, urine, and rotting food. The women are also put off by the myriad "Children, children, children—Heavens!"; to the sheltered visitors, there is something repugnant in the prolific reproduction of the poor. Brooks reveals their genuine feelings regarding the poor through references to their "love so barbarously fair," their "loathe-love," and their intent to refresh with "milky chill."

Brooks's use of capitals, lower-case letters, and italics is also noteworthy. Words beginning with capitals imply a dry objectivity. Thus, the capitalization of "Ladies," to refer to the visitors suggests a crushing, dehumanized force, without individual identity. (Brooks does not reveal until the end of the poem that there are two women). Other capitalized words include "Slum" and "Possibilities." To the Ladies, the Slum is simply a geographic area, not a human community. Similarly, "Possibilities" is an abstract concept, having no connection to specific persons with potential.

The lower-case spelling of "arrive" in the first line of the poem, "The Lovers Of The Poor arrive," diminishes the self-importance of the Ladies. Furthermore, "arrive" may be a play on the French *arriviste*, meaning social climber.

Finally, the italicization of "heavy" in "*heavy* diapers" and "*general*" in "*general* oldness" accentuates the difference between the Ladies' experience and the present situation. The phrase "*heavy* diapers" suggests that the busy mother in the apartment is less meticulous in child care than the Ladies are or would be, and the "*general* oldness" of the building is not picturesque, like that of the Ladies' mansions, but signifies decrepitude.

In her youthful writings, Brooks associated pink with a mountain maiden, an image connoting innocence and remoteness from the world. Twice, she refers to the pinkness of the Ladies—in their make-up and their "rose nails"—thus emphasizing their naïveté. She also mentions their "red satin hangings," associating red with the quiet anger they apparently feel, and "hangings" with slave punishment. Finally, she describes a rat as gray, the color of gloom. It is the rat that induces the Ladies to leave, feeling useless in this atmosphere of despair.

Summary

Writing from her own experience, Brooks captures black life in both its poverty and its beauty. Her ability to portray beauty comes from her use of varied poetic forms and linguistic devices such as diverse rhyme schemes and diction from earlier eras. In her three best-known collections of poetry, *A Street in Bronzeville*, *Annie Allen*, and *The Bean Eaters*, she shows personal growth. In the first collection, she is objectively descriptive, in the second, reflectively autobiographical, and in the third, more consciously aware of widespread social and racial problems. Her poetry has touched many readers, regardless of their color.

Bibliography

Brooks, Gwendolyn. *Report from Part One*. Detroit: Broadside Press, 1972.

Kent, George E. *A Life of Gwendolyn Brooks*. Lexington: University Press of Kentucky, 1990.

Lanker, Brian. *I Dream a World: Portraits of Black Women Who Changed America*. New York: Stewart, Tabori & Chang, 1989.

Madhubuti, Haki R., ed. *Say That the River Turns: The Impact of Gwendolyn Brooks*. Chicago: Third World Press, 1987.

Melhem, D. H. *Gwendolyn Brooks: Poetry and the Heroic Voice*. Lexington: University Press of Kentucky, 1987.

Rebecca Stingley Hinton

ROBERT OLEN BUTLER

Born: Granite City, Illinois
January 20, 1945

Principal Literary Achievement

Butler has written acclaimed novels and short stories about American and Vietnamese protagonists and their connections to Vietnam and the Vietnam War.

Biography

Robert Olen Butler was born in Granite City, Illinois, on January 20, 1945, the son of Robert Olen Butler, Sr., a theater professor at St. Louis University, and Lucille Hall Butler, an executive secretary. Granite City, a steel-mill town in the St. Louis area, attracted exiles from the deep South and the Midwest, bringing to the area what Butler terms "a collision of cultures." In the summers of his college years, Butler worked in the steel mills and found himself as comfortable talking baseball with the other workers as he was talking aesthetics with his father and his father's academic colleagues.

Butler received a B.S. in Oral Interpretation from Northwestern University in 1967. On his twenty-first birthday, Butler decided to write the words rather than act them. To this end, he enrolled in the University of Iowa to pursue a master's degree in playwriting. Immediately after receiving his M.A. in 1969, Butler enlisted in the U.S. Army, an experience that deeply affected his life and his writing. Trained as a counterintelligence special agent and a Vietnamese linguist, Butler gained "professional proficiency" in the language after a full year of study. The immersion course was taught by a Vietnamese exile who gave Butler a glimpse into the Vietnamese culture and the struggle of an exile. Butler served his tour of duty in Saigon as administrative assistant to a U.S. Foreign Service officer who was adviser to the mayor of Saigon.

Butler's early experiences with a wide variety of people while growing up in Granite City and his Army service during the Vietnam War are the two elements in his life that most strongly influenced his writing. In Vietnam, Butler came into contact with a wider variety of Vietnamese people than most Army men did. The quality of his contact with the Vietnamese and their culture was enhanced by his command of the language. His total immersion in Vietnam, its people, and its culture shaped the worldview that would become apparent in Butler's fiction.

Following his stint in the military, Butler worked as a substitute high-school teacher

for a year in his hometown. In 1975, he became editor in chief of the New York City-based *Energy User News*, an investigative newspaper he created. During this time, it occurred to Butler that he should be writing fiction, not plays. He enrolled in postgraduate work in advanced creative writing at the New School for Social Research in New York City, studying fiction writing with Anatole Broyard. He wrote short stories that were published in *Redbook*, *Cosmopolitan*, *Fame*, and *Genre*. He eventually turned to the longer and more satisfying form of the novel. During the daily train commute from his office in Manhattan to his home in Sea Cliff, New York, Butler wrote his first novel, *The Alleys of Eden* (1981), in longhand on a lap board. The novel was rejected by twenty publishing houses. One publishing house, Methuen, brought the book to the galley stage before canceling it. Publishers doubted the novel's marketability, believing that no one would want to read the story of an Army deserter and a Vietnamese prostitute. *The Alleys of Eden* was finally published to critical acclaim by Horizon Press.

In 1985, Butler assumed an assistant professorship at McNeese State University in Lake Charles, Louisiana, where he became the sole teacher of fiction writing in the university's master of fine arts in creative writing program. He settled in Lake Charles, a city with a community of Vietnamese exiles, with his second wife, Maureen, and his son from his first marriage, Joshua Robert.

Butler has received many awards for his fiction, most notably the 1993 Pulitzer Prize for Fiction for his 1992 collection of short stories, *A Good Scent from a Strange Mountain*. Additionally, Butler was a charter recipient, along with only three other fiction writers, of the Tu Do Chinh Kien Award given by the Vietnam Veterans of America for "outstanding contributions to American culture by a Vietnam veteran."

Analysis

In a 1993 interview, Butler noted that his military service, his intimate encounter with the people of Vietnam, and his intense experience with the ravishing sensuality of that country turned him into a fiction writer. Butler said, "I had the impulse—that is the impulse of art which is a deep but inchoate conviction that the world makes sense under its surface disorder or chaos—I wanted to write to articulate that vision."

Butler's experience in Vietnam served as the basis for three of his six major novels, *The Alleys of Eden*, *Sun Dogs* (1982), and *On Distant Ground* (1985). The major theme of this Vietnam War trilogy is the outsider abroad and at home, an alien in a country at war and an alien in his own country after the war. The three novels share characters, incidents, scenes, and symbols. In these novels, the protagonists are all soldiers who have served together as part of an American intelligence-interrogation unit stationed near Saigon. In *The Alleys of Eden*, Clifford Wilkes is an Army deserter who escapes from Vietnam during the fall of Saigon with Lanh, his lover, a Vietnamese bargirl. Wilson Hand, Wilkes's fellow soldier and the protagonist of *Sun Dogs*, carries the war with him in his soul to the oil fields of Alaska, where he is on an investigative mission that uncovers industrial espionage. *On Distant Ground* is the story of the court martial of David Fleming, a fellow enlisted man of Wilkes and Hand, who becomes obsessed with the notion that he has a son in Vietnam, whom he returns to Vietnam to find.

In this trilogy, which critic Philip D. Beidler has called "a master vision of Vietnam memory," Butler fashions archetypal scenes of war that personalize the Vietnam experience for the protagonists. In *The Alleys of Eden*, Clifford Wilkes is part of the American torture-interrogation squad (of which David Fleming is a member) that deals with a Viet Cong prisoner. The prisoner is stripped naked and lies near a stream. The American soldiers place a wet handkerchief over the prisoner's face to torture him during his interrogation. The prisoner suffers a heart attack and dies. For Wilson Hand in *Sun Dogs*, the scene is his kidnapping by the Viet Cong during a visit to an American-supported orphanage. The novel records Hand's ensuing solitary confinement and eventual rescue by David Fleming in a mission where all of Hand's captors are slaughtered. In *On Distant Ground*, the crucial scene occurs between David Fleming and a Viet Cong prisoner, Tuyen, who has scrawled "Hygiene is Beautiful" on a prison-cell wall. Fleming sees the graffiti as his mental link to Tuyen, and he liberates his foe, which leads to Fleming's court martial and eventual return to Vietnam to find the son he believes is the product of an affair he had with a Vietnamese woman. In each case, these scenes are interspersed in the texts, creating the effect that they might be the memories of the reader, which Butler says is his aim.

In *Countrymen of Bones* (1983) and *Wabash* (1987), Butler chooses the burden of American history as his theme. *Countrymen of Bones* takes place at Alamagordo, New Mexico, and a nuclear test site in the nearby desert. The conflict of the novel is between Darrell Reeves, an archaeologist who wants to preserve a burial-ground excavation, and Lloyd Coulter, a scientist and disciple of J. Robert Oppenheimer, the American physicist who helped to design the atomic bomb. The burial ground represents a vanished culture unspoiled by American culture; the test site represents the overpowering, destructive force of American culture. The conflict between Reeves and Coulter is also played out in their shared pursuit of a woman who represents the salvation of love for Reeves and an object of obsession for Coulter. *Wabash*, set in Wabash, Illinois, the fictional version of Butler's hometown of Granite City, Illinois, is the story of Jeremy Cole and his wife, Deborah. Jeremy Cole's story addresses the economic and political exploitation of workers and the attendant forces of revolution. Deborah Cole's story concerns itself with domestic conflict, as she navigates the less worlds of her relatives and her marriage in an attempt to reconcile the two. As in Butler's other novels, the possibilities of love in *Countrymen of Bones* and *Wabash* are redemptive forces that free the protagonists from the cultural dictates of society.

The Deuce (1989), Butler's sixth novel, is his first novel in which the point of view is that of a Vietnamese. It is written in the voice of a sixteen-year-old Amerasian boy, Tony Hatcher. Snatched from his bargirl mother in Saigon by his father, a former Army officer turned district attorney, Tony grows up as unhappy in affluence on the Jersey Shore as he was as a despised, mixed-blood child in Saigon. Running away from home, Tony finds himself in New York City, where he must come to terms with his dual heritage and with America. In *The Deuce*, Butler addresses the theme of a collision of cultures by showing two cultures united in the mind and body of a single human being.

This theme is again addressed in all fifteen of the short stories that make up Butler's *A Good Scent from a Strange Mountain*. Each of the stories is told from the point of view of a Vietnamese expatriate living in America, an experience that gives resonance to the historical term "New World." Just as the soldiers in Butler's Vietnam trilogy are aliens in a strange land, so are the diverse narrators of these stories of love and betrayal, myth and tradition, wartime and peacetime. Butler shows that the experience of Vietnamese Americans is the human experience, with all of its pain and joy.

THE ALLEYS OF EDEN

First published: 1981
Type of work: Novel

A U.S. Army deserter and a Vietnamese prostitute flee Saigon for America, where their relationship cannot withstand the clash of cultures.

Butler's first published novel, *The Alleys of Eden* explores his often repeated theme of the spiritual and cultural displacement of people by the Vietnam War. The book tells the story of U.S. Army Intelligence officer Clifford Wilkes and his girlfriend, Lanh, a Vietnamese bargirl.

When a prisoner he is interrogating dies of a sudden heart attack, Wilkes decides to desert; he feels that he can no longer believe in the United States, a country defined in his view by vanity and arrogance. He goes to live in an apartment on a Saigon alley with a bargirl named Lanh. She wonders why Wilkes loves her, since they are so different, both physically and culturally, from one another. Wilkes is as attracted to Lanh as he is to her country. For him, Vietnam has an integrity, a sense of self that he believes America no longer possesses. Lanh comes to understand this and tells Wilkes what he cannot articulate: that he can no longer go home because home is a place where a person feels innocent. She knows that Wilkes will no longer feel innocent in America. Butler writes, "The country he left was empty, the country he was in was doomed. . . ."

During the fall of Saigon, Wilkes and Lanh flee Vietnam for America and an Illinois town. In the United States, Wilkes is a fugitive and Lanh, who speaks no English, is overwhelmed. Everything about the Midwest scares Lanh, even the size of the people. She points out that she "did not feel Vietnamese in Vietnam," but she feels Vietnamese in America, a stranger in a strange world.

As her sense of cultural displacement intensifies, her relationship with Wilkes unravels. Wilkes tries to save their relationship by concentrating on the physical side of things. This works until he finds Lanh praying one day. He asks what she is praying for, and she answers that she does not know.

As Lanh's personality diminishes, Wilkes comes to understand that the woman he loves is being tortured, just as they believed they would have been tortured if they had remained in Saigon. The torture, however, is not physical; it is mental and is inflicted upon them both by the collision of cultures they find in America. Lanh goes to live with a Vietnamese family, where she at least has her language. Wilkes, who had expected to feel like a stranger in America, finds his growing retrospective alienation with Vietnam to be something he had not expected. Wilkes flees to Canada and leaves Lanh to live with the American representatives of her people, the Binh family.

In *The Alleys of Eden*, Butler writes about the American misadventure in Vietnam. The sexual collision between the American soldiers and Vietnamese prostitutes serves as a symbol of the war, just as the clash of cultures heightens the sense of a war fought on American soil. *The Alleys of Eden* provides a vision of what it is to be American and what it is to be Vietnamese.

SNOW

First published: 1992
Type of work: Short story

A Vietnamese American woman makes a personal connection with a Jewish widower and comes to understand that despite culture or religion, people are fundamentally alike.

In "Snow," a short story from his 1992 Pulitzer Prize-winning short-story collection *A Strange Scent from a Good Mountain*, Butler weaves the tale of an older Vietnamese refugee, Giàu, and a Jewish lawyer, Mr. Cohen. Butler's theme is once again the fracturing of community by the alienating sense of dislocation felt by outsiders.

On Christmas Eve, Giàu is working in the Plantation Hunan restaurant in Lake Charles, Louisiana. The product of a patriarchal society, she is a woman without a man, a position she finds uncomfortable. Everything about America makes her feel alien. In America, people are Christian; she is Buddhist. In America, people are always concerned about time; she had not seen a clock until she came to America (however, she likes the name of the "grandfather" clock, which conjures comforting images for her). She does not feel like those who live in the Vietnamese community in Lake Charles; she does not feel like a "real" American, like she supposes others do. Giàu compares herself to the building housing the restaurant, a former plantation home, noting that the life of a restaurant is not the life the house once knew.

Giàu remembers the first time she saw snow, while working in a St. Louis restaurant. The snow covered all that was familiar to her, frightening her. Just as she is frightened of snow, she is frightened to live her life without a man. When Mr. Cohen walks into the Plantation Hunan, she finds refuge in his face, as if it is a place to hide from the snow. She finds his voice reassuring, like a grandfather's voice. She asks why he is not celebrating Christmas. He explains that it is not the custom of Jews.

Mr. Cohen, a Polish man also displaced in America, is also afraid of snow, which reminds him of his father's death. His father's literal death is linked to the metaphorical death of his Polish and Jewish heritage through his displacement to America. Giàu understands this; it is how she too feels. When she saw the snow, she realized that her culture was lost to her. She adds, "I was dead, too."

"Snow" ends on an optimistic note when Mr. Cohen and Giàu agree to a New Year's Eve date. In the story's ending, Butler fuses images and metaphors, cultures and people. Giàu knows, just as her Vietnamese brothers and sisters know, that people should celebrate whatever holiday comes along. She sits in the restaurant, waiting for Mr. Cohen, listening to Grandfather, the clock, tell his story of time. She still has time to make her life whole, to recapture her culture. As two people displaced from their cultures, Giàu and Mr. Cohen can find wholeness and completion in one another as they together face the demands of their new world, the demands of America.

CRICKETS

First published: 1992
Type of work: Short story

A Vietnamese father learns to accept the Americanization of his son when he attempts to teach his son a Vietnamese game, Crickets.

From the short-story collection *A Good Scent from a Strange Mountain*, "Crickets" is the story of a Vietnamese family displaced to Lake Charles, Louisiana, and the rift that develops between a father who would like to retain his Vietnamese heritage and a son who prefers all things American. Butler repeats his trope of the collision of cultures, this time as embodied in a second-generation Vietnamese American.

Thiệu is a chemical engineer in a Lake Charles refinery. His American coworkers insist upon calling him Ted; he believes that they call him Ted because they want to think of him as one of them. Thiệu knows that he will never truly be one of them; everything about him and them is so radically different, right down to size. He gives in to the name change because he believes that he has done enough fighting for one lifetime.

As part of the acculturation process, Thiệu has given his son an American name, Bill. The son speaks no Vietnamese and is embarrassed when his father tells him goodbye in Vietnamese. In an attempt to instill some of his heritage in his son, Thiệu decides to teach his son one of his own childhood games from Vietnam, Crickets. Thiệu has difficulty in keeping his son engaged as he explains the game and as they search for crickets.

Thiệu tells his son that there are two types of crickets, charcoal crickets and fire crickets. The charcoal crickets are large and strong but slow and easily confused. The fire crickets are small and brown, not as strong as the charcoal crickets but very smart and quick. The fights between the two types of crickets take place in a paper tunnel made for the game. The game Thiệu explains to his son cannot take place, however, because they can find no fire crickets.

Bill loses all interest in the game when he sees that he has soiled his Reebok tennis shoes. Thiệu continues the search for fire crickets but finds none. He comes to believe that a fire cricket is a precious and admirable thing.

The game symbolizes the struggle between the Americans and Vietnamese in the Vietnam War. The charcoal crickets represent the Americans; the fire crickets represent the Vietnamese. Because he lives in America, Thiệu cannot find any fire crickets. Just as there are no fire crickets to fight the charcoal crickets, Thiệu decides not to fight his son's Americanization any longer. Thiệu understands that his son's concern over a pair of Reeboks, a symbol of America, is more important than his son's lack of interest in the game, a symbol of the Vietnam of Thiệu's past, a Vietnam that does not exist for Bill. The next morning, when Bill leaves for school, Thiệu tells him goodbye in English rather than Vietnamese.

Summary

In his novels and short stories, Robert Olen Butler probes the realities of the Vietnam War and its legacy. Butler scratches beneath the surface and reveals the human side of the Vietnamese, just as he reveals the human side of the Americans. The characters in Butler's Vietnam War fiction are haunted by the past, ambivalent about the present, and in search of truce for the various wars they carry with them.

Bibliography

Beidler, Philip D. *Re-Writing America: Vietnam Authors in Their Generation.* Athens: University of Georgia Press, 1991.

Broyard, Anatole. Review of *The Alleys of Eden*, by Robert Olen Butler. *The New York Times*, November 11, 1981, p.29.

Butler, Robert Olen. "The Process of Writing a Novel." *Writer* 95 (April, 1982): 11-13.

Dong, Stella. "The Cinderella Story of *The Alleys of Eden.*" *Publishers Weekly* 221 (January 1, 1982): 25-26.

Myers, Thomas. *Walking Point: American Narratives of Vietnam.* New York: Oxford University Press, 1988.

Packer, George. "From the Mekong to the Bayous." *The New York Times Book Review* 97 (June 7, 1992): 24.

Sartisky, Michael. "A Pulitzer Profile: Louisiana's Robert Olen Butler." *Cultural Vistas: Louisiana Endowment for the Humanities* 4 (Fall, 1993): 10-21.

Tom Petitjean

CHARLES WADDELL CHESNUTT

Born: Cleveland, Ohio
June 20, 1858
Died: Cleveland, Ohio
November 15, 1932

Principal Literary Achievement

The first African American novelist and short-story writer to produce a substantial body of fiction of widely recognized merit, Chesnutt was an important spokesperson on race relations at the turn of the century.

Biography

Charles Waddell Chesnutt was born in Cleveland, Ohio, on June 20, 1858, the first child of Andrew Jackson and Ann Maria Sampson Chesnutt. Charles' parents had met as members of a northbound wagon train of free people of color leaving Fayetteville, North Carolina, where legal and social restrictions imposed on free blacks had become intolerable. Andrew served with the Union forces as a teamster in the Civil War, after which the family moved back to Fayetteville, where Andrew opened a grocery store with the aid of his father, Waddell Cade, a white man and former slaveholder. Ann Maria died in 1871, the store failed soon after, and Charles was forced to drop out of the Howard School (which has since evolved into Fayetteville State University) to help support the family. Recognizing Charles's exceptional ability, his principal immediately hired him as a pupil-teacher at age fourteen. Chesnutt became the principal of the Howard School at age eighteen, then returned to the newly established State Colored Normal School in Fayetteville, a teacher-training institution for African American students, as a teacher and assistant to the principal.

Chesnutt married Susan Perry, a fellow teacher in 1878 and became principal of the Normal School in 1880, at the age of twenty-two. Discouraged by the unjust treatment of blacks in the South, by 1883 he had trained himself in stenography well enough to resign from his position and find work in the North. He eventually settled in Cleveland, where he worked as a legal stenographer and studied law, passing the Ohio bar examination in 1887 with the highest scores in his class. Chesnutt capitalized on his

stenographic and legal training to set up a court-reporting business, which quickly became profitable.

That same year, he published his first important story, "The Goophered Grapevine," in the August, 1887, issue of *The Atlantic Monthly*, and his career as a writer was launched. Chesnutt published more stories in 1888 and 1889 and gathered together three of them, along with four new stories, for his first book, *The Conjure Woman* (1899). The book was favorably reviewed and sold well, perhaps in part because of the interest generated by the public disclosure of Chesnutt's racial identity. He had never attempted to conceal his race, although he was often mistaken for a white man and could easily have "passed" as white, but he had refused to allow himself to be promoted as an African American writer because he preferred to have his work judged on purely literary criteria. His publishers decided to bring out a second volume of short stories before the end of the year, and *The Wife of His Youth and Other Stories of the Color Line* (1899) was released in time for the Christmas market. Two months after signing the contract for the book, Chesnutt closed his court-reporting business to devote himself full time to his writing. Unlike Chesnutt's more fanciful earlier stories, the tales in the second volume are generally serious in tone and contemporary in setting, focusing on the themes of miscegenation and the plight of people of mixed race in the United States. Perhaps because of the shift to weightier themes, the book was less successful with the public and the critics than *The Conjure Woman* had been. His two collections had made him enough of a reputation that another publisher commissioned him to write a biography of Frederick Douglass for high school students, and the book appeared in 1900.

Chesnutt next published two novels, *The House Behind the Cedars* (1900), the tragic story of a mulatto heroine who attempted to pass for white, and *The Marrow of Tradition* (1901); these books are now generally agreed to be his major literary achievement. Neither book sold well enough to enable him to support his family, however, and in 1902 Chesnutt reopened his court-reporting business. He continued to write, producing short stories and essays on racial problems as well as a third novel, *The Colonel's Dream* (1905). Chesnutt made the protagonist of this novel a white man, perhaps in hopes that his predominantly white audience would be more likely to identify with the character, but the book's pessimistic social analysis failed to attract favorable criticism or a wide readership. Chesnutt published little more fiction after this, although he worked actively for racial equality in local and national organizations and served on the General Committee of the National Association for the Advancement of Colored People (NAACP). In the 1920's, Chesnutt's work attracted belated interest from a new generation of readers, and *The House Behind the Cedars* and *The Conjure Woman* were brought back into print. In 1928, he was recognized by the NAACP with its Spingarn Medal for his literary and civic achievements.

Analysis

As Chesnutt predicted in a journal entry on May 29, 1880, several years before he actually published any substantial work, "The object of my writings would be not so much the elevation of the colored people as the elevation of the whites." He knew that militant preaching to white Americans would be received with indifference or hostility, and he concluded that it would be necessary to entertain his white audience before he could have any hope of leading them out of their prejudices: "The Negro's part is to prepare himself for recognition and equality, and it is the province of literature to open the way for him to get it—to accustom the public mind to the idea; and while amusing them, to lead people out, imperceptibly, unconsciously, step by step, to the desired state of feeling." The combining of these dual purposes, entertainment and moral education, constitutes the controlling strategy behind most of Chesnutt's fiction.

The stories collected in his first book, *The Conjure Woman*, appealed immediately to their predominantly white Northern audience as examples of two familiar popular genres, "local color" and "plantation" fiction. Local-color stories presented readers with detailed depictions of unfamiliar customs and places, often reproducing the distinctive dialect of a given region and social class. Plantation novels typically described the antebellum South as an idyllic and peaceful setting for the supposedly harmonious relations between benevolent masters and loyal slaves. Both genres were appealing sentimental fantasies for both Northerners and Southerners in a period of rapid and often threatening social and economic change during which the failure of Reconstruction policies and the reinstatement of an increasingly harsh racism in the South became apparent.

In *The Conjure Woman* stories, an elderly former slave, Uncle Julius, recounts the beliefs and practices of plantation slaves in the antebellum South. Uncle Julius' stories, delivered in his distinctive dialect, were cleverly designed at one level for the diversion of Chesnutt's target audience of middle-class white readers familiar with the Uncle Remus dialect stories of Joel Chandler Harris. As Chesnutt must have anticipated, most readers identified the first-person narrator, John, who becomes Julius' employer, with the voice of the author. Such readers assumed that Chesnutt was white and viewed the tales, as John does, as light local-color comedy, usually reflecting an attempt by Julius to gain money or privileges. More careful readers, however, could see that the tales Uncle Julius tells within this outer frame often constitute serious indictments of slavery and of the white characters' greed and abuse of power.

These two levels of interpretation, which correspond to Chesnutt's dual purposes of entertainment and moral education, are exemplified in the second tale in the book, "Po' Sandy." The tale is often regarded as the strongest of the conjure stories by modern critics who value Chesnutt's literary artistry and social criticism more than his contemporary audience did. Chesnutt appears to have fully realized the possibilities opened up by his creation of a fictional white audience for Julius' tales, and the frame includes the reaction of John's wife, Annie, whose compassion and understanding are much greater than her husband's. While John sees the story superficially, as a tall tale designed to trick him into letting Julius assume possession of an old building, Annie sees the serious indictment of the slave system that underlies the tale, which is for her more about the destruction of a slave family than about a conjuring feat. John remarks at one point that "Some of these stories are quaintly humorous . . . while others, poured freely into the sympathetic ear of a Northern-bred woman, disclose many a tragic incident of the darker side of slavery." As critics have noted, John's inability to sympathize with this tragic level unfortunately mirrors that of the complacent mainstream white audience Chesnutt addresses, while Annie's response dramatizes that of the ideal reader that he hoped to educate into being through his writings.

While a white audience could easily have missed much of the implicit social commentary of the stories in *The Conjure Woman*, most of the stories in Chesnutt's second book, *The Wife of His Youth and Other Stories of the Color Line*, are bold examinations of then-taboo subjects such as miscegenation and racial violence. The shift in approach does not really represent a new direction in Chesnutt's own ideas—many of the stories in the more pessimistic and realistic second book were written before the more optimistic first book was assembled—but rather indicates the extent to which he conceived of each book as having its own thematic unity. The sequence of his books nevertheless suggests an ever-increasing distance between Chesnutt, who insisted on taking a hard, realistic look at racial problems, and the popular audience, which was reluctant to read anything that was not presented with a sugar coating.

The themes of the second book of short stories are further explored in *The House Behind the Cedars*, which documents at greater length the social circumstances that provoke a mulatto woman to pass for white and the tragic consequences that follow. Chesnutt again hoped to educate his audience about a set of unfamiliar social and psychological conditions, with the hope of producing tolerance and reform. He further broadens his scope in *The Marrow of Tradition*, which introduces a much larger cast of characters from a broader spectrum of society. The novel is now recognized as an important example of early Social Realism in its effort to paint a comprehensive picture of the South at the turn of the century. *The Colonel's Dream* continues Chesnutt's emphasis on socioeconomic analysis, depicting the unsuccessful efforts of an idealistic white businessman to reform the social injustices in the South. As Chesnutt had written to his publisher after the limited success of *The Marrow of Tradition*, "I am beginning to suspect that the public as a rule does not care for books in which the principal characters are colored people, or written with a striking sympathy with that race as contrasted with the white race." His use of a white protagonist failed to make this sympathy more palatable to the public, and reviewers were more prone to attack the book for its pessimism thàn to praise it for its honesty.

THE CONJURE WOMAN

First published: 1899
Type of work: Short stories

The shrewd former slave Uncle Julius entertains, manipulates, and sometimes tries to educate his young Northern employers with humorous tales of conjuring in the antebellum South.

With the stories collected in *The Conjure Woman*, Chesnutt discovered a way to introduce into apparently humorous tall tales depictions of black characters who avoided the negative stereotypes then current in fiction and to include, beneath the comic surface, a level of social criticism. John, a young white man from the North, goes to North Carolina after the Civil War to find a suitable climate to help his wife's poor health and to buy a plantation for growing grapes. He and his wife meet Uncle Julius, an elderly former slave, who tells them anecdotes that revolve around instances of conjuring, or magic.

In "The Goophered Grapevine," Chesnutt's first major publication and still his most frequently anthologized story, Julius tells in minutely rendered dialect the tale of the slave Henry, whose health and appearance are magically linked with those of the bewitched, or "goophered," grapes that he has eaten from the plantation that John has come South to purchase. Henry's master takes advantage of the enchantment by selling him to a new owner every spring, when he is young and healthy, and buying him back every fall, when he becomes old. At one level, the tale is an attempt by Julius, who makes money selling the grapes, to dissuade John from buying the bewitched plantation; at a deeper level, however, the story can be read as social criticism of the owners' treatment of Henry, who withers away and dies.

Chesnutt again capitalizes on the device of having a dual audience discover dual meanings in "Sis' Becky's Pickaninny," in which a slaveowner first sells a baby's father and then trades the baby's mother for a horse, leaving the child alone in the world. A conjuring trick results in a relatively happy ending, to which John reacts by saying, "That is a very ingenious fairy tale, Julius." Annie, however, correctly sees the devastating critique of the inhumanity of slavery that underlies the fairy-tale elements. Implicit social commentary is also evident in "Mars Jeems's Nightmare," in which a slaveowner is temporarily transformed into a slave; his subsequent treatment at the hands of his own brutal overseer changes his view of slavery permanently. While the other tales in the book feature more comedy than tragedy, their depiction of sympathetic black characters in the context of their own folk culture allowed an ethnocentric white audience to learn something about the black experience in the South.

Chesnutt summarized the theme of his second book of short stories in a letter to his publisher written a few months before it came out:

> I should like to hope that the stories, while written to depict life as it is, in certain aspects
> that no one has ever before attempted to adequately describe, may throw a light upon the
> great problem on which the stories are strung; for the backbone of this volume is not a
> character, like Uncle Julius in *The Conjure Woman*, but a subject, as indicated in the
> title—*The Color Line*.

Chesnutt's more direct approach to these highly charged racial issues presented a challenge that the conservative reading public often proved unwilling to meet. Particularly shocking to contemporary critics were such stories as "The Sheriff's Children," in which a young mulatto, Tom, is arrested as a murder suspect in a small town in North Carolina about ten years after the Civil War. A lynch mob attempts to break into the prison to hang him without a trial but is driven away by Sheriff Campbell. Tom then gains possession of the sheriff's gun and reveals that he is the son of Campbell and a slave woman whom he had later sold. Just as he is about to shoot the sheriff, Tom is shot and wounded by Campbell's daughter and disarmed. Campbell spends the night contemplating his past and decides to atone for his moral crime of neglect against his son, whom he now believes to be innocent of the murder. When he returns to the jail the next morning, however, his son has torn off the bandage on his wound and bled to death in an apparent suicide.

Chesnutt focuses on the internal point of view of the relatively sympathetic white sheriff in the last third of the narrative, providing white readers with a moral role model within the story. Campbell's miscegenation and the lynch-mob scene, however, are more direct attacks on white society's treatment of African Americans than anything in the earlier book. Even in a story of superficially successful "passing" and miscegenation such as "Her Virginia Mammy," in which a young mulatto woman is kept ignorant of her black ancestry so that she may marry a rich white man, the emphasis is on the emotional cost to the black mother, who must never acknowledge their relationship, rather than on the daughter's happy future.

THE WIFE OF HIS YOUTH

First published: 1899
Type of work: Short stories

In these pioneering stories, Chesnutt explores a range of contemporary racial issues, including miscegenation and caste and color prejudice between and within ethnic groups.

Particularly interesting are a series of tales that analyze the hitherto seldom-explored subject of racial prejudice within the black community itself. "The Wife of His Youth" presents the positive example of a prominent and wealthy leader of the "Blue Vein Society" ("no one was eligible for membership who was not white enough to show blue veins"), who publicly acknowledges his long-lost wife, an illiterate former slave with very dark skin. "A Matter of Principle" complements "The Wife of His Youth" with the humorous negative example of a light-skinned mulatto whose bias against darker blacks costs his daughter a chance at a successful marriage.

THE MARROW OF TRADITION

First published: 1901
Type of work: Novel

Dr. Miller, a black physician, is called upon to help the dying son of the white Major Carteret, whose racist editorials had incited the riot in which Miller's own son was killed.

The main plot of *The Marrow of Tradition* is based on newspaper and eyewitness accounts of the lynchings that occurred during the election riots in Wilmington, North Carolina, in 1898. Chesnutt added a number of subplots that enabled him to explore a wider range of social issues more thoroughly than the short-story form had permitted. Dr. Miller, a talented black surgeon, and Major Carteret, an aristocratic white supremacist, are somewhat melodramatically brought together when Carteret, having indirectly caused the death of Miller's child with inflammatory race-baiting editorials that incited the riots, calls upon Miller at the end of the book to save the life of his own child. The connection between the two men is ironically underscored by the fact that they are married to half-sisters, one white and one mulatto. This parallelism of characters from opposite sides of the color line is echoed within the black community by the paralleling of the middle-class, moderate Miller with Josh Green, a militant black laborer.

Miller seems to represent an effort on Chesnutt's part to find a middle ground that will avoid the extremism of either Green or Carteret. Miller refuses to lead the black community in what he correctly perceives as a hopeless attempt at armed defense against the white lynch mob; at the end of the book, he agrees to help Carteret's child. Dr. Evans, a youthful white physician who lacks Miller's expertise and is himself powerless to help the child, ends the book with a cautious optimism about the Carteret child's condition that the reader is invited to apply as a prognosis for America's own condition with respect to the problems of race relations: "Come on up, Dr. Miller. . . . There's time enough, but none to spare."

Despite his evident intent to promote the moderate line, Chesnutt's involuntary admiration for Green's courage is unmistakable, and Green's heroic insistence that "I'd rather be a dead nigger any day than a live dog" is never convincingly discredited. Even the moderate Miller is acutely aware that Green exemplifies not savagery but love of liberty. While Miller's wife urges him to help the child, she emphatically refuses to accept her white half-sister's long-overdue offer to recognize their relationship and to offer financial restitution. Chesnutt's realistic depiction of the brutalities that kept black citizens in their social places, and his implication that black pride and resistance were appropriate positions, could hardly fail to strike genteel white readers and critics as bitter and excessive. Chesnutt himself considered the novel his best, and later critics have generally found the novel a milestone in the movement of the African American novel toward Social Realism.

Summary

Chesnutt failed to achieve his ambitious project of reforming the social consciousness of his white audience, but he nevertheless succeeded in earning national fame and the respect of the literary establishment. As Chesnutt himself said of his literary career, "My books were written, from one point of view, a generation too soon. . . . I was writing against the trend of public opinion on the race question at that particular time." Later generations of readers have proven more receptive to his insightful analyses of racial injustice. While his success in balancing the demands of entertainment and moral purpose has made the folklore tales of *The Conjure Woman* his more widely read work, critics have more recently come to appreciate the artistry and power of his later, more realistic short stories and novels.

Bibliography

Andrews, William L. *The Literary Career of Charles W. Chesnutt*. Baton Rouge: Louisiana State University Press, 1980.

Baldwin, Richard E. "The Art of *The Conjure Woman*." *American Literature* 43 (1971): 385-398.

Bone, Robert. *Down Home: A History of Afro-American Short Fiction from Its Beginnings to the End of the Harlem Renaissance*. New York: Putnam, 1975.

Chesnutt, Helen M. *Charles Waddell Chesnutt: Pioneer of the Color Line*. Chapel Hill: University of North Carolina Press, 1952.

Ellison, Curtis W., and E. W. Metcalf, Jr., eds. *Charles W. Chesnutt: A Reference Guide*. Boston: G. K. Hall, 1977.

Gibson, Donald B. *The Politics of Literary Expression: A Study of Major Black Writers*. Westport, Conn.: Greenwood Press, 1981.

Heermance, J. Noel. *Charles W. Chesnutt: America's First Great Black Novelist*. Hamden, Conn.: Archon Books, 1974.

Keller, Frances Richardson. *An American Crusade: The Life of Charles Waddell Chesnutt*. Provo, Utah: Brigham Young University Press, 1978.

Render, Sylvia Lyons. *Charles W. Chesnutt*. Boston: Twayne, 1980.

_____, ed. *The Short Fiction of Charles W. Chesnutt*. Washington, D.C.: Howard University Press, 1974.

William Nelles

FRANK CHIN

Born: Berkeley, California
February 25, 1940

Principal Literary Achievement
Chin's acclaimed dramas present the difficulties Chinese Americans face in negotiating the majority culture.

Biography

Frank Chew Chin, Jr., was born on February 25, 1940, in Berkeley, California, to a family prominent in the Chinese American community. His great grandmother owned a famous brothel, and his father was the president of the Chinese Six Companies, a combined business group and benevolent association. At the time, Chin's birth was exceptional; because of discriminatory laws, few Chinese women were allowed into the United States until the late 1940's.

At first, Chin's parents could not take care of him—his mother was only fifteen when he was born—and he was put in a foundling home. The home placed him with an impoverished white couple, with whom he stayed until his parents reclaimed him at age six. Even from that point, though, Chin's childhood was not to be an easy one, since his father was strict and beat the boy to discipline him. These early years had obvious effects on his writing, both in his portraits of tortured, poisoned relations between fathers and sons and in his depictions of Chinese American boys who feel they have lost contact with their Asian roots.

Chin attended the University of California at Berkeley from 1958 to 1961 and then went to work for the railroads, first for the Western Pacific and then, as a brakeman, for the Southern Pacific. He was the first Asian American to hold this latter position for the company. This was another important shaping experience for Chin, and his work makes repeated reference to railroad lines, both in connection to his own job and in discussions of the large part Chinese laborers played in building the Western railroads. In 1965, Chin returned to college at the University of California at Santa Barbara and received a B.A.

Through the late 1960's, the author taught in colleges and wrote for a broadcasting company. Also in this period, he founded the Asian American Theater Workshop in San Francisco. His first play, *The Chickencoop Chinaman* (pr. 1972, pb. 1981) was staged in New York City in the early seventies. This was another Chin first, since the

play was the first drama by an Asian American to be performed on Broadway. The work was acclaimed by the critics. Yet the event was also a traumatic one for the fledgling dramatist. He wanted his mother to come from California to attend the opening night, but Chin's father refused to permit her to leave, because he wanted her to attend a business party. On the way to the dinner, Chin's parents' car crashed, and his mother was killed.

Although the playwright's father accepted his son as a man, he never accepted him as a writer. Chin once commented that his father "never respected my writing. He died believing I never worked a day in my life."

Chin's next play, *The Year of the Dragon* (pr. 1974, pb. 1981), was also a critical success. He also coedited the anthology *Aiiieeeee!* (1974), the first literary collection to focus on Asian American writers. Chin, however, did not immediately follow up these successes, partially because of his own absorption in teaching and running his theater, and also because of a change in the literary climate. His militant writing, which castigated the mass media for stereotyping Asians, fell out of popularity with the public and lost acceptance from producers as the United States became increasingly conservative in the late 1970's.

Until the late 1980's, Chin devoted himself to teaching. In this period, he engaged in a drawn-out war of words with the Asian American novelist Maxine Hong Kingston. Their quarrel began when she asked him to write an endorsement for her first novel, *The Woman Warrior* (1976). Although he found merit in the novel, he could not sympathize with the general direction of her book, which seemed more aimed at endearing Kingston to white audiences than at recapturing or revivifying Chinese immigrant history. As her other novels appeared, he continued criticizing, especially scorning what he saw as her doctoring of Chinese mythology to fit Western misconceptions.

In the late 1980's, Chin returned to print with a book of short stories, *The Chinaman Pacific and Frisco R.R. Co.* (1988), and a novel, *Donald Duk* (1991), that worked to correct misinterpretations of the Chinese past. The novel presented a gallery of authentic Chinese heroes, while the earlier book went so far as to poke fun at Kingston in a short section that parodied her style and message.

Analysis

Frank Chin is centrally concerned with the psychological effects of assimilation on Chinese Americans who were born into the United States after World War II. He argues that the adaptation of Chinese Americans to their home was distorted by critical problems that Chinese immigrants have had since the nineteenth century in being accepted as equal to the children of European immigrants. Chin shows how real Chinese contributions to American life, such as the building of the railroads, have been downplayed or purposefully forgotten and how, in the place of real history, Chinese Americans have been saddled with degrading stereotypes.

This stereotyping plays into a second major problem Chinese Americans face, which involves their economic place. Either they do the real work of society—as laborers, cooks, and so on — and their activity is ignored, or they get high-profile jobs peddling the very stereotypes that disempower them. A character who holds this last type of job is Fred Eng in *The Year of the Dragon*. He gives tours of Chinatown and finds that, to make his business lucrative, he must repeat to his clients the same distortions they have heard about Asians from the media.

Chin is not a literary preacher who uses his work as a soapbox from which to make judgments; he is concerned with tracing the human effects of stereotyping and subordination. His views on the fate of Chinese Americans serve as a background to his portrayal of individuals and their families who are damaged by the roles they are forced to play in white America's reality and dreams.

A special quality of Chin's work is that he stresses the disastrous effects of prejudice more on the relations between family members than on individual psyches. Above everything, Chin focuses on the relations of fathers and sons. (Although Chin can portray vivid female characters, these are decidedly secondary to his interests.) This is why, of all the popular caricatures of the Chinese, the one Chin reverts to over and over is that of the fictional detective Charlie Chan, because central to this representation was the display of Charlie's relation to his servile number-one son.

Chin's discussion of stereotyping is a complex one. It is not so much that Charlie Chan films, for example, promoted the picture of Chinese sons as passive buffoons. Though this was bad enough, the real problem was that American-born Chinese sons, with no other available images of Chinese boys, began to believe in the stereotype. Thus, the protagonist of *Donald Duk*, who is sent to an American school where such stereotypes are promulgated, begins to hate other Chinese boys, who he thinks are physically weak and passive. The hero of *The Chickencoop Chinaman* is driven to despair by the parade of stereotypes in the media until he invents a Chinese role model, the Lone Ranger, a cowboy hero who never removes his mask—because, as the Chinese boy believes, he is concealing his Oriental eyes.

This second example suggests that Chinese sons do not simply submit to the endless negative images but may revolt against them, often putting them at odds with their uncomprehending fathers. Immigrant fathers, such as Pa in *The Year of the Dragon*, cannot sympathize with the feelings of the sons; the fathers are too steeped in original Chinese tradition to be really affected by American culture, and they are too impressed with the material success available in the United States to care about their images.

A division between the generations occurs because each requires a different degree of integration into their new society. The fathers are satisfied with economic acceptance, while the sons, who are necessarily more familiar with American ways, yearn for an unobtainable cultural acceptance. These disparate goals make for strife and misunderstandings in the family unit.

There is a clear change in Chin's attitude over the years. His earliest writings, his theater works, are unrelentingly bleak, showing protagonists who are painted into a corner by their own inabilities to either ignore or escape debilitating social strictures. In his later fiction, Chin does sketch avenues of psychic survival, ones that involve an honest appraisal of the Chinese place in America, a continued respect for the Chinese customs that can be salvaged in the new environment, and the choice of a career that can mediate between American and Chinese society. By the end of *Donald Duk*, the twelve-year-old protagonist has grasped these essentials. He has learned of the Chinese contribution to building the transcontinental railroad; has come to appreciate the significance of the traditional Chinese New Year; and has seen the viability of his father's choice of occupation. His father is a chef who is popular with Americans but who also makes time to be involved in sustaining his own ethnic community—as when he closes his restaurant except to his friends so that he can create dishes only the Chinese palate can properly savor.

Chin's style is protean. His writing becomes especially lyrical and surreal when describing media fantasy worlds, as when the Lone Ranger or Charlie Chan appears, but can be matter-of-fact and prosy when describing the everyday lives of immigrants. Nevertheless, his virtuoso handling of varied styles is subordinate to his continued focus on the perils facing the Chinese American boy who strains to adapt to an American system that has little regard for his people's history and less for his present need for self-validation.

THE CHICKENCOOP CHINAMAN

First produced: 1972 (first published, 1981)
Type of work: Play

A Chinese American filmmaker comes to Detroit, ostensibly in search of material but really looking for his own identity.

The Chickencoop Chinaman put Frank Chin on the map; it was a success and became the first play by an Asian American to be produced on Broadway. Yet the work is not one that would seem to recommend itself to the average theatergoer, given the play's dark theme, its depiction of the irreparable loss of a father, and its irresolute climax.

Ironically, of all Chin's works, this piece, which established his credentials as a Chinese American writer, is the one least concerned with the Chinese American experience. Rather, the play portrays the extravagant heterogeneity of the United States. Each character's life is an unstable ethnic melange. The protagonist, Tam Lum, a Chinese American, was reared in a black area of Los Angeles. Now, as a young man, he devotes his energy to making a film about his idol, an African American prizefighter.

The play does not celebrate this diversity. Instead, it counts the cost in unhappiness for those who have no clear-cut allegiances: These characters, who have lost their natal culture, have not been able to attach themselves to any other tradition. Tam is making a film to prove himself, but at bottom, he is not sure what he is proving or to whom he has to prove something.

If *The Chickencoop Chinaman* were a conventional play, its plot development would probably concern how the characters recontacted their base cultures and relocated their fathers. In Chin's alternative dramaturgy, however, the plot does not conclude the characters' searches but rather cuts the few ties they have left. In the most disheartening and poignant confrontation of the play, for example, Tam goes for an interview with Charley Popcorn, the purported estranged father of his film's subject. Tam has gotten substitute satisfaction from hearing touching stories of father-and-son affection from his boxer subject; now, though, he discovers that these stories were not reminiscences but fairy tales, since Popcorn was the fighter's manager but had no blood ties to him. In another blow to Tam, in a fantasy sequence he meets the Lone Ranger, whom he adored as a boy, thinking that the cowboy's mask concealed the fact that he was Asian. The Lone Ranger turns out to be white, and a racist to boot.

The play ends up in the air. The status of Tam's film project is in doubt, and no one has gained any clarity on their parentage or roots. Thus, Chin's play ends by underlining the points made at the beginning: Second-generation Americans are faced with a severe identity crisis seemingly out of all proportion to their ability to handle it.

THE SONS OF CHAN

First published: 1988
Type of work: Short story

The protagonist comes to Las Vegas on a dual mission: to interview a famous stripper and to kill Charlie Chan.

"The Sons of Chan" is the last story in Chin's short-story collection *The Chinaman Pacific and Frisco R.R. Co.* Chin's stories are the most stylistically idiosyncratic of his writings. Their prose is dense, allusive, and layered. In keeping with this individualism in style is the way that, in many of the stories, the protagonist concocts a subjective mythology. In the earlier *The Chickencoop Chinaman*, the hapless hero had tried to remold American pop iconography to his own ends; in the later *Donald Duk*, the hero locates a sustaining mythology by discovering forgotten pages from the Chinese past. In "The Sons of Chan," however, the hero dreams up his own personalized fantasy world, which is centered on the existence of a secret brotherhood; the imaginary actions are intercut with the more realistic events of the story's plot.

This brotherhood, The Sons of Chan, is made up of symbolic male children of Charlie Chan, that is, of Chinese American men who were crippled by media depictions of Asian sons. The vow of this order is to kill the actor who originally played Charlie Chan.

In the story, the symbolic attempt to break with the male stereotypes acquired in childhood intersects with the narrator's attempt to face down, in the real world, an example of the female type who has been put forward as the only worthy object of desire by American popular culture. This culture never portrays desirable Asian women but instead presents a pantheon of blonde, curvaceous love goddesses whose seductiveness has distorted the narrator's own romantic life. He has had affairs with and been married to only white women, never finding himself capable of loving a fellow Chinese. In coming to Las Vegas to interview a has-been stripper for a magazine, he is also coming to grips with his own warped sexuality.

Since a major facet of the hero's problems is that he cannot disengage his mind from these oppressive stereotypes, it is unlikely that his encounters with these archetypes will be productive. In fact, the meetings are abortive. In fantasy, he meets Chan, but he lets slip the opportunity to assassinate him; the hero cannot even arrange a meeting with the stripper.

The real moment of learning for the narrator occurs outside his fantasies. He runs into an older Chinese American woman who is on a picket line, and he feels drawn to her. Half charmed and half disgusted with her pidgin English and aging flesh, he sympathizes with her and ends up sleeping with her. Though his misgivings about himself are hardly laid to rest by this one-night stand, the episode does show him breaking with his evasive circling around media creations. He broaches the more fragile but potentially fuller relationship to someone he is meeting as a person, not as a reflection of programmed stereotypes.

DONALD DUK

First published: 1991
Type of work: Novel

A Chinese American boy overcomes his resistance to Asian things as he locates the usable parts of his heritage.

Donald Duk presents characters in positions similar to the ones they occupy in Chin's earlier works, but the novel reverses the characteristics of those that hold the positions. Specifically, his short stories and plays show a young Chinese American man who is constructing a viable tradition to put in place of the soul-destroying one given him by America; this construction is interfered with by a father figure, who may be a media image, such as Charlie Chan, who perpetuates the hurtful culture. In *Donald Duk*, however, it is the father who has located the viable, laudable tradition and the son who fights against it.

This change in who plays what role can be seen as accounting for the changed tone and even changed writing style of the novel. Chin's earlier works, which showed protagonists battling tenaciously but mostly unsuccessfully for an acceptable heritage while being dragged down by their American cultural baggage, moved spasmodically and ended inconclusively. *Donald Duk*, in which a workable Chinese American identity has already been established by the father and his peers, has a more linear, progressive plot, with the leading character following a clear trajectory.

The hero of the book, Donald, has been turned against Chinese traditions by the influence of the nearly all-white special school that he attends. He is so indifferent to his ethnic culture that he wantonly destroys one of the model planes his father has made for a Chinese New Year celebration. His father learns of his deed and tries to awaken Donald to the subtleties and enhancing aspects of their shared culture. Meanwhile, the father's teaching is supplemented by Donald's dreams, which put him back in the days of the building of the cross-country railroad. In his dreams, Donald finds out something about the Chinese people's real contribution to the American nation. By the end of the novel, Donald embraces his background, to the point of correcting his history teacher, who is ignorant of Asian American history.

As the novel presents a more definitive series of events than is seen in Chin's other fiction, so too is Chin's writing style less flashy and fragmentary, more workmanlike and plainer. This is not to say that one of these styles is preferable, either the earlier artsy one or the later simpler one; each is appropriate to its message and context. In *Donald Duk*, the point is that, through intelligent participation in and ongoing creation of a tradition, one can make a life that honors both individuality and one's ethnic group. The presentation of this message calls for a measured tone that is correspondent not with struggle but with struggle achieved.

Summary

Chinese immigrants to the United States would not have made the perilous voyage if they had not had high hopes. They were often disappointed. In Chin's opinion, however, it is not the immigrants but their children who were to feel the bitterest discouragement. His writings mull this theme, exposing how Chinese Americans are hit by both demeaning stereotypes and, often, occupational and social discrimination. Even at his most hopeful, Chin does not believe that the children can create an amalgam of American and Chinese ways. They must, instead, create a new Chinese culture, adapted to but not beholden to the largely antagonistic one of their new home.

Bibliography

Chan, Jeffrey Paul. "An Introduction to Chinese-American and Japanese-American Literature." In *Three American Literatures: Essays in Chicano, Native American, and Asian-American Literature for Teachers of American Literature,* edited by Houston A. Baker, Jr. New York: Modern Language Association of America, 1982.

Chin, Frank. "Uncle Frank's Fakebook of Fairy Tales for Asian American Moms and Dads." *Amerasian Journal* 18, no. 2 (1992): 69-87.

Feldman, George. "Spring's Five Fictional Encounters of the Chinese American Kind." *Publishers Weekly,* 238 (Feb. 8, 1991): 25-27.

Li, David Leiwi. "The Formation of Frank Chin and the Formations of Chinese

American Literature." In *Asian Americans: Comparative and Global Perspectives*, edited by Shirley Hune, Hyung-chan Kim, Stephen Fugita, and Amy Lin. Pullman: Washington State University Press, 1991.

McDonald, Dorothy Ritsuko. "An Introduction to Frank Chin's *The Chickencoop Chinaman* and *The Year of the Dragon*." In *Three American Literatures: Essays in Chicano, Native American, and Asian-American Literature for Teachers of American Literature*, edited by Houston A. Baker, Jr. New York: Modern Language Association of America, 1982.

James Feast

SANDRA CISNEROS

Born: Chicago, Illinois
December 20, 1954

Principal Literary Achievement

Cisneros was one of the first United States Latina writers to win a wide reading audience outside the Latino community.

Biography

Sandra Cisneros was born in Chicago, Illinois, on December 20, 1954, the only daughter in a family of seven children. Her mother, Elvira Cordero Anguiano, was a self-educated Mexican American who kindled her children's enthusiasm for reading by taking them to libraries. Her father, Alfredo Cisneros Del Moral, was a Mexican upholsterer who regularly moved the family between Chicago and Mexico City. In Chicago Catholic schools, where expectations for Mexican American girls were low, Cisneros was a below-average student, but she read voraciously and began writing early. After graduating from Loyola University in Chicago in 1976, she earned a master's degree at the prestigious Iowa Writers Workshop, where she learned "what I didn't want to be, how I didn't want to write."

Upon returning from graduate study to Chicago, she awakened to what she called the "incredible deluge of voices" that has become the hallmark of her writing. Her first three books are filled with a variety of voices, Mexican American voices mainly, telling their stories in an exuberant mixture of English and Spanish.

Her writing career started slowly. She earned her living as a teacher, college recruiter, arts administrator, writing teacher, and lecturer, following a nontraditional route for Latino women. Her choice to remain poor in order to write puzzled her father and brothers and often caused her to wonder whether she was betraying her beloved Mexican American culture by choosing a nontraditional life. She wrestled with the problems of how to be a liberated woman and remain a Latina.

She first published poetry and short fiction in feminist and Latino journals. *The House on Mango Street* was printed in 1984 by the Arte Publico Press in Houston, Texas. In 1987, Third Woman Press published her first volume of poems, *My Wicked, Wicked Ways*. These publications led to two grants from the National Endowment for the Arts and increasing public notice. *The House on Mango Street* began to appear in high school and college courses. Random House contracted to reprint a revised version

of *The House on Mango Street* in 1991 and published *Woman Hollering Creek* the same year. The latter title was selected by *Library Journal* as one of the best books of 1991, the year Cisneros received the Lannan Literary Award. Thereafter, her works began to appear in anthologies. During this period, she moved to San Antonio, Texas, where she found a rich source of voices for her stories and poems as well as an increasing independence that confirmed her in the choice of a nontraditional life, which she described as being "no one's mother and nobody's wife."

Cisneros came to see her writing as "terrorist activity," a means of helping people to see their lives more clearly. This help especially takes the form of showing both Latinos and whites that "we can be Latino and still be American."

Analysis

In a 1991 interview, Cisneros spoke of the "deluge of voices" she heard upon returning to Chicago after studying in the Iowa Writers Workshop. She said she was "fascinated by the rhythms of speech." Both her fiction and her poetry may be described as a deluge of voices, for virtually all of her fiction and some of her poems take the general form of the dramatic monologue.

A dramatic monologue is a literary work that consists of a speech such as one might hear in ordinary conversation, or especially in a play. One of the best examples is "*Los* Boxers," in which a talkative widower in a laundromat explains to a young mother how he has learned to do his laundry systematically, effectively, and cheaply, without any perception of the irony of his giving this information to a Latina—for whom such work is traditionally a life sentence, and who presumably still knows a good deal more about doing laundry than he does.

Cisneros' stories more often take the form of an internal monologue. The reader follows the speaker's inner thoughts as if he or she were saying them out loud in a distinctive voice; often the speaker is engaged in some specific actions while thinking. An example is "My Friend Lucy Who Smells Like Corn," a story that communicates the joys of youthful friendship in a poor neighborhood. The speaker breathlessly describes her friend while recounting past and current activities and adventures, including snatches of dialogue. She reveals her pleasures in playing at Lucy's house with her friend's eight sisters and tells of her wish for sisters of her own so that she could sleep with them "instead of alone on a fold-out chair in the living room."

Almost every story and many poems seem to be spoken aloud, even if there is not a specific dramatic situation. Even when a story clearly consists of recorded writing, as opposed to speech, Cisneros emphasizes a particular writing voice. For example, in "Little Miracles, Kept Promises," she presents notes left at shrines, notes thanking or making requests of various saints. Each note is a story told in a unique voice that reveals the personality of the writer, his or her situation and cultural background, and the writer's conception of the addressed saint as a listener. Though forms of the dramatic monologue and closely related letter forms are favorites for Cisneros, she occasionally tells stories in the third person, and many of her poems seem to be in her own voice, describing her own family and acquaintances.

Cisneros' main themes include the position of women in Latino culture, the problems of Latinas who want to live independent lives, and the problems of Latinos in U.S. culture.

Although Cisneros has clear political concerns that appear in virtually all of her work, her stories and poems are rarely political or moral tracts. Even the parable "There Was a Man, There Was a Woman" presents portraits without explaining the meanings readers should see in the depiction of the two characters. As she has said in interviews, one of her purposes as an artist is to change the way in which people see their world. Her works thus often present a picture of Latino life from a point of view that reveals aspects that ordinarily might be hidden. For example, in "*Los* Boxers," there is no moralistic voice that points out the irony of a middle-aged widower telling a mother how to do laundry. The man simply talks, and the irony is left for the reader to discover. As one thinks about such a story, with its new point of view on "women's work," further discoveries about political meanings in the story may emerge, such as, for example, what it means that a man finds the problems of doing laundry interesting to think and talk about. Furthermore, in the context of traditional Latino culture—in which the ideal woman passively serves men, obeying her father and then her husband, giving her life to housekeeping and motherhood—the story of a Latino advising a Latina about laundry takes on another dimension. For example, the story opens with a child dropping and breaking a bottle of soda, setting up a situation in which the mother, following orders, cleans up the glass and mops away the spill, while the man watches and lectures. He never thinks of helping her; in his culture, this is unthinkable, even for a man who has learned to do his own laundry. Because Cisneros usually avoids overt political statement, confining herself to pointed description or letting her characters speak, readers are encouraged to explore implicit meanings of the presented experience. Because Cisneros chooses to present especially revealing moments, the reader's exploration is nearly always rewarded with rich discovery.

THE HOUSE ON MANGO STREET

First published: 1983; revised 1988
Type of work: Novella

In a mid-twentieth century Chicago barrio, a Latina enters her teen years, struggling to become the person she envisions herself being.

The House on Mango Street is Sandra Cisneros' best-known work. Though it is made up of stories and sketches, some of which have been published separately, the collection has the unity of a novella. Cisneros has described the book as a connected collection, "each story a little pearl. . . . the whole thing like a necklace." In her own mind, Esperanza Cordero, the narrator, has one main problem: She wants to have a house of her own. As the story develops, the meaning of having a house of her own grows richer and more complex, until finally, she understands that she wants not only a literal house but also "a home in the heart." Furthermore, her one problem connects with many other problems that are clearer to the reader than to Esperanza, especially problems related to the roles and treatment accorded women in her culture and the problems of being Mexican American in U.S. culture.

Esperanza is the older of two daughters and has two brothers. Her wish for a house grows out of the family desire that is realized when they buy the house on Mango Street. This turns out not to be the home of which they have dreamed, with a large yard and many bathrooms, but the house they can afford, in a neighborhood being transformed into a ghetto. Esperanza's disappointment sparks her wish. She also realizes after moving to Mango Street that she does not want to live her life as do most women that she knows. She is named after her great-grandmother, a woman who refused to marry: "Until my great-grandfather threw a sack over her head and carried her off. Just like that, as if she were a fancy chandelier. . . . And the story goes she never forgave him." Having inherited her great-grandmother's name, Esperanza believes that she also has inherited her nature, a determination to be strong and to live independently. After young Esperanza is sexually assaulted at a carnival, she decides that she wants a house that belongs to her alone, not to any man. Her own bad experience confirms what she sees everywhere: that many women are seen as servants and property, their power and imagination imprisoned in houses that belong to husbands and fathers.

To her, a house comes to mean not only freedom from sexual oppression but also the freedom to pursue her vision of herself as an artist. Several times, Esperanza receives mysterious messages from seemingly spiritual sources that reveal what she must do to become an artist. Elenita, a medium, tells her mysteriously that she will have "a new house, a house made of heart." At the wake for her friend Lucy's baby sister, Esperanza meets three elderly sisters who see something special in her. They take her aside and tell her to make a wish. Seeming to know that Esperanza has wished to go away, they tell her, "When you leave you must remember to come back for the others. A circle, understand? You will always be Esperanza. You will always be Mango Street. . . . You must remember to come back. For the ones who cannot leave as easily as you." These messages tell her that she is destined to be a writer, to create an imaginary home out of the materials of her heart, which she will take with her wherever she goes and which will call her back to help those who are unable to leave. Near the end of the book, Esperanza's friend Alicia asks her a question: If she does not return to make Mango Street better—presumably a better place for women and for Latinos— then who will do so? Esperanza then begins to see that as a poet and storyteller, she will have a mission, to return not necessarily literally but certainly in her heart and mind, to make her people better known to themselves, to each other, and to the rest of U.S. culture.

WOMAN HOLLERING CREEK

First published: 1991
Type of work: Short story

A young Mexican woman is disillusioned by her marriage to a Mexican American man.

In "Woman Hollering Creek," Cisneros describes the experiences of an ideal Mexican wife, Cleófilas. Having grown up with her father, six brothers, and no mother, Cleófilas learns how to be a woman by watching *telenovelas* on television. She learns to expect that passion will fill her life. This passion will be the great love of her life, which will give it direction and meaning, so that "one does whatever one can, must do, at whatever the cost." This, she believes, is how life should be, "because to suffer for love is good. The pain all sweet somehow. In the end." To be complete as a woman, she need only wait for her lover to appear and carry her away into "happy ever after."

Her husband, Juan, carries her away from Mexico to Seguin, Texas, where she finds no community or family to support her, living in a comparatively isolated home and without independent means of transportation. Aware of the role of a good wife, she learns how to fit gracefully in with Juan's life. She cares for his house and bears a son, Juan Pedrito. Both she and Juan, however, are foreigners in Seguin. His work is menial and does not pay well enough for the minimum standard of life in Texas. By the time she is pregnant with their second child, he has taken to beating her regularly, partly as a way of dealing with his frustration and powerlessness.

As their relationship deteriorates, Cleófilas comes to realize that this marriage does not contain the passion she learned about in the *telenovelas*. She thinks about her situation while sitting next to Woman Hollering Creek, her baby in her lap; she sometimes wonders whether the woman after whom the creek is named cries out in pain or in rape. She finally realizes that she can do nothing herself to make the marriage right, and she wonders whether the arroyo was named after *La Llorona*, the weeping woman who drowned her own children, in the stories of her childhood.

Finally, she returns to her father, disillusioned, but still the passive woman depending upon men to care for her. To make her escape, however, she gets help from a woman who provides a glimpse of another way to live. Felice gives her a ride in her truck on the first part of her escape. That Felice lives alone, takes care of herself, and owns a truck—in short, that she lives much as a man does in Cleófilas' experience—astonishes Cleófilas. She continues to think about Felice long after her return to Mexico, and she tells others about this woman who, when they crossed the creek upon leaving Seguin, hollered like Tarzan: "It was a gurgling out of her own throat, a long ribbon of laughter, like water."

LITTLE MIRACLES, KEPT PROMISES

First published: 1991
Type of work: Short story

A collection of notes left at saints' shrines, ending with a long letter from a young woman who has achieved faith in herself.

"Little Miracles, Kept Promises" is a catalog of Cisneros' strengths and appeals as a fiction writer. The collection of notes left at saints' shrines may recall the letters of Nathaniel West's *Miss Lonelyhearts* (1933), but the tone of these is more consistently comic, showing well the witty and humorous side of Cisneros that appears in many of her stories and poems. For example, Barbara Ybañez threatens to turn the statue of San Antonio de Padua upside down until he sends her "a man man. I mean someone who's not ashamed to be seen cooking or cleaning or looking after himself." Rubén Ledesma somewhat reluctantly yet desperately appeals to San Lázaro, who was "raised from the dead and did a lot of miracles," to help him deal with his "face breaking out with so many pimples." These letters are especially rich in the variety of voices and tones they present, from the devout who speak to their saint as a friend, to the pious who lapse into almost meaningless formulas, to the inexperienced who are uncomfortable addressing a person they do not know personally, to the irreverent and skeptical.

These many voices lead finally to that of a young woman, Rosario, who has cut off a braid of hair that has never before been cut and pinned it by the statue of the Virgin of Guadalupe. Rosario is an image of Cisneros, the young Latina artist rebelling against the restrictive roles of women in her culture, especially as they have been reinforced by the massive cultural authority of the Catholic Church. She says that she has resisted religious belief until her discovery that the Virgin is not simply a passive sufferer but also one manifestation of woman as goddess, the powers of fertility, healing, creative energy. This discovery made it possible for Rosario to love the Virgin, and thereby not to be ashamed of her mother and grandmother and finally to love herself.

Of Rosario, Cisneros said, "That's me. . . . I'm very, very much devoted to the Virgin of Guadalupe, but not exactly the same figure celebrated in Church."

Summary

While Sandra Cisneros' subjects are her race, gender, and class, her stories and poems are not narrowly political. Rather than focusing on specific social problems and their remedies, Cisneros tries to be part of a more general solution, calling attention through lively and entertaining stories to how life is experienced, especially by Mexican American women. In her stories, she works at changing the ways her readers look at her worlds, helping them to imagine better ways to live. In this way, her work is related to that of major local color writers of the nineteenth century such as Sarah Orne Jewett.

Bibliography

Cisneros, Sandra. "From a Writer's Notebook: Ghosts and Voices: Writing from Obsessions, Do You Know Me? I Wrote *The House on Mango Street*." *The Americas Review* 15 (Fall/Winter, 1987): 69-73, 77-79.

Hoffert, Barbara. "Sandra Cisneros: Giving Back to Libraries." *Library Journal* 117 (January, 1992): 55.

Jussawalla, Ferosz, and Reed W. Dasenbrock, eds. *Interviews with Writers of the Post-Colonial World*. Jackson: University Press of Mississippi, 1992.

McCracken, Ellen. "Sandra Cisneros' *The House on Mango Street*: Community-Oriented Introspection and the Demystification of Patriarchal Violence." In *Breaking Boundaries: Latina Writings and Critical Readings*, edited by Asunción Horno-Delgado, et al. Amherst: University of Massachusetts Press, 1989.

Olivares, Julián. "Sandra Cisneros' *The House on Mango Street* and the Poetics of Space." In *Chicana Creativity and Criticism: Charting New Frontiers in American Literature,* edited by Maria Herrera-Sobek and Helena María Viramontes. Houston: Arte Publico Press, 1988.

Rodriguez-Aranda, Pilar E. "On the Solitary Fate of Being Mexican, Female, Wicked, and Thirty-Three: An Interview with Writer Sandra Cisneros." *The Americas Review* 18 (Spring, 1990): 64-80.

Sagel, Jim. "Sandra Cisneros: Conveying the Riches of the Latin American Culture. Is the Author's Literary Goal." *Publishers Weekly* 238 (March 29, 1991): 74-75.

Terry Heller

TOM CLANCY

Born: Baltimore, Maryland
1947

Principal Literary Achievement
Credited for creating the "techno-thriller," Clancy combines state-of-the-art military technology and superpower confrontation in his best-selling novels.

Biography

Thomas L. Clancy was born in Baltimore, Maryland, in 1947. His father, a mailman, and his mother, who worked in a department-store credit office, provided him with a middle-class upbringing. Toys, particularly toys featuring military technology, were more interesting to the young Clancy than athletics; he also became and remained a voracious reader.

After receiving his education in local Catholic schools, Clancy attended Loyola College in Baltimore, majoring in English. He later said that he always wanted to see his name on a book, although he never imagined that he would become a best-selling author. While in college, he was a member of the Reserve Officers' Training Corps (ROTC), but poor eyesight kept him out of the regular military, and he was denied the opportunity of serving in Vietnam, much to his regret. He married shortly after leaving college, and the need to support his growing family led him away from a literary career and into a more immediately financially rewarding occupation as an insurance agent. After gaining experience in Baltimore and Hartford, Connecticut, he joined his wife's grandfather's insurance agency in rural Maryland.

Clancy never entirely abandoned his quest to become a writer. He had a science-fiction story rejected, and in the early 1970's he began plotting a novel, a work that contained characters that would eventually populate his published books. During those years he also continued his extensive reading, particularly in science fiction and military manuals. Although he did well in business, by the end of the decade he concluded that the claims on his time were not that consuming, and he again turned to the task of getting his name on a book jacket.

In 1976, a naval mutiny had occurred on a Soviet frigate, the mutineers hoping to defect to Sweden. The mutiny failed, but the incident gave Clancy the inspiration for his first published novel. Written during several months in late 1982 and early 1983, the unknown author's *The Hunt for Red October* was published in 1984 by the Naval

Academy's Naval Institute Press, which had only recently decided to publish works of fiction. In retrospect, it was an unlikely publishing house to produce one of the best-sellers of the year. Clancy said that he thought the work might sell five or ten thousand copies, but eventually 300,000 copies were sold in hardback and two million in paperback. Film rights were purchased for $500,000, and the motion picture, which starred Sean Connery as a defecting Soviet submarine captain, was a popular hit.

The fame of *The Hunt for Red October* reached the upper levels of the political and military establishment in Washington. President Ronald Reagan called it "the perfect yarn." Caspar Weinberger, the secretary for defense, reviewed it favorably in *The Times Literary Supplement*. Clancy was invited to the White House, and the Pentagon gave him access to some of its major weapons systems; he spent time on a nuclear submarine and a naval frigate and drove an M-1 tank. All these experiences became grist for future works.

The books came rapidly. In 1986, he published *Red Storm Rising*, a novel about a third world war fought primarily in Europe between North Atlantic Treaty Organization (NATO) forces and the Soviet Union. In 1987, he put out *Patriot Games*, a story of terrorists from Northern Ireland, which also later became a popular film starring Harrison Ford. A highly placed Russian official who spied for the Central Intelligence Agency (CIA) was the focus of *The Cardinal of the Kremlin*, which appeared in 1988, *Clear and Present Danger*, about the Colombian drug trade, came out in 1989. *The Sum of All Fears*, published in 1991, pivoted around an international terrorist plot to explode a nuclear weapon during the Super Bowl game. *Without Remorse*, which returned to the era of the Vietnam War in the early 1970's, appeared in 1993. In addition, Clancy became a newspaper columnist and a popular lecturer. His continuing best-seller status saw the one-time insurance agent become one of the most recognized authors of the day, both in the United States and abroad.

Analysis

Clancy has stated that he does not like to analyze the themes of his books. "A theme to me is a question that a high-school English teacher asks," he told an interviewer, explaining that his literary concerns were with more essential matters. "In the real world, and that's what I try to write about as basically as I can, somebody has to get the job done." Nevertheless, there are obvious themes in Clancy's works. Clancy claims that, like most Americans, he is entranced with technology, and "the military happen to have the best toys." If so, perhaps it is not surprising that *The Hunt for Red October* became a best-seller. From the opening paragraph, the reader is caught up in the world of men at war, a world about which Clancy seems extremely knowledgeable, vastly more so than the lay reader. The attempt of the Soviet captain Mark Ramius to turn his nuclear submarine over to the Americans sees both sides caught in a web of circumstances that could lead to nuclear war between the superpowers. The author's expertise in military technology and in the minds and mores of those who fight—or, to use Clancy's words, those who must get the job done—is compelling and convincing.

The harnessing of the latest military technology to a plot in which a nuclear war is a possible outcome is a combination likely to attract many readers. Clancy, however, denies that he either invented what has been called the techno-thriller or that his writings should be so labeled. Clancy claims that he aims merely to be as accurate as possible; since he is writing about war and terrorism in the late twentieth century, technology must play a central role in his work.

Yet technology is not the master of humanity in Clancy's fiction. The machines can do only what men and women would have them do. Obviously, technology can be used for destructive and immoral purposes. Underneath the violence, there are pervasive elements of good and evil in Clancy's novels. Evil generally results from corrupt institutions, false ideologies, and immoral values. Although the author was strongly opposed to the Soviet Union and what it stood for—*The Hunt for Red October*, *Red Storm Rising*, and *The Cardinal of the Kremlin* all depict the Soviets as the enemies of American values and institutions—many of Clancy's Soviet characters are sympathetically drawn.

Yet the Soviet world portrayed in *Patriot Games* and *The Sum of All Fears* is not morally or spiritually equal to the West. In Clancy's works, the Soviet system devalues traditional religious and spiritual values; humans are no better than animals, and international terrorists are no more than common and vicious killers. Morality and immorality are central to Clancy's novels, and the good generally wins out. Neither pacifism nor neutrality, however, can preserve the West and its Judeo-Christian ethic; in Clancy's literary world, military values and strengths are necessary and imperative. Fortuitously for him, his early publications coincided with a political generation anxious to shake off the perception of American weakness and debility that followed the Vietnam War. It is no wonder that the Reagan White House found in Clancy a kindred spirit.

Clancy, however, has little respect for most politicians. Too often they are amoral, committed to their own careers. The unnamed president in *The Hunt for Red October* and *The Cardinal of the Kremlin* is often too pragmatic, but ultimately he makes the correct and necessary decisions. The same president is diminished in *Clear and Present Danger* because of his concern with his coming reelection campaign. President Fowler, his liberal successor, is worse, combining ignorance and arrogance, and he almost starts World War III by threatening to use nuclear weapons against the Soviets in *The Sum of All Fears*. Individual politicians may have vision and competence, but most are simply concerned with keeping their offices at any cost.

Although Clancy's books are populated by military figures, his alter ego in his stories is Jack Ryan, a civilian. Ryan, who has a doctorate in history and has made a small fortune in the stock market, saves the heir to the British throne in *Patriot Games*, becomes a consultant to the CIA, and eventually rises to a position of considerable influence in that organization. Ryan is not a superman—he has a fear of flying—but the convoluted plots of Clancy's books see Ryan forced into the active world of terror and war. He then becomes the man who, in Clancy's phrase, gets the job done.

Ryan is not the leading figure in all Clancy's books; however, he is the thread that ties the many subplots and numerous characters together. Clancy's works can thus be read as a whole. Not only Ryan but many other figures also appear and reappear, sometimes as major characters, other times in smaller parts. A character such as John Clark plays only a small—although crucial—role in *The Cardinal of the Kremlin*, but he has a much larger part in *Clear and Present Danger* and the lead role in *Without Remorse*.

Many have criticized the lack of character development in Clancy's works. While the dialogue is generally satisfying, many of his characters are often one-dimensional figures. Clancy is writing largely about desperate crises; action, not introspection, is perhaps expected. Jack Ryan, however, does evolve as the novels continue. By the time that *The Sum of All Fears* was published in 1991, Ryan was in his forties, working too hard at the CIA, neglecting his family, worrying about his inability to take his young son to a baseball game, and drinking too much. Even his marriage seemed in danger. The centrality of the family is an underlying theme in Clancy's works; Ryan's own family is the model modern family. His wife, Cathy, is an eye surgeon. They have two children. The ultimate crisis of *Patriot Games* sees Ryan forced to defend his family and home from a terrorist assault. The family personifies and preserves the moral and religious values necessary to society. It is a deeply conservative and traditional view that is perhaps related to the author's middle-class Catholic background; perhaps that synthesis of traditional values with the latest technology and the threat of total war explains his great popularity. He does tell a great yarn.

THE HUNT FOR RED OCTOBER

First published: 1984
Type of work: Novel

A Soviet submarine captain attempts to defect to the United States.

Clancy's first published novel, *The Hunt for Red October*, became a runaway best-seller. Writing in the early 1980's at a time of heightened Cold War tensions, Clancy touched a deep chord. Soviet submarine captain Mark Ramius is disillusioned by the Communist system and the Soviet state. His wife, a former ballerina, died on an operating table at the hands of a drunken doctor who, because of his Communist Party connections, was not punished for his misdeed. The leading Soviet expert in submarine tactics, Ramius, along with a number of his officers, decides to defect to the United States.

A number of themes common to Clancy's work appear in *The Hunt for Red October*. His knowledge of submarine technology and tactics carries the reader into an underwater world that, because of the technological framework, seems more fact than fiction. The Soviets do not want a nuclear war, but they might resort to war to recapture Ramius and his submarine, and military power divorced from morality could well destroy the world. Ramius, driven by family feelings and moral considerations, transcends a system that has proved to be an evil failure.

The key figure on the other side is Jack Ryan, a consultant to the CIA. Because he is only a professor of history, he lacks the authority government office might give him; he is neither a high-ranking military figure nor a politician. Ryan is an everyman, at least an everyman who is willing and able to do what is necessary. Eventually, Ryan boards the *Red October* and is forced to kill a committed young Communist who has been ordered to sink the submarine rather than have it fall into American hands. Although his submarine is damaged, Ramius sails his ship into an American port. Ryan has received an education in the necessity of using power, political and military, to maintain the good society: It is not enough merely to write about history.

As in all of his stories, Clancy brings together a number of subplots and numerous major and minor characters. Even if the politicians are not always dependable, the officers and men of the Navy invariably excel. They are well trained and motivated, and they work together for the greater good of the ship and the country. Clancy makes numerous comparisons between the Soviet system and the freedoms to be found in the West. The book is not so much a story of "good guys" and "bad guys" as a contest between a system that has failed and one that, in spite of individual human weaknesses, is the last best hope of humankind.

PATRIOT GAMES

First published: 1987
Type of work: Novel

A young American historian runs afoul of Irish terrorists after foiling their attack upon the Prince and Princess of Wales.

In part because of its success as a film, *Patriot Games* is one of Clancy's best-known novels. He began writing it before *The Hunt for Red October*, but it was not published until after his second hit novel, *Red Storm Rising*. *Patriot Games*, however, is the first chronological part of Jack Ryan's fictional biography. Some information is given about Ryan in *The Hunt for Red October*, but it is only in *Patriot Games* that his background is fleshed out. Clancy has admitted that in creating Ryan he has projected an idealized version of himself.

In a departure from his other novels, in *Patriot Games* technology, military and otherwise, plays only a secondary role. The story opens in London. Ryan and his family are enjoying a working vacation; his wife and daughter sightsee and shop while he researches his next work of history. At the end of a day, Ryan meets his family in a peaceful London park, but the plans for a pleasant evening are aborted by an explosion a few yards away. A radical Irish republican faction of dedicated Marxists has just assaulted the automobile carrying the Prince and Princess of Wales. Ryan, a former Marine officer, reacts instinctively, killing one terrorist and disarming another. Ryan himself is shot. For his heroism, he is given an honorary knighthood. Members of the terrorist group vow revenge, however, and eventually attack Ryan and his family after they have returned to the United States.

There are fewer subplots than in Clancy's other novels; Ryan remains the focus of the work. While still in the London hospital recovering from his wounds, Ryan is visited by the Prince of Wales, who feels guilty that he was unable to protect his wife personally. In American fashion, Ryan bucks up the prince, giving him renewed confidence in himself and his duties. In *Patriot Games* the importance of the family and all that it represents takes center place. The Windsors, who later visit the Ryans' home for dinner while on a tour to the United States, are presented as holding the same values and morals as Ryan and his wife Cathy. They might be royalty, but underneath they are just like the people next door. In contrast, the terrorists, rootless and homeless, lack those values necessary for society to survive. They are driven by perverted philosophies and motivated by blind hatreds. Clancy—and Ryan—are Irish Americans, but neither evinces any sympathy for radical Irish terrorists.

Clancy has the ability to touch the current concerns of his readers. The Cold War fears and the threats of terrorism were headline issues and events when his novels appeared. In *Patriot Games*, he capitalized on America's fascination with Prince Charles and Princess Diana. With Jack Ryan as an everyman becoming a knighted hero battling ruthless villains, the novel was almost guaranteed to be a best-seller and a hit film.

THE SUM OF ALL FEARS

First published: 1991
Type of work: Novel

An international terrorist group, hoping to re-create the Cold War era, explodes a nuclear device during the Super Bowl.

One of the strengths of Clancy's novels is their timeliness, and this characteristic is found again in *The Sum of All Fears*. Published in 1991, the book reflects the immediate post-Cold War world. The Berlin Wall has fallen; the Soviet Union is no more. Yet the world is not necessarily safer and more secure. New tensions and old rivalries have replaced the superpower antagonism. International terrorism is obviously not new—Clancy himself wrote about it in *Patriot Games*—but without the restraining influence of the Cold War, terrorism could well pose an even greater threat than in the past.

Ryan has risen to a position of considerable authority in the CIA. Unfortunately, the new president, Jonathan Robert Fowler, a liberal, and his national security advisor, Elizabeth Elliot, a leftist academic, see such agencies as the CIA as both incompetent and as relics of history that can be ignored and probably dismantled. Ryan, who is not a politician, does little to avoid alienating Fowler and Elliot. The conservative Clancy holds no brief for their liberal politics, but even worse than their politics is their lack of morality. When Fowler and Elliot become lovers, it becomes obvious to the reader that they are among Ryan's foes.

In *The Sum of All Fears*, the terrorists are a mixed group of German Marxists, radical Muslims, and a Native American. Each has slightly different motives, but all are wedded to a cause and an ideology foreign to Western values and institutions. As in most of Clancy's novels, technology plays a key role. The technological focus revolves around an Israeli nuclear weapon lost during the 1973 war with Syria. Rediscovered years later in a farmer's garden, the weapon is rebuilt, secretly shipped to the United States, trucked to Denver, and exploded during the annual Super Bowl game. In the aftermath, the president loses control of himself, first almost going to war against the Soviets, whom he suspects of setting off the device. When it is learned that the plot originated in the Middle East, perhaps at the instigation of an Iranian Muslim cleric, the president issues the order to bomb the cleric's hometown, the holy city of Qum, an act that would kill tens of thousands of innocent people. At the crucial point, Ryan steps in and vetoes the presidential order, and Fowler is replaced by the vice president. Although thousands have been killed in Denver, a world conflagration is narrowly avoided.

In this long novel, Clancy brings together all the themes that make his books so popular. There is no doubt about where good and evil stand. Technology is central to the story. The threat of nuclear weapons, a constant concern since the end of World War II, is shown to be a potential reality. Eternal vigilance is necessary, and someone must do what is required in spite of all obstacles. In the course of *The Sum of All Fears*, Ryan, driving himself too hard at work, almost destroys his own family through drink and inattention. At the end, he again puts his family at the center of his life and resigns from the CIA. Someone must do the job, but the human costs can be high.

Summary

Tom Clancy is only one of many writers who have used the background of the Cold War, the threat of nuclear conflict, international terrorism, and other current concerns to attract a wide reading audience. Clancy, however, has joined those fears to military technology in a manner that his rivals have not; he might deny it, but he does write "techno-thrillers." His first story was science fiction, and it was rejected. In a sense, though, he has been writing science fiction ever since—although it is science fiction that reflects the world of today rather than the world of tomorrow.

Bibliography

Anderson, Patrick. "King of the 'Techno-Thriller.'" *The New York Times Magazine,* May 1, 1988, 54.

Borger, Gloria. "The Hunt for Tom Clancy: Or, Why Recruits Are Hard to Find." *U.S. News and World Report* 108 (March 26, 1990): 27.

Greenberg, Martin H., ed. *The Tom Clancy Companion.* New York: Berkley Books, 1992.

Phillips, Christopher. "*Red October*'s Tom Clancy: After the Hunt." *Saturday Evening Post* 263, no. 6 (September/October, 1991): 16-19.

Ryan, William F. "The Genesis of the Techno-Thriller." *Virginia Quarterly Review* 69, no. 1 (Winter, 1991): 24-41.

Thomas, Evan. "The Art of the Techno-Thriller." *Newsweek* 122 (August 8, 1988): 60.

Eugene Larson

JUDITH ORTIZ COFER

Born: Hormingueros, Puerto Rico
February 24, 1952

Principal Literary Achievement

In her poetry and prose, Cofer communicates what a sensitive child growing up partly in Puerto Rico, partly in New Jersey endures.

Biography

When she was three or four, Judith Ortiz Cofer, born in Hormigueros, Puerto Rico, in 1952, began the routine that was to define her existence for a number of years. Because her father, J. M. Ortiz Lugo, was a career Navy man stationed on a ship from the Brooklyn Naval Yard in New York, Judith and her brother came with their mother, Fanny Morot Ortiz, to Paterson, New Jersey, where the family lived in "El Building," a vertical barrio. When the father was away on long cruises, the family often returned to Hormigueros in the southwestern corner of Puerto Rico, slightly inland from Mayaguez, staying there with Judith's grandmother.

When she was nineteen, Judith Ortiz married Charles John Cofer, a businessman. The couple has a daughter, Tanya. Following her marriage, Cofer continued her education at Augusta College, from which she received a bachelor's degree in 1974. Three years later, she earned a master of arts degree from Florida Atlantic University. Cofer attended the University of Oxford for part of 1977 on a scholarship from the English Speaking Union.

Fluent in English and Spanish, Cofer worked as a bilingual teacher in the public schools of Palm Beach County, Florida, during the 1974-1975 school year. In 1978, master's degree in hand, Cofer was named an adjunct instructor in English at Broward Community College in Fort Lauderdale, Florida. The following year, she was appointed an instructor in Spanish at the same institution. During this period, 1978-1980, she was also an adjunct instructor in English at Palm Beach Community College.

In 1980, having published her first collection of poems, *Latin Women Pray* (1980), as a chapbook, Cofer became a lecturer in English at the University of Miami at Coral Gables, a position she occupied until 1984, when she joined the Department of English at the University of Georgia as an instructor. By this time, Cofer had published two more chapbooks, *The Native Dancer* (1981) and *Among the Ancestors* (1981), and a three-act play also entitled *Latin Women Pray*, which was performed at Georgia State

University in 1984. Her poetry began to appear in anthologies, among them *Hispanics in the United States* (1982).

Having served as a regular staff member of the International Conference on the Fantastic in Literature from 1979 until 1982, Cofer was appointed a member of the Florida Fine Arts Council in 1982. During the summers of 1983 and 1984, she joined the administrative staff of the Bread Loaf Writers Conference in Ripton, Vermont, which she attended as a student participant in 1981 and as a John Atherton Scholar in Poetry in 1982.

The Bread Loaf experience, extending over four summers, did much to help Cofer fix her sights on publishing her poetry. *Peregrina* (1986) and *Terms of Survival* (1987) owe a substantial debt to the extensive critiquing sessions that characterize Bread Loaf, as does Cofer's fifty-seven-page contribution to *Triple Crown: Chicano, Puerto Rican, and Cuban American Poetry* (1987), for which she provided the section entitled "Reaching for the Mainland."

These collections and the Bread Loaf experience helped Cofer, in 1988, to garner a Witter Brynner Foundation Award for Poetry. This award was followed in 1989 by a fellowship in poetry from the National Endowment for the Arts. She used these grants to continue work on her poetry, to complete her novel, *The Line of the Sun* (1989), and to complete a collection of essays and stories, *Silent Dancing* (1990).

Cofer spent the 1987-1988 academic year as an instructor in the Georgia Center for Continuing Education, moving the following year to Macon College as an instructor in English. In 1990, she was the coordinator of special programs at Mercer University. Subsequently, she returned to the University of Georgia to teach writing in the school's English department.

Most of Cofer's work relates to her early experience, focusing both on her area of Puerto Rico and on Paterson, New Jersey, where she spent her childhood winters. The life of Marisol, the narrator in *The Line of the Sun*, parallels Cofer's life. The book examines the conflict a young girl feels when her father urges her to forsake her heritage and integrate into mainland culture while her mother presses her to cling to Puerto Rican ways, which reflect her true heritage.

Marisol is aided by her black-sheep uncle, Guzman, whose story Marisol is telling. Guzman comes to stay with the family in Paterson, and with his help, Marisol attempts an accommodation that will satisfy both parents. Worlds apart in thinking and social outlook from both of Marisol's parents, Guzman opens the impressionable Marisol's eyes to possibilities she had never considered. Although *In the Line of the Sun* is not strictly autobiographical, it is autobiographically accurate in its broader aspects.

Analysis

Judith Ortiz Cofer's writing is precisely right for its time. Hispanic American consciousness in the United States, already raised by such writers as Jesus Colon, Nicholasa Mohr, Rolando Hinojosa, Pedro Pietri, Piri Thomas, Tomás Rivera, and others, has been elevated to a new plane in Cofer's novels and poetry.

Her own life provided Cofer with the built-in conflict between two cultures that her writing successfully depicts. She has been able to place the two major elements of this conflict into the kind of symmetrical juxtaposition that permits her work to bristle with dramatic tension.

Her novel *The Line of the Sun* is equally divided between the stories of her family in southwestern Puerto Rico and in Paterson, New Jersey; the first half of the book is set in Puerto Rico, the second half on the mainland. In *Silent Dancing*, Cofer achieves an even greater contrast by intermixing stories of her island home with stories of her mainland home. Each story in this book has elements of both worlds in it, although each concentrates more on one of these worlds than on the other.

The contrasts Cofer builds are sharp and apparent. Puerto Rico is warm, both thermally and in terms of its people, whereas Paterson, New Jersey, is cold in the same terms. The autobiographical character in *Silent Dancing* is ever aware of Paterson's grayness, of its long, drab winters; the father is aware of Paterson's coldness to foreigners. To shield his family from this coldness and to avoid open hostility, he demands that his family members keep to themselves, realizing the near hysteria that the influx of Puerto Ricans into a formerly middle-class Jewish neighborhood has generated among the Anglos who remain.

The father, able to pass for an Anglo, stands in striking contrast to his wife and children, who are clearly Hispanic and cannot pass. The father has been assimilated; the mother never will be. Each has different hopes for the children. The father hopes they will gracefully, inconspicuously become typical Americans, the mother that they will preserve and reflect their Hispanic heritage.

The basic tensions in Cofer's work are heightened both by the obvious contrasts between two cultures and the contrasts between the perceptions of children and adults. Cofer handles these perceptions with disciplined consistency, revealing all that she needs to reveal, never allowing a child to have adult perceptions or an adult to have those of a child. She draws her lines clearly as she shapes her characters; she resolutely keeps them from intruding upon one another's turf.

Cofer acknowledges her great admiration of Virginia Woolf, who dealt with problems of personal isolation and alienation similar to those found in much of Cofer's work. Cofer, fortunately, had Puerto Rico to fall back on when her isolation and alienation threatened her equanimity; Woolf was less fortunate.

Cofer possesses the same sort of eye for physical detail that characterizes Woolf's writing. She presents her stories with an unencumbered sharpness of focus reminiscent of Woolf's best descriptive passages, yet with the sort of delicacy and decorum that Woolf attained in her most successful novels.

Cofer's poetry deals with the same dualities found in her short stories and in her play *Latin Women Pray*. The conflict that most engages her attention cannot be viewed in terms only of Hispanic culture versus mainstream American culture. In a sense, this surface conflict provides the pretext Cofer requires to frame her deeply felt, sweeping questions about humankind.

Cofer considers herself principally a poet. Much of her poetry is written in irregular lines of varied metrical schemes and lengths. Despite—or perhaps because of—this irregularity, Cofer's verse achieves a relaxed rhythm that suggests easy, free-flowing conversation.

Her poetic lines are wholly appropriate to the atmosphere she seeks to build. Cofer's ear for language is as good as her eye for detail, and the two combine happily in most of her poetry. Typical of the easy meter she achieves is a bitter yet matter-of-fact poem, "The Woman Who Was Left at the Altar." The spurned woman, having grown fat, makes her unused wedding gown into curtains for her room and makes doilies from her wedding veil. She roves the streets, chickens dangling from her waist; in her mind, their yellow eyes mirror the face of the man who shunned her. She takes satisfaction in killing the chickens she sells, because in that act, she is killing him, killing troubled memories that haunt her.

This narrative poem, gaining much of its power from what is left unsaid, achieves its major metrical impact by moving at its exact center from two anapestic feet to trochaic and iambic feet, all in one line; the next line is iambic dimeter:

> Since her old mother died, buried in black,
> she lives alone.

Cofer continues in the next lines with two dactylic feet, followed in the same line by two trochaic feet, and continuing to two lines equally varied metrically:

> Out of the lace she made curtains for her room,
> doilies out of the veil. They are now
> yellow as malaria.

These metrical irregularities are a fundamental part of Cofer's narrative poetic style. Her poems never seem strained or unnatural, despite their somewhat bewildering metrical scheme.

In her prose writing as in her poetry, moreover, Cofer is ever aware that words, whether written or spoken, have sound. She has an inherent sense of the cadences of human speech, and she captures those cadences with extraordinary verisimilitude.

THE LINE OF THE SUN

First published: 1989
Type of work: Novel

　　Marisol Vivente struggles between loyalty to her native Puerto Rico, from which she came, and loyalty to the United States.

Marisol San Luz Vivente, the protagonist in *The Line of the Sun*, Cofer's first novel, is an autobiographical character. Like Cofer, Marisol was born in southwestern Puerto Rico but, from an early age, spent much of her life in Paterson, New Jersey. The novel encompasses three decades, beginning in the late 1930's and ending in the 1960's, and traces the impact that these three decades have on three generations of a family.

Marisol's father, Rafael, works near New York City. His wife and children live with him. Marisol, through stories she hears from her mother, has enough direct and immediate contact with her heritage that she feels strongly impelled to cling to it—as her mother, who wants her to retain the values and culture of her forbears, thinks she should.

On the other hand, her Puerto Rican father, having struggled successfully to become assimilated, wants Marisol and her brother to adopt the manners and customs of the United States so that they can blend in as inconspicuously as possible, thereby assuring themselves better economic opportunities than would be available to them in their homeland. Marisol, at a highly impressionable age, has to deal with an inner conflict between her two cultures and, in doing so, has to consider the impact the resolution of her dilemma will have on her relationship with her parents and on her own future.

Into this situation, Cofer, writing vividly and poetically about the family, introduces Uncle Guzman, a relative about whom the parents have talked quite darkly. During the Korean conflict, Guzman's brother, Carmelo, was killed in combat. At about the same time, Guzman, fifteen and the wilder of the two brothers, was involved in a scandal in his native Salud, where he lived with a prostitute known as La Cabra. He fled his island for New York, going there as a migrant farmworker. Years later, he appears on the Viventes' doorstep in Paterson one Christmas Eve and stays with his relatives for several months. During part of this time, he is confined to bed after he is attacked by a neighborhood thug.

The introduction of Guzman, her father's best friend during adolescence, is necessary to the resolution of Marisol's conflict. She had known this uncle largely through reputation; the family talked about him in hushed tones. Guzman, quite unwittingly, enables Marisol to see in sharp focus the two major forces in her life and to balance them. He also finds peace by returning to Puerto Rico, where he marries La Cabra's daughter, Sarita, a saintly woman who takes satisfaction in redeeming Guzman.

Marisol's conclusion is that although she always carries her island heritage on her back like a snail, she belongs in the world of telephones, offices, concrete buildings, and the English language. This is essentially the decision Judith Cofer reached for herself during her own adolescence.

SILENT DANCING: A PARTIAL REMEMBRANCE OF A PUERTO RICAN CHILDHOOD

First published: 1990
Type of work: Autobiography

This personal narrative of growing up includes autobiographical tales set in both Puerto Rico and New Jersey, with relevant poetry following each tale.

Early in *Silent Dancing*, which in 1991 won the PEN/Martha Albrand Special Citation for Nonfiction and was included in New York Public Library's 1991 Best Books for Teens, Cofer warns her readers that she is not interested in "canning" memories. Rather, like Virginia Woolf in *Moments of Being* (1976), she writes autobiographically as a means of connecting with "the threads of lives that have touched mine and at some point converged into the tapestry that is my memory of childhood."

Silent Dancing is not an autobiography as such; it does not progress linearly from the moment of birth to the day before the final revision is completed. It is, rather, a collection of thirteen stories and a preface, with eighteen poems scattered amid the stories. The book's elements are interconnected but are also discrete. The sequence in which they are read need not be Cofer's sequence, although she obviously spent considerable thought on arranging the book's disparate components as she prepared her collection for publication.

"Casa," the lead story, explains elements of the book's genesis. The family has gathered, as it does every day between three and four in the afternoon, for *café con leche* with Mama, the term everyone uses in referring to Cofer's grandmother. In the comfortable parlor that Mama's husband built to her exact specifications, drinking coffee together provides the adults with the pretext for spinning yarns, ostensibly for one another but covertly for the edification of the children present.

Young Judith was an attentive listener; Cofer suggests that her desire to write stems from these three-to-four-hour sessions in her grandmother's inviting house in Puerto Rico. This story, like much of Cofer's writing, is exact in detail, warm and tactile in depicting human relationships. Mama is voluble, but as she talks, her hands work steadily on braiding her granddaughter's hair.

In sharp contrast to "Casa" and stories such as "Primary Lessons" or "Marina," set in rural Puerto Rico, are the stories about the author's life in a dark, crowded apartment in Paterson. In New Jersey, rather than being outdoors in a gentle climate, the children spend their winters huddled in a cramped living room around a television set. Despite its grayness, the New Jersey part of Cofer's existence has its compensations in both comforts and educational opportunities.

The conflict between two cultures that often are at odds provides the basic conflict for *Silent Dancing*. Cofer personalizes the conflict, yet she lends it a universality that exceeds the two specific cultures about which she writes.

THE LATIN DELI

First published: 1993
Type of work: Prose and poetry collection

Cofer intermixes poetry and prose throughout this volume, which deals with personal problems faced by Latin American women.

Readers of *Silent Dancing* and *The Line of the Sun* will encounter in *The Latin Deli* many of the personalities and situations familiar from Cofer's two earlier books. The delicatessen of the title is a *bodega* in Paterson where residents of El Building shop for such Puerto Rican comestibles as plantains and Bustelo coffee.

Most of the stories and poems in *The Latin Deli* are told from the perspective of a young girl torn between two worlds. The father, English-speaking and light-complected, is a working-class man who restricts severely the freedom of a daughter in whom sexual desire is awakening. The mother is a temporary resident of El Building, ever longing to return to Puerto Rico and refusing to learn English.

El Building is a vertical barrio, an attempt to preserve in Paterson some sense of the community its inhabitants have traded for the economic opportunities the mainland offers. The girl in most of Cofer's stories speaks English well, yet she endures discrimination directed against Puerto Ricans.

In "American History," the narrator, who is bright and more fluent in English than Spanish, is barred from classes for the gifted because English is not her native language. She develops a crush on Eugene, a boy from Georgia who is taking classes for the gifted. On the day of John F. Kennedy's assassination, she accepts Eugene's invitation to go to his house to study with him; Eugene's mother, however, asks her whether she comes from El Building, which is next door. When the narrator admits that she does, the mother bars her entry.

In "The Paterson Public Library," Cofer deals sensitively with a complex social problem: the tensions between blacks and Puerto Ricans. She explains that when Puerto Ricans fill jobs or move into vacant apartments, blacks often feel that those are jobs blacks might have gotten or apartments blacks might have occupied.

The narrator is terrorized by a black girl, Lorraine, whom she is forced to tutor at school. Even though Lorraine beats her up, the narrator understands the frustrations that motivate Lorraine's violence. The narrator, who resents being treated like a mental deficient because her accent is different, understands how Lorraine's brand of English also causes her to be misjudged by racist teachers.

In "The Myth of the Latin Woman: I Just Met a Girl Named Maria," Cofer focuses on what intelligent, well-educated women who are judged by ethnic stereotypes must endure. This piece, more sorrowful than bitter, speaks to members of any minority group.

The forty poems and fifteen stories in *The Latin Deli* are sensitive and searching. They demonstrate the increasing depth of an author who has spent her adult life exploring the impact of her early years poised between two cultures.

Summary

Judith Ortiz Cofer is no ideologue. She is, rather, a skilled teller of tales, a credible shaper of characters. Her writing never pontificates. Instead, it leads readers to form their own ideologies about the tensions that living as a part of two cultures, one cold, the other warm, engenders. Cofer writes with intense realism, softened only slightly by the high level of poetic insight that she brings to her prose and that sustains her poetry.

Bibliography

Bruce-Novoa, Juan. "Judith Ortiz Cofer's Rituals of Movement." *The Americas Review* 19 (Winter, 1991): 88-99.

Cofer, Judith Ortiz. "A *MELUS* Interview: Judith Ortiz Cofer." *MELUS* 18 (Fall, 1993): 83-99.

_____. "Puerto Rican Literature in Georgia? An Interview with Judith Ortiz Cofer." Interview by Rafael Ocasio. *Kenyon Review* 14 (Fall, 1992): 56-61.

_____. *Silent Running. Georgia Review* 44 (Spring/Summer, 1990): 51-60.

Marquez, Roberto. "Island Heritage." *The New York Times Book Review*, September 24, 1989, 46.

Wilhelmus, Tom. "Various Pairs." *Hudson Review* 43 (Spring, 1990): 151-152.

R. Baird Shuman

GUY DAVENPORT

Born: Anderson, South Carolina
November 23, 1927

Principal Literary Achievement

Widely recognized as one of contemporary American literature's most sophisticated postmodern short-story writers, Davenport is also known as a literary critic, translator, poet, and editor.

Biography

Guy Davenport was born on November 23, 1927, in Anderson, South Carolina. His father, Guy Mattison Davenport, spent most of his working life as a shipping agent in Anderson. His mother, Marie Fant Davenport, was a housewife. Although Guy Davenport keeps his private life very private, he seems to have had a happy childhood and recalls with pleasure summer days when he and his father scoured the South Carolina forest looking for Indian arrowheads.

Davenport attended Duke University, where he studied literature and languages including French, Latin, and Greek, graduating with honors in 1948. He then moved on to Oxford University's Merton College as a Rhodes Scholar and earned a B. Litt. degree in 1950. He subsequently served in the United States Army Airborne Corps for the next two years. He taught at Washington University in St. Louis, Missouri, from 1952 to 1955, moving on to further graduate studies at Harvard University from 1956 to 1961. He earned a Ph.D. in modern literature from Harvard in 1961. He taught at Haverford College in Philadelphia from 1961 to 1963 and accepted a permanent position at the University of Kentucky, where he remained for the rest of his academic career. He retired from Kentucky in 1991 after receiving a prestigious MacArthur Grant.

Besides teaching at the University of Kentucky, where he taught courses in modern literature, Davenport traveled extensively throughout Europe, especially France, gathering material for both his stories and his scholarly essays. In addition to his many literary essays and more than sixty short stories (some the length of novels), he wrote literary criticism and book reviews for many journals and magazines. He reviewed books for *National Review* for eleven years and also for *Life, The New York Times Book Review, Hudson Review, Poetry, Book Week, The New Criterion,* and the *Los Angeles-New York Times Book Review Service.* Though Davenport has retired from

teaching, he has continued to review books for *The New Criterion* and publish short stories in literary journals.

Analysis

The key to understanding the complex literary world of Guy Davenport is his commitment to understanding and using the lessons of the past in both his stories and his literary criticism. In his seminal essay "The Symbol of the Archaic," he most clearly articulates the need for modern humanity to save itself from the encroaching destructive effects of industrialization and mechanization by reawakening a passion for the "archaic," a passion that manifests itself in "a longing for something lost, for energies, values, and certainties unwisely abandoned by an industrial age." Davenport's project of reclaiming the ameliorating lessons of the past closely resembles similar efforts of other modernist writers such as Ezra Pound, James Joyce, and Charles Olson, and visual artists such as Pablo Picasso, Max Ernst, and Georges Braque. Davenport envisions these modernists as seriously trying to use the wisdom of the ancient Greeks, in particular, to heal the fragmentation in Western civilization resulting from the disastrous destructiveness of both World War I and World War II. Those wars, and the subsequent rise of fascism and communism that followed them, obliterated any remaining cohesive structures that had previously kept Western Europe unified. The artists and writers in whom Davenport is most interested are those who attempted to forge new literary and aesthetic methods and models to deal with and understand the fragmentation of the post-World War I era.

Davenport's most persuasive and brilliant essays on various aspects of the loss of a spiritual center that is grounded in the archaic imagination can be found in a number of essays in both *The Geography of the Imagination* (1981) and *Every Force Evolves a Form* (1987). In many of these essays, his persistent theme is the damage that an overly mechanistic society inflicts upon the feeling life and imaginations of human beings who have been cut off from the healing energies of geographical, cultural, and spiritual origins.

Davenport uses the same principles in formulating his uniquely compelling stories and novellas, which he has collected in books beginning with *Tatlin!* in 1974. Few short-story collections have been so praised; most reviewers confessed that they had seen nothing remotely like these six stories, which are united around the common theme of flight, both physical and spiritual, from the life-denying energies of Stalinism and capitalist industrialization. Davenport calls his highly individual use of collage "assemblages of history and necessary fiction," a modernist method that juxtaposes images of the past with the present to demonstrate the emptiness and aesthetic and spiritual poverty of the modern age. He acknowledges that his stories, particularly in *Tatlin!*, "are lessons in history." Davenport also uses the ideogrammatic techniques of poets Ezra Pound and William Carlos Williams and frequently combines them with the cinematic techniques of the experimental filmmaker Stan Brakhage, replacing traditional narrative and documentary methods with images that form a structure of their own as they accumulate throughout the stories. Davenport clearly asserts his view of what distinguishes human beings from the animal and vegetable world; the imagination, which he further defines as "what mankind makes of things." He has explained that "My theory of the imagination is this: that in the evolution of man this was the moment in which we became what we call human. That is, it's an amazing ability to see something with your eyes closed. Which is what imagination is . . . a power of communication so high that I can't think of humanity doing any better."

Concurrent with Davenport's reverence for the creative power of the human imagination is his persistent use of the theme of the "Fall." All of his stories throughout his six short-fiction collections could be said to treat, in one form or another, the consequences of humankind's Fall from a preternatural condition of Edenic happiness and ignorance into experience, time, and knowledge. His fictions attempt, then, to regenerate, fictively, an Edenic innocence that has been destroyed by the dehumanizing powers of so-called civilization and the Western obsession with rationality. Davenport's second collection, *Da Vinci's Bicycle* (1979), persuasively documents the ways in which people habitually marginalize, overlook, or ignore unique geniuses who are later discovered. He cites such figures as Leonardo da Vinci, the idiosyncratic Swiss poet and novelist Robert Walser, and Davenport's greatest philosophical influence, the French Utopian sociologist and philosopher Charles Fourier, to who he dedicated his fourth collection of stories, *Apples and Pears and Other Stories* (1984). Indeed, the longest and most intricately structured story in *Da Vinci's Bicycle* is "Au Tombeau de Charles Fourier" (at the tomb of Charles Fourier), which is a homage to the genius of Fourier as a visionary whose planned communities, such as Brook Farm, were tried in various parts of the United States but failed as a result of a lack of consistent and dedicated community support.

Davenport's next collection, *Eclogues* (1981) moves back in time to compare ancient Greek stories, with special emphasis on the "pastoral" elements in the eclogues of Virgil, Theocritus, and Plutarch, to modern Edenic pastoral communities of a fictional Dutch philosopher, Adriaan van Hovendaal. Van Hovendaal continues his attempt to regenerate a Utopian community in the Netherlands, a project that he first began in the longest story in *Tatlin!*, "The Dawn in Erewhon." Next to Fourier, Davenport's most crucial intellectual and spiritual influence is Samuel Butler, the English Utopian novelist whose *Erewhon* (an 1872 satire on Victorian society the title of which is an anagram of "nowhere") becomes the subtext for Davenport's long story about the need for human beings to free themselves of sexual guilt and shame.

Apples and Pears and Other Stories is considered by many critics to be Davenport's most brilliant collection, especially the 233-page title novella, which constitutes most of the book. *Apples and Pears* is a treatise organized along the lines of Fourier's favorite four-part structure, which he used in his major work, *Theórie des quatre mouvements et des destinées générales* (1808; *The Social Destiny of Man: Or, Theory of the Four Movements*, 1857). The main character is, again, the Dutch philosopher Adriaan van Hovendaal, whose Fourierist group has grown to eight members. Under van Hovendaal's gentle leadershp, the young members of the group spend their time enjoying camping trips in the forests and developing their artistic and intellectual powers. Nowhere does Davenport devote as much space in detailing the activities available to young people to enlarge both their physical as well as their mental and spiritual capacities as in *Apples and Pears*. The apples and pears as objects also symbolize the Fall and redemption, respectively, that take place in the Old and New Testaments. This work becomes Davenport's most important chapter in what he calls his "history of affection," since all the exercises of the adolescents throughout the story are aimed at deepening and enlarging their feeling for one another within the natural landscape around them.

Davenport's fifth collection of short stories is entitled *The Jules Verne Steam Balloon* (1987). The setting has moved from the sensually alluring Netherlands to a more northerly idyllic place, Denmark. Adriaan van Hovendaal has been replaced by a less sensual leader, Hugo Tvemunding, a doctoral student in theology and a teacher of classics in a Danish folk high school. A new moral note enters Davenport's fiction in this collection, especially in "The Bicycle Rider," a story that features a young man who is suffering from drug addiction and who finally dies because of his inability to participate in the rich emotional life around him. Davenport also invites his readers to compare the vocation of the artist to that of a religious leader insofar as both are involved in attempting to transcend the limitations of the mundane by the liberating power of the imagination.

Davenport's sixth collection of short fictions is entitled *The Drummer of the Eleventh North Devonshire Fusiliers* (1990). Of the five fictions in the volume, the longest, "Wo es war, soll ich werden" (where it was, there I must begin to be), examines the ways in which adolescents view life around them in its simplest terms and how the self-consciousness of adulthood destroys that purity of vision. These fictions are Davenport's clearest statements of his increasing concern over Western civilization's penchant for involving itself in potentially self-destructive political and military projects.

TATLIN!

First published: 1974
Type of work: Short stories

The six stories in this collection demonstrate Davenport's unique way of developing a story by means of collage and juxtaposition.

Tatlin! is the collection of short stories that made Davenport one of the most admired and studied fiction writers in contemporary American literature. Most of the reviewers who commented on the volume when it appeared admitted that they had seen nothing like these highly sophisticated and polished stories, either in subject matter or technique. The stories range from the title piece, about the founder of Constructivism and Russian Formalism, to a story about young boys who stumble on the Paleolithic cave paintings of Lascaux in "Robot," and move through the deep Greek past in "Herakleitos" to an imaginary past of the writer Edgar Allen Poe in "1830." The volume ends in an imaginative descent into Holland as a sensual "netherland" or underworld where a Dutch philosopher attempts to regenerate an earthly Eden by means of the body.

The second story in the collection, "The Aeroplanes at Brescia," was actually the first story that Davenport published and concerns a famous air show at Brescia, Italy, in 1909 in which most of the world's renowned pilots took part. The construction of the story has become as famous as the story itself; Davenport initially began it as an essay on Franz Kafka, but in the midst of his research, he discovered that Kafka's first published newspaper story was entitled "The Aeroplanes at Brescia." Though Kafka's story was a piece of journalism, Davenport views it as a typical Kafka short story and uses, in his own story, every sentence that Kafka wrote; however, Davenport makes important changes to suit his own style. Accompanying Kafka was Max Brod, a character in Davenport's story as well as Kafka's first biographer. Davenport also used every sentence of Brod's report of the air show at Brescia in his story. Again, he rearranges both Kafka's and Brod's sentences in highly imaginative ways to produce a composite narrative that fuses all of their perspectives into a typical Davenport story. He employs similar methods in many of the other stories in *Tatlin!*. In the title narrative, Davenport tells the story of the difficult life of Vladimir Tatlin, founder of Constructivism, an engineer, designer, painter, sailor, teacher, and folk musician—a veritable modern renaissance man whose genius was crushed by the life-denying strategies of Communism. Davenport, also a highly respected artist, interweaves his own drawings of Joseph Stalin, Vladimir Ilich Lenin, and Tatlin throughout the story, creating an intertextual collage of visual images and written passages.

The charming story "Robot" records the accidental discovery of the caves of Lascaux by six French peasant boys in 1941. The story is entitled "Robot" because that was the name of the dog of one of the boys who actually discovered the caves while chasing a rabbit. This story dramatically illustrates Davenport's persistent concern for the submerged archaic wisdom that lies hidden beneath modern civilization waiting for discovery. Because of this important discovery, it became clear that Western humanity had attempted to express itself through imaginative forms at a much earlier date than anyone had ever suspected.

The longest story in *Tatlin!* is "The Dawn in Erewhon." The story's title connects it to the famous English Utopian novelist Samuel Butler and his book *Erewhon*, an anagram of "nowhere." The fictional Dutch philosopher Adriaan van Hovendaal attempts to ecape his overly intellectual propensities by creating an Edenic community of three with a teenager boy and girl, Bruno and Kaatje. They travel to idyllic forests, carefully dividing up duties and enjoying themselves in clean but sensual activities. "The Dawn in Erewhon" is Davenport's first attempt to present the social ideals of Charles Fourier in a fictional form. Feelings and the claims of the body take precedence over all intellectual duties or exercises in the longest story in the collection.

ECLOGUES: EIGHT STORIES BY GUY DAVENPORT

First published: 1981
Type of work: Short stories

The eight stories in this collection illustrate the concept of societal unity as embodied in the pastoral tradition of ancient Greece.

As a translator of classical Greek and Latin texts, Davenport finds great affinity with the classical concept of pastoralism as a way of creating and enacting an Edenic society. Davenport harks back to the classical pastoral poetry of Theocritus and Virgil and of English pastoral poets such as William Shakespeare, Christopher Marlowe, and John Milton. All the stories contain a shepherd figure who helps to keep order and direction within the group and who maintains the beauty and structure of Arcadian society. There are humorous stories about the Greek philosopher Diogenes, who respects no one, not even Alexander the Great, whom he chides for blocking "his" sunlight. The most charming and intricately developed story, and the longest, is the concluding one, "On Some Lives of Virgil." The setting, the southwestern French city of Bordeaux, is key to understanding the theme of how geography influences the imagination and produces local aesthetic geniuses. In this story, the shepherd is the classical scholar Tullio, who leads his charges, again French teenagers who constantly experiment with innocent sexual pleasures, to examine some ancient French caves just outside Bordeaux. He teaches his students that true history is actually "the history of attention" and that they must pay attention to all forms of narrative, both written and oral, to understand and appreciate the complete historical canvas. "The Death of Picasso" finds Adriaan van Hovendaal and a student, Sander, discussing the significance of the painter's death in light of the fact that Picasso helped to create "modernism" as an amalgamation of the ancient and the contemporary.

THE JULES VERNE STEAM BALLOON

First published: 1987
Type of work: Short stories

Though the Fourierist communities have moved from the Netherlands to Denmark, a new moral note enters this collection, and evil is confronted and challenged.

This collection contains nine highly diverse stories that range from the pastoral Greek tale "Pyrrhon of Elis" to the avant-garde dramatic fragment "We Often Think of Lenin at the Clothespin Factory." Adriaan von Hovendaal is replaced by the Danish theology student Hugo Tvemunding, who also teaches at a high school and who is featured in "The Bicycle Rider," "The Jules Verne Steam Balloon," and "The Ringdove Sign." Davenport employs unusual narrative structures throughout the collection, such as a pastiche of quotations from the schoolbooks of Nazi children in "Bronze Leaves and Red" and a botanical listing of the components of Eden in "The Meadow."

The three longest stories concern themselves with Hugo's gradually emerging knowledge that he should not pursue his calling to the Lutheran ministry but should rather follow his leanings toward his vocation as an artist. He boldly confronts evil in the drug addiction of one of the more attractive young men, known as the Bicycle Rider, who eventually dies of an overdose because he has lost the ability to respond on a human level to his fellow companions. It is in this story that Hugo realizes fully what the purpose of art is and that an artist's first duty is to respond to the world as authentically as he can, regardless of how demanding those responses may become. The title story presents three male sprites, Tumble, Buckeye, and Quark, as messengers from beyond who come down to earth in their steam balloon to remind humankind that salvation lies in the ability to use imagination to transform the mundane into forms of visionary experience.

Summary

Guy Davenport's fictions are variations on the theme of the loss of innocence—the Fall from a childlike vision of the world into the adult world of experience and knowledge. The villains are always the mechanistic and dehumanizing forces in Western society, which continually threaten to eradicate the joyous and childlike sense of the marvelous that transforms boredom into celebration. The source of that energy has always existed and resides in the continuous rediscovery of the archaic—that is, of the wisdom found in the great art and literature of the ancient Greeks and Romans. Davenport wants nothing less than a new Renaissance, imitative of the fifteenth century one that transformed Europe from a Dark Ages society into one of the greatest and richest civilizations in existence.

Bibliography

Arias-Misson, Alain. "Erotic Ear, Amoral Eye." *Chicago Review* 35 (Spring, 1986): 66-71.

Bawer, Bruce. "Guy Davenport: Fiction á la Fourier." In *Diminishing Fictions*. Saint Paul, Minn.: Graywolf Press, 1988:234-245.

Kenner, Hugh. "A Geographer of the Imagination." *Harper's* 263 (August, 1981): 66-68.

Kramer, Hilton. "After the Archaic." *The New York Times Book Review* 86 (September 6, 1981): 7, 21.

Steiner, George. "Rare Bird." *The New Yorker* 57 (November 30, 1981): 196, 199-202, 204.

Patrick Meanor

Born: Akron, Ohio
August 28, 1952

Principal Literary Achievement

Although she has published fiction, Dove is known primarily for her Pulitzer Prize-winning poetry.

Biography

Rita Dove was born in the highly industrialized city of Akron, Ohio, on August 28, 1952. On her mother's side, the family had well-established roots in this northern urban center, and they had achieved a certain level of comfort and prosperity. Her father's side of the family had moved to the North during the great migration of African Americans that took place in the years after World War I. Brought up in a strict but loving environment, Rita Dove became a precocious and highly inquisitive young student. Her first attempt at writing was a childhood story entitled "The Rabbit with a Droopy Ear." The young author solved the rabbit's problem and straightened his ear by having him hang upside down from a tree.

The city of Akron left a deep and lasting impression on the young author's mind. The parks and hilly streets, the Goodyear rubber and tire factories, and the Quaker Oats oatmeal plant all became graphic images that she employed in the poetry and fiction of her mature life. In a real sense, Rita Dove never left Akron.

After completing high school in Akron, Dove moved to the college town of Oxford, Ohio, to continue her education at Miami University. The surrounding countryside, with its trademark barns and silos and its abundant corn and bean fields, also left her with vivid memories that she would later use in her writing. After her graduation from Miami University, Dove moved to Germany to continue her studies at the Universität Tübingen. While in Germany she met her husband, the novelist Fred Viebahn, with whom she had a daughter, Aviva. She returned to the United States to study at the prestigious Iowa Writers Workshop at the University of Iowa. In 1977, she received an M.F.A. in creative writing from Iowa and joined the ranks of the school's famous graduates, many of whom were regular contributors to literary publications such as *The American Poetry Review*, *Georgia Review*, and *Poetry*.

With this rich and complicated background, Dove began to publish widely in little magazines. Her first book of poems, *The Yellow House on the Corner* (1980), appeared

when she was twenty-eight, and it was soon followed by a second book of poems, *Museum* (1983). Both of these books bear the strong influence of the Iowa Writers Workshop: They contain many surrealistic poems and literary imitations in a style made famous by that university program. The poems are still undeniable literary accomplishments, but Dove had not yet come entirely into her own.

That situation was to change dramatically with the publication of her first book of prose, a collection of short stories entitled *Fifth Sunday* (1985), and a masterful volume of narrative poems entitled *Thomas and Beulah* (1986). Dove was clearly speaking in her own unique voice and following the inspiration of her own poetic muse, a fact recognized by a national literary audience; in 1987, she was awarded the Pulitzer Prize for poetry. In a short time, she published *Grace Notes* (1989), a singularly beautiful book of lyric poems, and *Through the Ivory Gate* (1992), a highly poetic novel that makes extensive use of autobiographical details. The years from 1980 to 1992 represent a period of remarkable literary growth and achievement for Dove; in the space of twelve short years, she produced six important volumes.

All this literary output was rewarded with many literary honors besides the Pulitzer Prize. Dove won a grant from the National Endowment for the Arts and a Guggenheim Foundation Fellowship, and she received the General Electric Foundation Award and the Ohio Governor's Award. In addition, Dove was presented with honorary doctorates from Miami University and Knox College. She has taught creative writing at Arizona State University and the University of Virginia and served briefly as a Fellow at the National Humanities Center in North Carolina. In 1993, Dove became the first black author to serve as poet laureate of the United States, an honor that also made her the poetry consultant to the Library of Congress.

Analysis

The title of Dove's *Grace Notes* might well serve as a metaphor for her basic strategy as a writer, for everything she writes is, to some extent, a "grace note," a subtle embellishment or addition to the basic "melody" of experience. Dove's attention as a poet is always on the overtones, the implications, the echoes, and reverberations of meaning that somehow surround even the simplest of plain facts. "Silos," the poem that opens the first section of *Grace Notes*, is a telling example of this powerful tendency in her writing.

At first glance, a group of silos may not seem like a very promising subject, after all. Silos are merely humble receptacles for storing grain. They are the plain, generic landmarks of the Midwest, largely ignored and unconsciously accepted by nearly everyone who sees them—except, that is, the poet. For Dove, the white silos represent a marvelous string of metaphorical possibilities, even if they are "too white and/ suddenly there." She rejects the obvious similarities, refusing to see the silos as "swans," "fingers," "xylophones," or "Pan's pipes." Instead, she sides with the children who recognize them as a huge "packet of chalk." She ends with her own favorite comparisons, suggesting erotic, surreal, and anatomical possibilities for looking at silos: "They were masculine toys. They were tall wishes. They/ were the ribs of the modern world." The point is that if Dove can make such an artistic production from the simplicity of silos, then anything becomes a possible—and fruitful—subject matter for her art.

Grace Notes as a title and silos as a subject are also ways of talking about the two poles that define the boundaries of Dove's writing—the aesthetic and the autobiographical. The concept of "grace notes" is eminently aesthetic, the product of a mind that is steeped in music. Indeed, musical references abound in Dove's work. The heroine of *Through the Ivory Gate* is a cellist. *Fifth Sunday*, Dove's short-story collection, contains a piece entitled "The Vibraphone" that concerns a classical pianist who turns to jazz and "new age" music. Thomas of *Thomas and Beulah* also happens to be a musician, a gifted mandolin player. Yet musical cues are not the only aesthetic concerns voiced in Dove's work. The cellist-heroine of *Through the Ivory Gate* is also a talented actress and puppeteer. *Grace Notes* even contains a poem entitled "Ars Poetica" (the art of poetry), as if to signal the reader that these poems are not only about things but also about the nature of art itself. In fact, Dove, although she wears her learning lightly, is a profoundly cultured woman who often makes delicate and appropriate references to the great composers and artists of the Western world. Each section of *Grace Notes*, for example, opens with an epigraph or quotation from such writers as Toni Morrison, David McFadden, Hélène Cixous, and Claude McKay.

The mention of African American writers such as Morrison and McKay brings the reader to the other pole of Dove's literary world—the realm of autobiography and the self. Dove is clearly not a "black" writer in the manner of such poets as Maya Angelou or Gwendolyn Brooks, nor is she overtly concerned with African American history in the manner of novelists Alex Haley and Richard Wright. Since Dove's mature work began in the rather late 1970's, she did not feel the need to repeat the highly charged political or social themes of earlier African American writers. Dove, then, could best be described as a middle-class African American author who is most concerned about representing art and autobiography in her work—not in putting forth a political agenda, no matter how valid or urgent.

Dove's work, however, never omits her African American heritage, nor does it sidestep the issues of racism or bigotry. Yet Dove's focus, in her poetry and in her fiction, is on the personhood of the voices and characters she evokes. One does not encounter African American stereotypes in Dove's work. Her characters and the voices one hears in her poetry speak wisely and with profound conviction; in fact, one might even argue that Dove has helped to redefine the image of African Americans in contemporary American literature.

Dove thus draws upon the totality of her own experience, as well as on the history and traditions of her own family, including a musician grandfather, an overbearing mother, and a proudly intellectual father. She recalls, in minute detail, the particulars of specific streets and houses in Akron, the noise and smells of industries, and the various shades of gray taken on by a sky filled with smoke, smog, snow, and the ever-present mists of the Great Lakes. In this connection, the silos from *Grace Notes* become one more talisman, allowing the poet to call up the past.

In like manner, Dove uses her memories of Phoenix and the Arizona desert landscape to great advantage in the flashbacks of *Through the Ivory Gate*, a novel in which the heroine lives in Akron before her family moves to Phoenix. She uses memories of Germany in "Poem in Which I Refuse Contemplation" from *Grace Notes*, a poem in which she receives a letter from her African American mother while she is living with her German mother-in-law. The result is a realistic transcription, with quotations from the actual letter, and also an artistic transformation in which autobiographical fact becomes artistic truth. This interplay between art and autobiography is the hallmark of Dove's work, creating everything that is beautiful, memorable, and most human in her writing.

THOMAS AND BEULAH

First published: 1986
Type of work: Poems

Thomas, an African American man, leaves the South for Ohio, marries Beulah, and rears a large family.

Thomas and Beulah is a tour de force, a virtuoso performance by a major poet operating at the height of her powers. *Thomas and Beulah* takes the form of a two-part book of narrative poems that collectively tell the stories of Thomas (in "Mandolin," the book's first part) and his wife Beulah (in "Canary in Bloom," the second part). The parts are meant to be read sequentially and offer the male and female perspectives on some seventy years of private history. The two parts are followed by a "Chronology" that provides an imagined framework of the critical years in the married life of Thomas, a mandolin player and talented tenor, and Beulah, his proud and sometimes unforgiving spouse. The poems are a mixture of lush imagery involving food, musical instruments, cars, and weather, as well as quotations from songs and specimens of actual "Negro" speech. Although the poems form interlocking units, many of them (such as "The Zeppelin Factory" and "Pomade") are self-sufficient and free-standing works of art that could be read individually, without reference to the book as a whole.

The story is a fairly simple one, even if the reader must fill in some gaps. Thomas takes a riverboat and leaves Tennessee. After two years of rambling and playing his mandolin, he settles in Akron, Ohio, where there are many good jobs, and where Beulah's family has already established itself after leaving Georgia. Thomas cuts a dashing figure, with his mandolin and fancy clothes, and becomes a womanizer. Beulah is naturally suspicious of him, but they eventually marry, and his dalliances with various women ("canaries") cease as he becomes a respectable family man, a member of the church choir, and, finally, a grandfather. Beulah takes up dressmaking. Thomas dies in 1963, the year of the March on Washington, and Beulah follows him six years later.

Thomas is captured in poems such as "Jiving" (about his mandolin playing), "The Zeppelin Factory," and "Aircraft" (about his work at the Goodyear plant). "Roast Possum," though, epitomizes the man and his unique speech, as he talks to his granddaughters in language that is both colloquial and literary. He uses similes and metaphors to dramatize the possum's ferocity ("teeth bared like a shark's" and "torpedo snout"), ending his description with a folksy twist as he notes that even the possum was no match "for old-time know-how."

Beulah comes to life in such poems as "Dusting," in which she dusts every item in the house while trying to recall the name of a long-forgotten boyfriend—Maurice, the final word of the poem. "Weathering Out" shows her wobbling around the house during the awkward months of pregnancy. Yet "Pomade" is perhaps the finest of the "Beulah" poems; in it, Beulah is revealed as a poetess who reminisces about a backwoods recipe for making pomade. She experiences a flashback that is triggered by Thomas' coming home with a catfish and tracking mud on her kitchen floor. At the end of the poem, while the catfish "grins/ like an oriental gentleman," she has an epiphany, a moment of pure spirituality, in which she momentarily feels herself "rolling down the sides of the earth."

GRACE NOTES

First published: 1989
Type of work: Poems

Everyday events and unnoticed objects can be turned into art if looked at properly.

On the surface, *Grace Notes* might almost seem to be a kind of poetic autobiography. As a book, it is neatly divided into five discrete sections, and this five-part format corresponds, in a general way, to phases in Rita Dove's life. The first section deals with childhood memories, the second with her thirtieth birthday, and the third with her daughter, Aviva. The last sections, however, do not seem to follow this pattern of personal evolutionary growth, at least not on first reading. Sections 4 and 5 contain poem with such titles as "Ars Poetica," "Medusa," "Genie's Prayer Under the Kitchen Sink," "Obbligato," and "Lint." Yet these poems also represent part of the artistic evolution of the poet, because the most sophisticated growth occurs on the spiritual and artistic planes. The final poems thus reveal general truths about art discovered by personal meditation on items as ordinary and ubiquitous as lint.

Grace Notes is such a remarkable example of poetic craftsmanship that it might almost serve as a textbook for literary devices. Similes and metaphors abound in this little masterpiece. In the poem entitled "Hully Gully," the moon is "riding the sky/ like a drop of oil on water." In "Horse and Tree," the entire poem becomes a complex metaphor linking horses and trees; the rider of a beautiful tree-horse experiences the magical sensation of "hair blown to froth."

Many of the poems in *Grace Notes*, however, deal with entirely personal matters—the poet as a ten-year-old child responding to flash cards, the poet's mother, and especially her daughter, Aviva. One of the most moving and tender poems in this group is the mother-daughter poem with the improbably long title of "After Reading *Mickey in the Night Kitchen* for the Third Time Before Bed." The poem describes the mother's responses to her three-year-old daughter's questions about sex and the mysteries of menstruation and genitals. "She demands," the poet explains,

> to see mine and momentarily
> we're a lopsided star
> among the spilled toys,
> my prodigious scallops
> exposed to her neat cameo.

If "scallops" and "cameo" can serve as metaphors for the most intimate parts of the female body, then a nasty cut on the arm can become an emblem for an opening in the poet's identity. She may be a proud African American person, but she nevertheless dwells on the puzzle of skin color. In "Stitches," after falling and receiving a gash on her arm, she immediately focuses on one thought: "So I *am* white underneath." But even this bloody moment of self-recognition is transformed immediately into "grace notes," as the ministering physician's teeth are seen as "beavery, yellow." He sews up her wound, and the "skin's tugged up by his thread / like a trout." In fact, the poet chides herself for being so clever in a moment of pain: "*You just can't stop being witty, can you?*" Yet the wittiness extends even to the punning title; her elaborate poetic "jokes" have, in effect, kept her and her audience in "stitches. Once again, Dove and her readers have been sustained by the exquisite grace notes that resonate powerfully—and unforgettably—in all of her poems.

THROUGH THE IVORY GATE

First published: 1992
Type of work: Novel

Virginia King, a recent college graduate, returns to her hometown to teach children about puppets.

Although Rita Dove is known primarily as a poet, *Through the Ivory Gate* offers eloquent proof that she is a talented storyteller capable of spinning a highly readable yarn. Virginia King, the sensitive and highly introspective young heroine of the novel, has just been graduated from college with an acting degree as well as a strong commitment to playing the cello. Unable to do either one professionally, she takes a brief job with a troupe of puppeteers. She lands a job in her hometown of Akron spending a month as an artist-in-residence at a local elementary school, where she instructs the children in the art of puppetry. One of the little girls idolizes Virginia and becomes strongly attached to her, as does Terence, the father of one of her young puppeteers. There are no startling, dramatic moments in the book; the month in Akron is largely an opportunity for Virginia to rediscover her childhood roots and relive (through flashbacks) the most important moments in her life. The point of the book seems to be the way that Virginia defines her life internally; she lives, as it were, in the confines of her powerful imagination and memory. Although she becomes romantically attached to Terence, she leaves Akron at the end of the month with her future still unclear. This interlude, though, has allowed her to take an inventory of her life, thereby defining herself as an artist. At last, she has found the courage to make this supreme commitment, and the book ends at the precise moment when her new life begins.

The title of the novel refers to a passage in which the Greek poet Homer describes all human dreams and fantasies as the process of passing through one of two gates, the gate of horn (for dreams that become reality) and the gate of ivory (for dreams that remain pure fantasy and illusion). Virginia's journey to self-discovery includes scenes of racial confusion: She throws away a new black doll in favor of a white one; later, she is rejected by a white friend with the stinging epithet "Nigger!" Her quest also includes many false starts in which she tries on other artistic hats, first as a baton twirler, then as an actress, and finally as a cellist. The novel is filled with discussions of art and technique (baton twirling, cello suites, and Javanese shadow puppets). As Virginia unravels these clues to her own psyche, she is simultaneously visiting her relatives and unlocking family mysteries—including the mystery of an incestuous affair between her father and her aunt Carrie (a scene based verbatim on the story "Aunt Carrie" from her earlier collection of short stories *Fifth Sunday*). One's true identity is always difficult to discover; as this novel beautifully demonstrates, however, the most elusive of all identities is that of the artist.

Summary

The character of Virginia King offers an important clue to the understanding of all Rita Dove's work. As Virginia cradles the cello to her body, she experiences the pure physical reality of the instrument—its contours, its weight, and its musical reverberations—but she is also transported by the purely intellectual pleasure of the music she is making. In like manner, she is deeply attracted to the physical beauty of Terence (as she was to Clayton, her first, ill-fated lover). With each man, though, the physical intimacy is merely a prelude to emotional transcendence: "When he touched her again their bodies merged into one long, yearning curve, and the sea rose up to meet them." Like her creator, Virginia King is living proof that art and life are not at distant removes from one another. What Rita Dove has shown, again and again, is that art is the most passionate and enduring expression of life itself.

Bibliography

Bellafante, Ginia. "Poetry in Motion." *Time,* May 31, 1993, 73.

Conde, Maryse, and Rita Dove. Interview by Mohamed B. Taleb-Khyar. *Callaloo* 14, no. 2 (Spring, 1991): 347.

Dove, Rita, "A Poet's Topics: Jet Lag, Laundry, and Making Her Art Commonplace." Interview by Felicity Barringer. *The New York Times,* June 20, 1993, p. E7.

McKinney, Rhoda E. "Rita Dove: Pulitzer Prize-winning Poet." *Ebony,* October, 1987, 44-45.

Vendler, Helen. "A Dissonant Triad (Henri Cole, Rita Dove, August Kleinzahler)." *Parnassus* 16, no. 2 (1990): 391.

Daniel L. Guillory

STANLEY ELKIN

Born: Brooklyn, New York
May 11, 1930

Principal Literary Achievement
Elkin is as concerned with the verbal texture of his finely crafted prose as he is with the tragicomic nature of his characters' lives.

Biography

Born in New York City on May 11, 1930, Stanley Elkin was reared in Chicago. His father Philip, a highly successful traveling salesman for a costume-jewelry concern and an equally accomplished raconteur, had a pronounced influence on Elkin's writing both in terms of style and subject. Just as important were the elder Elkin's fear of being thought less than he was and the four heart attacks that would cut short his career and then his life.

For all the rhetorical as well as geographical expansiveness of his fiction, Stanley Elkin has stayed close to home, first by choice, later by medical necessity. He attended the University of Illinois at Urbana, where he was awarded a B.A. in 1952, an M.A. in 1953, and, following a stint in the Army, a Ph.D. in 1961. It was during his military service that Elkin became interested in radio broadcasting, which figures so prominently in his third novel, *The Dick Gibson Show* (1971). In 1960, he joined the English faculty at Washington University in St. Louis, where he has continued to teach creative writing. Elkin began writing fiction while still a graduate student. His first published story, "A Sound of Distant Thunder," appeared in *Epoch* in 1957, and his first mass-market publication, "I Look Out for Ed Wolfe," appeared in *Esquire* five years later. That same year, Elkin, with financial assistance from his mother, went to Europe to write his first novel, *Boswell: A Modern Comedy* (1964). Although the collection *Criers and Kibitzers, Kibitzers and Criers* (1965) has proven his most enduring work (it has remained in print almost continuously, and many of its stories are frequently anthologized), Elkin has subsequently concentrated on novellas and especially novels. He has also written a screenplay, *The Six-Year-Old Man* (1968), a radio drama, *The Coffee Room*, a monologue for the Mid-America Dance Company, and a collection of essays, *Pieces of Soap* (1992).

The same year that his second novel, *A Bad Man*, appeared (1967), Elkin suffered his first heart attack. He was diagnosed as having multiple sclerosis while in England

2357

five years later. As his maladies both worsened and multiplied (he underwent quintuple and quadruple bypass surgery in the 1980's, was several times hospitalized for a collapsed lung, and was forced to use first a walker and then a wheelchair), the former hypochondriac managed to deal with his various ills in a manner that his longtime friend and colleague, the writer William Gass, has called "heroic." Elkin may have been unable to button his shirts, but he was still able to teach and write, producing *Searches and Seizures* (novellas, 1973), *The Franchiser* (1976), *The Living End* (interrelated novellas, 1979), *Stanley Elkin's Greatest Hits* (retrospective, 1980), *George Mills* (1982), *Early Elkin* (stories, 1985), *The Magic Kingdom* (1985), *The Rabbi of Lud* (1987), *The Macguffin* (1991), and *Van Gogh's Room at Arles: Three Novellas* (1993). This last appeared following a drug-induced "bout of temporary insanity" in April, 1991, an episode that left Elkin feeling not only humiliated (his other illnesses had already done that) but also, for the first time, embarrassed. Although he has been the recipient of numerous honors, including a National Book Critics Award for *George Mills,* Elkin has never achieved the kind of popular and commercial success that a writer so attentive to his craft, so steeped in the popular culture, and so sympathetic to the plight of his tragicomic characters deserves.

Analysis

Stanley Elkin is a diffucult writer to place within the scheme of existing literary categories. He is not, other than by birth and upbringing, a typically Jewish American writer in the tradition that stretches from Abraham Cahan to Saul Bellow. The rich verbal texture of his work notwithstanding, he is not an experimental writer (a term he especially dislikes); nor, despite the bleakness and grotesquerie of his fiction, does he think of himself as a black humorist. Moreover, for all the density of social detail in his stories and novels, Elkin does not see his fiction as being in any way sociological or his role as writer as involving any social obligations other than that of writing well. Despite, or perhaps because of, these many disclaimers, Elkin is an important if idiosyncratic writer whom Robert Coover has rightly called "one of America's great tragicomic geniuses."

At the heart of Elkin's fiction lies his sense of character and the ways in which character manifests itself. Elkin's style draws on and extends the American tradition of vernacular writing begun by Mark Twain and continued by such writers as Ring Lardner and Saul Bellow. Elkin, however, does not so much employ the vernacular perspective as exploit it, pushing it beyond the merely colloquial into the realm of what Elkin calls "heroic extravagance." This "rhetorical intensity," as Coover terms it, is one that Elkin shares with his characters, whose compulsive, even crazed "arias" serve "to introduce significance into what otherwise may be untouched by significance."

In Elkin's fiction, even in his essays, speech is character and character is speech. The typical Elkin hero is obsessive, isolated (frequently an orphan and therefore free to follow his obsession), powerless yet egocentric, and resentful yet oddly, even perversely sympathetic, most sympathetic in his (less often her) need to speak, to tell his tale. They are at once envious and insecure, humbled and vindictive, in a word, "driven," not by anything in particular but by need itself in a world of the "never enough." Not likable in any conventional sense, they nevertheless earn the reader's respect insofar as they embody, in Elkin's words, "the egocentric will pitted against something stronger than itself." At their best, at their most verbally egocentric, they become both "crier" and "kibitzer, " hapless whiner and hopeful joker.

Elkin's characters often have good, albeit grotesquely funny, reason to complain. In a way, they are all like the title character in "I Look Out for Ed Wolfe," who tries to determine his exact worth by converting everything he owns into cash only to learn that it is not much, certainly not enough. Bobbo Druff, in *The Macguffin,* finds himself "on the downhill side of destiny" despite his position as Commissioner of Streets. With his degree from an "offshore yeshiva," Jerry Goldkorn is the Rabbi of Lud, a cemetery complex in northern New Jersey. Marshall Preminger, in "The Condominium," finds himself similarly "left out." Boswell, the hero of Elkin's first novel, makes the mistake of taking literally the advice offered by the world-famous Dr. Herlitz and so becomes "a strong man" (a professional wrestler) in the first of his several attempts to achieve immortality. In *A Bad Man,* Feldman, the felled man, caters to the desires of others, legal and illegal, permissible and perverse, until a computer error sends him to prison. There, rather than throw himself on the warden's mercy, he throws himself back on his will. Rejecting the warden's advice to adjust to the world as it is, Feldman insists upon himself and his innocence. The protagonist of *The Dick Gibson Show* discovers quite by accident that not one person has been listening to his radio broadcasts, not even the station's owners or technicians. Later, as host of a late-night radio call-in show, he will enjoy a success that proves no less problematic, as his callers' obsessions begin to overwhelm him.

Control is also the key for Alexander Main in "The Bailbondsman." Against all that he can neither understand nor control in his own life, Main asserts his power as bailbondsman to choose who will go (temporarily) free and who will not. Unlike the ostensibly bad men who predominate in Elkin's fiction, Ellerbee in *The Living End* is saintly, excessively so. Killed by a robber, he is permitted a glimpse of heaven (which looks "like a theme park") before being unfairly sent to hell, "the ultimate inner city." Discovering there "the grand vocabulary" of pain, he learns to speak with the same intensity and extravagance as many of Elkin's other heroes, all of them suffering the bad luck that comes of just being alive. In this, they are indeed made in their maker's image: Elkin, with his bad heart and multiple sclerosis, as well as the God of *The Living End.* This is a God who has created heaven and hell, affliction and, finally, apocalypse, "because it makes a better story." Elkin's jokey fiction is suffused with intimations of mortality. In *The Magic Kingdom,* Simon Bale organizes a trip to Disney World for a group of English children suffering from various terminal diseases. The children's fate is cruel, and the novel itself is painfully, unsparingly funny, but the pain, here and elsewhere in Elkin's fiction, is to a degree offset by the characters—and the author's— affirmation of life and spirit of defiance.

This is not to say that Elkin's fiction resolves itself in any conventional way.

Beginning with nothing more than a situation (and in the case of at least one story, nothing more than the word "bailbondsman"), Elkin does not develop his stories and novels in terms of plot and the Enlightenment ethos it implies. Instead, following the rule of whim and the muse of serendipity, he proceeds on the basis of opposition, of "action and respite, tension and release," obsession and resistance, of "what the character wants to happen and what he does not want to happen." Elkin's protagonists move through their worlds comically repeating themselves, "the stammer of personality" asserting itself over and over.

A POETICS FOR BULLIES

First published: 1965
Type of work: Short story

Against the logic of submission and adaptation, the young protagonist defines himself in terms of his own perverse desires and supercharged rhetoric.

Of the nine stories in *Criers and Kibitzers, Kibitzers and Criers*, "A Poetics for Bullies" was the last to be written and the one Elkin likes best. The story marks Elkin's breakthrough from his earlier, more realistic and generally more sedate style to the approach that characterizes his later work. The story's young protagonist-narrator is the unlovable but irrepressible Push the Bully. Push imposes his perverse will and vision on others, all of them, like Push, grotesques: Eugene, with his overactive salivary glands, fat Frank, Mim the dummy, Slud the cripple, Clob the ugly. A trickster as much by compulsion as by choice, Push claims that were magic real, he would use it to change the world, but because it is not real, he spends his time asserting himself and disillusioning others. Although this "prophet of the deaf" seems in many ways a younger version of one of Saul Bellow's "reality instructors," he also resembles the typical Bellow hero, Eugene Henderson, for example, in *Henderson the Rain King* (1959), whose clamorous "I want, I want" is Push's own. "Alone in my envy, awash in my lust," Push feels forever the outsider, though not in any clearly existential sense; he is more the perennial new kid on the block than the absurdist antihero of Jean-Paul Sartre and Albert Camus.

As if to prove Push right, an actual new kid, John Williams, immediately gains the acceptance that Push both desires and despises. Tall, blond, and handsome, the well-traveled and well-dressed Williams cuts a princely figure. A version of the main character in the slightly earlier "On a Field Rampant," Williams is a "paragon" of virtue and Christlike lover of all, including those defectives whom Push loves to hate. He puts Frank on a diet and Slud in the gym, and he even tries to befriend Push, who has always tried to live his life so that he "could keep the lamb from the door." Push decides to fight Williams, "not to preserve honor but its opposite"; willing to risk the pain he has always avoided, he is determined that his nemesis will not turn the other cheek. In this, Push claims, he is only following natural law: "Push pushed pushes." Push succeeds; Williams strikes back, only to then extend his hand in friendship. "Hurrah!" cry the others, like the chorus of children at the end of Fyodor Dostoevski's *Bratya Karamazovy* (1879-1880; *The Brothers Karamazov*, 1912). After a moment's hesitation, however, Push rejects all offers and pleadings; he chooses instead to follow his own inexorable self rather than adapt and submit: "Logic is nothing. Desire is stronger." Bully in no ordinary sense, Push is the "incarnation of envy and jealousy and need," ready to "die wanting," possessing nothing more and nothing less than "the cabala of my hate, my irreconcilableness."

THE FRANCHISER

First published: 1976
Type of work: Novel

The apotheosis of self-effacement, Ben Flesh tries to live without desire and therefore without personality.

If Push the Bully represents one extreme of character in Elkin's fiction, then Ben Flesh, protagonist and narrator of *The Franchiser*, represents the other. "A Poetics for Bullies" and *The Franchiser* are also representative of two other aspects of Elkin's writing. One is generic; there is the story's depiction of "acute character" manifesting itself in a crisis situation versus the novel's presentation of "chronic character" manifesting itself over a serendipitously (or whimsically) developed series of episodes. The other difference is autobiographical. "A Poetics for Bullies" and the other stories in *Criers and Kibitzers, Kibitzers and Criers*, were all written before "anything bad" had ever befallen Elkin; *The Franchiser* was written after the author had suffered heart attacks, temporary blindness, and multiple sclerosis.

"Deprived of all the warrants of personality," Ben is a man "without goals, without obsession, without drive" but in possession of a substantial inheritance from his wealthy godfather. That inheritance enables Ben, who has "no good thing of his own . . . to place himself in the service of those who had." For Ben, this means buying franchises (buying names), in effect becoming Evelyn Wood (speed reading), Fred Astaire (dance studio), Mr. Softee (ice cream), Colonel Sanders (chicken dinners), America's Innkeeper (Holiday Inn), and the like.

Ben's efforts to define himself in terms of others prove as unsatisfying as his attempts to control his various, mainly outdated or poorly located businesses, the inflation-prone economy, the weather, even his own body. The prime rate rises, the temperature soars, energy suddenly becomes scarce, and Ben learns that he has multiple sclerosis. His illness is diagnosed in, of all places, the tropical fever ward of a hospital in South Dakota, where a fellow patient offers him this stiff-upper-lip advice: "Be *hard*, Mr. Softee." Ironically, even perversely, that is precisely what Ben is doing, as the disease hardens patches on his brain.

His own health deteriorating and his eighteen nearly identical godcousins dying of bizarre maladies, Ben finally takes leave of his anonymity long enough to stake nearly all of his other franchises on a Travel Inn located in the town of Ringgold, Georgia. The inn, of course, fails, but not before Ben, putting his ear to the doors of the few occupied rooms, discovers that romance, even in its most perverse forms, is "as real as heartburn." He is amazed and delighted, but his "ecstasy attack," while clearly an affirmation of life, is also a chemically induced symptom of his worsening multiple sclerosis. "Nope," Ben says to himself in the novel's closing pages, "he couldn't complain." Would that he could, for (the novel suggests) he should. Lacking Push the Bully's rage and resentment, however, Flesh can only sigh, tragicomically resigned, perversely contented.

HER SENSE OF TIMING

First published: 1992
Type of work: Novella

Confined to a wheelchair, a political geographer finds himself in the land of farce, where he discovers the actual extent of his helplessness.

Best known as a novelist and frequently anthologized as a writer of short stories, Elkin has also produced a significant body of work in a form, the novella, that most contemporary American writers have, perhaps for commercial reasons, avoided. That Elkin should find the novella form so appealing is understandable, for it allows him to combine the emphasis on situation and acute character that typifies his short stories with the spatial freedom of the novel so necessary to the development of his poetics of resentment and obsession. What especially distinguishes "Her Sense of Timing" is how painfully close Elkin, never an autobiographical writer but always willing to draw on personal material, is working to the autobiographical bone. He takes his own increasing state of helplessness and dependency (on the drugs used in the treatment of his heart disease and multiple sclerosis, on his wheelchair and stair-glide, above all on his wife Joan) and asks a simple question: What would happen if a character who is not the author but who is like him in terms of age, personality, academic affiliation, and medical history suddenly found himself home alone, abandoned by a wife who, after thirty-six years of marriage and a decade or so spent caring for her disabled husband, decided that she had had enough?

Although he can understand Claire's leaving, political geographer Jack Schiff greatly resents her going and resents most her leaving on the very eve of his annual party for the graduate students he in fact does not particularly like. With Claire gone, Schiff must, quite literally, fall back on his own limited resources and abilities (including his ability to exploit others). Forced to "shift" for himself, he will come to understand better than ever before not only his humiliating helplessness but also the farcical nature of his situation. He takes pratfalls despite the presence of an expensive medical alert system, which he has installed the day Claire leaves and which the cunning, conniving Schiff will abuse, claiming a medical emergency when in fact he wants only someone to empty his urine container and close the front door. Schiff is adept at beating the system, at taking revenge by taking advantage. Elkin makes Schiff's situation at once convincing, comical, and emotionally affecting. " 'I'd like,' said Schiff, sorry as soon as he permitted the words to escape, 'for my life to go into remission.'" Failing that, the coward will once again turn bully, playing his handicap as if it were a trump card. In doing so, he seeks not just to assert himself; he seeks to avenge himself, though invariably in petty ways. In Elkin's fiction of obsession and resentment, the ways are always petty. The pettiness serves as further proof of the powerlessness that his characters feel so acutely and struggle against so mightily.

Summary

The Book of Job, Elkin has claimed, "is the only book . . . because all books are the *Book of Job*," and the best proofs of this assertion are the books Elkin himself has written. Thematically, they make the case for the position taken by one of William Faulkner's characters, that "between grief and nothing, I will take grief." Stylistically, Elkin's books make a virtue and an art of excess, of obsession, of the extraordinariness of the ordinary, and above all of naked human need. It is an art that is at once defensive and self-assertive, a way of out-grotesquing life's grotesquerie, all of its bad jokes, including the painful M.S. that Elkin painstakingly transforms into MS, malady into manuscript.

Bibliography

Bailey, Peter J. *Reading Stanley Elkin*. Urbana: University of Illinois Press, 1985.

Bargen, Doris G. *The Fiction of Stanley Elkin*. Frankfurt, West Germany: Lang, 1979.

Dougherty, David C. *Stanley Elkin*. Boston: Twayne, 1990.

Gass, William. Afterword to *The Franchiser*, by Stanley Elkin. Boston: David Godine, 1980.

MacCaffery, Larry. "Stanley Elkin's Recovery of the Ordinary." *Critique: Studies in Modern Fiction* 21, no. 2 (1978): 39-51.

Robert A. Morace

RICHARD FORD

Born: Jackson, Mississippi
February 16, 1944

Principal Literary Achievement
As a leading novelist and short-story writer, Ford has become a model in narrative style and structure for other American writers.

Biography

Richard Ford was born February 16, 1944, in Jackson, Mississippi, shortly after his parents, Parker Carrol Ford and Edna Akin Ford, moved there from Arkansas. By the time Ford was graduated from high school, his father had died suddenly of a heart attack and his mother decided to return with her son to Arkansas. The conditions of his youth—growing up in the Deep South as an only child, living alone with his widowed mother—contributed much to the tone and content of the fiction he was to write in later years. His essay "My Mother, In Memory" (1987), reflects on the events of his early years and on the influence of his relationship with his parents.

After Ford received his B.A. in 1966 from Michigan State University, he worked for a year as a writer for a sports magazine, an occupation that was to influence his novel *The Sportswriter* (1986). It was two years after his graduation that he determined to abandon his intention to be a lawyer and to become a writer instead. The same year, he married Kristina Hensley, a fellow student at Michigan State who subsequently became a professor of urban affairs and political science as well as a planner for several American cities. In 1970, Richard Ford earned an M.F.A. from the University of California at Irvine, where he studied creative writing with novelists Oakley Hall and E. L. Doctorow. He taught for one year at the University of Michigan before the publication of *A Piece of My Heart* (1976), his first novel.

In 1979 and 1980, Ford held a position as a lecturer at Williams College, followed by two years as a lecturer and George Perkins Fellow in Humanities at Princeton University, where he completed *The Ultimate Good Luck* (1981). This second novel, set in Mexico, exemplifies his tendency to use a variety of locales and represents his turning away from the Southern environment of his childhood.

Though Ford began to direct serious attention to the short story only with "Going to the Dogs" (1979), he wrote his first short story, never published, when he was seventeen. From 1979 to 1986, he spent much of his time writing short works of fiction,

although he was also at work on a third novel. *The Sportswriter* represents yet another departure in setting, in type of protagonist, and in some of its themes. This novel brought him wide recognition both in the United States and abroad as a major fiction writer. The next year, the stories he had written in the 1980's were published in the collection entitled *Rock Springs* (1987). His fourth novel, *Wildlife* (1990), is his first with a teenaged protagonist and thus shows the influence of his short stories, in many of which a young man is the central figure.

In addition to his fiction, Ford has produced a number of essays that comment on the craft of writing, on other authors, on members of his family, on sports and hunting, and on a variety of other topics ranging from motorcycles to rock musicians to friendship. In the 1990's, the range of his mastery of genres has been indicated by his publication of another short story, "Jealous" (1992), his first novella, *The Womanizer* (1992), and personal and critical essays in several periodicals.

Ford has lived with his wife in a variety of locales, including New York, New Jersey, Rhode Island, rural Mississippi, and Montana, and this geographical flexibility is reflected in his fiction. They reside for most of the year in New Orleans, where Kristina Ford is director of city planning, but he works for long periods in other places.

Analysis

Richard Ford's theory of fiction arises from what the poet Wallace Stevens called the "rage for order." Ford sees life as essentially chaotic and the writing of fiction as the act of taking the often disordered material of experience and creating a new setting, atmosphere, and order for it. His discontent with the way life is, he states, leads him to attempt to find an alternative. Thus, he says, fiction has moral implications because it implies hope of a better future, a better existence. The moral element of his work involves his concern with the proper responses to certain situations, the good or evil of a character's deeds, and a concern for how those deeds will shape a character's future. His final test for good art concerns the idea of unification, a belief that somehow the novel or the story may restore order to an otherwise chaotic and destructive pattern of existence. Although he professes a distrust of ambiguity, the endings of his works, like those of Nathaniel Hawthorne and Henry James, may lead two equally sensitive readers to two contrasting interpretations of the actions and responses of the characters.

While Ford has denied any religious implications or unified view of the world in his works, more than one critic has insisted that such elements are to be found there. Certainly, people in his novels and stories ponder more than most fictional characters the ethical significance of their acts and the acts of others. In contrast to those contemporary authors who believe in no ideal existence beyond the immediate reality, Ford portrays people who, in the face of the slings and arrows of outrageous fortune, find hope for the future, a belief in love, and a recognition of the importance of human relationships. In addition, certain recurrent themes, optimistic in their tone despite the stark environment and the often disturbing nature of the action, are to be read in his work. There is a continuing concern with loyalty among people, with courage, and with the ability to accept whatever fate hands one, however hard it may be. In this respect, Ford's work seems similar to that of Ernest Hemingway, although it is finally more optimistic.

Ford has insisted that "drama arises from individuals attempting to accommodate to an environment or to a place where they want to be, need to be, or must be." This relationship of characters and setting is reflected in work after work of Ford's. His protagonists often are placed in some alien environment in which they attempt to find an identity as well as a sense of belonging. In *A Piece of My Heart*, for example, the two protagonists, Robard Hewes and Sam Newel, men from different backgrounds and with different personalities, find themselves for two quite different reasons living on an uncharted island in the Mississippi River. Out of the conflict between the two men and their new environment, both the drama of the story and the philosophical theme develop.

Despite the fact that only one of his novels and a few of his stories have Southern settings, the influence of the region of his birth on Ford's work is apparent in several elements: a belief in the significance of place in life and fiction; a particular kind of moral vision; and the issues and themes he has chosen to employ. He has commented on more than one occasion that, despite the variety of his residences through the years, he still considers himself a Mississippian and likes Southerners for a variety of reasons, a major one being that they often speak in a way that does not truly reflect their minds. The discrepancy between a character's words and his actions, a major concern of many twentieth century authors, is also evident in much of his fiction.

Ford's interest in character is as wide-ranging as his use of settings. In *A Piece of My Heart*, for example, Sam Newel is a law-school graduate who is trying to make sense of his life, while Robard Hewes is a laborer drawn to the new environment by his lust for a young woman. *The Sportswriter*'s protagonist, Frank Bascombe, on the other hand, is established in an occupation; despite the earlier death of a son and his subsequent divorce, he manages to enjoy life, though he senses that something is missing. In marked contrast, *The Ultimate Good Luck* has a protagonist who finds himself in an alien environment, Mexico, trying to effect the release of his brother-in-law, who has been imprisoned for drug dealing.

Ford's fascination with Sherwood Anderson's short stories, one of the major influences on his work, grew out of his love of two Anderson works, "I Want to Know Why" and "I'm a Fool." In both stories, young men endeavor to come to terms with growing up and discovering the many confusing facts of life. Most Ford stories and novels could be subtitled "I Want to Know Why," for his characters are always engaged in an attempt to find answers to many questions: What are human beings? What is their purpose? What is their place? What should they do? How can they find direction for their lives?

Much of the power of Ford's work lies in his remarkable control of style. In an era when many fiction writers seem unconcerned about the exact meaning of words, Ford's prose employs diction as exact as Hemingway's, a finely tuned use of language that often startles with its force. Ford has several times expressed in interviews and articles his desire to avoid irony, that is, never to speak indirectly but to attack his subject head-on, using concrete words to evoke images that are immediately identifiable and not subject to misinterpretation. The reader finishes a Ford novel with the sense of having been led deep into the consciousness of a character, sometimes quite different from the reader, and of knowing that character as intimately as a family member, a friend, or one's own self.

THE SPORTSWRITER

First published: 1986
Type of work: Novel

A decent, caring man without irony moves through the confusing events of his life searching for the right action, the right attitude, the haven of rest.

The Sportswriter is Richard Ford's most acclaimed novel, the one that firmly established him as a major American writer. Ford asserts that the novel was written in answer to his wife's question, "Why don't you write a book about someone happy?" His intention was to produce a protagonist without irony who always says what he believes. Frank Bascombe is a failed novelist turned sportswriter, which he thinks of as not "a real profession but more of an agreeable frame of mind, a way of going about things rather than things you exactly do or know."

The "sport" of this novel is life itself, with the games grown-up boys play employed as metaphors for actions and ideas much more important than weekend pursuits in stadiums and gymnasiums. *The Sportswriter* bears some resemblance to Walker Percy's Christian existential fiction, although Ford denies any religious intention. Frank is an "anticipator" who dwells in the realm of possibilities, a typical trait of Southerners, according to Percy. Frank is also a man who values life for its own sake, despite the despair that is part of it, and who puts a premium on mystery, that element of life one cannot explain. Though he is a decent man, his life would be judged by many standards to be a failure: His marriage ended in divorce; his current love affair is on the rocks; two previous careers have been unsuccessful; and his choice of sportswriting as a substitute is almost accidental.

Nevertheless, Frank has never lost the ability to hope: "I've always thought of myself as a type of human weak link, working against odds and fate," he says, "and I'm not about to give up on myself." The death of one of his three children has left him vulnerable but never pathetic. He is a modern antihero, so credible that it is easy to empathize with him and almost impossible not to sympathize with his plight.

This is a novel of character rather than action; there is a suicide and a humorous scene in which Frank is briefly trapped in an outdoor phone booth that is attacked by a young man in a car, but the action is generally subdued. Ford's portrayal of characters is grounded in a keen perception of human weaknesses and virtues. *The Sportswriter* is a philosophical novel that comments on life in general and contemporary American life in particular. The style is subtle, often poetic, filled with aphoristic statements, as when Frank states, "Writers—all writers—need to belong. Only for real writers, unfortunately, their club is a club with just one member."

ROCK SPRINGS

First published: 1987
Type of work: Short stories

The ten short stories in *Rock Springs* portray protagonists attempting to understand themselves and their relationship to the often hostile environments in which they dwell.

Rock Springs is a collection of stories Ford wrote during the 1980's. There are no heroes in the traditional sense in these short works, nor are there villains. Some readers might be inclined to label the characters "victims," for certainly the environment and the influence of other people determine the characters' actions, often for the worse. Yet Ford should not be confused with the naturalistic authors of the early 1900's who portrayed hapless human specimens under a microscope.

Though the situations in which characters find themselves seem, for the most part, not of their own making, rather than being dehumanized or victimized, they become more credible and sympathetic. Many are loners struggling to find some meaning in limited lives lived out against a harsh environment. In the title story, Earl, the narrator, is a petty criminal fleeing bad-check charges in Montana with his girlfriend and his daughter. As his troubles mount—his car breaks down and his girlfriend decides to leave him—he experiences a self-revelation. He comes to see himself as a victim of happenstance, unable to take charge of his life: "There was always a gap between my plan and what happened, and I only responded to things as they came along and hoped I wouldn't get in trouble." Like many Ford stories, "Rock Springs" concludes as it begins, with a question that remains unanswered.

Like several protagonists in the stories, Les, the narrator of "Communist," is a teenager. On an illegal expedition to hunt migrating Siberian geese with his mother Aileen and her friend Glen, he acquires a painful truth about life and himself. When Glen decides to leave a wounded bird to die, Aileen rejects him, explaining her action by asserting, "We have to keep civilization alive somehow." Years later, remembering the incident, Les thinks, "A light can go out in the heart. All this happened years ago, but I can still feel now how sad and remote the world was to me." With "Communist," Ford perfected the type of ending that is a hallmark of his stories: The protagonist analyzes past events because, like Sherwood Anderson's character, he wants to know why. Anderson's influence is clearly evident in *Rock Springs*, and Ford has often expressed admiration for Anderson's plain diction and his fondness for simple American people. All these elements permeate Ford's own fiction in his choice of character and the style of his narration.

In *Rock Springs*, Ford reveals hopes and desires of characters whose limited lives belie their depth of feeling and capacity for love. Most of the endings are to some degree positive, for they involve hope on the part of characters that some understanding of reality is possible. No matter how insignificant their lives and acts appear on the surface, Ford makes readers observe, listen, and identify with these people. He believes that a short story should treat readers to language, make them forget their problems, and give "order to the previously unordered for the purpose of making beauty and clarity anew."

WILDLIFE

First published: 1990
Type of work: Novel

Sixteen-year-old Joe, the narrator, witnesses the breakup of his parents' marriage and attempts to understand them, himself, and the purpose of his existence.

The wide-open spaces, the mountains, the forest fires in *Wildlife* serve not only as backdrops and symbols but also as catalysts for the action of the novel. The lives of four main characters—Joe Brinson, his parents, and the man with whom his mother has an affair—are shaped by their environment. The action occurs in 1961 in Great Falls, Montana, which for Joe is "a town that was not my home and never would be." This sense of disorientation and alienation is central to the message of Ford's novel.

Wildlife is a rite-of-passage novel in which Joe, remembering events that occurred when he was sixteen, confronts life, death, change, and truth. His father, who moved the family to Montana during an oil boom in hopes of bettering their lot, finds a job fighting fires in the mountains. During his absence, Joe's mother briefly takes a lover. In an important passage, Joe considers the average youth's ignorance of his parents, "which can save you from becoming an adult too early." On the other hand, he believes that shielding oneself is a mistake, "since what's lost is the truth of your parents' life and what you should think about it, and beyond that, how you should estimate the world you are about to live in."

Faced with his mother's infidelity and his father's rage, Joe must make choices that most young people are spared. The significance of decision-making in this novel relates Ford's work to the existential belief that human beings create their identities through the choices they make. Without the aid of any authority, Joe alone must decide for himself, and his decision may be the wrong one, may even be fatal. His isolation is intensified by the mobility of his family and his consequent lack of longtime friends or other relatives in whom to confide. Alone, he faces unavoidable change, and with his new knowledge, he suffers the inevitable "fall" from the grace of childhood. Joe's strength derives from what his mother terms "inquiring intelligence." "Everything will always surprise you," she tells him, and when he has faced his dilemmas and acted, perhaps wisely, perhaps not, he seems well on the way to shaping a meaningful life for himself.

In *Wildlife*, Ford strongly evokes the troubled and puzzling teenage years of a boy on the border of maturity. With a spare, carefully shaped prose style that reflects the setting of the action and the quality of the problems and choices Joe faces, Ford creates a character and situations with which many young people can no doubt identify.

Summary

Richard Ford's philosophy of art involves his belief that the creative artist is driven to create order in a world that is essentially chaotic. The writing of fiction is, for him, an act of finding meaning in events that otherwise merely confound the participant and the observer.

Dealing with characters who are usually out of the mainstream of American life, writing in a language controlled and even subdued, Ford evokes sympathy from his readers, who must recognize, in the painful and persistent questionings of his protagonists, their own attempts to understand life. Ford's novels and stories, centered on events that are often depressing in nature, nevertheless celebrate the persistence of the human longing to be a part of the world and to find ultimate answers.

Bibliography

Ford, Richard. "What a Sea of Stories Tell Me." *The New York Times Book Review*, October 21, 1990, 1, 32-34.

Gray, Paul. "Trials of a Transient Household." *Time* 135 (June 4, 1990): 86.

Prescott, Peter. "I Dreamed Our House Caught Fire." *Newsweek* 115 (June 11, 1990): 64.

Seabrook, John, and Maude Schuyler Clay. "Of Bird Dogs and Tall Tales." *Interview* 19 (May, 1989): 104-107.

Weber, Bruce. "Richard Ford's Uncommon Characters." *The New York Times Magazine* 137 (April 10, 1988): 50-51, 59-65.

W. Kenneth Holditch

CHARLES FULLER

Born: Philadelphia, Pennsylvania
March 5, 1939

Principal Literary Achievement
One of the leading playwrights of his generation, Fuller became only the second African American to win the Pulitzer Prize in drama.

Biography
Charles Henry Fuller, Jr., was born in Philadelphia, Pennsylvania, on March 5, 1939, the son of Charles Henry and Lillian (Anderson) Fuller. Born the son of a printer, Fuller was educated in Philadelphia, attended Villanova University, then served in the U.S. Army from 1959 to 1962. In 1962, he married Miriam A. Nesbitt, and they had two children, Charles III and David. He resumed his studies at LaSalle in Philadelphia from 1965 to 1967 and went on to become the cofounder and codirector of the Afro-American Arts Theatre in Philadelphia from 1967 to 1971. In 1982, LaSalle awarded him an honorary degree after the stage success of *A Soldier's Play* (1981). Honorary degrees than followed in 1983 from Villanova University and in 1965 from Chestnut Hill College as Fuller became one of Philadelphia's most famous writers. He was appointed professor of African-American studies at Temple University in Philadelphia.

Fuller's plays began to appear during the late 1960's. In 1968, his two-act play *The Village: A Party* was produced in Princeton, New Jersey, in October; in March of 1969 it was produced in New York City as *The Perfect Party*. In 1972, a collection of six of Fuller's one-act plays was produced in New York City under the title *In My Many Names and Days*. Other plays that followed in 1974 included the one-act *First Love*, the two-act *In the Deepest Part of Sleep*, and the three-act *The Candidate*. In 1976, his three-act play *The Brownsville Raid* was produced in New York City by the Negro Ensemble Company, and in 1978, his two-act musical *Sparrow in Flight* was produced in New York. Another two-act play, *Zooman and the Sign*, won an Obie Award. In 1980, Fuller completed the teleplay for Ernest J. Gaines's *The Sky Is Gray*, based on Gaines' short story about an African American farm boy learning about his place in the world. In 1981, Fuller's two-act *A Soldier's Play* was produced by the Negro Ensemble Company to high critical acclaim and went on to win the Pulitzer Prize in drama. It was later adapted to the screen by Norman Jewison, who invited Fuller to

write the screenplay. *A Soldier's Story*, the film that resulted in 1984, went on to capture Academy Award nominations for Best Picture, Best Adapted Screenplay, and Best Supporting Actor. In 1987, Fuller wrote a screenplay for *A Gathering of Old Men*, a television adaptation of an Ernest Gaines novel. In 1988, Fuller completed a play series entitled *We*.

Fuller has earned a number of grants and awards besides the Obie Award in 1981 and the Pulitzer Prize in drama in 1982. Also in 1982, he won the Audelco Award as best playwright. That same year, *A Soldier's Play* won the New York Drama Critics Circle Award, the Outer Circle Critics Award, and the Theatre Club Award. The film adaptation, *A Soldier's Story*, won the Edgar Allan Poe Mystery Award for 1985. Fuller had grants from both the National Endowment for the Arts and the Rockefeller Foundation in 1976. He was named a Guggenheim Foundation fellow for 1977-1978. He has also been active in the International Association of Poets, Playwrights, Editors, Essayists, and Novelists (PEN), the Writers Guild of America, the Dramatists Guild, and the Dramatist Guild Foundation.

Analysis

Charles Fuller has written a number of tough, uncompromisingly honest plays that can be disturbing to both black and white audiences. His works deal with such controversial issues as miscegenation, racism, reverse racism, and ruthless inner-city violence. He has shown an unflinching determination to scrutinize the consequences of easy liberal solutions to human problems that might occur in the black community and that need to be carefully examined. His plays address the issue of racial justice, to be sure, but he is also keenly aware of the rights of the individual.

The Brownsville Raid, for example, is a three-act play based on a historical incident that occurred in 1906, when a U.S. Army regiment was dishonorably discharged when the black soldiers refused to confess to inciting a riot in Brownsville, Texas. There was no evidence that the men were responsible for the riot, and the men's records were cleared some sixty-six years later when the Army reexamined the case and determined that a gross injustice had been committed. In the play, career Army Sergeant Mingo Saunders has faith that the Army will protect his men, but that faith is betrayed.

Fuller's interest in the conflict between men and institutions is also evident in his other, more widely recognized work in a military setting, *A Soldier's Play*. The play is mainly about justice, military justice and racial justice, but it also concerns integration in an army that is moving toward the last months of World War II. That goal is not to be achieved, of course, for at least another decade, but Fuller's play is historically accurate in suggesting that initial goals of civil rights were achieved in the military, which was in advance of society at large. The irony of *A Soldier's Play* is that the black soldiers win the right to fight—and then die in combat in Germany.

Fuller pushes the envelope of integration in *The Village: A Party* by focusing upon the issues of racially mixed couples working to achieve a utopian social experiment, an experiment that works until the leader of the community falls in love with a woman of his own color and becomes a threat to the experiment. In this play, a relationship based upon love cannot succeed unless the colors of the partners are properly matched. The idealistic participants in this experiment do not account for the irrationality of human emotion.

Fuller has never glorified African Americans simplistically, for he is painfully aware of the problems that beset the black community. *Zooman and the Sign*, for example, dramatizes the consequences of ghetto violence by portraying the death of a twelve-year-old girl who is killed by a stray bullet in a neighborhood gang fight. In the play, the father of the dead girl faces the same fear and apathy that one might expect to find in any neighborhood of any city, frightened citizens afraid of becoming involved, even for the good of their neighborhood. When the father posts a sign on his front porch begging neighbors who witnessed the killing to come forth, he is ostracized by cowards who accuse him of "bringing the neighborhood down." Part of the problem is a reluctance of blacks to cooperate with the police, but this cultural sticking point could also be considered an excuse to avoid taking action. This is a discomforting play that takes on openly such problems as armed teenagers on the streets. Zooman himself, the murderer, is a brutal fifteen-year-old thug, but he is also a victim of his environment. He is depicted as something more than merely a heartless villain.

Fuller turned to the reality of the streets for *Zooman and the Sign* and to the reality of history for *The Brownsville Raid*, but he made a significant dramatic advance with *A Soldier's Play*. The work reflects the atmospheric "reality" of African American troops serving in the Deep South during World War II, but it also takes the form of an American tragedy, with two potentially tragic protagonists, Sergeant Waters and Private First Class Melvin Peterson, both of whom have absolute notions of what constitutes proper behavior for African Americans in charge of a black company, Waters hates ignorant "geechies" who perform for whites in expected ways he considers demeaning and embarrassing. He is obsessed with changing such behavior. He believes that the only way for a black man to succeed in a white world is to adapt white ways, to imitate white speech and assimilate white ambition. He is profoundly embarrassed by country blacks and by black culture in general, since he has spent his life attempting to escape from it.

Waters attempts to change a good-natured country black named C. J. Memphis, but he ends up driving the man to suicide. For this, Waters is hated by his soldiers, two of whom, Peterson and Smalls, encounter him on a country road and shoot him dead. Peterson, the assassin, kills Waters because he cannot condone Waters' behavior. At one point, he asks Waters, "What kind of colored man are you?" He challenges Waters, and the two of them fight at one point, but in fact Waters, who beats Peterson in the fight, also respects him for his spunk and courage. Peterson, however, despises the sergeant and feels no remorse. Both men are dehumanized by their idealism, but Waters is forced to understand his error in judgment in his treatment of C. J. and therefore reaches a moment of discovery, thus fulfilling a part of the classic Aristotelian tragic formula. He ruins his life and is made to understand why this has happened. His fate is tragic before his death. But even before his abuse of C. J., Waters is presented as being desperately unhappy. The most perceptive reading of his character comes from the unschooled C. J. who says of him, "Any man ain't sure where he belongs must be in a whole lotta pain."

As critics were quick to notice, the play is a tragedy disguised as a mystery that also explores the dynamics of racism. *A Soldier's Play* won the Pulitzer Prize in drama in 1982, no doubt because it represents an advance in both form and substance. In 1984, it was transformed into a motion picture that earned three Academy Award nominations for Best Picture, Best Supporting Actor, and Best Adapted Screenplay. The film opens up the play and makes a few changes, the most substantial of which are the removal of a bitterly ironic final monologue by Captain Davenport, the investigating officer, and the fact that in the film both Peterson and Smalls are captured, giving Davenport a final opportunity to confront the murderer with the following words, "Who gave you the right to judge? To decide who is good enough to be a Negro, and who is not?" These questions drive home the nature of the tragedy and also the similarity between Peterson and the man he kills. The film is excellently crafted and wonderfully acted; it both simplifies and clarifies the meaning of the original play. The film was made at a cost of $6 million and earned more than $30 million at the box office, becoming a runaway crossover hit. It set a significant precedent and marked the beginning of the 1980's renaissance of serious black films.

Charles Fuller played a significant role in bringing about that renaissance. He earned an Obie Award for *Zooman and the Sign* as well as the Pulitzer Prize and other awards for *A Soldier's Play*. It is particularly surprising, therefore, that by the early 1990's, only one of his plays remained in print. He is surely one of the most gifted playwrights of his generation, regardless of color, and a major theatrical talent.

THE VILLAGE: A PARTY

First produced: 1968
Type of work: Play

A tragic study of idealists living in a racially mixed community as a social experiment who turn upon their leader when he wavers in his principles.

The Village: A Party is a two-act play that was first produced in Princeton, New Jersey, in 1968, then produced five months later in New York City in 1969 under the ironic title *The Perfect Party*. It is an important early play for Fuller because it raises questions of black awareness that resurface in *A Soldier's Play*. The cast consists of ten characters: five couples, husbands and wives who have founded an integrated, racially mixed community. They come together to celebrate the birthday of their charismatic leader—who, it turns out, has fallen in love with a black woman and wants to leave the white woman he has married.

The other couples are shocked. They see their interracial experimental community as an apparent success, and they are afraid of what will happen to the community's image if they allow their leader to defect from his dream and betray the principles upon which the community was founded. To protect the purity of the experiment, the other couples murder the leader at the birthday party, then insist that his white widow marry another black man.

The play questions the ideal of integration as a realistic solution to the problem of race by suggesting that integration can in fact magnify emotional tension. The individual is made subservient to the community in this play, and the idea of a marriage based upon love is replaced by the notion that one must sacrifice all to satisfy the ideal of integration; the individual will is not to be tolerated. As in *A Soldier's Play*, some characters are attempting to force others to live by their notions of what may be considered right. As Dan Sullivan wrote in his review of the Princeton production for *The New York Times* (November 13, 1968), "Utopia has become not just a ghetto but a cell-block." The play was controversial in what it had to suggest about miscegenation and also in what it suggested about idealogues so determined to change the world by their example that the life of an individual was deemed inconsequential. In this play, Fuller demonstrated a courageous tendency to question ideals that might be disturbing to both white and black audiences.

ZOOMAN AND THE SIGN

First published: 1979
Type of work: Play

A decent, working-class family seeks revenge for the death of their twelve-year-old daughter, who has been struck down by a stray bullet in a gang shooting.

The play, set in Philadelphia, begins with a rapping monologue delivered by the jive-talking "Zooman," Lester Johnson, a teenaged thug who has just killed a little girl in a gang shootout. "She was in the wrong place at the wrong time," he says, expressing no remorse for having killed the twelve-year-old. Zooman's monologues continue to punctuate the action, but the main dramatic focus is upon the angry and grief-stricken family of Zooman's victim.

Rachel and Reuben Tate (a bus driver who has been estranged from his wife because of an affair with another woman) are mourning the death of their child Jinny; they are joined in their grief by Uncle Emmett and their fifteen-year-old son Victor. Emmett is a hothead who argues for revenge, "an eye for an eye," but Reuben is more restrained, exclaiming, "We're not head hunters!" Rachel wrongly blames herself for having allowed the child to play outside. Victor says nothing in this argument but asks his friend Russell if he can find him a gun, which Russell agrees to do.

When a neighbor, Donald Johnson, stops by to offer condolences, the audience learns that Reuben had been a light-heavyweight boxer and something of a local celebrity of one time. Jackson tells Reuben that no one on the block would tell the police that they had seen anything. The Tate family knows that there were in fact witnesses, and they are disturbed by their neighbors' silence.

In his second monologue, Zooman confesses that "I shot the little bitch 'cause I felt like it!" The audience learns that Zooman and his friend Stockholm served time for raping a schoolteacher, a crime that Zooman claims they did not commit. It is later revealed that Zooman has committed other crimes as well, including armed robbery, and that he is a hard and brutal case. He seems to be the egotistical personification of evil.

Meanwhile, Reuben has attempted to contact the neighbors to find a witness to the shooting, but they are all afraid to come forward. Ash Boswell, a family friend, explains that "black people don't like to deal with the police." The family frustration is heightened because Reuben had been seeing another woman, and Rachel knows about this. For the present, however, they are united in their grief.

Jinny wanted her parents back together. Ironically, her death has given them a common purpose, but the parents do not agree upon what course of action should be taken. Rachel wants to move to another neighborhood, but Reuben knows they cannot afford such a move and seems determined to improve their present neighborhood. They are devastated that neighbors they have known for fifteen years will not come forward to help them identify Zooman as the shooter. Victor has heard rumors that Zooman did the shooting. Reuben has a sign made to hang on his porch, a sign that reads: "The killers of our daughter Jinny are free on the streets because our neighbors will not identify them." The sign proves to be controversial; many of the neighbors are offended.

In act 2, Russell advises Victor not to go after Zooman. He tells Victor that the neighbors are angry about the sign because "it brings the whole neighborhood down." Russell regrets having given Victor the weapon and is reluctant to provide ammunition. When neighbors begin throwing bricks at the family's front door in protest, Victor brandishes the gun, but his mother disarms him. Reuben and Emmett return from a bar, where they have been in a fight over the sign. Emmett has apparently broken his arm in the fight and needs to be taken to the hospital.

At the funeral service, some people write threats about the sign in the register, and tension builds. The Tates suspect that Jackson or his wife might have witnessed the killing. Jackson denies this but tells Reuben some of the neighbors are organizing a march to tear the sign down. The police call to say that one of the culprits, the fifteen-year-old Stockholm, has been apprehended, adding that he has confessed and named Zooman as the murderer. Rachel tells Reuben that she wants him to leave if he will not take the sign down. Finally, Zooman comes to take down the sign himself and is shot through the window by Uncle Emmett.

Justice is done, perhaps, and Zooman no doubt observes his fate, but the point is made that his death will not bring Jinny back to life. The play also makes it clear that Zooman himself was a victim of his environment; all that sets him apart from Jinny's brother Victor is that Victor has had a stronger home life. The play ends with another sign. "Here, Lester Johnson was killed. He will be missed by family and friends. He was known as Zooman." Hence violence breeds violence. The killing has continued, and the neighborhood has not really been improved.

A SOLDIER'S PLAY

First produced: 1981 (first published, 1982)
Type of work: Play

At first, *A Soldier's Play* seems to be a murder mystery in a military setting, but the play is in fact both a modern tragedy and a commentary on racist attitudes in America.

A Soldier's Play is set on an Army base at Fort Neal, Louisiana, in 1944, near the end of World War II. A black soldier, Master Sergeant Vernon C. Waters, has been murdered at night on a country road near the base. The black soldiers and their white officers believe that the killing was racially motivated and probably the work of the Ku Klux Klan. In order to avoid tension between the black soldiers on the base and the local civilians, Colonel Nivens, the base commander, has not ordered a full investigation; the murder is not given the same kind of attention it would have been if a white soldier has been the victim. Captain Taylor, his subordinate, believes justice should be served, however, and he has reported the killing to Army headquarters. Consequently, an officer is sent from Washington, D.C., to investigate the murder.

The Department of the Army dispatches a bright Howard University-trained military attorney, Captain Richard Davenport, who happens to be an oddity for the time, a black officer. Both Colonel Nivens and Captain Taylor are worried about how local whites will react to Davenport. Nivens is convinced that the killers were white, and he assumes that Davenport will go after these racist murderers with a vengeance, causing problems in the white community. Nivens, however, does not understand the man Washington has sent.

Davenport's investigation is thorough, meticulous, and fair. He discovers that Waters was a hard taskmaster, feared by most of his men and despised by some of them. The story is revealed in flashbacks in which Waters alienates his men by picking on a well-liked, good-natured country boy named C. J. Memphis, whom he sends to the brig on a trumped-up charge. C. J. is held there and intimidated by the sergeant. Waters is embarrassed by C. J. and his Uncle Tom ways. C. J. is a gifted musician and also the best batter on the company's baseball team; he is a walking, talking stereotype of a talented, self-deprecating black man, and Waters hates the type. He frames C. J. to get him thrown into the brig so he can intimidate him and change his ways. Yet the physically strong C. J. is psychologically weak. Driven to desperation in prison, C. J. commits suicide. Waters, who has a conscience after all, suffers guilt for what C. J. has done and turns to drink. His presumption is his tragic flaw; it causes his downfall and, ultimately, his death.

Gradually, Davenport begins to suspect that Waters might have been murdered by his own men, who blamed him for the death of C. J. The team falls apart and loses its chance to be the first all-black team to play the New York Yankees during an exhibition. Waters loses the respect of his men and then his own self-respect. Although Davenport suspects that Waters might have been murdered by his own men, Captain Taylor is pressing him to prosecute two white officers, Lieutenant Byrd and Captain Wilcox, who were placed at the scene of the crime shortly before the killing took place.

The issue becomes one of justice, not race, though the theme of racial justice is an important secondary one. Davenport is a good and dedicated lawyer who follows the evidence to where it takes him, discouraging though that may be. By the end of the play, one of the culprits has been apprehended; in a final monologue, the audience is told that the murderer will be captured a week later in Alabama, leaving the impression that justice will be done in military circles. Yet there are other, larger social problems that are left unresolved. As Davenport's final monologue makes clear at the end of the play, the entire all-black company is doomed, even though they have won the right to fight the Germans in Europe. Davenport explains at the conclusion that the men of the company, the "entire outfit—officers and enlisted men—was wiped out in the Ruhr Valley during a German advance."

Moreover, Sergeant Waters is honored as a hero; he is believed to be the first black soldier from his home town to die in action, since his death was wrongly reported. Thus, although the play celebrates a victory for the black soldiers, who win the right to fight for their country, the story ends with an ironic denouement that is devastating. The moral victory and the resolution of justice are made to seem hollow by the final monologue, which was removed from the film version. Fuller was given the opportunity to reinvent his drama for the screen and in doing so managed to clarify the message, even though the tone of the conclusion was substantially changed.

Summary

Charles Fuller's probing examinations of the corrosive effects of racism have earned him the admiration of critics and the attention of a wide audience. The popular success of his best-known work, *A Soldier's Play*, in both its stage and film versions demonstrates that serious—even disquieting—literature need not be the exclusive province of academics and the avant-garde. Fuller has transcended the limitations implied in such labels as "black playwright" to earn recognition simply as one of America's most accomplished dramatists.

Bibliography

Cooper, Carol. "*Soldier's Story* Salute." *Film Comment* 20, no. 6 (November-December, 1984): 17-19.

Gottfried, Martin. "A Powerful Play in 'Brownsville.'" *New York Theatre Critics' Reviews* 37, no. 25 (December 6, 1976): 77-78.

Kael, Pauline. "Three Cheers." In *State of the Art*. New York: E. P. Dutton, 1985.

Kerr, Walter. "A Fine New Work from a Forceful Playwright." *The New York Times*, December 6, 1981, p. B3.

Rich, Frank. "Negro Ensemble Presents *Soldier's Play*." *The New York Times*, November 27, 1981, p. B3.

Sullivan, Dan. "In Switch, Princeton Offers New Plays and Club Here an Old One." *The New York Times*, November 13, 1968, p. 39.

Van Gelder, Lawrence. "Intermarriage Under a Microscope." *The New York Times*, March 21, 1969, p. 42.

Weales, Gerald. "American Theatre Watch 1980-1981: *Zooman and the Sign*." *The Georgia Review* 35, no. 3 (Fall, 1981): 600-601.

Welsh, Jim. "*A Soldier's Story*: A Paradigm for Justice." In *Columbia Pictures: Portrait of a Studio*, edited by Bernard F. Dick. Lexington: University Press of Kentucky, 1992.

James M. Welsh

ERNEST J. GAINES

Born: Oscar, Louisiana
January 15, 1933

Principal Literary Achievement
Gaines is celebrated for his simple but poignant and intensely sympathetic depiction of poor blacks in rural Louisiana.

Biography

Ernest James Gaines, the first son of African American parents Manuel and Adrienne Gaines, was born on January 15, 1933, in Oscar, Louisiana, a small town a few miles northwest of Baton Rouge. He grew up in former slave quarters on River Lake Plantation, where, for six years, he attended a one-room elementary school before enrolling in the Augustine Catholic School in nearby New Roads.

At the end of World War II, his mother moved to California to be with her second husband, Raphael Colar, a merchant seaman, leaving Gaines behind to be reared by his invalid aunt, Augusteen Jefferson, who had a formative influence on the boy. Although she had never walked in her life, she had extraordinary resiliency and great faith, and Gaines credits her with teaching him fundamental values, above all, about suffering with courage and dignity.

Like so many rural blacks, after school and over the summer Gaines worked in the sugar-cane and cotton fields, but many of his evenings were given over to reading and writing for his aunt and her illiterate acquaintances. From them, he derived a strong sense of a native, oral tradition and his own heritage.

Upheaval followed in 1948, when, at fifteen, he moved to Vallejo, California, to live with his mother and stepfather. The move was traumatic for Gaines, who has dwelled on his departure from the quarters and who later returned in his depiction of characters with experiences paralleling his own.

Prompted by his stepfather's fear that he might fall in with bad company, Gaines spent long, lonely hours in the public library, reading voraciously while trying to cope with his yearning to return to Louisiana. There, too, he made his first serious attempt at fiction, writing the initial draft of what eventually became *Catherine Carmier* (1964), his first novel.

After completing high school and beginning college, Gaines was drafted into the Army, serving in the Pacific from 1953 to 1955; then, after his discharge, he entered

San Francisco State College to study English. While there, he published his first story, "The Turtles," which helped to win for him a Wallace Stegner Creative Writing Fellowship for graduate study at Stanford University. Strongly influenced by the writing of Ivan Turgenev, James Joyce, and William Faulkner, at Stanford Gaines began bringing into focus his own artistic vision.

That vision became sharper in 1962, when he returned to Louisiana and strengthened his desire to write about the places and people of his boyhood years; he hoped to write from an honest but sympathetic perspective that no white writer of the rural South had been able to assume. His first novel, *Catherine Carmier*, did not win much critical attention, and Gaines followed it by abortive attempts to write about his adopted San Francisco culture. Thereafter, he wisely turned again to writing about Louisiana, about the people and places in his heart.

In 1966, Gaines was awarded a National Endowment for the Arts grant, and over the next two years he published a novel, *Of Love and Dust* (1967), and a collection of short stories, *Bloodline* (1968), one of which, "A Long Day in November," was also published separately as a children's story in 1971. Thereafter, he began garnering considerable acclaim and several awards, including a California Commonwealth Gold Medal Award (1972), the Louisiana Library Award (1972), a Guggenheim Fellowship (1974), and an honorary doctorate from Denison University (1980).

While writer-in-residence at Denison, he published his best-known novel, *The Autobiography of Miss Jane Pittman* (1971). It was followed by *In My Father's House* (1978) and *A Gathering of Old Men* (1983), which, like *The Autobiography of Miss Jane Pittman*, was adapted as a television play and helped to introduce his work to an expanding international audience.

In 1983, Gaines became writer-in-residence at the University of Southwestern Louisiana in Lafayette, about sixty miles from his birthplace. He has continued to divide his time between Lafayette and San Francisco, where he also has a home.

During the 1980's, Gaines won several additional awards, including three more honorary doctorates and, in 1989, the Louisiana Humanist of the Year Award, presented by the Louisiana Endowment for the Humanities in recognition of his dedication both to his craft and to his teaching. Fame also brought him travel and lecturing obligations, so that it was only after a hiatus of ten years that he was able to finish his long-awaited novel *A Lesson Before Dying* (1993).

Analysis

Ernest Gaines is a raconteur of the agrarian South, specifically of the black experience in rural Louisiana during the three decades following World War II. His chief setting, former slave quarters located near the town of Bayonne, closely mirrors the actual surroundings of Gaines's boyhood: the quarters on River Lake Plantation and the town of New Roads. This world, remote for most readers, becomes in Gaines's novels a literary microcosm, inhabited principally by blacks, Creoles, and Cajuns, all treated with a simple honesty and direct style that are the hallmarks of his fiction.

Prevalent themes in Gaines's fiction have also spring from his own experience. His male characters often search for an identity at a time when change was hard-won and self-esteem required the courage to reject a demeaning place in a world in which wealth, prestige, and power belonged exclusively to whites. For many southern black males growing up in those turbulent years, escape from poverty and racial servility often involved flight to the North or West, but at great emotional cost and with a deep sense of alienation and loss.

Gaines makes clear that many of the younger blacks in that era had little real choice, for the life their parents and grandparents knew was gone. Slowly but relentlessly, blacks who had eked out an impoverished but dignified living from the land were being pushed into the soggy bottoms, onto land unfit for serious cultivation. The inheritors, mostly Cajuns, were swallowing up the good lands, farming for profit with mechanized equipment, tearing down the houses of the poor blacks and plowing over their graves.

Less deracinated by these events, the black women in Gaines's novels are more adaptable, particularly the older ones. Most of them cling to their Christian faith tenaciously, drawing strength from the church, which many young black men, like Jackson Bradley in *Catherine Carmier*, come to abandon. The women endure in part because the conditions do not really so deeply erode their sense either of purpose or identity. They can live a bare, frugal existence because they gain much strength from their community, their extended families, which they strive to hold together. The younger black men, their prodigal sons, either set out on solitary quests for a new source of pride and dignity or succumb to an early defeat, even a violent death.

Against this background, Gaines spins highly personal stories of individuals and families profoundly affected by change and exacerbated racial tensions, a complex problem because of miscegenation and the existence of a large Creole and mulatto population. The separatist attitude of Creoles, like Raoul in *Catherine Carmier*, is often as intransigent as that of many bigoted whites.

Remarkably, the bitterness that might surface in this world is usually muted. Although omnipresent and insidious, the racial caste system is not something its principal victims dwell upon or use as a psychological crutch. For most of them, the system is a fundamental fact of life, and though they dream of change, they are pragmatists, finding dignity despite the system and revealing moral strength confronting it.

There are few real villains in Gaines's fiction, even among the persecutors. The worst of men, such as Luke Will, the redneck bully in *A Gathering of Old Men*, are mindless and craven. Most, such as Fix Boutan from the same novel, are bound to a familial and racial code, however misguided, by a strong sense of honor. These, too, are victims of caste, for they cannot see that they are morally bankrupted by their blind arrogance and hate.

Such characters play only secondary roles, however, for Gaines's avowed purpose is to focus on the poor blacks, not their persecutors. To that end, Gaines evolved a disarmingly plain and direct style, a "voice" to match the simple, unsophisticated lives of his principals, most of whom have no hope of sharing the whites' bounty. Inspired by the rhythm and phrasing of blues musicians, the harangues of Pentecostal preachers, and recorded interviews of former slaves, Gaines uses short sentences, colloquial cadences, and unpretentious diction with a lyricism that is both insistent and intense. His preference is for monosyllabic, ordinary words of everyday speech, and his progress through a tale is seldom encumbered by elaborate description or extensive introspection by his characters. It is a style that he has mastered, and with it he evokes both humor and pathos.

It is also a style suited to Gaines's baldly realistic, uncomplicated plots, which often focus on the impact of one critical event or relationship in the experience of simple people who normally live uneventful, even placid lives. With the exception of *The Autobiography of Miss Jane Pittman*, which covers a span of roughly one hundred years, the plot time frame is narrow, as in *A Gathering of Old Men* and *A Lesson Before Dying*, but Gaines builds the real story in the event's uncertain, soul-searching aftermath.

Two characters who repeatedly enter Gaines's fictive world are a young, educated black male, seeking purpose while impaled on the horns of a moral dilemma, and an older, righteous black woman, urging him toward the harder, self-sacrificing choice. They are Jackson Bradley and Aunt Charlotte in *Catherine Carmier*, Gaines's first novel, and Grant Wiggins and his aunt, Tante Lou, in *A Lesson Before Dying*. In one guise or another, they appear in almost everything that Gaines has written; it is primarily through them that the author has worked to cope with a fundamental ambivalence toward his own heritage. It is on this, his own spiritual odyssey, that Gaines has revealed that he is one of the most humane and compassionate novelists in America.

THE AUTOBIOGRAPHY OF MISS JANE PITTMAN

First published: 1971
Type of work: Novel

A resourceful, engaging black woman survives a century of adversity and little joy to become a strong moral presence in her community.

The Autobiography of Miss Jane Pittman remains Gaines's best-known work, partly because of Cicely Tyson's portrayal of Jane in the 1974 televised adaptation of the novel. It is Gaines's most panoramic and episodic book, tracing the long life of its protagonist from her youthful emancipation to her old age in the 1960's.

The novel purports to be the recorded history of the protagonist herself, leading many to conclude that she was a real person, but she is actually a composite portrait Gaines drew from several inspirational sources, including his aunt, Augusteen Jefferson. Miss Jane's narrative threads through important public events, providing a backdrop of historical names and dates against which, through adversity and triumph, Jane grows in stature from an ignorant young slave to a wise old woman.

Her saga begins with no inkling of geographic reality, merely the desire to find the Union soldier who, in dubbing her "Jane Brown," had removed her stigma as a slave. She quickly learns that freedom means that she must forage for herself, not an easy task in a land full of marauding whites bent on exterminating black vagrants.

She teams up with Ned, a younger boy whose mother has been slaughtered, and together they follow her elusive dream. With the end of Reconstruction and the onset of the Jim Crow era, Ned migrates to Kansas, committed to helping his fellow blacks, who have been forced once again into economic subjugation. Jane enters into a common-law marriage with Joe Pittman, a sharecropper and the great love of her life. They move near the Texas border, where Joe has a job breaking horses, but after Joe is killed, Jane settles near Bayonne, the epicenter of Gaines's fictive world.

Ned returns to Louisiana, rekindling in Jane a hope that had dimmed with Joe Pittman's death. Teaching the need for justice and change, he is soon marked for death. Within a year, Ned is gunned down by a Cajun assassin, Albert Cluveau, who, ironically, had befriended Jane.

In the final parts of the narrative, Jane's focus shifts from episodes in which she is the main participant to stories of other people living on the Samson plantation, her last home. She describes the various teachers who come to the one-room black school, including Mary Agnes, a Creole who inspires an ill-fated love in Robert Samson, the son of the white plantation owner. She also reflects on black heroes, including Joe Louis and Jackie Robinson, and other public figures, including Huey Long. Her main focus, however, is on Jimmy, who, like Ned before him, goes away to be educated, returns to preach against segregation, and is killed by lawless whites. It is his spirit that lives on in Miss Jane, who, at the novel's end, plans to carry on against racial injustice.

In Miss Jane, Gaines etched a compelling literary character who penetrates socially sanctioned wrongs with brash innocence. Yet her attraction lies less in that than in her wonderful earthiness and irrepressible determination to survive. She is an authentic, poignant, and engaging character who has left an indelible imprint on American literature.

A GATHERING OF OLD MEN

First published: 1983
Type of work: Novel

A group of elderly black men, defying tradition, reveal unprecedented courage when they gather to protect another man whom they believe has shot and killed a Cajun farmer.

Unlike *The Autobiography of Miss Jane Pittman*, which has an epic sweep, *A Gathering of Old Men* limits its primary action to a single day and to locales in and around the plantation quarters near Bayonne. It is only in Lou Dimes's last narrative, a sort of epilogue, that the reader is carried past the climactic day on which a group of old black men gather to protect their friend, Mathu. They assume that Mathu has killed Beau, a white farmer and son of a powerful Cajun patriarch, Fix Bouton.

The old men congregate at Mathu's house, each carrying a shotgun and confessing to the crime. They have an ally in a young white woman, Candy, who has prompted the gathering. She also claims to have shot Beau, fearing that Beau's killer, once identified, will fact brutal retribution. The men hold to their charade, braving the abuse of Sheriff Mapes and frustrating all of his attempts to intimidate them. Although he believes that only Mathu is capable of the act, Mapes slowly gains grudging respect for the men because they have dared to defy him.

Candy, too, must face the implications of the men's stand. As her friend Lou Dimes tells her, Mathu is now free of her, free of her protection, which, however well-intentioned, in its way has been as demeaning for blacks as the brutal intimidation of men such as Mapes and Beau Bouton. The black men are finally able to stand alone, with dignity and pride, beholden to nobody.

Complications in the novel introduce two other white men with sharply contrasting attitudes about what should be done about revenging the death of Beau Bouton. Gil Bouton, brother of the victim and a star football player at Louisiana State University, counsels restraint; Luke Will, an ignorant redneck, tries to flame bigotry into action against the old men. Although Fix is chagrined by his son's views, he declines to act. Disgusted, Luke leads a party of his friends to the quarters in an attempt to force Mapes into handing Mathu over to them. Mapes is wounded in the ensuing gunfight, and Luke and Charlie Biggs, who actually shot Beau, are both killed, ending the crisis.

The novel is narrated from the viewpoints of fifteen different characters, including several of the old men, whose accounts are full of good-natured ribbing in an engaging folk idiom. These men, with memorable nicknames such as Cherry, Dirty Red, Chimley, and Rooster, lend broad humor to the novel, so that its grim events, even the gunfight, have a seriocomic cast. That humor, at times self-deprecating, simply counterpoints their increasing sense of pride, for at the end they clearly stand triumphant, taller than they ever had before.

A LESSON BEFORE DYING

First published: 1993
Type of work: Novel

Enjoined by others to help another black man to face his impending execution with dignity, a teacher struggles with his own loss of faith and sense of purpose.

A Lesson Before Dying is set in the late 1940's, in the former slave quarters of the Marshall plantation and the town of Bayonne. Gaines takes his reader back to a time when racial segregation was both legal and endemic in the South, a time when black people could barely hope for recognition of their humanity, much less find justice in a court of law.

It is in this world that a dirt-poor, semiliterate black man, Jefferson, is accused of murdering a white liquor-store owner. In the Bayonne courthouse, Jefferson is quickly condemned to death by an all-white jury. Although he is innocent, the verdict is never in doubt. Even his attorney characterizes Jefferson as subhuman, claiming that electrocuting him would make no more sense than electrocuting a hog.

Jefferson's godmother, Miss Emma, aided and abetted by Tante Lou, prevails upon Tante Lou's nephew, Grant Wiggins, to help Jefferson face death like a man, with dignity. Grant, the teacher in the quarters where Jefferson lived, is very reluctant to undertake the task, but the women and Grant's girlfriend Vivian convince him that he has no choice but to try.

Grant's initial efforts are disappointing. Jefferson has accepted his lawyer's depiction of him as a hog, and he resists all attempts to help him break through his self-loathing. Furthermore, in order to help Jefferson, Grant must cope with his own doubts about his role, both as man and teacher. The task also puts his own pride at grave risk, as he must seek the cooperation of white men such as Henri Pichot and Sheriff Guidry, who want to stifle his "smartness."

Lashed by the righteousness of Tante Lou and Reverend Ambrose, his chief tormentor, Grant persists and finally succeeds in befriending Jefferson, largely through simple kindness. He bolsters Jefferson's courage, helping him to face Gruesome Gerty, the portable electric chair, with unflinching dignity.

The novel thus ends with hope, both for Grant, the protagonist, and for the South. Grant has learned that his teaching is not in vain, that his education has given him the power to help others discover their humanity. He has also earned the respect and potential friendship of a young white deputy, Paul, who holds out the promise for a future racial harmony.

Except for a few segments in which *A Lesson Before Dying* subtly slips into a third-person point of view, the novel is presented in the first person from the point of view of its protagonist, Grant Wiggins. The reader thus closely audits Grant's own progress from doubt and moments of self-hatred to an honest confrontation with his feelings of anger and bitterness, love and shame. His growth parallels that of Jefferson, who, by facing death bravely, at the end has become his teacher's teacher.

Summary

In 1993, Gaines was the recipient of a MacArthur Foundation Award, an honor given to persons for their selfless contributions to humankind. Gaines's fiction argues that he is a deserving choice, for his works are strong indictments of racial bigotry and inhumanity. They offer a quiet plea for sanity, for racial harmony and understanding. More than that, they are testimonies to the strength of the human spirit, not only in blacks, but in all men. Lastly, they are works of great humor and compassion, rich in the folklore of oral tradition, told, through many different voices, with masterful skill.

Bibliography

Babb, Valerie Melissa. *Ernest Gaines*. Boston: Twayne, 1991.

Bruck, Peter, and Wolfgang Karrer, eds. *The Afro-American Novel Since 1960*. Amsterdam: B. R. Gruner, 1982.

Callaloo 1, no. 3 (1978). Special issue on Ernest J. Gaines.

Gaudet, Marcia, and Carl Wooton. *Porch Talk with Ernest Gaines: Conversations on the Writer's Craft*. Baton Rouge: Louisiana State University Press, 1990.

Harper, Mary T. "From Sons to Fathers: Ernest Gaines' *A Gathering of Old Men*." *College Language Association Journal* 31 (March, 1988): 299-308.

Simpson, Anne K. *A Gathering of Gaines: The Man and the Writer*. Lafayette: Center for Louisiana Studies, 1991.

Turner, Darwin T. "Black Fiction: History and Myth." *Studies in American Fiction* 5 (1977): 109-126.

John W. Fiero

WILLIAM GASS

Born: Fargo, North Dakota
July 30, 1924

Principal Literary Achievement
Although Gass is a distinguished philosopher of language, he is known primarily for his original and experimental short stories and novels.

Biography
William Howard Gass was born in Fargo, North Dakota, on July 30, 1924, the son of William and Claire (Sorensen) Gass. With two brief exceptions, Gass has spent most of his life in the Midwest, the place most frequently evoked in his works of fiction. From 1943 to 1946, Gass served in the U.S. Navy, principally in China and Japan. He left the Navy in 1946 with the rank of ensign, and in 1947 he finished his undergraduate studies at Kenyon College in Ohio. He then enrolled in graduate studies in philosophy at Cornell University in New York, specializing in the philosophical analysis of language, a preoccupation that would become the central focus in his works of fiction.

While working on his Ph.D. in philosophy at Cornell, Gass supported himself by working as an instructor of philosophy at the College of Wooster (in Wooster, Ohio) from 1950 to 1954. On June 17, 1952, he married Mary Patricia O'Kelly with whom he had two sons and one daughter. In 1954, he received the Ph.D. from Cornell and immediately took a new teaching position as a professor at Purdue University, where he taught until 1969. The period at Purdue was an especially productive one for Gass. During this time, he published his highly original first novel, *Omensetter's Luck* (1966), and a critically acclaimed book of short stories, *In The Heart of the Heart of the Country* (1968). In 1968, Gass also published an important novella, *Willie Masters' Lonesome Wife*, which appeared in the pages of *TriQuarterly* magazine. In 1969, he married again, to Mary Alice Henderson, with whom he had two daughters.

In 1969, Gass also began a long and fruitful association with Washington University in Saint Louis, Missouri, a period marked by a flood of publications having to do with his philosophy of language and general theories of fiction. He also wrote a prodigious number of reviews and critical articles on contemporary and classic works of fiction. Gass was writing regularly for such influential publications as *TriQuarterly*, *The New York Review of Books*, *The New York Times Book Review*, *The Nation*, and *The New*

Republic. These scholarly articles and reviews became the basis for his important works of nonfiction and often served as chapters in such books as *Fiction and the Figures of Life* (1970); *On Being Blue* (1975), his most famous and frequently quoted work of nonfiction; *The World Within the Word* (1978); and *The Habitations of the Word: Essays* (1984).

The collective importance of these works of nonfiction for the student of Gass's work cannot be overstated; in them, Gass created his own complex theory of fiction as an end in itself, thus establishing himself as one of the chief practitioners and theoreticians of the New Fiction, a style practiced by such writers as Donald Barthelme, Richard Coover, John Barth, and John Gardner, among others.

Gass's work in all these arenas—teaching, literary creativity, and scholarly publication—began to attract more and more attention, as well as many coveted awards, prizes, and honorary positions. In 1965, he won the Standard Oil Teaching Award at Purdue University, followed by Sigma Delta Chi Best Teacher Awards at Purdue in 1967 and 1968. The *Chicago Tribune* also recognized Gass in 1967, giving him an award for being one of the best Big Ten university teachers. In 1969, he was awarded a prestigious Guggenheim Fellowship, and in 1974, he received the Alumni Teaching Award from Washington University.

The awards were not limited merely to William Gass's teachings skills, outstanding though they were. His fiction and essays began to receive more and more national recognition, as suggested by the following honors: The National Institute of Arts and Letters Prize for Literature (1975); the National Medal of Merit for Fiction (1979); and the National Book Critics Circle Award for Criticism (1986). Gass was also asked to serve as a member of the Rockefeller Commission on the Humanities from 1978 to 1980 and as a member of the literature panel of the National Endowment for the Arts from 1979 to 1982. Gass has also been awarded honorary degrees from Kenyon College (1974), George Washington University (1982), and Purdue University (1985).

Analysis

Anyone who has read the first page of Gass's famous *On Being Blue* must recall the dazzling, virtuoso performance of the author, who manages, in the first few paragraphs, to evoke every possible connotation of the word "blue," including the blues and such phrases as blue laws, blue stockings, blue blazers, and blue pencils. This playfulness with language, this delight in turning words around and examining them as if they were resplendent prisms or baffling puzzle cubes, is characteristic of Gass's fiction.

Again and again, one is struck by the fact that Gass's short stories and novels, however enticing and entertaining they may be, somehow evade the standard storytelling function of most narratives. Gass's stories are not so much about something as they are explorations of how to look at something, how to discover the multiple possibilities inherent in the simplest moment or action. In a real sense, Gass is a proponent of art for art's sake. He is not interested in delivering a familiar moral or preaching a popular message, and he is rarely interested in realism as such.

A typical Gass story makes relatively few historical or chronological references to the everyday world. His narrative plots tend to be spare and minimal, even though a great deal seems to happen in each story. The reader thus may be hard put to summarize or encapsulate a Gass story, yet that story will leave its audience with an indelible sense of having experienced a richly imagined world—or a sense of having lived in the mind of an unforgettable character. Much of Gass's fiction is focused on the choices and thought processes of such characters. Gass often creates a kind of stream of consciousness in which every perception, doubt, dream, fear, or memory of a character bursts upon the page in a rushing torrent of words. Once again, it is the individual word, with all of its associations and musical reverberations, that becomes the principal unit of composition.

In a real sense, then, Gass's language-oriented technique is his basic theme: Everything he writes in some way reflects on his fundamental notion that words do not merely create reality; they are, finally, the only reality. This technique does not, however, absolutely exclude other interpretations or thematic possibilities. Gass is certainly moved by the theme of human loneliness and alienation; he is fascinated by the spectacle of individuals cut off psychologically or socially from the rest of society. He is equally fascinated by the impossibility (or near-impossibility) of arriving at any fundamental truth in human life. His works often suggest that ambiguity, misunderstanding, and confusion tend to be the norm.

This skepticism on Gass's part may well result from his professional training as a philosopher in general, or from his specific attention to the philosophy of language. After all, one of the most important philosophers of the twentieth century, Ludwig Wittgenstein, theorized that language is a game that people learn to play by virtue of their humanity. The rules of the language game are arbitrary, for words can mean anything the speaker wants them to mean, as Lewis Carroll's Alice, for example, discovers on her confusing journey through Wonderland.

Despite his spare plots, general themes of uncertainty and misunderstanding, and love of individual words (a kind of poet's attention to craftsmanship), Gass does not leave the reader in a sort of literary vacuum, a minimalist universe with only bare outlines and skeletons. In fact, Gass provides one of the richest textures of detail in contemporary American fiction. His fictions positively bristle with details about weather, facial appearance, architectural details, slang terms, odd names, nicknames, bits of song and poetry, and passages from the Bible. Perhaps the secret of Gass's success is that he invites the reader to make a fresh interpretation or reordering of the wealth of details always present in his narratives.

Therefore, what Gass provides most consistently is an overwhelming sense of the richness and complexity of day-to-day life. The subject most frequently evoked by that rich detailing is Gass's native Midwest, the region where he has spent most of his life. Midwestern weather, snowstorms, sunsets, fields, flowers, trees, farm buildings, and turreted Gothic mansions abound in his fiction. For all his avant-garde experimentation, Gass always keeps his attention on what he calls the "heart of the heart of the country."

Gass has always maintained a kind of love-hate relationship with the Midwest. On the one hand, its pastoral beauties and traditional patterns of social life have fascinated him and provided him with the raw material for his experimental storytelling. On the other hand, however, he has utterly rejected the smallmindedness, bigotry, and cultural conservatism that often characterize small-town life in the heartland. One might observe that Gass's literary experimentation and philosophical independence might not have occurred in the first place if he had not experienced a kind of artistic claustrophobia in his youth.

In "A Revised and Expanded Preface," written in 1981 for the second edition of his classic work, *In the Heart of the Heart of the Country and Other Stories* (originally published in 1968), Gass speaks passionately and sometimes bitterly about his origins. Racial slurs ("nigs, micks, wops, spicks, bohunks, polacks, kikes") abounded in his hometown. Gass's response to this poisonous atmosphere (which he described in many of his later works) was to seek refuge in art. He read widely and deeply, developing a taste for modern writers such as Franz Kafka, James Joyce, Marcel Proust, Thomas Mann, and William Faulkner—in short, all the masters of twentieth century literary experimentation. In the process, he determined to become a writer himself and to define himself as an artist with "a soul, a special speech, a style." For Gass, there is no discontinuity between his life as an artist and the rest of his existence; the two are inseparably intertwined. "I was born somewhere in the middle of my first book," he explains. The rest of his life can be seen as a brilliantly successful process of self-discovery through one artistic creation after another.

THE PEDERSEN KID

First published: 1968
Type of work: Novella

An adolescent boy survives a blizzard in the Midwest and thereby finds his own identity.

On the surface, at least, "The Pedersen Kid" is a relatively simple tale. A Scandinavian family, the Jorgensens, are trying to keep warm during a howling blizzard, which has virtually rendered them snowbound. The family consists of Ma (Hed), a kindly, self-effacing woman, and Pa, a boorish, drunken lout who hides his whiskey bottles all over the house and expresses his displeasure by dumping the contents of his chamber pot on the heads of his victims. Jorge, their son and the narrator of the tale, fears and despises him, as does Big Hans, the hired hand who works for the family and lives in the house with them. It is Big Hans who finds the Pedersen kid, half-buried in a snowdrift in front of the Jorgensen farmhouse. Although he first seems to be dead (the first of many ambiguities in the story), Ma revives the young child (his exact age is another ambiguity—he could be two or even four years old) with the help of Big

Hans and Jorge. Pa awakens, fuming as always, but eventually he, Big Hans, and Jorge determine to visit the Pedersen family to notify them of the child's rescue—and to verify if they have been killed or put in the cellar by a mysterious character called "yellow gloves" by the Pedersen kid.

The bulk of the narrative is taken up by their visit to the Pedersen farm in the midst of a blinding blizzard, itself a kind of symbol for the confusion and ambiguity of the entire situation. Pa drops his whiskey bottle in the snow, and Jorge finds a dead horse, which they all realize does not belong to Pedersen. They all conclude, without any real evidence, that the dead horse must have been ridden by the murderer of the Pedersens, although even the fact that the family has been murdered has not been established. The entire meaning of the story is revealed at that juncture, because Jorge (on whose point of view the reader is forced to rely) speculates that the horse may be the murderer's, or it may belong to Carlson or Schmidt—nothing is clear. Pa and Big Hans dig a tunnel to the barn, and finally all three of them stumble toward the house, but Jorge thinks rifle shots have been fired, killing Big Hans and Pa. In any event, they fall behind in the snow, and Jorge makes no attempt to rescue them or to verify their condition, preferring the relative warmth of the Pedersen cellar (which contains no corpses) and the empty house. The story ends there, with Jorge riding out the storm, uncertain of his fate or that of his companions, because at any moment he could be eliminated by "that fellow."

Like other precocious and highly imaginative narrators—Huck Finn and Holden Caulfield readily come to mind—Jorge invents a complex and often contradictory universe. Yet that world is always thrilling and vivid precisely because of its uncertainty. Like Jorge, the reader will want to thank the mysterious "yellow gloves" for the "glorious turn" he has given to what would have been a hopelessly ordinary little world.

OMENSETTER'S LUCK

First published: 1966
Type of work: Novel

A harness-maker named Brackett Omensetter arrives in the isolated town of Gilean, Ohio, and immediately becomes an object of curiosity and gossip.

Omensetter's Luck is a highly complex and original novel that enchants and mystifies the reader on nearly every page. The novel actually takes the form of three closely related tales, the last two progressively longer than their predecessors, all somehow dealing with the mysterious central figure of the book. The three tales (subdivided into chapters) include "The Triumph of Israbestis Tott," "The Love and Sorrow of Henry Pimber," and "The Reverend Jethro Furber's Change of Heart." Just as in "The Pedersen Kid," Gass places his story in the familiar terrain of the Midwest, in Gilean, a small, imaginary community on the Ohio River at the turn of the century.

The broad details of the story are simple enough: Brackett Omensetter, a dark, burly harness-maker, arrives in Gilean during a season of drought, rents a home from Henry Pimber, and takes a job with Mat Watson, the blacksmith. A flood arrives, and the Omensetter house survives, in spite of its perilous location near the river bottom. The myth of Omensetter's luck begins. Omensetter's reputation as a kind of magician or possessed man (a fiction created by the half-demented and jealous Reverend Furber) is enhanced when he cures Henry Pimber of lockjaw by using a poultice made from ordinary beets. Later, Henry Pimber hangs himself in a tall oak tree, Omensetter's recently born son contracts diphtheria, and Omensetter finds Henry's body at the same time that he refuses to seek a doctor's help for his own son. The novel concludes with the departure of both Reverend Furber and the Omensetter family. Amos, the Omensetter infant, miraculously survives his diphtheria, and "Omensetter's luck" is forever established as a kind of catchphrase in the inbred community of Gilean.

Gass employs a number of literary techniques in this novel, another story of ambiguity and misunderstanding. Omensetter's luck is merely a projection of the town's superstitions and insecurities. The literary technique that Gass uses most frequently to bring this town and its unique residents to life is the device of the catalog or list of items, a technique that goes all the way back to the ancient poetry of Homer. In Gass's novel, the catalog is used to show how people literally create reality by piling one piece of data atop another. In Gilean, the world is made up of lists.

Israbestis ("Bessie") Tott, the ancient postmaster of Gilean, is a kind of living historian, carrying lists of people's possessions (the opening scene of *Omensetter's Luck* is an auction). Henry Pimber will make a detailed list of Omensetter's possessions on the day of his arrival in town. Reverend Furber makes lists of flowers, mourners at a funeral, and jars of preserves on a shelf. Names, though, constitute the primary data is this list-making process.

In his famous preface to *In the Heart of the Heart of the Country*, Gass admits that he collected names as the germs or catalysts for stories, including names such as Jethro Furber, Pelatiah Hall, George Hatsat, and Quartus Graves. So it is not surprising to see some of those names (such as Jethro Furber) figure prominently in his later work, nor is it strange to read the catalog of names supplied by the oddly named Israbestis Tott at the beginning of the novel, including May Cobb, Kick Skelton, Hog Bellman, and Madame DuPont Neff. For Gass, the world is made up of words, as suggested by the title of his book of essays, *The World Within the Word* (1978). Words possess the magical power of invocation: They can call things into being. Names are the most powerful of all words, able to call forth the whole town of Gilean, Ohio.

IN THE HEART OF THE HEART OF THE COUNTRY

First published: 1968
Type of work: Short story

A frustrated lover and poet makes a detailed and documented journal of life in a small Indiana town.

In "In the Heart of the Heart of the Country," Gass not only makes short lists of names and objects, but he also creates the very structure of the tale from his ingrained habit of list-making. The story, in brief, becomes a list of lists. There is no regular storyline or even normal paragraphing but rather a series of journal-like entries, each one with its appropriate subtitle such as "People," "Weather," or "Place." There is only one voice, that of the unidentified poet-narrator, who is living in the dismally boring town of B. . . , Indiana (identified in the preface to the whole volume, *In the Heart of the Heart of the Country*, as Brookston, Indiana). As in *Omensetter's Luck*, the texture of the world is composed of words and, particularly, of words turned into poem-like lists. There is again that same preoccupation with names, including Mr. Tick, the narrator's cat, and such hilarious names as "Gladiolus, Callow Bladder, Prince and Princess Oleo, Hieronymous, Cardinal Mummum, Mr. Fitchew, Spot." The narrator also lists all the possessions of an old man in Brookston, a kind of pack rat who has saved everything, even the steering tiller from the first, old-fashioned car he owned.

The narrator is saver of things, too, a poet without a lover or a job who painfully plods through each day, examining the minutest details of his environment (clouds, trees, buildings) until they become a kind of poetry. This process of saving things through documentation is especially evident in the entries marked "Data," which culminate with a magnificent list of all the social clubs and civic organizations in Brookston, from the Modern Homemakers to the Merry-go-round Club. One theme that emerges clearly in this story is the idea that something can be so boring that it actually becomes interesting—if one has the artist's eye and the ability to have "intercourse by eye." Another theme is the loneliness and isolation (often self-imposed) of the American artist. In the preface, Gass observes, "The contemporary American writer is in no way a part of the social and political scene."

Thus this famous story, for all of its well-articulated pain and loneliness, is ultimately a celebration of the power of art to elevate and transform even the plainest elements of a little Midwestern hamlet. "In the spring the lawns are green, the forsythia is singing, and even the railroad that guts the town has straight bright rails which hum when the train is coming," the narrator says.

Summary

In a marvelous book called *The Fabulators* (1967), the distinguished critic Robert Scholes suggested that the best writers of the late twentieth century were not realistic storytellers so much as artists who were motivated by the embellishments and multiple possibilities in any story. He called this process "fabulation" and identified the work of Kurt Vonnegut and John Barth as prime examples.

Like the fabulators, Gass has entertained and edified his readers by showing them the story behind the story—and the unending possibilities of meaning contained in even the simplest of words. Like all true geniuses, he took an established form, narration, and made something new and beautiful with it, something that no one had yet anticipated.

Bibliography

Bellamy, Joe David, ed. *The New Fiction: Interviews with Innovative American Writers*. Urbana: University of Illinois Press, 1974.

Holloway, Watson L. *William Gass*. Boston: Twayne, 1990.

McCaffery, Larry. *The Metafictional Muse: The Work of Robert Coover, Donald Barthelme, and William H. Gass*. Pittsburgh: University of Pittsburgh Press, 1982.

Saltzman, Arthur M. *The Fiction of William Gass: The Consolation of Language*. Carbondale: Southern Illinois University Press, 1985.

Vidal, Gore. *Matters of Fact and Fiction: Essays, 1973-1976*. New York: Random House, 1977.

Daniel L. Guillory

SUSAN GLASPELL

Born: Davenport, Iowa
July 1, 1876
Died: Provincetown, Massachusetts
July 27, 1948

Principal Literary Achievement

A pioneering and prolific American feminist novelist, journalist, short-story writer, and Pulitzer Prize-winning playwright, Glaspell advocated freedom of expression and was cofounder and codirector of the influential Provincetown Players.

Biography

Mystery surrounds the birthdate of Susan Glaspell. Was she born in 1876 or 1882? Glaspell always asserted that the latter date was correct, and it was often used in past studies. Recent evidence suggests, however, that the earlier date is accurate. Why she would deny a linkage to the nation's centennial and make herself appear younger has never been explained. Susan was born to Elmer S. and Alice Keating Glaspell in Davenport, Iowa. Her father's family was among the first of the Davenport settlers. Her father was solidly middle-class with some affluence, but he was not a wealthy man. Her parents instilled in their daughter a love of the region that she would retain to the end of her life.

Glaspell was educated in the public schools of Davenport. She then went to Des Moines, Iowa, to attend Drake University. She was graduated in 1899 with a Ph.B. degree, having studied literature, classics, and the Bible. By all accounts, she was popular; she was also noted for her storytelling abilities and gained experience as a writer. Her first job after graduation was as a reporter for the *Des Moines Daily News*. While there, she met and befriended Lucy Huffaker, who became an influential and lifelong friend. Glaspell worked at the paper for two years, became expert at political writing, and had her own column, "The News Girl," which began with political commentary and then strayed to fictional forays and personal observations. The column's success prompted Glaspell to quit her job at the newspaper in 1901, return to Davenport, and earn a living as a freelance writer. The "Freeport" stories, twenty-six in all based on the city of Davenport, were escapist and romantic works filled with local color and unexpected plot twists.

The turning point in her private and literary career occurred in 1907, when she met George Cram Cook, a charismatic man. Nicknamed "Jig," he opened her eyes to new forms of literary expression, especially in the theater. They married six years later on April 14, 1913, in Weehawken, New Jersey. Both Glaspell and Cook had become involved with several free-thinking, nontraditional groups, most notably the Monist Society and the Liberal Club. Between the time they met and married, Glaspell published her first novel, *The Glory of the Conquered: The Story of a Great Love* (which Cook heartily disliked) in 1909, a second novel; *The Visioning*, 1911, and *Lifted Masks*, a collection of short stories, in 1912.

In 1915, two years after their marriage, Glaspell and Cook cofounded the Provincetown Players at the Wharf Theatre in Provincetown, Massachusetts. They had summered there the year before and had put on some amateur theatricals. Now the new little group, patterned after the New Theatre movement in Europe, began a quest to produce works by new playwrights. Many artists became attracted, and attached, to the Provincetown Players. some of the most notable were Robert Edmond Jones, John Reed, Edna St. Vincent Millay, Edna Ferber, Theodore Dreiser, Djuna Barnes, and, most important, Eugene O'Neill. In 1916, the Provincetown Players, which also took on the name "The Playwright Theater" at O'Neill's request, opened in New York City in Greenwich Village. The playbill included Glaspell's best short play, *Trifles*, and O'Neill's *Bound East for Cardiff*, the first of his "S.S. Glencairn" quartet. The Provincetown Players, which continued as an organization until 1929, became an important theater laboratory that took creative risks with budding playwrights, actors, and designers.

On March 22, 1922, Glaspell and Cook, having recently dropped their association with the Provincetown Players (now led by O'Neill, Jones, and Kenneth Macgowan), moved to Greece. Cook had always dreamed of moving to Delphi and creating theater where classical drama had once flourished. Less than two years later, on January 24, 1924, Cook died in Delphi and was buried there.

Glaspell returned to Provincetown to resume her professional literary career as a novelist. She married writer Norman Matson in 1925 (they divorced in 1931) and collaborated with him on several works, most notably a play, *The Comic Artist*, in 1927. A year earlier, she had published *The Road to the Temple*, a loving biography of her first husband. Glaspell was awarded the 1931 Pulitzer Prize in drama for her play *Alison's House* (1930), produced by Eva Le Galliene. Three years later, she was briefly appointed Midwest Director for the Federal Theater Project. Glaspell remained in Provincetown writing novels, the last one, *Judd Rankin's Daughter*, published in 1945, until her death from pneumonia on July 27, 1948.

Analysis

Glaspell had a remarkable literary career that spanned almost five decades. She began writing short stories in high school. On graduation from college, she became a reporter writing political columns; she continued her output of short stories and then switched to novels. It was as an experimental playwright, however, that she found her own distinctive and innovative style, which would win her fame and a permanent place in American dramatic literature. Throughout her long literary career, Glaspell remained consistent, always dealing with Midwestern themes and attitudes and employing unusual women as her leading characters. Her earliest short fiction, published at the turn of the century, reveals her talent for local color, a trait that made her work admirably suitable for such popular women's magazines as *Good Housekeeping*, *Ladies' Home Journal*, and *Harper's Bazaar*. The stories had certain recurring qualities. They were primarily escapist reading, perennially optimistic, and sentimental in nature. Glaspell often included last-minute plot switches or humor to offset saccharine sentiment. Romance and romantic problems appear in many, with obstacles to true love (usually young) removed at the last moment. In her early short fiction, Glaspell never attempted to shock or moralize to her readers. In 1912, she published *Lifted Masks*, a collection of thirteen short stories.

Glaspell's best short fiction was written between 1916 and 1919. Two of her best stories, "Finality in Freeport" (1916) and "The Escape" (1919), are set in Freeport, a fictional place modeled after her hometown, Davenport. In the first, she pokes fun at the city's bluestockings who attempt to censor literature because of some new ideas, underscoring the conflict between freedom and morality. In "The Escape," a freethinking, pacifist woman refuses to be caught up in the jingoistic fervor of World War I. Glaspell's entire output of short fiction, with one exception, was written for popular magazines of the day and reflects the editorial demands and public expectations of such entertainment. The single exception, now considered a classic, is "A Jury of Her Peers," which was adapted from her earlier one-act play *Trifles* and concerned an Iowa woman accused of killing her husband. Its depiction of the locale is realistic and demonstrates a complete unity of plot, characters, and conflict.

Trifles was the second play Glaspell wrote after she collaborated with her husband on *Suppressed Desires* (1915); in all, she wrote fourteen plays. Unlike in her short stories, which had a predictable framework, in her plays Glaspell experimented with the dramatic form despite her lack of dramatic experience or training. She wrote short dramas and comedies before switching to full-length plays. The one-act plays, eight in all, appear to be tentative efforts. She seemed more comfortable writing satiric or comic sketches rather than serious ones; her serious works sometimes come across as vague, and the idealism behind them at times seems ill-defined.

Glaspell found a stronger dramatic voice and greater confidence switching to full-length drama, but her experiments in the shorter form paid off handsomely with *Bernice* (1919). As in *Trifles*, the main character, Bernice, is never seen (she dies before the play opens); it is her death and its impact on the main characters that fuels the play. Glaspell creates a play of little dramatic action, strong mood, and interesting people. Her second play, *Inheritors* (pb. 1921), is a historical piece covering the lives of three generations. Against a Midwestern college background, the heroine supports independence of thought against narrow-minded provincialism, which is represented by faculty and students.

Glaspell's next play, *The Verge* (1921), is perhaps her most difficult to comprehend.

The heroine, Claire, is a wife and mother who rejects all societal restraints and murders her lover; the play builds to a shocking conclusion. After two less than satisfactory plays—*Chains of Dew* (1922) and *The Comic Artist* (1928)—she wrote *Alison's House*, produced in 1930. The play is based loosely on the life of poet Emily Dickinson; the title character is already dead, and her life and work are shown through the eyes of family, friends, and strangers.

Glaspell's major weakness as a playwright is one of too much intellect. She sometimes creates static, "talking" drama, with characters who cannot articulate their feelings or emotions. Yet she also creates a strong modern drama populated with fascinating people, particularly strong-minded women. Her plays are experimental, treating topical themes, and contain strong idealism. Unlike her contemporary and friendly rival, Eugene O'Neill, Glaspell never strays from her American heritage, and she successfully merges American beliefs and ideas with mysticism and a oneness with the eternal.

Glaspell's nine novels, published between 1909 and 1945, can be neatly categorized within three distinct periods. Despite the wide separation of time, all of them take place in the Midwest and contain a melodramatic situation, with strong women (often artistic) searching for fulfillment and coming into harmony with the universe. The first period (1909-1916), like her early short fiction, used romantic love to heal and unify. The best play from this period is *Fidelity* (1915), in which a Freeport woman runs off with a married man to Colorado, returning home eleven hears later to face family, friends, and society. Love does not conquer all here, as Glaspell's heroine follows her own principles instead of society's; the author compares and contrasts early Midwest veracity with its present prudishness.

The second period (1928-1931) produced Glaspell's least interesting work. The novels in question—*Brook Evans* (1928), *Fugitive's Return* (1929), and *Ambrose Holt and Family* (1931)—focus away from love and deal with individuals battling society. Her faith in the Midwestern tradition permeates the work, as do her political liberalism and Christian ethics.

Glaspell's last cycle of novel writing (1940-1945) offers a clearer, more coherent vision of her life and art. Her last and best work is *Judd Rankin's Daughter* (1945), in which three main characters represent different aspects of the Midwest. The book reveals Glaspell's major strengths as a regional novelist who captures the pioneering spirit, the physical beauty, and the colorful characters of Midwestern life.

A JURY OF HER PEERS

First published: 1917
Type of work: Short story

In an Iowa farmhouse, investigators gather evidence against a woman charged with murder, but two women discover the truth and sympathize with the accused.

All critics agree that Susan Glaspell's "A Jury of Her Peers," is far and away her best short story. First published in *Everyweek* on March 5, 1917, the work is a faithful adaptation of her play *Trifles*, produced the year before by the Provincetown Players. Her husband, Jig Cook, decided to stage two one-act plays for the company. He already had Eugene O'Neill's *Bound East for Cardiff* but needed another, and he told Glaspell to write one. She protested because of her lack of experience as a dramatist and the pairing with O'Neill. Reaching into her past as a courthouse reporter in Iowa, she remembered covering a murder trial and her impressions of entering the kitchen of the accused. She had meant to write about the experience as a short story but had never gotten to it.

> So I went out on the wharf . . . and looked a long time at that bare little stage. After a time the stage became a kitchen—a kitchen there all by itself. I saw just where the stove was, the table, and the steps going upstairs. Then the door at the back opened, and people all bundled up came in—two or three men, I wasn't sure which, but sure enough about the two women, who hung back, reluctant to enter that kitchen.

The play was a big success of Glaspell and the Provincetown Players; it remains her best play. It is considered one of the finest short pieces written for the American theater and is frequently anthologized.

Glaspell had only to make minor changes in adapting *Trifles* to a short story. As with some of her other literary work, the main character is never seen. The setting is the Iowa farm of Minnie Wright. She has been charged with murdering her husband. Her guilt in committing the crime is never questioned. Three men—a sheriff, a county prosecutor, and a neighbor—have come to gather evidence to support the prosecution. Two women—wives of the sheriff and neighbor—accompany the men. Their purpose is to pick up effects for Minnie.

Glaspell skillfully shows how the men and women look at the household differently. While the men seek evidence to convict her, the two women come across trifles such as a disordered household, an irregular quilting pattern, and a strangled canary, and they conclude that such details are indicative of Minnie's motivations for the murder. The women gossip openly about Minnie's abusive and authoritarian husband and discuss why they sympathize with her desperate act. Glaspell creates a courtroom in that Iowa farmstead, and the women become jurors who decide that Minnie is not guilty. They base their judgment not on legality but on simple humanity and compassion. The women decide not to reveal their evidence to the male investigators out of respect for Minnie's long suffering.

ALISON'S HOUSE

First produced: 1930 (first published, 1930)
Type of work: Play

The survivors of a famous poet must decide whether or not to publish her poems about her unfulfilled love for a married man.

Alison's House, the last produced play by Glaspell, was first presented at the Civic Repertory Theater in New York City on December 1, 1930. The production, produced and directed by Eva Le Galliene, ran for forty-one performances and won for Glaspell the 1931 Pulitzer Prize in drama—a decision that outraged some critics who disliked her play and thought it too literary.

Alison's House concerns a noted fictional poet, Alison Stanhope, who has been dead for eighteen year when the curtain rises. Her poetry, published after her death, has brought her posthumous fame. The play begins on December 31, 1899, in the library of the Stanhope estate. John Stanhope, Alison's brother, is selling the property, and there is much confusion as family members gather to say goodbye and pick up keepsakes. One of the recently arrived relations is Elsa, Alison's niece and John's daughter, who scandalized the family some years earlier by running off with a married man. A Chicago newspaper reporter, Ted Knowles, has also come to do a story on Alison; he is curious to know if all Alison's poetry has been published. Slowly, the dark secret buried inside the house comes to life. Alison's family has withheld some of her poetry. Agatha, Alison's spinster sister and close friend, decides to burn down the mansion to destroy the papers and bury the secret. Failed in her attempt, she gives Elsa the unpublished poetry and dies shortly after of a heart attack. The final act takes place in Alison's old room. Alison's secret is revealed: She was in love with a married man, but unlike Elsa, she sublimated her secret passions into poetry. The play ends with Elsa planning to publish Alison's lost poetry because it belongs to the world and the new century.

Glaspell based the play loosely on the life of the New England poet Emily Dickinson, but she moved the setting to Iowa. Unable to use Dickinson's poetry, Glaspell freely borrowed from the work of Ralph Waldo Emerson. She again used one of her favorite literary devices; the title character Alison Stanhope, is never seen, but her presence is felt through the other characters. The newspaper reporter Knowles sums it up best:

You know, I think all your family have something of the spirit of Alison Stanhope. . . .
Yes, coming in fresh, I can tell better than you. It's as if something of her remained here, in you all, in—in quite a different form.

The dramatist ends the play on the note of rebirth and love. The play is tightly constructed and adheres to the classical dramatic unities. Through the various characters, Alison becomes a reality, an ideal who brings hope and regeneration.

JUDD RANKIN'S DAUGHTER

First published: 1945
Type of work: Novel

Midwestern beliefs and values clash and coalesce through the dynamically different personalities of conservative Judd Rankin, his liberal daughter Frances, and her nonconformist cousin Adah.

Judd Rankin's Daughter was the last of Glaspell's nine novels. The last three—*The Morning Is Near Us* (1940), *Norma Ashe* (1942), and *Judd Rankin's Daughter*—were written close together; each of the three features a memorable heroine looking to rediscover her Midwestern heritage in order to better understand the present. In the first two books, the protagonists must struggle through the corruption and dissipation of their early idealism to a gradual reawakening in themselves. *Judd Rankin's Daughter*, which is not representative of most of Glaspell's work, delineates a much more complex and interesting heroine involved with the major problems of modern life.

Judd Rankin's Daughter is about three wonderful people: Judd Rankin, a lovable old Iowa farmer and philosopher who has finally written a book about people living in the Midwest; Frances Rankin Mitchell, his liberal daughter, who is living in Provincetown, Massachusetts, and who blends both Midwestern and Eastern values; and Cousin Adah Elwood Logan, a nonconforming sophisticate whose love lives on long after her death.

The novel opens with the anticipated death of Cousin Adah. She lived a rich and happy life, had lovers before and during marriage, and kept a salon where writers and workers could meet. Frances is present as witness to the death of someone she loved, someone who symbolized freedom and a piece of the pioneering spirit of women. A young soldier arrives at the deathbed wishing to speak to Cousin Adah about the meaning of life. Frances tries to comfort him and warns against following ideologies. Her adoption of this spiritual son brings Frances to understand her biological son, Judson, who has returned from the Pacific. He now hates his parents, particularly his father, whom he believes helped to provoke the war.

Frances is forced to reexamine her beliefs. Her husband hates Judd for his conservative, isolationist views. Her friend, a left-wing writer, is slowly turning into a fascist. Her best friend reveals herself to be anti-Semitic. Her son's accusations about her husband's politics combine with Frances' other concerns to shatter her complacency. She visits her father in Iowa to pull her life together and seek his help with her son.

Judd writes a powerful letter to his grandson that changes his mind, and Frances' dearest wish is realized on New Year's Eve, when her father, husband, and son are reunited.

Glaspell's last literary work is marked by a mature fluidity of style that reveals her as an artist of integrity. She offers up a prevailingly hopeful picture of honest people and grass-roots wisdom, and she does so in a pleasant, witty, and thoughtful manner. *Judd Rankin's Daughter* reveals the faith in the American heritage, particularly the Midwestern tradition of common sense, that suffuses Glaspell's art.

Summary

Susan Glaspell was a truly prolific writer. During her lifetime, this remarkable feminist wrote fourteen plays, nine novels, forty-three short stories, numerous essays, a biography, and a children's tale. Although successful in a variety of literary genres, Glaspell is best known for her dramatic works. The Pulitzer Prize-winning playwright created a new theatrical voice and dealt with contemporary issues. Glaspell is also remembered as the inspirational force behind the founding of the Provincetown Players and for her continuous encouragement of new playwrights, particularly Eugene O'Neill.

Bibliography

Dell, Floyd. *Homecoming*. New York: Farrar & Rinehart, 1933.

Deutsch, Helen, and Stella Hanau. *The Provincetown: A Story of the Theatre*. New York: Farrar & Rinehart, 1931.

Hapgood, Hutchins. *A Victorian in the Modern World*. 1939. Reprint. Irvine, Calif.: American Reprint Services, 1991.

Heller, Adele, and Lois Rudnick. "Jig Cook and Susan Glaspell: Rule Makers and Rule Breakers." *Nineteen Fifteen, the Cultural Moment: The New Politics, the New Woman, the New Psychology, the New Art, and the New Theatre in America*. New Brunswick, N.J.: Rutgers University Press, 1991.

Makowsky, Veronica. *Susan Glaspell's Century of American Women: A Critical Interpretation of Her Work*. New York: Oxford University Press, 1993.

Vorse, Mary Keaton. *Time and the Town: A Provincetown Chronicle*. 1942. Reprint. New Brunswick, N.J.: Rutgers University Press, 1991.

Waterman, Arthur E. *Susan Glaspell*. New York: Twayne, 1966.

Terry Theodore

JOHN GUARE

Born: New York, New York
February 5, 1938

Principal Literary Achievement
A New York born-and-bred dramatist, Guare writes increasingly sophisticated farces about the impact of the American Dream on lives by contemporary cultural forces.

Biography

John Guare was born in Manhattan on February 5, 1938, to John Edward and Helen Clare (Grady) Guare. Shortly after his birth, his parents moved to Forest Hills, Queens, where he attended St. Joan of Arc Parochial School and, when old enough, was taken to mass every day by his mother.

Guare's father worked on Wall Street and had in earlier years been employed as office boy for George M. Cohan. Guare speaks of his very bright and unhappy parents, of listening to constant arguments between them and of hearing stories about his Hollywood uncle, Billy Grady. He heard stories about his uncle's having secretly signed Elizabeth Taylor to star in *National Velvet* (1944) and about Grady's managing the careers of Ruby Keeler, W. C. Fields, and Will Rogers. Exposed early to religion and Hollywood, he learned from direct experience about "Catholicism and show biz," which he referred to as "full of dreams and phoney promises."

Guare was graduated from Georgetown University in 1961 and went on to receive his M.A. in English at Yale University in 1963. He was a fellow at Yale University's Saybrook College from 1977 to 1978 and adjunct professor from 1977 to 1981. He lectured, as well, at New York University and City College of New York.

His serious interest in the theater emerged following a series of experiences that included service with the Air Force Reserve, a job with a London publisher, and extensive hitchhiking through Europe that concluded in Cairo, Egypt. While in the service, he stopped going to Mass. In Rome, he read newspaper accounts of the pope's impending visit to New York in 1965, and in Cairo, he received a letter from his parents about the pope's ride through Queens on his way to speak at the United Nations. The letter pushed into perspective the events of his own life in a Joycean epiphany. He fell to imagining his mother's reaction to the visit and "was suddenly intensely in touch with myself and my past." He returned to New York in July of 1966, having written

act 1 of his first New York success, *The House of Blue Leaves* (1971). In its completed form, the play is crowded with images of his life up to 1965.

Unable to finish the play because of the death of his father shortly after his return, he did accede to having the first act staged at the O'Neill Playhouse in Connecticut. He became active in the protests against the Vietnam War and was once knocked unconscious by a kick from a policeman's horse. Troubled by the fact that there were decent people on both sides of the protests, Guare once more left for Europe, where he finished *The House of Blue Leaves*, returning home in 1970 to enjoy its production at the Off-Broadway Truck and Warehouse Theater in New York in 1971. The play was then successfully revived in 1986 at the prestigious Lincoln Center Vivian Beaumont Theater, which soon became his stage home in New York. His other two major plays, *Six Degrees of Separation* (1990) and *Four Baboons Adoring the Sun* (1992), were produced there as well.

His lesser plays include *Muzeeka* (1967), the musical *Two Gentlemen of Verona*, for which he wrote the lyrics (1971), *Marco Polo Sings a Solo* (1973), *Rich and Famous* (1976), *Landscape of the Body* (1977), *Bosoms and Neglect* (1979), *Lydie Breeze* (1982), *Gardenia* (1982), *Women and Water* (1983), and *Moon Over Miami* (1988). He has, as well, joined with playwrights Austin Gray, Romulus Finney, Jean Claude Van Itallie, Edward Albee, and Christopher Durang, each writing a segment of *Faustus in Hell* (1985) and with seven writers, among them David Mamet and Wendy Wasserstein, in adapting stories from Anton Chekhov in a production entitled *Orchards* (1987).

Guare served as playwright-in-residence at the New York Shakespeare Festival Public Theater in 1976 and 1977; his other activities include coeditorship of the Lincoln Center *New Theater Review*. He has received many honors for his plays, including a Tony Award two Obie Awards, two New York Drama Critics Circle Awards, and an Award of Merit from the American Academy and Institute of Arts and Letters. For his screenwriting, he has been honored with the New York, Los Angeles, and National Film Critics Circle Awards. A fellow of the New York Institute for the Humanities and a member of the council of the Dramatists Guild, Guare lives in New York with his wife, the former Adele Chatfield-Taylor.

Analysis

Guare's play titles are an important indication of the theatricality of his style, suggesting dynamism that is spectacular in its sensory and artistic images. In *The House of Blue Leaves*, there are the American icons of song, food, and a bomb; in *Six Degrees of Separation*, a double-sided Wassily Kandinsky painting; and in *Four Baboons Adoring the Sun*, an incredible massing of art and myth imagery: an Egyptian sculpture (from the Louvre) of four baboons staring blindly into the sun; a nearly naked, singing Eros, skirting the rim of the stage throughout; the assigning of mythical names to children; and, finally, the play's locale, archaeological digs in Sicily, to which a recently married couple have brought their nine children from previous marriages.

Images, musical and visual, are Guare's vehicles for messages involving the yearnings of his characters for material success and then for something spiritual beyond the disillusionments that contemporary values have either denied or provided them. In the first of Guare's trilogy of major plays, fame haunts Artie Shaughnessy but in the end denies him, and he is left with the ashes of his life. In the second, affluence and the good life are Ouisa Kittredge's, but she discovers them to be hollow. In the third play, Penny McKenzie takes Ouisa's questioning a step further in the form of a spiritual quest that includes all eleven members of her newly formed family.

With his strong academic background, Guare has gradually moved his latest characters beyond the borders of America and the twentieth century to the time and space of mythical reality. In one play, realism and myth blend in an Icarus character who flies too close to the sun and falls to his death. Yet even in Guare's early plays, there is the Greek sense of lives haunted by the pursuit of truth and the eventual acceptance of the sometimes disastrous consequences of that search. Deaths occur in all three of his major plays.

In his portrayal of urban and suburban America, Guare paints with a highly theatrical brush. In his plays nuns maneuver to see the pope while a political activist plots to bomb him, even as domestic problems vie with national events for attention. Complacently affluent couples have their lives disrupted by an imposter posing as Sidney Poitier's son. Disrupted families seeking harmony in Sicily find not only that their pasts haunt them but also that their problems continue into the present.

Guare combines visual techniques with musical ones, an important aspect of his personal life. The dissonances in the Shaughnessys' lives are matched by the jangling ditties that Artie constantly plays and sings throughout *The House of Blue Leaves*. The soliloquies (like operatic arias) in *Six Degrees of Separation* function as Hamlet-like self-questionings. The antiphonal dialogues, the soliloquies, and the chants of Eros successfully fuse the dissonances into a music of life in *Four Baboons Adoring the Sun* as in no other of Guare's plays.

Structurally, Guare's plays reflect the techniques of absurdist theater, with disconnected plots unhindered by logic or chronology. Guare abandoned the episodic structure of the two acts in *The House of Blue Leaves* for a ninety-minute, intermissionless form in *Six Degrees of Separation* and *Four Baboons Adoring the Sun*. The result is a drama in which the themes are so sharply focussed and images so crowded that their density and brilliance can be blinding if, like Guare's four baboons, one stares too long and too hard.

Like Chekhov's uses of the seagull and the cherry orchard and Tennessee Williams' uses of a glass menagerie and a streetcar, Guare's blue leaves and baboons provide him with images that reveal truths reaching into lives of each character. His titular imagery is reinforced within the plays by his use of the arts. Music, important in Guare's life, is a natural part of his plays. A painting in one play and a sculpture in another may seem contrived to some. Yet in combination, domestic realism, myth, and art provide, respectively, emotional, intellectual, and visual rewards for those who choose to "stare into the sun."

Guare's overall theme is the American suburban family in all of its aspirations and losses. The dysfunctional Shaughnessy family—composed of a wayward son, an insane wife and mother, and a husband and father who works at a zoo and entertains Hollywood dreams—is bombarded by the media. The family in *Six Degrees of Separation* has realized its dream, only to undergo disturbing intrusions by those who have not enjoyed its affluence. In *Four Baboons Adoring the Sun*, two middle-class families—one headed by a university professor of archaeology and the other by a congressman—are the victims of divorces. In a marriage of two of the divorced parents, there is an attempt to unify the disparate experiences of each group of children, for whom there looms yet the marriages of the other two divorced parents, with further family relationships to be embraced or rejected.

Guare's comment on society reaches a sophisticated savagery in its portrayal of the supposed insularity of the successful family in *Six Degrees of Separation*. The same society contains a drug-and-crime culture to which the privileged have become so impervious that only the imposters can penetrate it. A struggling young couple, newly arrived in New York to make their way in the theater world, become innocent victims of the same scams made necessary, it would seem, by the insularity of wealth and fame.

Yet the largest truth in Guare's suburban universe is, perhaps, found in the questioning and the quest, respectively, of a Ouisa and a Penny in the hope of attaining some solution to the problems. Such solutions may ultimately be found only in the mythical truths, so old and yet so persistently relevant.

THE HOUSE OF BLUE LEAVES

First produced: 1971 (first published, 1971)
Type of work: Play

The collision of dreary middle-class reality with ideals of Hollywood success destroys the world of an untalented song writer.

What happens in the lives of the family of a middle-aged zoo keeper, Artie Shaughnessy, in Queens, New York, on October 4, 1965—the day of the pope's journey through Queens—is the result of an explosive combination of a lifetime of dreams and realities. Blending historical and personal events, Guare describes the play in his introduction as "a blur of many years that pulled together under the umbrella of the Pope's visit."

Based on Guare's father (who referred to his Wall Street job as a "zoo"), Artie comes home from his job to an untidy house. At home, he devotes his time to playing and singing corny jingles that he has written, with dreams of Hollywood success constantly on his mind. His household consists of his insane wife, Bananas; his mistress, Bunny Flingus, who lives in the apartment below; and his eighteen-year-old son, Ronnie, currently a serviceman stationed in Fort Dix, New Jersey.

Artie, with the knowledge of Bunny, is in the process of making arrangements to put Bananas into an asylum. Ronnie arrives, unnoticed, with a box of explosives intended for the pope but which, in the course of the play's manic action, go off accidentally, killing three visitors, two nuns, and a visiting Hollywood actress. Ronnie, Bunny, and three visiting nuns maneuver to get as near the pope as they can, each for personal reasons. Among the frenetic events and images of the play, one of the most hilarious is that of the nuns, whose dreams of seeing the pope in person are thwarted; one ends up photographing another who is hugging the television picture of the pope.

The play's title derives from Artie's description of a tree near the asylum to which he plans to remove his insane wife. To get out of the rain, he walks under the tree, the leaves of which turn into birds "waiting to go to Florida or California." After the birds' flight to another tree, the bare tree bursts into blossom again. Like those unrealistic blue leaves, the fantasies of Guare's characters keep returning, their insistence suggesting a permanence denied them in the practical world.

Guare's style, that of the dream in which anything can happen, brings together in one rich, highly detailed tapestry the diverse color and strands of his own life—Catholicism, politics, and art. He points to Ronnie's childhood scene with Uncle Billy—the one member of his family whose Hollywood dreams have been realized—as "an exact word-for-word reportage" of a boyhood event. The image of Billy hovers over the play from start to finish, its destructive influence symbolized by Ronnie's bomb. Dedicating the play to his parents, Guare seems to exorcise their hold on him: "I liked them, loved them, stayed too long, and didn't go away." His comment is a perverse variation of a song written by his father for Guare's mother before Guare's birth.

SIX DEGREES OF SEPARATION

First produced: 1990 (first published, 1990)
Type of work: Play

A confidence man posing as the son of Sidney Poitier causes chaos and moral self-questionings by his audacious invasions into the lives of privileged urban American families.

In *Six Degrees of Separation*, a young black man named Paul educates himself in order to pull off a daring scam. He enlists the aid of a high-school friend and accumulates the addresses of a number of wealthy New York families. He becomes familiar with the names of family members, their possessions, and customs. He is trained by the friend, now a student at the Massachusetts Institute of Technology (MIT), to speak the language of the upper class. Fully armed with a knowledge of upper-class tribal customs and rites, he passes himself off as a friend of the families' offspring enrolled at Ivy League universities.

Like Don Quixote of old, he sallies forth, but without the Don's ideals. He goes so far as to stab himself before intruding at the home of Ouisa and Flan Kittredge, sophisticated and affluent dealers of art. When he appears, he is bleeding, pleads having been robbed, and invokes friendship with their children, Tess and Woody, including knowledge of a "double" Kandinsky painting that hangs on their wall. He exudes the kind of charm, knowledge, and manners expected of a son of Sidney Poitier. His success consists of acquiring the façade of a member of the social tribe to which the Kittredges belong. Furthermore, he whets the interest of his victims by posing the possibility of their playing in a new film his "father" is in New York to cast (Guare's reinvention of a detail in *The House of Blue Leaves*) and by tales of how their children, away from home, freely discuss their parents.

Paul's downfall begins when he is discovered in Tess's bed with a male prostitute he has taken in off the streets. Other discoveries involve two families who had been similarly defrauded and, finally, a struggling Mormon couple from Utah, Rick and Elizabeth, who are in New York to study acting. This latter scam ends in Rick's suicide, and Paul eventually fails in his goals.

As in Greek tragedy, past events are the subject for a reevaluation of the present. The past is reenacted by means of short, abrupt, tension-creating lines of dialogue and by monologues delivered in asides directly addressed to the audience. Ouisa, in particular, as Guare's version of the Greek chorus, reveals moral questionings that throw her self-centered existence into a tailspin.

The play's title derives from Ouisa's ruminations about the comforting theory that only six "degrees"—six people—separate one from everyone else on the planet. The quandary is to find those six and thus to realize the connection. She experiences the dilemma, and her theory is the basis for Guare's simultaneously funny and searing exploration of contemporary mores and manners.

FOUR BABOONS ADORING THE SUN

First produced: 1992 (first published, 1993)
Type of work: Play

A recently married American couple bring to Sicily their nine children from previous marriages in an attempt to forge familial and individual identities beyond those offered by American culture.

The questioning of the rewards of success in the lives of Ouisa and Flan Kittredge in *Six Degrees of Separation* are again enacted in *Four Baboons Adoring the Sun*. Here, however, the couple—Penny and Philip McKenzie—and their children (ranging in age from thirteen to seven) are younger. Philip has left his successful "empire" as an archaeology professor at a California university, and Penny has severed her typical suburban existence "off Exit 4 of the Connecticut Turnpike" as wife of a congressman. Having realized the rewards of the American Dream, both need, more than anything, change and love, and they wish the same for their children.

In Philip's words, there are two universes—Universe A, which is "all facts and reasons and explanations," and Universe B, the universe of childhood, which is essentially mythic. It is this mythic level to which the play aspires. In no other play has Guare so richly invested the style and symbols of myth; for example, the family's children are given mythic names (the most important of which is Wayne's appellation of Icarus). The mythical ambience is created immediately with the appearance of Eros, Guare's version of the Greek chorus. As background to the action, Eros is onstage throughout, chanting aspirations and forebodings in the tradition of the chorus. Beyond Eros, there is a replica of a 4000-year-old granite Egyptian sculpture of four baboons who have stared at the sun until they are blinded. Wayne (Icarus), in a forbidden love with his new sister Halcy, feels trapped in a labyrinth his father has created. He climbs a nearby mountain and falls to his death.

The exotic myth imagery in the play blends with the poetically framed dialogue, in which realistic contemporary American speech is stylized in the manner of the stichomythia of classical drama. Realism and myth are one as the eldest children question the parents in incantatory lines:

Wayne: Did you hate Mom?
Halcy: Did you hate Dad?
Penny: No.
Philip: Yes.

The antiphonal nature of the questions and responses in which parents and children participate transforms the play into a ritual without diluting the realism of their respective situations. The play ends with Eros chanting about choices he offers and with parents and children choosing their futures. Penny, like Philip's Wayne, chooses to "leap into space." Philip, like Penny's Halcy, chooses not to leap, and he will return to his university.

Summary

Guare was influenced by Chekhov and Henrik Ibsen in his younger years, and he acknowledges the existence, from Aeschylus on down, of what has been labeled in the twentieth century as the Theater of the Absurd. He goes on to say that "the absurd is that which generates music." In the ditties composed and sung by Artie Shaughnessy, in Ouisa Kittredge's poetic reachings for a reality beyond that she has known, and in the McKenzie family's realization of a mythic reality, Guare has caught the music of life in the suburbs of contemporary America, in its lofty aspirations and its phoniness—all exposed at some point to the harsh glare of the sun.

Bibliography

Bosworth, Patricia. "Yes for a Young Man's Fantasies." *The New York Times*, March 7, 1971, p. II1.

Cohn, Ruby. *New American Dramatists: 1960-1990*. 2d ed. New York: St. Martin's Press, 1991.

DiGaetani, John L. *A Search for a Postmodern Theater: Interviews with Contemporary Playwrights*. New York: Greenwood Press, 1991.

Guernsey, Otis L., ed. *Playwrights, Lyricists, Composers on Theatre*. New York: Dodd, Mead, 1975.

Harris, William. "For John Guare a Return to Roots in the Comic Style." *The New York Times*, June 10, 1990, p. II7.

Rich, Frank. "Desperate for a Reason to Live in an Alien World." *The New York Times*, March 19, 1992, p. C15.

Susan Rusinko

JOY HARJO

Born: Tulsa, Oklahoma
May 9, 1951

Principal Literary Achievement

As one of the leading contemporary Native American poets, Joy Harjo has contributed to a broader understanding of her people's struggle to survive within American culture.

Biography

Joy Harjo was born in Tulsa, Oklahoma on May 9, 1951, the daughter of a Creek Indian father, Allen W. Foster, and a Cherokee French mother, Wynema Baker Foster. She enrolled as a member of the Creek tribe and at the age of sixteen moved to Santa Fe, New Mexico, to attend the Institute of American Indian Arts.

She became increasingly interested in writing, and in 1975, while she was a student at the University of New Mexico, her first book was published. *The Last Song* includes nine poems set in Oklahoma and New Mexico that articulate her deep connection to the land. Harjo lived in Oklahoma and, as she told Geary Hobson in a 1979 interview, those memories are forever with her. "When I was a little kid in Oklahoma, I would get up before everyone else and go outside to a place of rich, dark earth next to the foundation of the house. I would dig piles of earth with a stick, smell it, form it. It had sound. Maybe that's where I learned to write poetry."

In 1976, she received her B.A. in poetry from the University of New Mexico and in 1978 received her M.F.A. in creative writing from the University of Iowa. That same year, she was awarded a fellowship from the National Endowment for the Arts and returned to teach at the Institute of American Indian Arts for a year.

What Moon Drove Me to This?, Harjo's second book, came out in 1980. It was her first full-length book and included all the poems from *The Last Song* as well as new ones. In this collection, she continued to use Native American images to expose the truths beneath the surface of ordinary experiences, especially those of women. She also introduced a personality, Noni Daylight, who sees clearly because she moves between realms of time and space.

While continuing to write, she also taught at other institutions. In 1980 and 1981, she was a part-time instructor in creative writing and poetry at Arizona State University. Returning to the Institute of American Indian Arts, she taught there from 1983 to

1985. In 1983, her best-known volume, *She Had Some Horses*, was published. In it Harjo refines her earlier images and ideas into clearly defined poems revolving around the theme of freedom through self-knowledge. The title poem is one of Harjo's most-anthologized works.

From 1985 to 1988 she taught at the University of Colorado and from 1988 to 1990 at the University of Arizona. In 1989, she collaborated with photographer Stephen Strom on *Secrets from the Center of the World*. Her prose poetry describing the beauty and truths of the land accompanies his photographs of the Four Corners area in Navajo Indian country.

In 1990, she began teaching at the University of New Mexico as a full professor. That same year, her latest book, *In Mad Love and War*, appeared. A departure from her previous writing, the volume moves beyond Native American symbols and images and contains narratives about people whose lives have failed, affecting the balance and order of those who survive.

In addition to writing and teaching, Harjo is accomplished in several other areas. She has done much screenwriting and has written teleplays, public-service announcements, and educational television programs. In 1985, she wrote the film script *Origin of Apache Crown Dance* and coauthored another, *The Beginning*. She continues to contribute to literary journals and has edited several, including *High Plains Review*, *Tyuonyi*, and *Contract II*. In 1986, she made the tape *Furious Light*, on which she read selected poems accompanied by music. Music is an important part of her life; she plays the saxophone and the flute and has performed in rock, big-band, and jazz bands.

Harjo also travels to many readings, workshops, and literary festivals, so her work reaches a larger audience than does that of many poets. She serves on several advisory boards, including the Native American Public Broadcasting Consortium and the New Mexico Arts Commission. In addition to her several visiting professorships and writer-in-residence posts, she has participated in the Artists-in-the-Schools program, which exposes public school students to working artists of all kinds.

Harjo has received many awards and grants in addition to her National Endowment for the Arts Fellowship. She is the recipient of the American Book Award from the Before Columbus Foundation, the Poetry Society of America's William Carlos Williams Award, and the American Indian Distinguished Achievement Award. She has two children, Phil and Rainy Dawn.

Analysis

Joy Harjo's Native American heritage is an important part of her writing. In her poetry, she often uses Creek Indian myths and symbols. By setting these within the larger context of American life, she illustrates the fears that lie below the surface of actions and events. Many of her poems tell about the lives of people, especially women, in which the natural order of things has been violated. Her images and musical poetic techniques emphasize the emotions present in these situations, and her themes point out a desire for harmony and order. To Harjo, realizing these fears is the first

Magill's Survey of American Literature

step to the self-knowledge needed to be free and empowered.

Using traditional Native American images juxtaposed with images of modern America enables Harjo to emphasize the clash of values. In her first collection, _The Last Song_, the poem "3AM" describes two Indians in the Albuquerque airport standing amidst the chrome and lights surrounding an airline ticket counter. They want to find their way back, "and the attendant doesn't know that third mesa is part of the center of the world." The Indians are at odds with the rest of the world, unable to find direction anywhere. Mainstream culture does not recognize ways other than its own. In "White Bear," a later poem from the 1980 work _She Had Some Horses_, Harjo uses the same theme, describing a woman ready to board her flight in Albuquerque who stops in the tunnel leading to the plane. She sees her whole life as a state in between staying and leaving, forever existing in the grey area of not knowing who she is. Life becomes a continual balancing act.

For many Native Americans, this ambiguous existence leads to lives in which they cannot realize their dreams. In "The Woman Hanging from the Thirteenth Floor Window" from _She Had Some Horses_, Harjo describes the Indian woman's precarious position as representing "all the women of the apartment/ building who stand watching her." The section of the book in which the poem appears is called "Survivors" because the people described are victims. Only those who can conquer that victim mentality and the fears and the ambiguities that accompany it will survive the clash of values and the disruption of nature and order. _In Mad Love and War_ details the lives and deaths of people whose heroic deeds live on to infuse the living with the spirit of conquest.

To deal with this subject matter, Harjo uses several recurring images throughout the body of her work. In her second book, she introduced the figure of Noni Daylight, a mystical personage who can move within all spheres, real and mythical, throughout time and place. Because Noni can go anywhere, she can see things from any perspective. Harjo continued to use this figure in her 1980 collection, as in "Kansas City," in which Noni is a "dishrag wrung out over bones watching trains come and go." The moon, another of Harjo's favorite images, takes many guises: lover, spirit, guide, and woman. In an early poem, "Going Toward Pojoaque, a December Full Moon/ 72," the moon is a spirit, a "winter ghost . . . so bright I could see the bones in my hand." In a later poem, "Moonlight," from the 1980 book, the moon is a cruel lover; "the last time I saw her was in the arms of another sky." Perhaps the image Harjo is best known for is the horse, which she used for her most popular poem, "She Had Some Horses." Harjo uses the horse in many poems, working with all the qualities associated with the animal: strength, freedom, grace, fury, stubbornness. Horses represent these different aspects of life and also of individual people. The symbol is as ancient as the Native American culture, harking back to humanity's prehistoric beginnings.

Harjo uses these images to focus on several themes, all of which are related to the central one of survival. Throughout her collections of poetry, she sees nature as disrupted and people as needing order and balance to restore their lives to wholeness.

This wholeness includes a connectedness with the past, so she mingles the past and the present, as well as the mythic and the ordinary, in the same poems. Looking at things from this vantage of wholeness enables people to see more clearly and to articulate fears. Naming fears, in turn, allows people to deal with them positively. In "I Give You Back," the final poem in *She Had Some Horses*, Harjo writes, "I release you. . . ./ I am not afraid." Losing the fear is the first step toward empowerment.

Her 1990 work becomes more strident. The poems still use Native American landscapes and symbols, but they reach beyond these references. The narrators tell stories of those survivors who have failed because of political violence. They are being eradicated by modern society, but their voices remain as an inspiration for those who live on. They will be heard, like Alva and the others in "For Alva Benson, and for Those Who Have Learned to Speak," who, despite hardships, raised their voices and found an identity. This preoccupation with social concerns led some critics to object that Harjo was becoming too "politically correct" in dealing with the causes. Her main theme, however, has remained the same: survival. In the 1990's, she has simply used different terms.

SHE HAD SOME HORSES

First published: 1983
Type of work: Poem

Using the horse as a many-faceted symbol, Harjo celebrates truths about the human spirit.

"She Had Some Horses," Harjo's most frequently anthologized work, is the title poem from the 1983 collection of the same name. In it, she achieves a beautiful, chantlike quality by repeating the three words "She had horses" at the beginning of each line. She also uses the phrase "she had some horses" as a one-line refrain following each stanza. These poetic techniques not only unify the poem but also add emotional impact to its theme, a celebration of human nature in all of its aspects. The many characteristics attributed to the horses represent the many complicated facets of the human spirit.

In the first stanza, the horses are described as things that can be broken, ephemeral things that are hard to pin down: "bodies of sand," "splintered red cliff," and "skins of ocean water." These are natural elements that can be damaged but will reemerge in some form. This is the cycle of nature, and the human spirit too follows this pattern.

In the next section, Harjo juxtaposes these images to human characteristics that are aggressive, protruding, and sharp: "horses with long, pointed breasts," and "horses who licked razor blades." These images, in contrast with those in the first stanza, reveal the threatening nature of humanity's intrusion on the delicate balance of the natural order.

Harjo continues to symbolize human traits in the next two stanzas, which cover a wide range of human activity. "She had horses" who "danced in their mothers' arms," "waltzed nightly on the moon," "liked Creek Stomp Dance songs," and "told the truth, who were stripped/ bare of their tongues." These phrases refer to Native American myths and images, but as actions they also apply to any human being.

In the next stanza, Harjo refers to names, "horses who called themselves 'horse' '' and "horses who had no names." A name identifies a unique human being. As people experience life, their identities go through changes. In one period of life, one name may apply; in another period, perhaps another is more suitable. Changing names points up the complex ways in which people see themselves. Like the changing images of nature in the first stanza, human nature is difficult to pin down.

In the next two stanzas, Harjo's images become darker. She speaks of destruction and fear: "Horses who screamed out of fear of the silence" and "who/ carried knives to protect themselves from ghosts." Their fear is intense, but they are powerless; they "waited for destruction" and "waited for resurrection." In the last stanza, Harjo becomes more bitter. She speaks of the horses "who got down on their knees for any saviour" and who "climbed in her/ bed at night and prayed as they raped her." This is the climax of the poem, as the complex images of the human spirit tumble in upon each other.

The poem ends in a direct two-line statement followed by a different refrain: "She had some horses she loved./ She had some horses she hated./ These were the same horses." The horse, with its many associations and symbols, stands for things in all people. Love and hate can coexist. Recognizing this complexity makes each woman a true individual. Harjo's women are strong and have the capacity to name and face even fears of destruction. As with the wild horse, the power lies within each of them, waiting to be released.

JAVELINA

First published: 1990
Type of work: Poem

Like the javelina, a wild boar whose feeding grounds have been usurped by civilization, the Native American must fight to survive in a society that has violated the natural order.

"Javelina," from the 1990 book *In Mad Love and War*, is an example of Harjo's prose poetry. The poem consists of four "paragraphs," with a two-line stanza appearing between the second and third. Harjo aligns herself firmly with those "born of a blood/ who wrestled the whites for freedom" and who have "lived dangerously in/ a diminished system." Comparing a young woman with the wild boar, the javelina, she tells the story of a displaced young Native American couple coming to the city.

Harjo introduces the javelina in the first stanza. At dusk, the animal comes out to feed. History, though, has violated the natural order of things. Housing developments have encroached upon the desert, so the javelina has learned to live and forage among the trappings of civilization. The setting then switches to the city. The poet describes driving the streets of South Tucson, an area of poor housing and ethnic minorities, where she identifies with a young Indian woman who is standing at a pay phone holding a baby. The poet imagines why the girl may be there: Perhaps her car has broken down, or perhaps she needs a job. Like the wild boar, the woman seeks sustenance in an alien environment. The poet feels a kinship with both the animal and the woman. Both know the displacement of the natural ways by the white civilization, which does not allow them room to grow.

The poet wishes that she could stop the car and tell the young woman that all will be well for her and her child, that "*the mythic world will enter*" and the "*wounded spirit*" will turn into a beautiful butterfly. Yet the poet knows better. The girl has lost hope and would not believe such dreams of a happy future.

The poet leaves as the girl's husband arrives with more change for the phone. The poet remembers the years that she has prayed for life-giving rain, which symbolically brings hope for the beaten spirit of the Native American as it does literally for the dry crops and waiting animals in the desert. The poet then turns her thoughts again to the javelinas, imagining the animals speaking of "the coolest promise of spiny leaves." This dream is tempered by reality: "Their prevalent nightmare has entered recent genetic memory, as the/ smell of gunpowder mixed with human sweat." The poem ends with a comment from an elder javelina "with thick tusks of wisdom." He knows the desert without the white presence: "*It is sweeter than the/ blooms of prickly pear. It is sweeter than rain.*"

Into the words of the animal, Harjo puts her passionate feelings about the ways in which the balance of nature has been destroyed by a system that forces people to become scavengers. Like the javelina foraging for food, the Native American skirts the edges of a wealthy society. Like the javelina, which is unseen by most people, the talents of the young Native American girl go unnoticed; she has been made to think that she has nothing worthwhile to say. The vitality that she could bring to society is lost. Like the javelina, however, Native American culture and people are tough. As the poem illustrates this truth, it also asserts the right to an orderly society open to all people.

FOR ANNA MAE PICTOU AQUASH, WHOSE SPIRIT IS PRESENT HERE AND IN THE DAPPLED STARS (for we remember the story and must tell it again so we may all live)

First published: 1990
Type of work: Poem

The dreams of those who died violently will not be lost, but will endure as inspiration to the living.

"For Anna Mae Pictou Aquash, Whose Spirit Is Present Here and in the Dappled Stars (for we remember the story and must tell it again so we may all live)" appeared in Harjo's 1990 volume *In Mad Love and War*. The poem is a narrative describing the poet's reaction to the story of a woman whose message and dreams were silenced by an early, violent death. Harjo juxtaposes Native American images of nature with contemporary urban images to re-create the true story of Anna Mae Aquash in the hope that the story will remain forever as inspiration.

Harjo appends a note to the text to explain the poem's context. In February, 1976, the body of a young woman was found on the Pine Ridge Reservation in South Dakota. An autopsy attributed the death to exposure, and the unnamed body was buried. Later, after friends and relatives discovered that Anna Mae Aquash, a young woman who had been active in the American Indian Movement, was missing, they demanded another autopsy. This time, evidence revealed that the woman's death had been caused by a bullet fired into the back of her head at close range. Anna Mae Aquash's killer was never found.

Harjo begins the poem by describing her amazement at finding beauty when nature arises at the end of winter. She compares a small crocus emerging from the ground with the way she herself feels each morning when she awakes. She comments that it is natural to understand this scheme of things, in which, despite destruction, nature continues and "everything and nothing changes."

Next the poet directly addresses Anna, "the shimmering young woman/ who found her voice" after she was threatened with harm if she continued to speak. She did continue, like an "elegant weed," a persistent plant that cannot be tamed. Although she was cut down like a weed, her spirit continues, "present in the dappled stars." This spirit, prancing with the energy of an untamed horse, remains with people who pursue truth. The spirit persists even in cold, unlikely places, such as "steely cities," thriving where nothing seems to grow, "nuzzling the frozen bodies of tattered drunks/ on the corner."

In the midst of big-city traffic, the poet remembers Anna's second burial, which was conducted in the Lakota Indian dialect, "a language that could/ free you." Heard by Native Americans everywhere, her message lives on, especially among the women, who, because of their intimacy with birth and death, understand well the changing of the seasons. They know that they are poised to understand centuries of buried anger.

Recalling the death of Anna brings all of these feelings to the surface to be articulated: "we have just begun to perceive the amazed world the ghost dancers entered/ crazily, beautifully." The poem ends with new understanding of the meaning of Anna's death. Like other poems in the collection, it reflects Harjo's Creek Indian heritage and her close identification with those whose lives and dreams have been thwarted in the pursuit of truth.

Summary

In a 1989 interview, Joy Harjo remarked that "I write poetry because it is a way to travel into internal landscapes/starscapes which also become the external. It helps in traveling between many worlds and helps in speaking them."

By creating images that bridge the gap between Native American concepts of the world and those of mainstream culture, Harjo's poetry reveals what happens when the two worlds collide. Her work illuminates the harmony and balance necessary not merely for Native Americans or women but for all people.

Bibliography

Balassi, William, John F. Crawford, and Annie O. Eysturoy, eds. *This Is About Vision*. Albuquerque: University of New Mexico Press, 1990.

Bruchac, Joseph. *Survival This Way: Interviews with American Indian Poets*. Tucson: University of Arizona Press, 1987.

Gwynn, R. S., ed. *American Poets Since World War II*. Vol. 120 in *Dictionary of Literary Biography*. Detroit: Gale Research, 1992.

Hobson, Geary, ed. *The Remembered Earth: An Anthology of Contemporary Native American Literature*. Albuquerque, N.Mex.: Red Earth Press, 1979.

Scarry, John. "Representing Real Worlds: The Evolving Poetry of Joy Harjo." *World Literature Today* 66 (Spring, 1992): 286-291.

Ullman, Leslie. "Seven Poets: Reviews." *Kenyon Review* 13 (Spring, 1991): 180-182.

Louise M. Stone

MICHAEL S. HARPER

Born: Brooklyn, New York
March 18, 1938

Principal Literary Achievement

While Harper's poetry is crucially connected to African American history and music, his use of language and form places him in the mainstream of contemporary American poetry.

Biography

Michael Steven Harper was born in Brooklyn, New York, on March 18, 1938, the son of Walter and Katherine (Johnson) Harper. He was reared in a household that treasured music, and he met several prominent jazz musicians when he was a young boy. After his family moved to Los Angeles in 1951, he combined a variety of jobs (postal clerk, aspiring professional football player) with a personally designed program of enthusiastic, eclectic reading, including African American poets such as Sterling Brown, Langston Hughes, and Gwendolyn Brooks. He entered Los Angeles City College in the late 1950's and was graduated with a B.A. from California State College in 1961. He proceeded to a graduate degree in 1963 before entering the M.F.A. program in writing at the University of Iowa.

He began to teach in 1964 as an instructor in English at Contra Costa College in San Pablo, California, where, he has said, he felt that "my poetry began to be distinctly my own . . . when I was teaching and able to look at poetry as something I loved to do and probably could do all my life." He was married in 1965 to Shirley Buffington, and he took a position as poet-in-residence at Lewis and Clark College in Portland, Oregon, from 1968 to 1969. While there, he prepared the manuscript of his first book of poetry, *Dear John, Dear Coltrane*, which was published by the University of Pittsburgh Press in 1970. Before accepting a position as associate professor of English at Brown University in 1970, Harper spent some time traveling in Mexico and Europe.

As he began to publish regularly in the 1970's, Harper received recognition from the literary community, including a Black Academy of Arts and Letters Award in 1972 for his second volume of poetry, *History Is Your Own Heartbeat* (1971), a Guggenheim fellowship in 1976, a National Endowment for the Arts creative writing award in 1977, and a nomination for a National Book Award for poetry, as well as the Melville Cane Award in 1978 for *Images of Kin: New and Selected Poems* (1977).

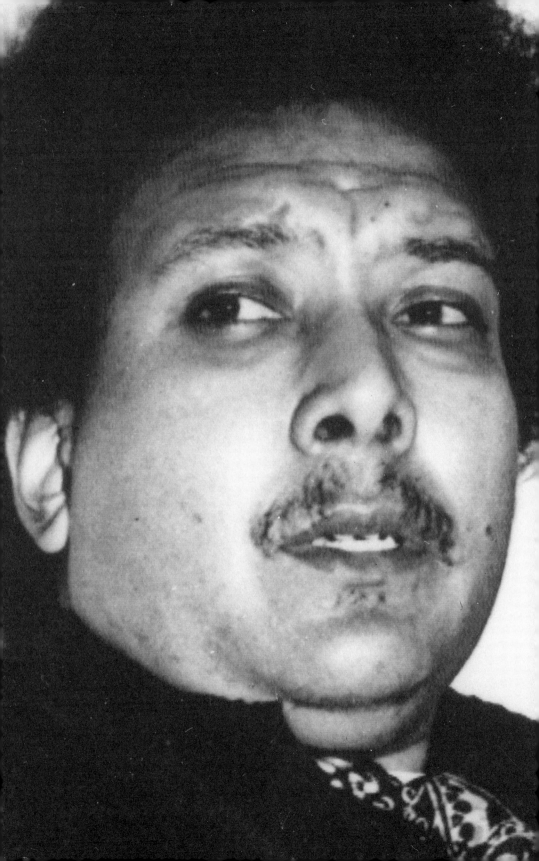

During the 1970's and 1980's, Harper held positions as a poet-in-residence, visiting writer, and distinguished professor of English at several universities in the United States and in Europe and Africa. In 1983, he became I. J. Kapstein Professor of English at Brown University.

The publication of *Healing Song for the Inner Ear* in 1985 (along with the release of a videotape, *The Poetry of Michael Harper*, which he made for the Brockport Writers Forum in 1985), his contributions to numerous anthologies, and his work on numerous editorials boards have established Harper as an important American writer.

The experience of life as an African American has been a major part of Michael Harper's work, but Harper has always vigorously resisted an obligation to write according to the expectations or demands of any particular group. In an interview, he complained about "people who are in influential positions" who ask "people who have been kicked in the teeth how it feels." Harper goes on to say that "the first act of liberation is always to destroy one's own cage," and he has refused to accept any categorization of his work.

His insistence on defining his art as a part of a "totality larger than man" has led him toward a poetics that depends on several important principles of coherence. The most encompassing is an awareness of his relationship to history, including the historic experiences of African Americans and the crucial individual historical moments of his own life. Without ever assuming that he is a "spokesman" for his community, he has accepted the social obligation of addressing historical incidents that seem of particular importance in his judgment. He was moved to write "Grandfather" (1974) both to honor the life of his own grandfather and to correct the "false weight given to elements of the Civil War and its aftermath" that he had seen in D. W. Griffith's 1915 film The Birth of a Nation. Poems about the abolitionist John Brown, the experiences of soldiers in World War II and in Vietnam, and the murder of black children in a Birmingham church, as well as poems celebrating heroic figures from African American history such as Harriet Tubman and Sojourner Truth, are a part of Harper's effort to help people see where they have been so they can know where they must try to go. "When there is no history," Harper says in *Debridement* (1973), "there is no metaphor"; a nation without historical knowledge is "blind," trapped in ignorance.

Harper also regards kinship—his family (in the literal and largest human sense)—as an essential element in understanding history. His title *History Is Your Own Heartbeat* suggests "that there is a relationship between a single beating heart and all hearts beating," and he builds outward from his "Images of Kin," using the Aristotelian principle of the universality of intense individual experience. In addition to his well-known poem about his grandfather, Harper has written with insight and poignancy about his immediate family, looking with compassion at his wife's mother in "Blue Ruth: America" (1971) as she recovers from a serious operation; reflecting in sorrow on the death of his second son in "We Assume: On the Death of Our Son, Reuben Masai Harper" (1970); writing in love and remembrance for his brother Jonathan in "The Drowning of the Facts of a Life" (1985). He has also widened the family circle to include noteworthy members of his cultural family, finding appropriate language and the right angle of perception to cite and explain the significance of important, often heroic figures from black history, including Paul Robeson, Willie Mays, Alice Walker, Richard Wright, Malcolm X, and Bessie Smith.

While he has accepted the traditional role of the poet as the speaking memory of an often-suppressed culture, the distinctly personal features of Harper's poetry derive from a response to the heritage of the African American community that is an expression of what has moved and touched him in some profound way. Although many black artists have written with insight and enthusiasm about jazz, Harper's relationship with modern jazz has a special quality, exemplified in the title poem of his first book *Dear John, Dear Coltrane* (1970). "I loved John Coltrane, and I loved his music," Harper has said, "I loved the kind of intensity he brought to his playing and I loved his commitment." In the lives and performances of the great black contemporary musicians whom he discusses, addresses, eulogizes, and often brings to a radiant reality in his poetry, Harper has found a modern icon for the African American community, a hero-figure with many human flaws. In jazz, he has found a continuing of the most vital, enduring legacies of an Afrocentric heritage. From such music—which is itself based on a fusion of ancient rhythms and modern modes—he has built a style of expression that is an individual version of a dynamic cultural energy source.

Harper has explained his uses of jazz structures by saying that the jazz idiom is "the best equivalent I could think of" for an oral poetry designed to be spoken or sung. Techniques of repetition, innovation, recapitulation, and exploration are further examples of parallels between jazz composition and Harper's work, but Harper is not trying to imitate or reproduce the sound of jazz. What is more important is the spirit that informs jazz. As Harper has put it, Coltrane "played through pain to a *love supreme*," using the title of one of Coltrane's most important albums as an emblem of his own vision of ideal existence. In his epigraph to *Images of Kin*, Harper almost cryptically observes that "A friend told me/ he'd risen above jazz/ I leave him there." His rueful tone indicates his disappointment that an African American could renounce such a fundamental part of the black cultural experience.

The structures of Harper's poems, and many of the technical devices he has employed, may find some correspondences in music, but they are also very much a function of Harper's knowledge of the entire tradition of poetry. His involvement with the jazz life goes beyond such influences; rather, jazz is the central symbol of black experience in his life and art.

DEAR JOHN, DEAR COLTRANE

First published: 1970
Type of work: Poem

John Coltrane, the great musician, is celebrated as an emblem of the struggle of black artists to speak the truth of their cultural experience.

From the first book of poetry he published, which used the name of John Coltrane in its title, through the fourth section of *Healing Song for the Inner Ear* (1985), which is called "My Book on Trane," and beyond, Michael Harper has written about the legendary composer and performer as a mythic but human figure whose life contains many of the most vital and troubling elements of black experience. "Dear John, Dear Coltrane," which is both an address to the spirit of the artist and a paen to his achievement, carries as an epigraph the title of one of Coltrane's most important albums, *A Love Supreme*. Harper quotes the phrase four times, establishing a rhythmic figure as a base against which much of the poem works as a form of improvisation or melodic variant. The long first stanza begins, in Harper's words, "as a catalogue of sexual trophies for whites," in which the anatomy of a slave in death or auction is reduced to the dubious market value of its separate parts. "Black men are potent," Harper explains, "and potency is obviously a great part of Coltrane's playing."

As the stanza continues, however, the price of this power is inverted so that it becomes a burden that a black man must accept or suffer, resisting the hatred and fear of racists and the tendency toward acquiescence of people beaten through centuries of oppression. The poem follows Coltrane from the countryside of his birth near Hamlet, North Carolina, to the "electric city"—symbol of sin, excitement, self-destruction, self-revelation, and redemption. "You pick up the horn/ with some will and blow/ into the freezing night:/ *a love supreme, a love supreme.*" This is a picture of initial success, the agony and pain of racial discrimination transmuted through musical magic into a song of exaltation.

The second stanza moves deeper into the "painful private life of black musicians." "Dawn comes," and to keep the mundane, daytime world at a distance a little longer, the musician is tempted to extend the euphoria of night and music with drugs. A struggle between "impotence and death" results in the entire life of the musician; "heart, genitals and sweat" become a fuel that burns in his saxophone, a kind of "cannibal" that consumes but that "makes you clean." The chorus, "*a love supreme*," works as a pause before the next melodic variation.

In the third stanza, written entirely in italic type, Harper imagines Coltrane's responses to questions about his power and commitment. A fearful query, "*Why you so black?*," is answered with a proud, self-evident proclamation, "*cause I am.*" The concluding stanza recalls Coltrane near the end of his short life, too sick to play comfortably but playing nevertheless. The final image of Coltrane's artistic commitment literally consuming and destroying his body but ennobling his spirit is a metaphor for black experience. "Your diseased liver gave/ out its purity,/ the inflated heart/ pumps out, the tenor kiss,/ tenor love."

The last chorus, which recapitulates the poem by restating the epigraph, the motivating force behind the struggle, "*a love supreme*" is like a motto for Harper's aspirations.

GRANDFATHER

First published: 1974
Type of work: Poem

The poet celebrates the strength of his grandfather, who lived honorably and independently in spite of many obstacles.

Harper describes the genesis of "Grandfather," from the collection *Nightmare Begins Responsibility*, as the showing of the D. W. Griffith film *The Birth of a Nation* in a college film course. He recalls his anger at the instructor's attempt to emphasize the technical achievement of the film while ignoring its racist, inaccurate presentation of the events following the Civil War. Harper was determined to tell the story of his grandfather and his father (who was born in 1915, the year of the film's release) as a testament to the reality of black life after the Civil War.

The first long stanza is primarily a recounting of factual information describing how his grandfather's "neighbors surrounded his house" planning to "burn/ his family out," as if this act of hatred could be the birth of their racist nation. This act is set in contrast with the humanity of the man himself, depicted with a simplicity that shows how his calm courage deflects the blind anger of the mob, a "posse decomposing" in confusion. There is a sudden shift from the past of the poem's initial setting to a present in which Harper envisions his grandfather, now in old age, still strong enough to win a footrace against the boy who will write the poem.

The last stanza of the poem continues in a mood of recollection, as Harper narrows the focus to the mundane but necessary acts of existence that define the reality of a man's life. His language becomes more lyrically evocative, as he is moved by the images of his grandfather. In spite of the grandfather's resilience and fortitude, he—like so many black men—finds "the great white nation immovable," and "his weight wilts," Yet this is not an expression of defeat, because the man has left an impression on "his grandson's eyes." As he says of his own father, whose "recollections in part were consummated in my writing," he was in his actions "their embodiment and their legacy"—an example of what Harper hopes to achieve in his art.

PEACE ON EARTH

First published: 1985
Type of work: Poem

In presenting the voice and thoughts of the mythic John Coltrane, Harper meditates on the power of poetry to illuminate human existence.

The last poem from Harper's collection *Healing Song for the Inner Ear*, "Peace on Earth" concludes a triad in which Harper moves beyond his previous addresses to and descriptions of jazz giants to enter the mind and soul of John Coltrane. Using a structure of separate image clusters produced by groupings of two and three lines, Harper not only recapitulates the highlights of Coltrane's life and work but also maintains a correspondence between the music and his own poetry, finding parallels between Coltrane's compositions and many of his own efforts.

Like the melodic motifs of a jazz composition, the twin themes of the sublime, transformative force of artistic inspiration fused with the idea of an artist's responsibility to the cultural legacy of his community are interwoven throughout the poem. The poem begins with an image of spiritual transcendence, as the speaker declares that moments of inspiration are closely connected to an attitude of religious reverence. "Tunes come to me at morning/ prayer," he says, extending the thought to include the nature of an individual's obligation to human decency by recalling how he "prayed at the shrine/ for the war dead broken/ at Nagasaki." This reference carries the poem beyond a specific local culture to an international linkage of human beings. The immediacy of his personal response, "the tears on the lip of my soprano/ glistened in the sun," establishes a close identification between the artist and his instrument, or the poet and his use of language.

After setting the conditions of the meditation, the artist mentions that "In interviews/ I talked about my music's/ voice of praise to our oneness," stressing the commonality of human experience, and by inference, the solidarity of a specific cultural community. The poem focuses on the forces of creation and their effect on the creator. Speaking in awe of the power surging through the process of artistic expression, the speaker mentions "cymbals driving me into ecstacies on my knees." He describes his collaborator, "the demonic angel, Elvin/ answering my prayers on African drum," contributing to a partnership that echoes the call-and-response connection between a chorus leader and chorus. This idea is extended further in the way in which the musicians responded to the words of Martin Luther King, Jr., in their music, as "we chanted his words/ on the mountain, where the golden chalice/ came in our darkness."

The latter sections of the poem move deeper into the artist's consciousness. Driven by an instinctive vision, he recalls that he "pursued the songless sound/ of embouchures on Parisian thoroughfares," realizing that no other experience could match the sense of illumination of creative effort: "no high as intense as possessions/ given up in practice." The wrenching, unsettling difficulties of the demands the musician placed on himself are expressed in his admission that he worked "without deliverance/ the light always coming at 4 A.M." Yet he knows that he had no alternative—"how could I do otherwise"—since he was involved in a much larger motion, "my playing for the ancestors." The ultimate justification for his work, his life, is expressed in one of Harper's favorite phrases, the name again of the Coltrane composition that is at the heart of all worthwhile human activity: "A LOVE SUPREME."

Summary

In *Nightmare Begins Responsibility*, Michael Harper explicitly explains his credo as an artist: *"These are my first values: Understanding, Conscience, and Ability."* By "understanding," he means a compassionate appreciation of human suffering, both personal and historical, which remains a fundamental fact for African Americans in a still-racist society and for all human beings in an imperfect world. His poetry is guided by his determination to find appropriate language to express this pain. By "conscience," he means the obligations of the artist to transform this understanding into a vision of hope and possibility. By "ability," he means the responsibility inherent in his capabilities as an artist and the necessity of committing himself completely to their fullest development in his poetry.

Bibliography

Cooke, Michael G. *Afro-American Literature in the Twentieth Century: The Achievement of Intimacy*. New Haven, Conn.: Yale University Press, 1984.

Henderson, Stephen, ed. *Understanding the New Black Poetry*. New York: William Morrow, 1973.

Lee, Don L., ed. *Dynamite Voices*. Vol 1. in *Black Poets of the 1960's*. Detroit: Broadside Press, 1971.

Mills, Ralph J. *Cry of the Human: Essays on Contemporary American Poetry*. Carbondale: University of Illinois Press, 1974.

O'Brien, John, ed. *Interviews with Black Writers*. New York: Liveright, 1973.

Stepto, Robert, and Michael S. Harper, eds. *Chant of Saints: A Gathering of Afro-American Literature, Art, and Scholarship*. Urbana: University of Illinois Press, 1979.

Turner, Alberta, ed. *Fifty Contemporary Poets: The Creative Process*. New York: David McKay, 1977.

Leon Lewis

ROBERT HAYDEN

Born: Detroit, Michigan
August 4, 1913
Died: Ann Arbor, Michigan
February 25, 1980

Principal Literary Achievement
Hayden spoke to such prominent themes as the civil rights struggle and African American history, choosing to create by combining voices to give a multidimensional density to his examinations.

Biography

Robert Hayden was born Asa Bundy Sheffey to Asa and Ruth Sheffey on August 4, 1913, in the Paradise Valley slum section of Detroit. He kept his birth name only briefly; his father immediately deserted the infant, and when he was eighteen months old, his mother left him with neighbors, the Haydens, so she could pursue her stage career in another state. His foster parents rechristened him Robert Earl Hayden.

Although the Haydens reared Robert as their own son, his foster mother often reminded the boy how much he owed her for taking him in when his own mother had rejected him. The boy's emotional life was complicated by the frequent reappearances of his natural mother, who eventually moved back to Detroit. The mother and foster mother often struggled over the boy, vying for his affection.

When he was a youth, his extreme myopia prevented him from participating in sports with other children, and this, combined with the difficulties of his home life, drove him increasingly to books. In school, he showed interest in poetry and drama, doing poorly only in physics.

Though he was a good student in high school, his race and his family's poverty during the Depression meant that he would not have an easy time getting a college education. From 1932 to 1944, he went to school at Detroit City College and the University of Michigan, punctuating his stints in academia with periods doing research for the Works Progress Administration's Federal Writers Project and for another government agency. During this period, he deepened his knowledge of African American history, and in 1946 he married Erma Morris, a pianist and teacher, to whom he remained married for the rest of his life. He also joined her in becoming a member of the Baha'í World Faith.

In 1944, Hayden obtained an M.A. from the University of Michigan, where he had the good fortune to study under W. H. Auden. Two years later, he became a professor at Fisk University in Nashville, Tennessee.

Throughout his college years, he had been publishing poems in such magazines as *The Atlantic Monthly*, placing pieces in poetry anthologies, and winning occasional awards; his work, however, was still largely unknown. Though he began to win more important awards, such as the Ford Foundation grant he received to travel to Mexico in 1954, for the next twenty years after his university appointment, he labored in undeserved obscurity, at least in the United States. While neglected in his homeland, Hayden was winning acclaim abroad. He was widely translated, his second book of poetry, *A Ballad of Remembrance* (1962), was published in London, and in 1966 he was awarded the Grand Prize for Poetry at the World Festival for Negro Arts in Dakar, Senegal.

Toward the middle of the 1960's, Hayden's work became better known in the United States with the publication of his *Selected Poems* in 1966 and *Words in the Mourning Time* in 1970. Yet this recognition by the literary and academic establishment did not endear Hayden to the young, militant African American poets who were associated with the Civil Rights and Black Power movements. At an African American writers' conference held at Fisk in 1966, the more radical writers took turns pillorying Hayden for not drawing enough on the black experience and for being an overly literary inhabitant of an ivory tower. When Hayden told an audience that the assembled should stop thinking of themselves as merely black writers, Melvin B. Tolson, another senior African American poet, denounced him, saying, " I'm a black poet . . . and I don't give a tinker's damn what you think."

Things calmed down in the 1970's. Hayden moved from being a professor at Fisk to teaching at his alma mater, and in 1970 was nominated for a National Book Award for *Words in the Mourning Time*. This was followed by perhaps his highest honor, an appointment as consultant in poetry to the Library of Congress. Throughout the 1970's, Hayden was showered with accolades and tributes, and he taught as a visiting professor or writer-in-residence at many schools and conferences. He died of respiratory embolism in Ann Arbor, Michigan, on February 25, 1980.

Analysis

Robert Hayden repeatedly affirmed that he did not want to be labeled simply as an African American poet who wrote about and for black readers. In his work, he said,

> I am not so interested in pointing out what is singularly black or Afro-American as in pointing out something about the way people live . . . Perhaps we've had to go through a phase of ethnicity, but now we must move to our common heritage.

This could hardly mean that Hayden, who had grown up in a black slum, who had faced racial obstacles throughout his career, and who had steeped himself in African American history would ignore or downplay the black experience in his work. On the contrary, most of his significant poems are careful reflections on this experience.

Rather, his emphasis on "common humanity" is to be seen in how he presents this ethnic experience within a broad philosophical framework and in how he reserves special attention for molding a personal language and style that draw on, without being subsumed by, black English.

One of the major focuses of Hayden's work is religion. A turning point in the poet's life came when he abandoned the fundamentalist Christianity of his youth to embrace the Baha'í religion, a faith that emphasizes the underlying unity of all religious credos and of all races. The Baha'í religion provided a pattern of belief that would inform many of Hayden's poems. In *Words in the Mourning Time*, for example, it is only a faith in the evolving brotherhood of all peoples that leads the poem's speaker out of the despair brought on by a meditation on America's troubles.

A second religious motif found in Hayden's work, on to which he was sensitized by his own journey from the religion of his youth to the one of his adulthood, is that of the personal crisis that results in a change of faith. Hayden is acutely aware of how an ethical orientation may grow, and, in the process, possibly cause a change in religious allegiance. This is illustrated in "The Ballad of Nat Turner," a 1962 poem that concentrates on the antebellum slave-revolt leader's conversion experience. Wandering in the woods, Turner has a vision of a war in heaven between good and evil angels that transmutes into a battle between slaves and masters, with the slaves eventually winning the victory. Thus Turner's Christianity—a faith that, as disseminated by the masters, stressed forbearance and acceptance of life's yokes—is transformed by Turner's vision into a radicalized liberation theology.

Equally important as a theme for Hayden was the black struggle for freedom. Rather than seeing this struggle in parochial terms as one limited ethnic fight, the poet sets it within humanity's perpetual striving for justice. Thus in the poignant "Frederick Douglass" (1949), Hayden's aim is not so much to eulogize a great leader as to emphasize that Douglass will neither be properly celebrated or even correctly understood until the world has escaped all oppression and freedom has become "reflex action." Whereas in "Words in the Mourning Time" he links antiblack racism in the South with anti-Asian racism in Southeast Asia, in his poem about Douglass, he situates the African American struggle for freedom in illuminatingly wide parameters.

This contextualization of one struggle within a wider horizon is carried out by Hayden at the linguistic level through a unique blending of voices and idioms. His work sometimes gives distinctly African American diction pride of place, but as only one element that is part of a felicitous mixture of styles and voices.

His mixing of discourses appears in the way that some of his most powerful poetic vehicles involve a shifting among voices. This is displayed clearly in a poem that has often been identified as his masterpiece, "Middle Passage" (1945). The poem describes the voyages of slave ships carrying human cargo from Africa to plantations in the Americas. Not only does the poem recount the sufferings of the captives, but it also alternates these viewpoints with accounts given by the slave traders themselves. In presenting these accounts, Hayden never takes the sides of the purveyors of human flesh, but he is willing to adopt their viewpoints in some passages. The technique allows him to present a much wider picture of the slave trade as well as to provide a wider feeling for the human tragedy of the whole enterprise, which dehumanized all involved.

Even where Hayden eschews the use of more than one speaker, he artfully mixes different types of language. An example of Hayden's combinatorial style is "El-Hajj Malik el-Shabazz (Malcolm X)" (1967), in which the poet weaves together in one voice a heightened Romantic diction, slang, and phrases from the American Black Muslim movement and the religion of Islam as practiced in the Middle East. Such poems give the reader the impression that a single voice is picking its way through the varied, interconnecting dialects of the United States in order to create one unified, mighty speech.

It should be said that in such relatively monovocal presentations, the leading part is supplied by a nuanced, ambiguous voice loved by academics. Hayden's decision to use this voice as his principal one brought him into disfavor with those African American writers who called for an identifiably black tone in literature. Yet it is worth arguing that this one voice best represents Hayden's own stance as one who, in his writing, wanted to take a step away from his own and his race's specific life experiences in order to be able to return with redoubled clarity and feeling.

MIDDLE PASSAGE

First published: 1945; revised in Collected Poems, 1985
Type of work: Poem

A historical collage re-creates the voyages of slave ships taking Africans to the New World.

In "Middle Passage" Hayden mingles the voices of multiple speakers to depict the voyages of slave traders bringing Africans across the Atlantic. He had been deeply moved by "John Brown's Body," Stephen Vincent Benet's epic 1928 poem about the Civil War, and he especially marked a passage in which Benet stated he could not fairly describe the titanic battle from the African American viewpoint. Such a depiction, Benet declared, waited upon a black pen. It became Hayden's ambition to write such an epic, and though he was never to write a full-scale work on this theme, "Middle Passage" became the largest and most compelling of the fragments of his promised epic.

Since the turn of the century, there have been at least two other great American fragmented epics, T. S. Eliot's 1922 masterpiece *The Waste Land* and Hart Crane's 1930, *The Bridge*, both of which influenced Hayden. Eliot used a collage of voices and mangled quotations to suggest the disunity of the twentieth century. Hayden uses the same techniques, but he turns their implications in another direction by suggesting that it is the past, not the present, that is fragmented; he views the past as a time when tribal Africans lost their culture and slave-traders their humanity. The distorted quotations mingled in Hayden's text, taken from the works of William Shakespeare and from gospel hymns, do not, as in Eliot's poem, suggest the amnesia of the present. Rather, they used to assail the integrity of the material itself. Christian lines, for example, seem hollow when they are presented as prayers uttered by slave-traders.

In the less despairing *The Bridge*, Crane sought to locate figures who embodied the best in American life. Hayden finds such an inspiring figure for his poem in Cinque, a character based on a real-life captive who led a successful rebellion on a slave ship.

"Middle Passage" consists of three sections, each of which is centered on a statement of a slave trader. In the first section, a crew member unconsciously reveals the brutalizing effects of the trade, and in the second, the complacency of slave-traders is shown. In the last section, however, a flicker of surprise appears in the mind of a slave trader who observes the Africans' intelligence and passion, exhibited in how they matched the merchants for guile and savagery in carrying out their rebellion. Significantly, neither Cinque nor any of the other slaves speaks in the poem, indicating their ominous, forced silence in the historical record.

The poem ends on a note of tempered hope. A crew member who is speaking about getting the slaves extradited—Cinque's boat crashed in the United States —notes that he was opposed by the lawyer John Quincy Adams, who had implied in his case that slaves have a right to rebel. This hints that the poem's repeated refrain, "Voyage through death/ to life upon these shores," can be read in a less ironic way than might at first seem indicated. The phrase may symbolically refer to the historical "voyage" that African Americans would take through the Civil War and, much later, through the civil rights struggle to achieve a freedom that really is a life won through deaths.

WORDS IN THE MOURNING TIME

First published: 1970
Type of work: Poem

The poet laments the burgeoning violence and chaos afflicting his homeland but is consoled by seeing this as part of a divine preparation.

In "Words in the Mourning Time," Hayden comes to terms with the tempestuous, violent 1960's. Explicitly, Hayden is mourning the deaths by assassination of Martin Luther King, Jr., and Robert Kennedy; implicitly, he is concerned with the damage done to the body politic by enduring injustice. He alludes to the riots that had rocked African American ghettos, sparked by King's death but nourished by years of inequality. Further, as a poet, Hayden is concerned with the destruction of language that results when words are pressed to service in an ignoble cause. He decries the distortions used to justify the war in Vietnam: "Killing people to save them, to free them?" the poet asks.

In traditional mourning for a loved one, a person moves through horror at the death to a grudging understanding of nature to, in some cases, a deeper appreciation of spiritual realms. This is the path Hayden follows in his ten-part poem, drawing on his ability to play with multiple voices, though not so much to ventriloquize different speakers as to move through various styles of writing.

In the first six sections, the poet recites a litany of contemporary American problems. This is hardly a monotonous cataloging since the writer keeps changing tacks as he drives home his message: An aphorism in section 2 suggests an ugly alliance between platitudes and violence; section 3 contains the arresting image of a wasted beggar whose peeling flesh mixes with his food; section six includes an attempt to personify the black rage of the times in the antic figure of Lord Riot.

In parts 7 through 9, the author seeks for positive meaning in the historical situation. Part 7 is given in the voice of Bahál'u'lláh, the founder of the Baha'í faith, who leads the poet to the guiding insight that those who act brutally are not so much savages as people misguided in their search for meaning. In this second step of mourning, Hayden understands humanity from a deeper angle.

In the final section, what at first appears to be Hayden's own voice lamenting contemporary difficulties turns out to be Bahál'u'lláh's voice ruing the conditions of the ancient Middle East. The final vignette is that of the prophet himself making a decision to live righteously. Hayden indicates that people of integrity must persevere in trying to bring enlightenment to all the world's lost souls. Thus, he ends with a reaffirmed spiritual purpose.

RUNAGATE RUNAGATE

First published: 1949
Type of work: Poem

> Harriet Tubman, who helped slaves escape, is portrayed both as a character and through the effect she had on her charges and on enemies.

Hayden tended to shy away from the martyrology practiced by some militant African American writers who presented highly varnished depictions of the heroes of black history. In "Runagate Runagate," however, he did paint a glowing portrait of Harriet Tubman, an African American abolitionist who smuggled slaves from the South to the free North before the Civil War.

All ethnic and racial groups have enshrined ideal members who have accomplished great things. It became the special province of radical black writers of the 1960's to supply such champions for their race, heroes who, these writers correctly claimed, had been neglected by the dominant culture. These militant writers often dismissed Hayden for the lack of revolutionary flourishes in his verse, and they also looked in vain through his works for idealized depictions of African American historical figures.

When Hayden did present such figures, as in his allusions to Cinque in "Middle Passage," the portrait was neither touched up—the atrocities practiced by Cinque's followers are not glossed over—nor direct (Cinque, for example, is described only through the words of his opponent). Without compromising his commitment to indirection or objectivity, in "Runagate Runagate," Hayden does give a larger-than-life, though not overly flattering, picture of a valiant woman.

Again Hayden plaits together a number of voices, often hostile ones, to give a rounded picture of both the woman and her surrounding circumstances. There are snippets from advertisements for runaway slaves along with quotations from spirituals and wanted posters.

The poem falls into two sections. The first, which does not mention Tubman, is concerned with sketching the milieu in which slave hunters and fleeing slaves coexisted. The description is focused by the stream of consciousness of a harried but determined escaped slave who is crashing through thickets and swimming rivers to escape pursuing hounds. In this part of the poem, the lines taken from spirituals appear as tonics to strengthen the escapee's resolve.

The second section is less generic, pinpointing Tubman as the leader who is ferrying fugitives to the North. The voice now comes from an escapee under Tubman's direction. The slave's voice is counterpointed by the words on a wanted poster that describe Tubman: "Alias Moses, Stealer of Slaves." Ironically, by calling her "Moses," the masters adopt the slaves' own way of reading the Bible, according to which the slaves see themselves as Israelites under unjust Egyptian bondage.

In the end, though, Tubman is not so much idealized as merged with the forces of nature. Hayden describes how the shadows of fugitives blend with the dark trees and how their voices mix with the bird calls they imitate. These comparisons act not so much to lift Tubman higher as to suggest that the impulse to freedom is as inexhaustible as nature's impulse to grow.

Summary

Although short-sighted critics once decried Robert Hayden's lack of poetic commitment, his verse did turn upon profoundly political themes. What was especially objectionable to such critics was that Hayden never adopted a blaring tone. In fact, his chosen style, the mingling of different voices and tones, precluded this. Yet the polyphony that was his signature style itself embodied a radical democracy in verse; he did not present his readers with one set poet's voice but made them discover that whatever beauty and truth could be found was the product of interlacing voices.

Bibliography

Davis, Arthur P. "Robert Hayden." In *From the Dark Tower: Afro-American Writers, 1900 to 1960*. Washington, D.C.: Howard University Press, 1982.

Magill's Survey of American Literature

Fetrow, Fred M. *Robert Hayden*. Boston: Twayne, 1984.

Harper, Michael S., and Robert B. Stepto, eds. *Chant of Saints: A Gathering of Afro-American Literature, Art, and Scholarship*. Urbana: University of Illinois Press, 1979.

Hatcher, John. *From the Auroral Darkness: The Life and Poetry of Robert Hayden*. Oxford, England: George Ronald, 1984.

Williams, Pontheolla T. *Robert Hayden: A Critical Analysis of His Poetry*. Urbana: University of Illinois Press, 1987.

James Feast

Principal Literary Achievement

Helprin has been credited with, and criticized for, reintroducing carefully written stories with positive values and happy endings to late twentieth century American literature.

Biography

Mark Helprin was born on June 28, 1947, in New York City. His father, Morris Helprin, worked in the film industry, eventually becoming president of London Films. Eleanor Lynn Helprin, Mark's mother, was a successful actress, starring in several Broadway productions in the 1930's and 1940's. When Mark was six, the family left New York City for the prosperous Hudson River Valley suburb of Ossining, New York.

Having parents working in the creative arts was an ideal environment for the development of a writer. According to Helprin himself, his father often pestered him until he told a satisfactory story, true or not, of his school day. Helprin attended Harvard University, earning his English degree in 1969. After that he attended Stanford University briefly, moved to Israel for a few months, and then returned to Harvard, where he completed a master's degree in Middle Eastern studies in 1972. During another nine months in Israel, he became a dual citizen and was drafted into the Israeli Army. Though he did not see any combat duty, it was an experience he would use in many of his stories and novels. Upon leaving Israel, he attended Princeton University and the University of Oxford for short periods.

Helprin first realized that he had a talent for writing when he was seventeen. He wrote a description of the Hagia Sophia, a cathedral in Istanbul that he had never seen, and was so proud of the result that he decided that writing was something he could do, and do well. He went on to write numerous short stories that he submitted to *Harper's* and *The New Yorker*. After a dozen rejections, *The New Yorker* accepted two at once: "Because of the Waters of the Flood" and "Leaving the Church."

Those two stories, and eighteen others, were published in 1974 in the collection *A Dove of the East and Other Stories*. This volume, with its wide range of characters, settings, and themes, received generally good reviews. The late writer John Gardner

was impressed with Helprin's handling of various cultures and wrote that Helprin "seemed to be born and raised everywhere."

A novel, *Refiner's Fire, the Life and Adventures of Marshall Pearl, a Foundling*, came out in 1977 to mixed reviews. This was a rambling, picaresque novel of improbable events skillfully rendered. Detractors faulted the book for having too much in it; one reviewer complained that it had "enough matter in it for three or four novels, but far too much for one." Most, though, could not help but admire Helprin's lyrical style and imaginative use of language.

In 1981, another volume of Helprin's short stories appeared, many of them again reprinted from *The New Yorker*. *Ellis Island and Other Stories* cemented Helprin's stature as a major writer. This collection, like *A Dove of the East*, contains powerful stories of a wide range of characters, from contemporary cowboys in Israel to a captain of a sailing ship in the 1850's, to a would-be mountain climber in Germany. The title story, "Ellis Island," about a turn-of-the-century immigrant to New York, has the episodic nature of *Refiner's Fire* and also introduces some of the fantastic elements Helprin further developed in his next work.

Though Helprin considered himself "prize-proof" because of his refusal to join writers' groups and endorse other books, the publication of *Ellis Island* brought him many accolades. Helprin received the Prix de Rome from the American Academy of Arts and Letters and the National Jewish Book Award. *Ellis Island* was nominated for the American Book Award and the PEN/Faulkner Award for Fiction.

Winter's Tale (1983) became a best-seller, even reaching the paperback racks at grocery-store checkout counters. This novel, set in a fantastic version of New York City, spans the century from 1900 to the year 2000, touching on the big themes of death, rebirth, love, and justice. Helprin's next two projects, *Swan Lake* (1989), a collaboration with noted children's illustrator Chris Van Allsburg, and the novel *A Soldier in the Great War* (1991) also quickly hit the best-seller lists.

This success was destined to continue. On the strength of these books, Helprin negotiated a remarkable contract with Harcourt Brace Jovanovich. For a reported two million dollars, paid up front, Helprin agreed to give the publisher three more novels and two volumes of short stories, an arrangement that gave the author an unusual degree of income and stability for the next several years.

Helprin married Lisa Kennedy in 1980. In 1986, they and their two daughters moved from New York to a spacious new home in Seattle, Washington. The writer who said that he enjoyed writing more than anything certainly enjoyed a measure of critical and financial success rare among serious writers.

Analysis

The reader of Mark Helprin's work is immediately struck by sentences such as the following from the short story "A Room of Frail Dancers" (1981): "Once, far away, he had seen an endless column of tanks moving in rays of sun, and their dust cloud had risen like the voices of a choir." This sentence demonstrates several features of Helprin's acclaimed style and offers a glimpse of one of his main themes as well.

The most striking device in this example is the simile using synesthesia, or combining of the senses, to compare the tanks' dust cloud to singing voices. Surprising and thought-provoking metaphors such as this abound in Helprin's work. Sometimes his fertile imagination piles two or more onto one referent. There is also an example here of the author's use of hyperbole, or poetic exaggeration, in the "endless column of tanks" the column is not truly endless, but merely seems so to the observer. Helprin often uses this device to describe the wonders of childhood, as in "A Vermont Tale" (1981), or to instill a childlike perspective in adults. The novel in which this device expands to become the driving force of the story, *Winter's Tale*, has been described by one reviewer as a "children's book for grown-ups."

This example also hints at Helprin's uncommon use of the imagery of light. Most of his descriptions of setting include at least a few words about how the light looks; *Winter's Tale* begins in the "light blue flood" of dawn and dissolves, at the end, into another dawn with an ocean of "pale shimmering gold."

Finally, the sentence quoted above also demonstrates Helprin's ability to turn commonplace or even tragic aspects of human existence into things of beauty. In this case, the movement of tanks, ugly machines going about the terrible business of war, becomes a thing of beauty through an image suggesting, ironically, an act of religious worship. The capacity to see the beauty in all things is one facet of a passionate love of life, and one that Helprin advocates throughout his work. The main character in the short story "Ellis Island," an unnamed immigrant to New York in the early 1900's, explains it best:

> So, I worked in the kitchen, I didn't care. In fact, I came to enjoy it. I saw every scene as if it were a fine painting. That, I suppose, is one of the benefits of a life of the mind—when you can turn the kitchen from homeliness into a thing of beauty. With patience, all motion becomes dance; all sound, music; all color, painting.

The trick, it seems, is to maintain a distance from the subject, and to view life as art.

Life can also be illuminated by the nearness of death. As an avid mountain climber, Helprin himself appreciates, and shows in his characters, that life becomes most precious when it is in danger of being lost. In *Winter's Tale*, Peter Lake's lover is terminally ill when he meets her. She is burning up with fever; here Helprin paints an image of the body as machine, overstoked and destroying itself from too much heat, too much life. She gains from this existence a calm contemplativeness and a heightened pleasure in living. In one of the most striking sections of *A Soldier of the Great War*, the title character, Allesandro, is awaiting execution, having been condemned to death for deserting his post in the Italian Army. The narration slows and the writing becomes lyrical, describing the almost suspended animation of the prisoners waiting for death, day after day, on an island in the beautiful Mediterranean Sea. As other condemned prisoners react with madness or despair, Allesandro achieves a transcendental peace. He even develops the courage, when he is miraculously reprieved at the last minute, to offer his life in exchange for that of a friend who has a wife and children.

In addition to this acceptance of death, Helprin also considers death to be a great injustice, the ultimate enemy in the great war of life. This is especially true when death claims the young and innocent. One way to deal with this injustice, he feels, is through exploring the possibility of rebirth or resurrection. This is one of the major themes of *Winter's Tale*. Peter Lake returns, after apparently having been dead for eighty years, to be a catalyst as New York City is burned and then reborn into the twenty-first century. Then he gives his life to resurrect a five-year-old girl who had died of a fever, a child symbolic of all the unjustly taken.

Among the old-fashioned values that Helprin's work promotes are responsibility and commitment. Most of the romantic relationships in these novels and stories are true loves, often begun as love at first sight. In one of the few stories where marital infidelity is portrayed, "A Vermont Tale," the narrator's veiled confession, told in a parable of two loons, becomes a cautionary tale about the perils of unfaithfulness. More often, Helprin's protagonists are faithful and true, sometimes for years after the lover has been lost, apparently dead. In *A Soldier of the Great War*, Allesandro's commitment and enduring hope is rewarded when his lover, who had seemingly died in an air raid years before, turns up, along with the son she had been carrying at the time. In this case, hope and faith are rewarded with an apparent resurrection.

To be fair, many critics view Helprin's style and message with a cynical eye. His prose has been called sugary and overblown, and he has been accused of showing off, of dazzling the reader with literary tricks and wordplay at the expense of the story. The stories themselves, and especially the novels, have been criticized for being too heavy-handed, with the author intruding on the story to point out the morals and messages. Some reviewers find his positive attitude a bit naïve and say that his victories, resurrections, and golden dawns are too easily won. Others, though, are refreshed or even moved by these tales of love and hope in an age of increasing trouble and despair.

A DOVE OF THE EAST

First published: 1975
Type of work: Short story

A man risks ridicule and death to tend a wounded bird and recalls the disappearance of his young bride during World War II.

The title story of Helprin's first published collection, "A Dove of the East," is a beautiful story of love and courage set in Israel some years after the 1967 Six-Day War. Leon Orlovsky is a French Jew who has settled in the occupied territory of the Golan Heights and become a scout for a crew of cowboys. His job is to ride ahead of the herd, finding a route to water and fresh forage. He enjoys his work, taking pleasure in the solitude and the harsh beauty of his surroundings despite the persistent threat of Syrian snipers and saboteurs.

One evening, Leon finishes his day with an outburst of wild riding and an unexplained outpouring of emotion ranging from exhilaration to violence to tears. In the morning, he finds a beautiful dove, critically wounded apparently after having been trampled during Leon's wild ride of the night before. He decides that he must stay with the bird, to keep it company as it heals or, more likely, dies. Leon wonders why, and how, he can do this for a simple bird, shirking his responsibility to his comrades and exposing himself to ridicule and danger.

A long flashback then tells the story of Leon's relationship with Ann, with whom he fell in love at first sight (a common occurrence in Helprin's stories) when both were quite young. They courted, were married, and had started on what would seem to be a wonderful life together until the interruption of World War II. Here, as with the Syrian guerrillas in the earlier part of the story, the enemy is simply the war, an impersonal force like a hurricane that sweeps over individual humans.

As Leon and Ann were fleeing Paris to the south of France, the train on which they were riding suffered a brutal air attack. Leon was wounded; upon regaining consciousness, he found the train, and Ann, gone. In the chaos of war-torn Europe, he was never able to find Ann again or discover her fate. Crushed by the loss of her, he is able to survive only by harboring a hope that she will someday reappear.

At the end of the story, Leon hears riders approaching. The reader never learns whether they are his enemies or his comrades, nor is the ultimate fate of the dove revealed.

Though the story is rich in symbols, correspondences, and meanings, one possible interpretation is that the dove represents to Leon innocence and beauty destroyed by random, unfeeling fate, just as his perfect relationship with Ann was inexplicably ended. Courage and hope in the face of tragedy are among the glories that Helprin sees in the world of "a God whose savage beauty made sharp mountains of ice and rock rise suddenly out of soft green fields."

WINTER'S TALE

First published: 1983
Type of work: Novel

This is a sweeping story of love and adventure in a fantastic New York City, from 1900 to the turn of the twenty-first century.

Winter's Tale is set in a surreal version of New York City and its surroundings. Many of the places are real, and the story begins in the early 1900's. In this book, however, Helprin lets his penchant for exaggeration run free. The winters are longer and colder, the buildings higher, and the world generally more glorious than in real life. The city is sometimes encircled by an impenetrable cloud wall that could be a gateway to another universe.

Into this world sails the infant Peter Lake, Moses-like, to grow and find his way. Peter becomes a mechanic, tending the machines of the city, and later becomes a thief who breaks into the home and the heart of Beverly Penn, who becomes his true love. She is terminally ill and soon dies. Peter later escapes death with the help of his flying white horse and disappears into the depths of the sky. He reappears, nearly a century and many pages later, to help shepard the city through the death of one century and the birth of another at the turn of the year 2000.

The city itself is a major character in the novel, with its teeming humanity, mechanical heartbeat, and seasonal moods. The story opens in the early 1900's with the dawn of the mechanical age; the highest achievements of human art and science are the magnificent bridges linking Manhattan with the rest of the world. The book ends with the new millennium, and the bridge builders also return from the neverland of time to attempt a new technology, a bridge made of light. The bridge's architect "would not say where this bridge will lead, preferring to leave that to my imagination—as I will leave it to yours."

This book is often considered a failure for its convoluted plot and lack of a coherent theme. Indeed, the author seems to have overreached himself, attempting a transcendental, visionary tale of death, rebirth, love, and justice. Many elaborate side stories and subplots seem to clutter the novel. The problem, if it is one, is that all the digressions and meaningless details are fascinating. Indeed, one of the reader's chief pleasures is following the twists and turns of Helprin's prodigious imagination. The beauty of the language is also reason enough to read the book, with its bits of sly humor and startling similes on every page.

A SOLDIER OF THE GREAT WAR

First published: 1991
Type of work: Novel

An elderly Italian man tells the story of his life and of his search for love and beauty amid the horrors of World War I.

Mark Helprin's third novel, *A Soldier of the Great War*, is a huge book, and opening it is less about starting to read than beginning to live another life. Its 792 pages encompass the story of a well-born Italian, Allesandro Giuliani; it is the tale of his early life and loves and of his experiences in World War I. Unlike Helprin's previous novel, *Winter's Tale*, there is no fantasy here, and only a little hyperbole or humor. Like Helprin's other works, though, this book is written in his acclaimed gemlike lyrical style, perhaps even more polished here.

The smooth writing and luminous images reinforce one of the main themes of the novel: the desirability of finding beauty and the joy of living, in nearly any situation. Allesandro is a student, and later a professor, of aesthetics, and his concerns about art and life, and the author's eye for the beautiful, infuse the book with light. In one scene, after Allesandro, as a soldier, has been sentenced to hard labor in a marble quarry for desertion, the description of the quarry in action at night, with searchlights glinting off blocks of marble being transported high in the air on cables, is nothing less than dazzling. The exhausting, backbreaking labor is accepted by Allesandro as a way of feeling truly alive.

War itself is a major theme of the book, and Helprin's ambivalent feelings about it are clear. War is at once a brutal waste of human life and resources and a testing ground that can bring out the best in individuals. The battle scenes are frightening and realistically drawn, yet there is always space for a noble act of mercy or a radiant sunrise. Allesandro fights valiantly or tries to escape, whichever seems to be appropriate to him at the time. He also accepts totally the consequences of his actions, as when he uncomplainingly faces execution for desertion.

The absurdity of war is clearly shown in the character of Orfeo, a strange and probably mad scribe in the office of Allesandro's lawyer father. Orfeo ends up working for the Department of War, where he edits the military orders he transcribes, saving Allesandro from his execution and virtually directing the war by his personal whims.

Finally, the novel, though set in the horrors of war, is filled with the positive values that Helprin holds dear. Almost all the characters are good people who are trying to do what is best for themselves and their loved ones. Families experience tragedy and survive in love. Allesandro finds love at first sight with a nurse who cares for him when he is wounded, but then he loses her in an air raid. Like Leon in "A Dove of the East," he is sustained for years by the seemingly impossible hope of finding her again, though here he miraculously does.

A Soldier of the Great War is an old-fashioned book, full of positive values and written in sparkling prose. It is a life, an adventure, and a love story that is not soon forgotten.

Summary

After finishing nearly any of Mark Helprin's novels or stories, the reader is left with the feeling that despite tragedy and misfortune, life is as it should be. The author's love of life and his joy of using language sweep the reader up into the world of imagination. Though some critics think that Helprin's style is overdone and his happy endings are too unrealistic, others find his work an antidote for the nihilism, despair, and purposely artless writing that is characteristic of much contemporary fiction. The reader is uplifted by Helprin's stories and given new eyes with which to see a world filled with mystery and beauty.

Bibliography

Alexander, Paul. "Big Books, Tall Tales." *The New York Times Magazine* 140 (April 28, 1991): 32.

Bell, Pearl K. "New Jewish Voices." *Commentary* 71 (June, 1981): 62-66.

Butterfield, Isabel. "On Mark Helprin." *Encounter* 72 (January, 1989): 48-52.

Keneally, Thomas. "Of War and Memory." Review of *A Soldier of the Great War*, by Mark Helprin. *The New York Times Book Review*, May 5, 1991, 1.

"Mark Helprin's Next 10 Years (and Next Six Books) with HBJ." *Publishers Weekly* 236 (June 9, 1989): 33-34.

Rubins, Josh. "Small Expectations." Review of *Winter's Tale*, by Mark Helprin. *The New York Review of Books* 30 (November 24, 1983): 40-41.

Solotarfoff, Ed. "A Soldier's Tale." Review of *A Soldier of the Great War*, by Mark Helprin. *The Nation* 252 (June 10, 1991): 776-781.

Joseph W. Hinton

OSCAR HIJUELOS

Born: New York, New York
August 24, 1951

Principal Literary Achievement
The most prominent contemporary Cuban American author, Oscar Hijuelos received a Pulitzer Prize for his second published novel.

Biography
Oscar Hijuelos, one of two children of Pascual Hijuelos, a hotel employee, and Magdalena Torrens Hijuelos, a homemaker, was born in New York City on August 24, 1951. Both his parents had immigrated to the United States in the 1940's from Cuba's Oriente Province. Hijuelos grew up in Manhattan and attended a Catholic elementary school and a public high school. Throughout his adolescence, he played in bands with other Latino, mostly Puerto Rican, musicians. Hijuelos received both his B.A., in Asian history in 1975, and his M.A., in English in 1976, from City College of the City University of New York.

After graduation, he supported himself with odd jobs. An amateur archaeologist, he traveled widely and lived in Italy for a few years. In 1985, Hijuelos was awarded both a creative writing fellowship from the National Endowment for the Arts and the Rome Fellowship of the American Academy and Institute of Arts and Letters. His first book, the largely autobiographical *Our House in the Last World* (1983), earned him $6,400. His second, *The Mambo Kings Play Songs of Love* (1989), won him fame, fortune, and a Pulitzer Prize in fiction, the first given to a Latino author. The popular novel was also nominated for the National Book Award and for the annual fiction prize of the National Book Critics Circle. In 1990, Hijuelos was awarded a prestigious Guggenheim Foundation grant to continue writing fiction.

Though he did not write its screenplay, Hijuelos did play a bit part in director Arne Glimcher's *The Mambo Kings* (1992), a film adaptation of the novel, but the author as actor ended up on the cutting-room floor. Despite musical contributions by Tito Puente, Linda Ronstadt, and Los Lobos, the film was a commercial and critical failure. Hijuelos' third book, *The Fourteen Sisters of Emilio Montez O'Brien*, received widespread attention when it was published in 1993, but it did not match the commercial or critical success of *The Mambo Kings Play Songs of Love*.

Hijuelos has expressed particular admiration for the writings of Guillermo Cabrera

Infante, Jorge Luis Borges, and Mark Twain. Asked by an interviewer about the sources of his inspiration, he replied: "You see your characters everywhere." He recalled how seeing a heavyset man with three children carrying a bass fiddle led to the creation of Cesar Castillo, protagonist of *The Mambo Kings Play Songs of Love*. Hijuelos' acquaintance with a Dominican elevator operator who could sing as well as Frank Sinatra but who never got the opportunities to break into show business led to Cesar's brother Nestor. The character Bernardito Mandelbaum, a Jew who passes for Latino, originated in a childhood friend of Hijuelos. "I'm not your typical-looking Latino," observed the fair-skinned Hijuelos, who traces his ancestry to Galicia in Spain, "so I sort of moved like a spy through two worlds."

Analysis

Like Mexican American writers Sandra Cisneros, Richard Rodriguez, and Gary Soto, Oscar Hijuelos emerged at an opportune moment, when the burgeoning U.S. Latino population had also piqued an interest in books by Latino authors. His first two books are classic American immigration narratives, though his characters hail from Cuba instead of Russia, Italy, or Norway. His third novel follows the lives of a family created by a mother from Cuba and a father from Ireland.

In *The Mambo Kings Play Songs of Love*, as Cesar Castillo, green from Havana, walks about the streets of 1949 New York, he is unnerved by its polyglot clatter—"a constant *ruido*—a noise—the whirling, garbled English language, spoken in Jewish, Irish, German, Polish, Italian, Spanish accents, complicated and unmelodic to his ear." *The Mambo Kings Play Songs of Love*, like *Our House in the Last World*, focuses on the community of first- and second-generation Cubans living in New York in the decades after World War II. An Irish landlady named Shannon is a minor exception, but Bernardito Mandelbaum, an American Jew who embraces Cuban culture, in spirit is not. His third novel, *The Fourteen Sisters of Emilio Montez O'Brien*, expands the story into another generation that ceases to speak Spanish and whose ancestral homeland is Ireland as well as Cuba.

A Few Moments of Earthly Happiness was Hijuelos' working title for his third book, but it might apply as well to all of his fiction, which is populated by hapless, lonely characters driven by desire and haunted by the realization that life is brief and satisfaction even briefer. The engine of the plot is sometimes sexual desire, as in the obsessive philandering graphically detailed in *The Mambo Kings Play Songs of Love*. Yet the driving force of Hijuelos' fiction is always a longing for something either unattainable or impermanent.

In *The Mambo Kings Play Songs of Love*, desire is largely male, centered in the sexual athlete Cesar's large and insistent penis. Hijuelos does create sympathy for the thwarted longings of Delores Fuentes, the bookish woman Nestor marries merely as a surrogate for his missing María. Critics, however, still complained of Hijuelos' failure to create a strong and sympathetic female character. As if to appease his critics, Hijuelos next offered a world populated and shaped mostly by women. *The Fourteen Sisters of Emilio Montez O'Brien* matches the machismo of its predecessor with an attempt at representing feminine sensibilities. Yet much of the novel is dominated by Emilio Montez O'Brien, another obsessive womanizer.

In *Our House in the Last World*, Alejo Santinio courts his future wife at the movie theater, where she works as a ticket girl, but the radiant images on the local screen in Holguín, Cuba, do not prepare them for the drabness and drudgery of the life they encounter in the United States. *The Mambo Kings Play Songs of Love* continues Hijuelos' study in unfulfilled desire—not merely Cesar's grotesque sexual adventuring but also the unrequited love that Nestor translates into the Mambo Kings' most enduring creation, the haunting song that the band performs for Desi Arnaz during their enchanted visit to his television program. Called "Beautiful María of My Soul," it is an aching evocation of the ravishing woman who never ceases to haunt the amorous young Nestor, years after she abruptly and mysteriously abandoned him in Cuba. Like the William Shakespeare sonnets that vow to outlive the physical beauty of the poet's beloved, it is both a monument to mutability and frustration and a tribute to the redemptive might of art.

For all the hardships that their characters endure, each of Hijuelos' novels offers the possibility of transcendent grace through a brief brush with celebrity. After he leaves Cuba, Alejo Santinio encounters nothing but disappointment and failure. His single luminous moment occurs in 1961, with the unexpected visit of Nikita Khrushchev to the hotel kitchen where Alejo toils. Years later, the humble Cuban immigrant lives on, in triumph, in the glossy photograph that captures him beside the famous Russian. Similarly, a broadcast tape beautifies Cesar and Nestor Castillo during the single moment that denies the frustration and banality of their lives, their appearance on network television with the glamorous Desi Arnaz. Photographs and films perpetuate Emilio Montez O'Brien's brief career as a film star, a buddy of the charismatic Errol Flynn.

Publicly exuberant, Nelson O'Brien takes to private tippling, as insulation against his chronic melancholy, the same sort of anguish over the vanity of human wishes with which Cesar Castillo's life concludes. "Ally yourself with progress and tomorrow!" exhorts *Forward America*, the inspirational manual that becomes Cesar's guidebook soon after his arrival in New York. "The confident, self-assured man looks to the future and never backwards to the past." Hijuelos, like Nathaniel Hawthorne, Herman Melville, William Faulkner, and many other writers of classic American fiction, addresses the theme of the revenge of the past on the optimist. Ambitious for fame and fortune, Hijuelos' characters end up afflicted by the melancholy of futile desire. Whether or not their author's sudden fame itself endures, his books offer the mortal pleasures of articulate anxiety. They are a wistful, wise reminder that more than ninety miles separate Cuba and the United States and that a sea of trouble divides ambition from accomplishment.

OUR HOUSE IN THE LAST WORLD

First published: 1983
Type of work: Novel

Hijuelos traces the fortunes of the Santinios, a family that migrated from Cuba to Spanish Harlem in the 1940's.

A *Bildungsroman* and *Künstlerroman* about an unhappy family of Cuban immigrants struggling in Spanish Harlem, Hijuelos' first published novel culminates with Hector Santinio's declaration of redemptive literary ambition: "I think that one day I would like to write a book, something that would so please my mother and my Pop, if he was still alive." *Our House in the Last World* is just such a book, a text that, for the autobiographical Hector Santinio, as for his author Hijuelos, preserves and honors the tribulations of a working-class family struggling to succeed in a strange new land.

Letters from his sister in New York inspire Alejo Santinio with dreams of adventure and prosperity. In 1943, he and his wife Mercedes depart Holguín, their small hometown in Cuba's Oriente Province. Yet the reality of life in Manhattan is much harsher than Alejo, forced to take a menial, low-paying job in a hotel, had imagined it. Alejo's one transcendent moment in an otherwise dreary existence comes when Soviet Premier Nikita Khrushchev steps into the hotel kitchen and is photographed beside him. A romanticized memory of their house in the last world—the lost world of pre-Castro Cuba—becomes a constant source of torment for Alejo and Mercedes in New York. Yet the two Santinio sons, Horacio and Hector, do not share their parents' Hispanic associations. After contracting a serious illness during a visit to Cuba, Hector even comes to associate Cuba and the Spanish language with evil.

Hector, who is drawn into fierce battles with his father, is embarrassed by and resentful of the crudeness of his parents. His alienation from his parents is exacerbated by a visit to an affluent, confident aunt and uncle in Miami. It is only with the death of his father and the strengthening of his literary ambitions that Hector becomes reconciled to the Santinio legacy. Like many other young men's debut novels, *Our House in the Last World* is the story of a son's coming of age by coming to love the father he had fought and the culture into which he was born. Hector's older brother Horacio has an Irish American girlfriend named Kathleen whose family refuses to allow him past their door because he is Cuban. Hijuelos populates the neighborhood with Irish and Puerto Rican street gangs, but they are always seen from outside. What makes the book particularly distinctive is its vivid inside account of how first- and second-generation Cuban Americans adapt to life in the United States.

THE MAMBO KINGS PLAY SONGS OF LOVE

First published: 1989
Type of work: Novel

In a final, boozy night of life, an aging Cuban immigrant recollects his early glory, when he and his younger brother were promising musicians.

Hijuelos' original working title for his second novel was *The Secrets of a Poor Man's Life*. The version published as *The Mambo Kings Play Songs of Love* shares those secrets in ornate prose that is often graphically erotic. The book, which became an enormous commercial and critical success and was adapted into a 1992 film, recounts the foiled ambitions of Cesar and Nestor Castillo. The ambitious young musicians arrive in New York from Havana in 1949 and, calling themselves the Mambo Kings, begin to establish careers in the lively postwar Latino nightclubs. While telling the Castillos' story, Hijuelos also provides a vivid evocation of the music, clothing, idioms, and food of a particular time, place, and community.

Most of the novel is an elaborate flashback from a night in 1980 that the elderly Cesar spends in the Hotel Splendour, a Manhattan flophouse that has deteriorated as much as he has. It is here, during his final, boozy hours, that Cesar listens to the recording that he and his brother made in 1956 and recalls sexual escapades in that same room with Vanna Vane, Miss Mambo of June, 1954. At the end of the day, he reconstructs a thwarted life the themes of which are sex, love, memory, and music.

That life's single instant of grandeur occurs in 1955, when Cesar and Nestor are invited to put in a brief musical cameo as fictional cousins of Desi Arnaz on the popular *I Love Lucy* television show. They perform "Beautiful María of My Soul," a wistful song composed by Nestor that evokes the memory of a ravishing woman who abruptly and mysteriously abandoned him in Cuba. Though he marries the bookish Delores Fuentes in New York, Nestor never overcomes his melancholy over the loss of his beloved. Shortly after the Mambo Kings' auspicious television debut, the despondent Nestor is killed in an automobile accident. Cesar, who works in a meat-packing plant and then as superintendent of an apartment house, gives up playing songs of love. "Beautiful María of My Soul," however, has been preserved on record, while the Castillos' triumphant visit to the set of *I Love Lucy* survives in reruns. Listening to the recording and watching the television program, Eugenio, Nestor's only son, marvels at art's power to immortalize, to overcome his father's death and his uncle's self-destructive, alcoholic self-pity. For Eugenio, the cathode tube has performed a veritably Christian miracle: "the resurrection of a man, Our Lord's promise which I then believed, with its release from pain, release from the troubles of this world." So, too does Hijuelos' novel perform the literary miracle of capturing the aspirations and exasperations of its thwarted characters' fleeting lives.

THE FOURTEEN SISTERS OF EMILIO MONTEZ O'BRIEN

First published: 1993
Type of work: Novel

Children of an Irish father and a Cuban mother, Emilio Montez O'Brien and his fourteen sisters grow up in Cobbleton, Pennsylvania, and move out into the world.

The opening sentence of Hijuelos' third novel proclaims that "the house in which the fourteen sisters of Emilio Montez O'Brien lived radiated femininity." That radiation is powerful enough to cause horses to throw their riders, cars to skid into ditches, and a plane to fall from the sky. Patriarch Nelson O'Brien senses himself condemned to solitude in his own crowded home, and his proficiency at generating daughters perplexes and perturbs him. He rejoices when his final, fifteenth, child turns out to be a son. For Emilio, surrounded and coddled by a mother and fourteen sisters, woman sets the standard—"What was ugly in life, he thought male."

As a title, *The Fourteen Sisters of Emilio Montez O'Brien* is misleading. With an expansive, rhapsodic style, the novel does celebrate fecundity, but it does not give equal time or attention to all fourteen sisters. Emilio, though not born until midway through the novel, is the object of as much narrative interest as any of the other O'Brien offspring. Though he begins with a chart listing all the O'Brien children and their years of birth, Hijuelos does not distribute his story equally among every member of the clan; the chronicle is partial to Margarita and Emilio. Margarita, the first O'Brien child, is old enough to be mother to the youngest, who as an infant is in fact suckled by his older sister. Margarita is a creature of exquisite, insatiable longing, through sexual and romantic trials that span the century. Emilio is an Olympic philanderer whose brush with vulgar glamour—he makes forty-two B-films in five years during a meteoric Hollywood career—suffuses the story with melancholy over mutability. For the other O'Briens, a simple set of traits suffices: Helen is a beauty, Irene "ever-plump" and omnivorous, Veronica compassionate, Violeta "pleasure-bound and promiscuous."

Early films are a primal influence on the O'Brien children, whose father Nelson owns and operates Cobbleton's Jewel Box Movie Theater. The entire family is, in effect, generated through still film; in Santiago, Cuba, in the summer of 1900, sixteen-year-old Mariela Montez is brought by her father to sit for a portrait in Nelson O'Brien's photography studio. Mariela marries the handsome Irishman and moves with him to Pennsylvania. As an epigraph, the novel offers Nelson's explanation of why, as late as 1937, he continues to use a shuttered, folding-bellows camera. The archaic instrument, he claims, most faithfully and effectively captures the sadness, joy, and worry of its subjects. The camera is an obvious analogy to Hijuelos' own literary device for arresting the fleeting images of existence—the sadness, joy, and worry experienced by each of the O'Briens. *The Fourteen Sisters* is an old-fashioned collation of life studies, a patient record of moments from ten decades. Photography often provides its pretext for narration.

When, at various stages of their lives, Nelson, who continues with his camera work even after opening the Jewel Box, assembles his family for a group portrait, Hijuelos proceeds to tell the story behind the picture. After retiring as an actor, Emilio, following in his father's line of work, becomes "photographer of the stars" in Los Angeles, and much of the rest of the story is generated by either the new prints that Emilio produces or the old ones that he ponders.

Summary

Nestor and Cesar Castillo gaze forever from fictive footage of the *I Love Lucy* show, Alejo Santinio lives on beside Nikita Khrushchev in a snapshot, and the O'Brien sisters and brother are also apprehended through a lens. For Hijuelos, memory is photographic, if imperfect, and his storytelling is inspired by and analogous to Nicéphore Niépce's dream of retaining traces of light—and life—on paper. In rich, resonant English prose, the three Hijuelos novels provide a snapshot of the ambitions and frustrations of Cuban Americans during the twentieth century.

Bibliography

Barbato, Joseph. "Latino Writers in the American Market: In the Aftermath of Winning a Major Literary Prize, a Minority Culture Faces a Welcome Threat: Mainstreaming." *Publishers Weekly* 238 (February 1, 1991): 17-20.

Earle, Peter G. "Back to the Center: Hispanic American Fiction Today." *Hispanic Review* 58 (Winter, 1990): 19.

Fein, Esther B. "Oscar Hijuelos's Unease, Worldly and Other." *The New York Times*, April 1, 1993, p. C19.

Hunnewell, Susannah. "A House Filled with Women." *The New York Times Book Review*, March 7, 1993, 6.

Shorris, Earl. "In Search of the Latino Writer." *The New York Times Book Review*, July 15, 1990, 1.

Steinberg, Sybil. "*PW* Interviews Oscar Hijuelos." *Publishers Weekly* 236 (July 21, 1989): 42-43.

Steven G. Kellman

CHESTER HIMES

Born: Jefferson City, Missouri
July 29, 1909
Died: Moraira, Spain
November 12, 1984

Principal Literary Achievement

Although a pioneer in African American protest fiction, Himes is best known for his series of detective novels set in Harlem.

Biography

Chester Bomar Himes was born in Jefferson City, Missouri, on July 29, 1909, to an industrial arts professor and a music teacher who disagreed on social strategy. His dark-skinned father strove for acceptance in a black subculture; his almost-white mother rejected secondary status and made repeated efforts to "pass" as white. Continued confrontations forced his father into increasingly demeaning jobs, ending as a laborer in segregated Cleveland when Himes was ten. Himes felt responsible for family failure, especially when his older brother was blinded in an accident.

After beginning premedical training at Ohio State University, Himes found he could not make the transition to a college environment, largely because he felt obsessed with social success while at the same time isolated between two hostile cultures, neither of which accepted him. He began frequenting the underworld of speakeasies and bordellos, taking on the image of the undergraduate "bad boy" and provoking a number of confrontations with faculty, administrators, and other students. Eventually he led his fraternity into a red-light district brawl that had to be broken up by police. This brought expulsion. To support himself, Himes took to petty crime. He was soon arrested for armed robbery and sentenced to twenty years in the penitentiary, by then almost a case study of the chronic malcontent.

In prison, he witnessed beatings, murder, and riots. A fire during an uprising took more than three hundred lives. He turned to writing as a refuge, before long placing his stories in major publications, especially *Esquire*. Upon parole in 1935, Himes emerged into the Great Depression, where jobs were practically nonexistent for former convicts, especially if they were black. In 1938, the Federal Writers Project appointed him to write a history of Cleveland, which, though completed in 1941, was not published. With the outbreak of World War II, he went to California, which promised,

but failed to provide, discrimination-free war-industry jobs. There he finished and published his first novel, *If He Hollers Let Him Go* (1945), the first of five novels tracing the effects of Jim Crow culture on nominally free blacks. In these books, he drew freely on his own experiences, reaching a high point with *The Primitive* (1955). He also wrote for the labor movement, for the *Cleveland Daily News*, and for the Communist Party.

In 1955, Himes fled to France, a haven for black artists. Even there, however, he found small welcome until he began producing his "Harlem Domestic" thrillers for a French publisher. *For Love of Imabelle* (1957) was a smash in France and led to the publication of the series in the United States. The series eventually ran to ten titles, including also *The Real Cool Killers* (1959), *The Crazy Kill* (1959), and *Cotton Comes to Harlem* (1965). Himes continued to live and write in Paris for several years, although a stroke disabled him in 1965. He spent the final fifteen years of his life in Spain, where he completed the two volumes of *The Autobiography of Chester Himes* (1972-1977). In his later years he was severely afflicted with Parkinson's disease, from which he died in 1984.

Analysis

The literary accomplishment of Chester Himes falls into three categories, each of which is distinct. The work of each phase often seems incompatible with the work of others, almost as if he were three different writers at different stages of his career. A close look, however, suggests that these differences reflect profound changes in his life; that understanding leads, in turn, to the recognition that Himes's writing was always and in every way deeply rooted in his life. His work profoundly reveals his growth and change as an artist.

The first phase includes his short fiction (gathered in *The Collected Stories of Chester Himes*, 1990) and the five semiautobiographical novels written after his release from prison and before his expatriation in 1955. Taken together, these constitute his contribution to the fiction of black protest, except that this was hardly a well-defined category at the time. Further, both short and long fiction were produced by mainstream publishers, as his early acceptance by *Esquire* shows. From 1935 to 1946, the magazine published a story by him practically every year, at the very time that it was establishing its reputation for printing the absolute best in American writing, regardless of category. Since the author was identified not only by name but also conspicuously by prison number, however, his status and subject matter clearly had much to do with his success especially since he continued to be identified in this way long after his release.

Sensationalism, then, may have had something to do with Himes's acceptance, at least at first. Yet most fiction of the 1930's was sensationalistic, as a glance at the works of Ernest Hemingway and William Faulkner shows. Moreover, Himes's stories retain much of their interest today, plainly disclosing the qualities that attracted editors then as well as now. The first published of them, "To What Red Hell" (1934), shows a command of narrative pacing, apt selection of detail, taut dialogue, and compressed phrasing that Hemingway might well have envied—and which Himes should have remembered in the toils of some of his longer fiction. At any rate, this graphic account of a prison fire contains memorable character sketches and dialogue on almost every page.

"To What Red Hell" is remarkable in another way. Most of Himes's writing grows completely out of racial consciousness, indeed out of an awareness of the profound reaches of racism. Yet although this story registers racial identity more completely than some fiction, the race of the central character is never absolutely established, and the story ends with the suggestion that racial differences have somehow been transcended in responding to emergency. In this respect, Himes accomplishes the kind of interracial tolerance projected by Faulkner's fiction. A number of other *Esquire* stories focus on this sense of transcendent unity.

Other stories of the same period, however, focus more directly on registering the pains of discrimination, and in this they foreshadow the major characteristic of the five early novels. These books—*If He Hollers Let Him Go* (1945), *Lonely Crusade* (1947), *Cast the First Stone* (1952), *The Third Generation* (1954), and *The Primitive* (1955)—all single out ways in which segregation constrains and restricts blacks, even when overt discrimination is done away with. The first two novels examine limitations in employment and education; they conclude that blacks routinely are forced to compete against a stacked deck. *Cast the First Stone* has been called a classic prison novel, and some of the scenes catch exactly the way in which discrimination persists even in a supposedly classless society. The last two, more explicitly autobiographical, deal with the coming of age of a young black and with a mature interracial affair, respectively. Although each contains some of Himes's best material—*The Primitive*, especially, features a timeless vividness of language and some of the most acute sexual psychologizing in fiction—both are inconsistent in character development and flat and stagy in presentation. Most of these books have attracted enough readers to have been twice reprinted; in general, though, they lack the finish and integration of the short stories.

Himes's second phase is made up of the single novel *Pinktoes* (1961) and the set of nine novels he composed for the French publisher Marcel Duhamel between 1957 and 1970. These novels, which have an extremely confusing publication record, were commissioned by Duhamel when he discovered Himes barely surviving in France. Once *Cast the First Stone* had been suspended in publication even after extremely promising advance sales—some critics objected to the overt racist confrontations in the book—Himes had abandoned America, feeling rejected both as a writer and as a man. Yet the Paris that had proved hospitable to earlier African American exiles such as Richard Wright and Ralph Ellison turned its back on Himes. Duhamel rescued Himes by asking for a thriller set in black America. Locking himself in his hotel room for three weeks on a diet of three bottles of wine daily, Himes produced *For Love of Imabelle*, which Duhamel published in French as *La Reine des pommes*. The two had found the recipe for Himes's greatest success.

The series was a success, both in France and in the English markets. In the beginning, Himes attempted to follow the hardboiled pattern established by Raymond Chandler, the American mystery novelist whose books included *The Big Sleep* (1939) and *Farewell, My Lovely* (1940). Himes, however, set his work in Harlem rather than Los Angeles. He created dual heroes in the black detectives Coffin Ed Jones and Grave Digger Johnson, and he reproduced the life of the ghetto in language uniquely his own—fresh, vivid, direct, accurate, spiced with street metaphors that reflected black consciousness. Once he liberated his imagination from the need to establish a theme and purpose, he set it free to reproduce the life of the streets. In this respect, he more than rivaled Hemingway and Chandler. Two of the novels, *Cotton Comes to Harlem* and *The Heat's On* (1966), were made into Hollywood films, the first in 1970, the second (as *Come Back, Charleston Blue*) in 1972. The most striking feature of these books, partly reflected in their idiosyncratic language, is the abounding humor, the energy of their creativity. As much as any of Himes's books, they display the grim and sordid reality of ghetto life; but they also show the spirit of people who refuse to allow their physical and psychological surroundings to defeat them.

The third phase of Himes's literary career produced his autobiographical writings, the two-volume *The Autobiography of Chester Himes*. Freed again from the need to draw specific conclusions, he tells his story honestly and directly. Perhaps because by this time he had come to terms with his life, he comes across in these pages as a man for whom humor was always—or at least ultimately—more important than outrage.

THE COLLECTED STORIES OF CHESTER HIMES

First published: 1990
Type of work: Short stories

This assembles the stories Himes wrote between 1933 and 1978, including a number of unpublished and undated titles.

Until *The Collected Stories of Chester Himes* was published, Himes's writings in this genre were largely unknown and difficult to find. Thus, his achievements in this field suffered the kind of neglect that plagued Himes throughout most of his life. It is difficult to account for this neglect. The market for the short story peaked in the 1930's and 1940's, and since his stories were picked up by leading magazines, he would seem a prime candidate for anthologizing and collecting. Yet he gained less exposure than most writers of the period, many of whom are still celebrated for limited production. Himes published thirty-four major stories between 1934 and 1948, but he was ignored. In comparison, J. D. Salinger had gained a national reputation by 1953 on the basis of nine stories.

The easy explanation for this disregard would be to conclude that it was racially motivated. Yet many other black writers found print during this time, and some, such as Countée Cullen, Langston Hughes, Zora Neale Hurston, and Gwendolyn Brooks, had national followings. Himes, of course, was sometimes strident, though he was certainly not alone in this. Still, the short story has been a form for which black writers in general have achieved little recognition, even during the Harlem Renaissance of the 1920's and the Black Power movement of the 1960's and 1970's. Even after Himes's detective novels gained wide circulation, his stories remained unappreciated.

Yet his distinctive qualities appear from the beginning. "To What Red Hell" (1934) re-creates the scene of a prison fire so vividly that the reader almost feels the heat and certainly feels the panic of the trapped convicts and the desperation of those trying to rescue them. Himes reproduces the situation so apparently effortlessly that it is easy to overlook the degree of skill involved. Himes also refuses to flinch in the face of unsettling details. No one who reads this story will be able to forget the revulsion of the central character for the dead and dying, his inability to control his fear-ridden reactions to the unforeseen, or his instinctive release of petty prejudices even while reacting to emergency.

Other vivid prison and crime stories appeared in *Esquire*, including "The Visiting Hour" (1936), "Every Opportunity" (1937), "The Night's for Crying" (1937), "The Something in a Colored Man" (1943). "Headwaiter" (1937), first published in *Opportunity*, explores the necessarily repressed feelings of a black headwaiter who is forced to defer to an exclusively white clientele while overseeing an equally exclusively black waiting staff. In "Face in the Moonlight" (published in *Coronet* in 1941), Himes reproduces the awake-at-night reflections of an inmate, carrying off the neat trick of not revealing his race while including racist aspects of his thought patterns. With the outbreak of war, Himes turned occasionally to depicting the democratizing effects of combat even while acknowledging the ineradicability of inbred racism, as in "Two Soldiers" (1943). The bulk of his sixty stories, however, deal with black sensibility in a segregated and prejudiced society, revealed directly through taut dialogue, riveting detail, and finely honed language.

THE CRAZY KILL

First published: 1959
Type of work: Novel

Coffin Ed Jones and Grave Digger Johnson unravel a mystery in Harlem involving a body found in a shopping cart filled with bread.

The Crazy Kill was the third novel in the "Harlem Domestic" ("Serie Noir") series. It is typical of the series in beginning with an apparently inexplicable act of violence that triggers a network of reactions in the intricately interrelated underworld of Harlem. Superficially, the incident seems baffling, an act of random violence generated by the sodden meanness and madness of the streets. Yet the linked reactions suggests it results from the interconnections that bind all these passionate lives together. The outcome reveals that these events are more than the random trails of individual lives; they are part of a system with its own internal code of justice and order. In the end, order is reestablished and justice prevails—but emphatically not the order imposed from without by the official society and its black agents. Beyond that, the novel draws the reader into a world dense with dramatic personalities and alive in the bright edges of concrete details.

The opening of the novel juxtaposes two scenes in Harlem late on a Saturday night: A thief steals a moneybag from the car of a supermarket manager; a preacher at a wake in a neighboring apartment oversees the theft, leans out the window to see better, and falls out, landing in a shopping cart filled with bread. He recovers, returns to the party—where tempers are already flaring because of various sexual tensions—and accuses a guest who has left of having pushed him out of the window. As he gestures from the window toward the cart, others notice another body lying in it. The body turns out to be that of the brother-in-law of the man who has just succeeded the object of the wake as the local racketeering boss.

Overtly, the novel is concerned with determining who did the murder, how, and why. The writer's focus, though, is not on the mechanics of the plot but on the world in which it takes place. Obviously, it is a world in which the bizarre is commonplace, the outrageous everyday. People fall out of windows in stop-action sequence; as in a cartoon strip, they perform perfect half-gainers into a providential shoppingcart; later, that saved body is replaced with a murdered one. Further, everyone—except for the white supermarket manager and the white police sergeant—fails to note any irony in the passage. It is almost as if surrealism has come to life; or, better, as if these lives have been invested with a special reality. Characters, settings, and atmosphere are all sketched in with the bold outlines of caricature. This oversimplifies Harlem and the quality of life there, to be sure, but it also endows it with life, humor, and love. The language may reduce Harlem to the level of a circus, but the circus is bold, loved, and zestful.

It would be hard to maintain such a precedent-defying opening, and Himes in fact does not quite carry it off. The plot takes unusual, baroque turns, and the contorted character relationships twist deviously. Typically, detectives Jones and Johnson do not really solve the mystery. Rather, it solves itself, or the characters who generated it resolve it—which is exactly as it should be in a novel primarily directed toward demonstrating the self-consistency and death-defeating vitality of the black spirit in Harlem.

COTTON COMES TO HARLEM

First published: 1965
Type of work: Novel

In mid-1960's Harlem, detectives Johnson and Jones deal with the robbery of a back-to-Africa financing scam, the loot from which disappears in a bale of cotton.

The seventh novel in Himes's detective series, *Cotton Comes to Harlem*, is generally considered the best of the set, ranking with the works of Dashiell Hammett and Raymond Chandler. Like the others in the series—and like the stories of Chandler—this follows a standard pattern. A public scene in Harlem is visited by an act of overt violence, which catalyzes the major characters to restore the status quo and reassert their control. Meanwhile, the official representatives of the law that supposedly governs the streets, black detectives Coffin Ed Jones and Grave Digger Johnson, carry on a formal investigation, which eventually explains the mystery—but only after the principal actors have already worked it out in their own way. Ultimately, Harlem proves to possess its own self-generating and self-protective powers of restoration, which reside in the spirits of the black people who live there.

The opening scene of this novel is explosive. Deke O'Hara, a politician and recent ex-convict, is working the streets with an updated, glitzy version of Marcus Garvey's back-to-Africa program. He is supposedly selling shares in a colony to be established in Africa for African Americans discontented with America. Since discontent is endemic in Harlem, he has a ready market—but the profits from his scheme, theoretically invested in the company, are intended for his own pockets. Before he can capitalize on his plan, however, his movement is hijacked by a white gang in broad daylight. A frantic chase ensues, scattering innocent bodies in its wake, but the getaway truck escapes, having dropped a bale of cotton that contains the money.

Multiple lines of inquiry spread out: the police want O'Hara, O'Hara wants the hijackers, the hijackers want to recover the lost bale, the common people want to recover the money they have invested. In their quests, the various characters make contact with others, who set off on quests of their own. In the middle of everything else, another organization sets up shop in Harlem, this one fronted by whites: the Back to the Southland (BTS) movement, supposedly dedicated to establishing protected enclaves in the South for blacks who long to return to the security of plantation life. It is, of course, only a front for the hijackers, who are attempting to recover the bale of cotton.

Himes's real emphasis is on the endlessly resourceful people of Harlem, from scheming reverends to amoral prostitutes to manipulative grandmothers. A wonderful exuberance pervades this novel, perhaps best represented by Uncle Bud, an itinerant bagman who acquires the bale of cotton without knowing what he has. When asked jokingly what he would do with the missing $87,000, he answers that he would probably go to Africa. That is exactly what he does at the end of the novel. By playing dumb when everyone around him is on the make in one form or another, by using exactly what is meant by native wits, he does more than survive, he triumphs.

The novel triumphs equally. It reveals all Himes's narrative strengths and achieves a surpassing excellence in use of language to create a society. Himes does more than merely catch the unique cadences of the street talk of 1950's Harlem; he preserves that Harlem by catching its language.

Summary

It is a true cliché to say that Chester Himes has not gained the recognition he deserves. It is a compound truth, for even when he has been successful—as he certainly was with his detective novels—he practically gave his rights away, and he profited little from the film versions of his work that made others rich. At the time of his death, he remained largely unknown, and most of his books had dropped out of print.

He may not ever have written a book worthy of his talent. His most enduring legacy is probably his Harlem series, which deserves recognition but which will probably continue in neglect, because his fine critical intelligence can be misconstrued as uncomplimentary to the African American culture he truly loved.

Bibliography

Himes, Chester. *The Autobiography of Chester Himes*. 2 vols. Garden City, N.Y.: Doubleday, 1972-1976.

Littlejohn, David. *Black on White: A Critical Survey of Writing by American Negroes*. New York: Viking Press, 1966.

Lundquist, James. *Chester Himes*. New York: Frederick Ungar, 1976.

Margolies, Edward. "Chester Himes's Black Comedy: The Genre Is the Message." In *Which Way Did He Go? The Private Eye in Dashiell Hammett, Raymond Chandler, Chester Himes, and Ross Macdonald*. New York: Holmes & Meier, 1982.

——————"Race and Sex: The Novels of Chester Himes." In *Native Sons: A Critical Study of Twentieth-Century Negro American Authors*. Philadelphia: J. B. Lippincott, 1968.

Milliken, Stephen. *Chester Himes: A Critical Appraisal*. Columbia: University of Missouri Press, 1976.

James Livingston

ROLANDO HINOJOSA

Born: Mercedes, Texas
January 21, 1929

Principal Literary Achievement
Focusing on his birthplace just north of the Texas-Mexico border, Hinojosa has captured the essence of what it is to be a Mexican American.

Biography

Although Rolando Hinojosa's father, Manuel Guzmán Hinojosa, was born in the United States—as Manuel's own parents had been—Manuel was distinctly Mexican American in his outlook. Mercedes, Texas, the border town where the author was born and where his father's family had lived since the 1740's, fell three miles north of the border when the United States-Mexico boundary was drawn in 1845. Manuel's family owned "accidental" United States citizenship, remaining loyal always to the Mexican government.

Rolando's mother, Carrie Effie Smith, arrived in Mercedes in 1887, when she was six weeks old. Her father, a Union soldier in the Civil War, brought his family to Mercedes from Illinois. Carrie, reared in a bicultural and bilingual environment, was equally comfortable speaking Spanish and English. She bore two daughters and three sons (one of whom died early). Rolando was the youngest child.

Carrie taught school; Manuel, who fought in the Mexican Revolution, worked variously as a farmer, a shepherd, a dancer, a dairyman, a policeman, and owner of two dry-cleaning establishments. Manuel suffered a stroke in his forties and died instantly; Carrie Smith lived to be eighty-eight.

Rolando's early education was in private, Spanish-language schools, which his parents hoped would increase his knowledge of his Mexican heritage and reinforce his pride in it. This early training played a significant role in making Hinojosa the ethnic writer he became.

Surrounded by older Mexicans struggling to survive, Rolando became a perceptive listener to the yarns they loved to spin. He developed an early appreciation of how Mexican Americans in small border towns live, but he needed distance to understand what he had absorbed. Upon completing high school in 1946, he joined the Army and left Mercedes. His two-year military commitment completed, he entered the University of Texas at Austin, but he was redeployed shortly and served in Korea. Separation

from Mercedes deepened Hinojosa's understanding of the Rio Grande Valley and its people.

Upon discharge, Hinojosa returned to the University of Texas, receiving a bachelor's degree in Spanish in 1953. His first post-college job was teaching at Brownsville (Texas) High School. The diversity of his teaching responsibilities—Spanish, Latin, history, government, and typewriting—combined with substandard pay forced him to quit and become a laborer in a chemical plant.

Between 1954 to 1958, he read everything he could, including the major Hispanic and Russian classics, continuing a pattern his parents had instilled in their children. He married in 1956. That union, which ended in divorce, produced one son, Robert Huddleston.

After another brief stint of high-school teaching, Hinojosa was encouraged by the dean of humanities at New Mexico Highlands University in Las Vegas to begin graduate work, which he did in 1962. He received the master's degree in 1963, the year he married Patricia Louise Mandley. This union produced two daughters, Clarissa and Karen.

Rolando and his new wife set out for the University of Illinois in Urbana, where he entered the doctoral program in Spanish. He received a Ph.D. in 1969, completing a doctoral dissertation on Benito Perez Galdos during a two-year (1968-1970) teaching stint at San Antonio's Trinity University. This was the beginning of Hinojosa's fruitful academic career.

Although he was a strong doctoral student, Hinojosa did not relish the thought of becoming a literary theorist. He knew that he wanted to write, to create stories from his background. In 1970, he met prize-winning Hispanic novelist Tomás Rivera, who encouraged Hinojosa to submit *Estampas del valle y otras obras/Sketches of the Valley and Other Works* (1973) to Quinto Sol Publications, which published it and, in 1972, awarded its author the press's literary prize for fiction, which Rivera had won in 1970. In 1983, a revised version of the book was published in English as *The Valley*.

Hinojosa's advancement in the academic world was meteoric. He served as the chair of the department of modern languages (1970-1974), dean of the college of arts and sciences (1974-1976), and vice president for academic affairs (1976-1977) at Texas A&I University; as professor of English and chair of the program in Chicano studies (1977-1981) at the University of Minnesota; and as Ellen Clayton Garwood Chair in English beginning in 1981 at the University of Texas at Austin.

During Hinojosa's time at the University of Minnesota, his wife completed a law degree there. In 1988, she left him and, with their daughter Clarissa, moved to California. During the seventeen years from 1973 to 1990, Hinojosa published nine works of fiction, all with small presses, although major publishers courted him.

Analysis

Superficially, one might compare Hinojosa's major work, "Klail City Death Trip," to Marcel Proust's *À la recherche du temps perdu* (1913-1927; *Remembrance of Things Past*, 1922-1931). Proust's magnum opus consists of seven interrelated novels;

"Klail City Death Trip," too consists of a number of discrete individually titled works.

Hinojosa's novels are not novels in the sense that Proust's are. Proust observes the conventions of the traditional novel, having the expected protagonist and sequential plot. Each of the seven parts of *Remembrance of Things Past* is written in prose, each in French. Most of the installments of "Klail City Death Trip," too, are written in prose, but half of the third book in the series, *Korean Love Songs from Klail City Death Trip* (1978), is poetry.

Hinojosa wrote the first two elements of his series—*Estampas del valle y otras obras* and *Klail City y sus alrededores* (1976; *Klail City: A Novel*, 1987)—in Spanish; they were translated into English by Gustavo Valadez and Rosaura Sanchez respectively. Hinojosa did not write *Korean Love Songs* in Spanish, because the book is set in a milieu half a world away from Mercedes, and English seemed to the author to be a more appropriate vehicle of communication than Spanish. Yet he wrote his fourth installment, *Mi querido Rafa* (1981; *Dear Rafe*, 1985), in Spanish, then translated it himself for the English language edition.

The next two works in the series, *Rites and Witnesses* (1982) and *Partners in Crime: A Rafe Buenrostro Mystery* (1985), were written in English. The author wrote *Claros varones de Belken Fair Gentlemen of Belken County* (1986) in both Spanish and English, and the book is printed with Spanish on one page and English on the facing page.

In speaking of the larger work of which each of these installments is a part, one can probably feel comfortable in designating the whole series a novel. Hinojosa has gone on record as saying that he conceives of the series as one novel with many parts. The individual parts of the series are quite brief, seldom exceeding one hundred fifty pages and sometimes coming in at fewer than one hundred.

It is difficult to generalize on Hinojosa's style. Speaking, however, in broad terms—and acknowledging that exceptions exist—one can say that much of Hinojosa's work adopts an interview style. That is, as in *Becky and Her Friends* (1990), a given volume may emphasize one character, yet the book is so arranged that in the subdivisions, each headed by the name of a person, the reader is given a personal insight into Becky's character and reputation by the person speaking.

In the case of *Becky and Her Friends*, twenty-seven characters (including Becky and her first husband, Ira Escobar) speak. Some have little to say; their sections might consist of less than one page. Others are more voluble, but no section is inordinately long. It is interesting that Becky's second husband, Jehú Malacara, whom Hinojosa's readers already know well through his twenty-three long letters to Rafe Buenrostro in *Dear Rafe*, is not among the cast of characters who give their impressions of Becky.

Some of Hinojosa's short works have more than a hundred characters in them. The aesthetic explanation for this is that the author is attempting to re-create the ambiance of a close knit Tex-Mex community in which people are interrelated, in which everyone knows everyone else's business and has a strong and definite opinion about it.

The result may seem chaotic to anyone reading about it, yet Hinojosa's books are not difficult to follow. Because most of the characters recur from work to work, the demands the author places on readers makes it possible for them to keep track of the individual characters without too much trouble.

The nature of Hinojosa's storytelling is such that his work is filled with contradictions, but this is because life is filled with contradictions. People are not consistent, and this author makes no effort to impose a false consistency upon his characters. Furthermore, Hinojosa, a singularly intelligent writer well schooled in literary criticism, is fully cognizant of the holes that critics might punch in his novels.

Because of this, he has consciously avoided publishing with major publishing houses, preferring to work with small, specialized publishers who allow him greater control over his work than most major publishers would permit. Hinojosa's writing has been more celebrated abroad than at home, perhaps because a more vigorous literary avant-garde exists in Europe than in the United States.

It is the conflicting voices in Hinojosa's writing that create and sustain the dramatic tension essential to its progression. In all of his work, he writes from a base outside mainstream American experience. This is not the literature of Boston Brahmins or Newport socialites. It is, rather, the literature of an ordinary, bilingual-bicultural populace confined within an area that makes up Hinojosa's microcosm. When the stories leave this circumscribed setting, as they do in *Korean Love Songs*, they are still about citizens of Klail City (Mercedes, Texas) who are, through necessity, acting out their roles in the broad context imposed by a military action on a distant continent.

Hinojosa has been called an ethnopoetic and a sociopoetic writer. Both designations apply to his work. He is perhaps the most successful literary exponent of Chicano life in the Southwestern United States. He focuses more on people than on ideology, although ideologies emerge through the interplay of the characters he develops within the continuing and interlinking course of his novels.

KOREAN LOVE SONGS FROM KLAIL CITY DEATH TRIP

First published: 1978
Type of work: Poems and prose sketches

Rafe Buenrostro, drafted from Klail City to fight in the Korean War, recounts in poetry and prose his wartime experience.

Rafe Buenrostro, Rolando Hinojosa's autobiographical character in this third installment of the Klail City series, steps outside the cultural context in which readers were first introduced to him in two earlier novels, *Sketches of the Valley and Other Works* and *Klail City y sus alrededores*. Because this story is removed from Rafe's accustomed Tex-Mex environment with its bilingual-bicultural atmosphere, Hinojosa wrote it in English rather than Spanish.

Korean Love Songs is a daring book. The first half consists of a series of poems, mostly in free verse, that recount the horrors of combat in which Rafe is involved. A bitter irony pervades the poems. Juxtaposed to mass destruction one finds a fragmented, small-minded military bureaucracy that seems at times bent on making the last days of military men under dire threat as miserable as it can, all in the name of maintaining discipline.

"Chinaman's Hat (Hill 329)" focuses on soldiers who run from enemy fire, abandoning their weapons in the field. As an object lesson, the high command decrees that the 88th Field Battalion, for its "own good and discipline," be forced to march back under guard to retrieve its abandoned weapons. This poem captures the terror of war, demonstrating the inability of officers to command their troops to hold fast in the face of almost certain death.

Enlisted men, deaf to the commands of their officers, flee as fast as they can from an enemy that is eventually destroyed by Air Force bombing. They leave their dead behind as well as their firearms. This poem, much in the style and tone of the World War I poetry of Wilfred Owen, is graphic, bitter, without hope. Human devastation lurks in every line; overshadowing the entire poem is the knowledge that there will be a tomorrow, more battles, other senseless deaths.

Even more chilling is "Night Burial Details," a Dantesque poem about the dead with their foolish grins lying on a rain-soaked battlefield. The body bags are of high quality, their hasps the best that money can buy. An urgency motivates the burial details: Tomorrow will be hot, and unburied bodies emit a sickening stench.

Pits the size of a football field have been dug and filled with lime some forty miles away. The burial details remove dogtags and empty wallets of the things that soldiers carry—money, pictures, condoms. They tag wristwatches and rings, bag the occasional rosary and missal. They note the macabre, ironic humor of the fallen soldier who, on the back of a naughty French postcard, has written that in case of accident the president of the United States, 1600 Pennsylvania Avenue, Washington, D.C., should be notified.

War poetry, if it is honest, has usually produced the most strident antiwar sentiments in print. The poems and sketches in this collection perpetuate that tradition.

MI QUERIDO RAFA/DEAR RAFE

First published: 1981 (English edition, 1985)
Type of work: Novel

Jehú Malacara writes twenty-three long letters to Rafe Buenrostro, who is recovering from war injuries in a nearby military hospital.

Dear Rafe consists of three parts. In the first section, Jehú Malacara, a well-known public figure and loan officer in Klail City, writes twenty-three letters to Rafe

Buenrostro, his cousin, who is recovering from wounds received in the Korean War. Rafe is confined to the veteran's hospital in William Barrett, Texas.

The second part of the book is composed of sketches in which twenty-three citizens of Klail City reflect upon Jehú, all from their unique perspectives. These two sections occupy forty-six and sixty-five pages respectively. The third section, three pages long, consists of a penultimate note (designated as such) and a brief sketch, "Brass Tacks Are Best; They Last Longer."

In his letters to Rafe, Jehú gossips about what is happening in Klail City, relating some of the intrigue associated with his boss, Noddy Perkins, who is manipulating the forthcoming elections. Through Jehú, Rafe (and readers) receive an inside view of how the monied class in Klail City exploits the Mexican American working class.

Jehú, still young enough to be principled, eventually oversteps the bounds that Noddy sets for him and is fired. Noddy relents and rehires Jehú, but this arrangement does not last long. Jehú's conscience unmans him, and he resigns from a job with a future in order to attend college.

Jehú's letters, although they lack the flair and the urgency of Pamela Andrews' or Clarissa Harlowe's incendiary missives in Samuel Richardson's *Pamela, or Virtue Rewarded* (1740) and *Clarissa: Or, The History of a Young Lady* (1747-1748), achieve similar ends: They highlight a moral dilemma and effect a resolution.

The second half of the book reports on the results of interviews conducted by P. Gallino, a Klail City writer, who solicits comments from twenty-three local residents regarding their opinions about Jehú Malacara's unexpected and unaccountable departure from Klail City, where his prospects seemed singularly promising. Gallino remains the objective reporter throughout his extensive interviews, through which the reader, in the style typical of Hinojosa, is made to see Jehú, Klail City, and its residents from multiple points of view.

As in much of Hinojosa's writing, the author introduces a character—in this instance, Jehú Malacara—who is permitted to reveal in some detail salient elements of his own personality and value system. Jehú's revelations accomplished, Hinojosa makes this character the subject of conjecture by a broad variety of other townspeople who know him in various contexts, thereby projecting a complex mosaic that simulates a balanced view of the character.

This is Hinojosa's first attempt to produce a bilingual book. *Dear Rafe* consists of an intermixture of English and Spanish, which, in itself, becomes at times a strident social statement.

BECKY AND HER FRIENDS

First published: 1990
Type of work: Novel

When Becky leaves her husband, Ira Escobar, and marries Jehu Malacara,
twenty-six townspeople comment on her behavior.

One day, completely out of the blue, Becky Escobar tells her husband, Ira, that she
has decided he is not going to live with her and their children any longer. A similar
event occurred in Hinojosa's life in 1988, when Patti, his wife of twenty-five years,
unexpectedly filed for divorce and left for California, taking their daughter Clarissa
with her.

Becky is extremely calculating in ending her marriage so abruptly. She has a moving
company pack Ira's belongings, which are out of the house by the time he returns home
from his job as a county commissioner. What follows are the reactions of twenty-six
townspeople (including both Ira and Becky) to the end of a marriage that was generally
considered stable.

As in all of Hinojosa's novels, the cast of characters is familiar. Readers of the whole
series have met most of them before and will certainly have formed opinions about
them, although some of the characters change significantly from book to book.

The author involves himself in the narrative immediately in the first section, "Lionel
Villa," where he begins by saying, "Let's drop in on Lionel Villa and hear what he
has to say regarding Rebecca—alias Becky—Escobar." This informality persists in
most of the twenty-six sections that follow.

Lionel is Becky's uncle and is probably, therefore, a biased witness. His testimony,
however, is counterbalanced by that of such a broad collection of other townsfolk that
any bias he may have hardly matters. In the end, it seems inevitable that the truth will
out.

Becky, in a real sense, is a feminist heroine, a product of a decade in which women
have rejected their subservient roles and have struck out on their own. The comments
that the townspeople make about Becky's decision to leave Ira reach far beyond the
separation of two people, suggesting clearly that the changing role of women will
inevitably lead to a new way of viewing the social structure of communities such as
Klail City.

Eighteen months after leaving Ira, Becky marries Jehú Malacara, now a prominent
bank official. They move, with Becky's children, from Klail City. Becky, who during
her marriage to Ira had belonged to the accepted civic organizations in Klail City, had
been brought up bilingually. As her social status had improved, she had lost her
Spanish and had spoken only in English.

With her split from Ira, however, Becky abandons her clubs and takes lessons to regain her Spanish. In doing so, she recaptures her heritage. Becky obviously is struggling to redefine herself and to establish an identity based not upon her husband's position but upon her own.

Summary

Rolando Hinojosa has an encompassing aesthetic vision that is based upon achieving an understanding of society through achieving an understanding of its common people. Neither an idealist nor an ideologue, Hinojosa has captured the pulse of a community. By depicting that community through the perceptions of a representative sampling of its members, he has defined what it is to be a Mexican American in southern Texas in the last half of the twentieth century.

To tell his stories effectively, Hinojosa has devised an original format for the novel. Similar approaches have been taken by other writers, notably William Faulkner, who, like Hinojosa, invented a county and populated it with fictional characters drawn directly from life.

Bibliography

Calderón, Héctor. "On the Uses of Chronicle, Biography, and Sketches in Rolando Hinojosa's *Generaciones y semblanzas*." In *The Rolando Hinojosa Reader: Essays Historical and Critical*, edited by José David Saldívar. Houston: Arte Público Press, 1985.

Houston, Robert. Review of *Dear Rafe*, by Rolando Hinojosa. *The New York Times Book Review*, August 18, 1985, 20.

Saldívar, José David. "Our Southwest: An Interview with Rolando Hinojosa." In *The Rolando Hinojosa Reader: Essays Critical and Historical*, edited by José David Saldívar. Houston: Arte Público Press, 1985.

——————. "Rolando Hinojosa's *Klail City Death Trip*: A Critical Introduction." In *The Rolando Hinojosa Reader: Essays Historical and Critical*, edited by José David Saldívar. Houston: Arte Público Press, 1985.

Saldívar, Ramón. "*Korean Love Song*: A Border Ballad and Its Heroes." In *The Rolando Hinojosa Reader: Essays Historical and Critical*, edited by José David Saldívar. Houston: Arte Público Press, 1985.

R. Baird Shuman

LINDA HOGAN

Born: Denver, Colorado
July 16, 1947

Principal Literary Achievement
A leading Native American poet, Linda Hogan transcends a merely political voice by incorporating into her poems her deep respect for and love of the natural and spiritual worlds.

Biography

Linda (Henderson) Hogan was born on July 16, 1947, in Denver, Colorado, the daughter of Charles and Cleona (Bower) Henderson. Her mother was a white woman from Nebraska, but Hogan identified most strongly with her Chickasaw father and his family, who lived in rural South-Central Oklahoma. She and her parents frequently visited Oklahoma; in one interview, the poet stated that Oklahoma felt like home to her, a place where she was loved, "cared for, wanted." She was nevertheless a solitary child, choosing to spend much of her time alone outdoors.

Hogan's grandfather was a bronco rider, and her grandmother, descended from a nineteenth century head of the Chickasaw nation, was what Hogan calls "a caretaker of the people." During the 1930's, her grandparents lost their allotment land, which they had farmed, to foreclosure. To support themselves, her grandfather worked as a janitor for a church, and her grandmother sold eggs in town. This family experience helped Hogan to understand how American society blames victims for their own poverty and hunger, a common topic in her work. From her grandparents, Hogan also learned that there was an alternative to her working-class city lifestyle: She learned, she has said, "better ways to love, to take care of life," to appreciate the beauty of nature as well as how to survive poverty and hardship.

During Hogan's childhood, little value was placed on formal education, because her Native American family had different values from the dominant white society. Although she did not read much as a child, she grew up in a strong oral tradition, encouraged by her father, her uncle, and her grandmother, all of whom were storytellers. As she said in one interview, "I wasn't interested in literature, but I did listen to stories, and I still do. I listened carefully and acutely, and I heard what was behind words, and voices. . . ." Many of her poems are based on these family stories or reflect her childhood experiences.

The first time Hogan tried to write a poem was in a high-school writing class. She was unfamiliar with modern poetry, so, she has recalled, she "looked up words in the dictionary, using words like 'cherubim' and 'seraphim'." After Hogan was accused of plagiarism by her teacher, her mother testified that the work was original. Yet Hogan did not write another poem until she was in her late twenties, and she abandoned the use of traditional rhyme and set meter.

While in her late twenties, Hogan worked in Washington, D.C., with orthopedically handicapped children as a teacher's aide. During her lunch hours, she would sit in the nearby woods and write. This early work helped Hogan to reconcile her rural, working-class background with her suburban lifestyle. She wrote about the children with whom she worked, about "what it was like to be beautiful souls inside bodies that didn't work"; she felt that this writing helped her to make contact with her own life in a fundamental way.

In 1975, Hogan went back to school and took a creative writing class. At this time, she was working on a long poem that she eventually organized into her first book, *Calling Myself Home* (1979). Before this work was completed, she attended the University of Colorado, where she encountered two encouraging writing instructors. Hogan earned her master's degree in creative writing in 1978 from the University of Colorado, but she has said that she really became a writer when "I began to look for my own ideas, for critical work in books, and rejected what I heard in class."

Linda Hogan then worked as poet-in-residence from 1980 to 1984 for the Colorado and Oklahoma arts councils and as assistant professor at Colorado College from 1982 to 1984. In 1984, she was appointed associate professor of American and American Indian studies at the University of Minnesota. Yet it was her Native American and working-class experiences (as a nurse's aide, dental assistant, waitress, homemaker, secretary, library clerk, and more) that encouraged her to use accessible, colloquial English in her poems. She believes that poetry should not be restricted to the well-educated. Hogan's books of poetry—*Calling Myself Home* (1979), *Daughters, I Love You* (1981), *Eclipse* (1983), *Seeing Through the Sun* (1985), and *Savings* (1988)—as well as her short and long fiction—*That Horse* (1985) and *Mean Spirit* (1990)—all weave together aspects of her life and memories in everyday language.

Analysis

In "Native American Women: Our Voice, the Air" (1981), Linda Hogan wrote:

> The literature contemporary Indian women write is a necessity. It is existence and survival given shape in written language. It is more than poetry and prose. It is an expression of entire cultures and their perceptions of the world and universe.

Like many Native American authors, Hogan struggles with themes of history and oral tradition (and how the past affects daily life), themes of return (to the home or to the self), themes of identity or self-definition (often involving the reconciliation of two cultures or the continuation of tribal identity), and themes of metamorphosis or transformation. All these themes, however, are simply aspects of a preoccupation with genocide, a concern of critical importance to American Indian authors. As the noted Native American scholar Paula Gunn Allen has pointed out,

> The impact of genocide in the minds of American Indian poets and writers cannot be exaggerated. It is a pervasive feature of the consciousness of every American Indian in the United States, and the poets are never unaware of it. Even poems that are meant to be humorous derive much of their humor directly from this awareness. American Indians take the fact of probable extinction for granted in every thought, in every conversation.

This awareness is vibrantly present in Hogan's poem "Blessing" (1978), in which she writes, "Blessed are they who listen when no one is left to speak."

Hogan's understanding of the issues of genocide forces her to deal with the politics of Indian survival, which she links with the survival of the natural world. In fact, one device used in many of her poems is an identification with nature or with animals; for example, "Evolution in Light and Water" (1985) proclaims,

> Dark amphibians
> live in my skin.
> I am their country.
> They swim in the old quiet seas
> of this woman.
> Salamander and toad
> waiting to emerge and fall again
> from the radiant vault of myself,
> this full and broken continent of living.

The phrase "I am their country" proclaims the unity of the Native American people and the natural world. If the Native American ways or people become extinct, then the natural world will also be lost.

The themes of protecting the natural world and of awareness of human suffering are reflected in many of Hogan's poems in *Daughters, I Love You*, in which the specter of nuclear accident or holocaust is present. This volume commemorates some of Hogan's experiences with her family at a 1980 antinuclear protest in the Black Hills of South Dakota.

Despite these overwhelming concerns, Hogan is by no means an elitist; she empathizes with all human suffering and cannot accept the apathy of modern society. In the poem "Workday" (1988), she describes going to work at the university, riding the bus, eating lunch, chatting, and going home at night, all the while conscious of hungry children, imprisoned women, torture victims, lost children—in short, all the horrors of modern society. As she leaves the bus, she sees women alone in their homes and men coming home, "the shoulders/ which bend forward and forward/ and forward/ to protect the heart from pain." Thus, Hogan is aware of the walls people erect to protect themselves from other people and the natural world. These are exactly the barriers she wants to transform. In "Wall Songs" (1985), she wishes all walls will disappear under the growth of bridges between people, a process she compares with the disappearance of manmade roads under the natural force of animal-filled jungle growth. As she states, "boundaries are all lies."

The poem "All Winter" (1988) represents Hogan's concern with the continuance of tribal identity and her sense of tribal history. In it, she remembers how the winter snow absorbed her predecessors, whose voices have gone underground. She recalls a man named Fire whose ancestors "live in the woodstove/ and cry at night and are broken." She speaks of her unity with every creature and knows "how long it takes/ to travel the sky,/ for buffalo are still living/ across the drifting face of the moon." The poem ends with the spirits in the night air pointing out "the things that happen,/ the things we might forget."

As Allen explains, transformation is the oldest tribal ceremonial theme and has existed in ancient Europe, Britain, and America. Some of Hogan's poems (especially in *Calling Myself Home*) use transformation to celebrate the continuance of tribal identity, love, or the natural world. For example, she is like the changing subject of "Man in the Moon" (1978): Although yesterday poor and thin, tomorrow "his house/ will fill up with silver/ the white flesh will fatten on his frame." In "Celebration: Birth of a Colt," Hogan watches the transformation of potential life into its realization, "that slick wet colt/ like a black tadpole/ darts out/ beginning at once/ to sprout legs." Hogan's work also reflects the transformation of the ways of Native Americans to survive the modern world. She laughs at the white society's stereotype of Indians; she wants portrayals of believable Indians who, for example, have bumperstickers on their cars.

Paula Gunn Allen has pointed out that American Indian writers often have trouble finding readers who can appreciate the meaning of their work, because the experience and vision of Indians and other Americans are so different. Hogan, though, can understand broader concerns, as she demonstrated in "Workday." One example of the difference between Indian and mainstream American perceptions is the fundamental assumption about the existence of spirits in the world. As her worldview was developing, Hogan became conscious of having visions (of spirit people, past events, or the destruction of the earth). With the help of a mixed-blood Indian friend who had similar experiences, she finally realized that these visions formed part of her heritage as an American Indian. Hogan views the world through this spirit-centered consciousness, which creates the tone and the substance of her poems. This vision shows her the importance of the survival of both the tribal and the natural worlds, underscoring her belief that political commitment is the complement of her natural spirituality.

PLANTING A CEDAR

First published: 1985
Type of work: Poem

The poet mediates on nature's society, white society, their similarities, and her position in both.

"Planting a Cedar" was written while Hogan was living in a large city (Minneapolis). This represents a change in her working style; her earlier work was composed in a quiet environment, rather than in a noisy urban one. As a result, the poem exhibits what Hogan calls "faster language" in comparison to her earlier work. This phrase, she explained, means that the flow of her words is faster, at a "clipped pace," and that she uses more jargon and humor. The form of her poems changed as well; she explained that she will use a cliché and then "use it against itself."

"Planting a Cedar" begins with the image of black ants, "the old dark ones/ fierce as slaves," hurrying from underneath a stone to protect the "new white larvae/ from danger or sun." The young larvae are "surrounded by white swaddling" through which they must eat their way to the outside world. Hogan compares these young insects pushing at walls to human children, who are "covered in so many words/ there is nothing left for them to know." With this image, Hogan seems to be describing modern American urban culture, in which children must find their own way through a wordy barrage of information.

The poem's narrator then says that she "did not mean to disturb plain life/ or sit this long/ beside the stone's country. It is late." After being lost in the natural world, she has become aware of the passage of time and the presence of city life: men with rattling lunch pails returning home, where women have taken in laundry "blowing from the lines." She did not intend to remain so long by the stone, but at the same time, she never intended to find herself living in the city, "wrapped around the little finger of this town/ I wear like a white lie."

For Hogan, "the white lie" is both city life and its concrete skin. Her nature-centered consciousness never lets her forget that the earth is still present under the concrete, which means that there is still hope for the world. As she stated in one interview, "All that concrete is just a thin little layer on this huge planet. It is nothing. It is a white lie." The use of the word "white" in this phrase is an example of Hogan's clever use of a cliché against itself. The phrase "white lie" usually means a lie concerning something trivial; Hogan says that the concrete and the cities are trivial when compared to the enormous bulk of the earth. This phrase, however, also reflects Hogan's view that white society tries to deny the existence of nature and Native Americans. Thus, the cities with their cars and concrete are "white" lies perpetrated by white society to enforce this denial.

BEES IN TRANSIT: OSAGE COUNTY

First published: 1983
Type of work: Poem

Hogan expresses sorrow for the losses of the Osage people, who have been driven away from their lands by the greed and ruthlessness of whites.

"Bees in Transit: Osage County" reflects Linda Hogan's interest in the so-called Osage murders, which were researched by the Osage scholar Carol Hunter. Hogan based her first novel, *Mean Spirit* (1990), on this work. The novel is set in Oklahoma during the 1920's, soon after the discovery of oil on the allotment lands of the Osage people, and provides a fictionalized account of the lives of Osage landowners who were murdered, most probably for their oil rights. By the novel's end, the Osage people were abandoning their former town life and the white world, leaving behind the luxuries they had purchased with their oil money. A major theme of the novel is the suffering of the Osage women, some of whom were courted by white men interested only in their land rights and some of whom were murdered outright.

The suffering of the Osage women is also depicted in Hogan's poem "Bees in Transit: Osage County," first published in the volume *Seeing Through the Sun*. This poem begins with the image of "a hundred white bedroom chests/ being driven to the county dump," a reminder of the possessions that the Osage left behind. Like these white chests, beehives draped in white sheets are transported by truck away from their home and abandoned. "The air is filled with workers/ on strike," and the cold air meets the smoke of a brush fire. Green Osage oranges fall, "hitting earth/ where dark women, murdered for oil/ under the ground/ still walk in numbers/ through smoky dusk." As the author Helen Jaskoski has noted, this work displays Hogan's feeling for history in the light of her spiritual awareness: Prompted by the spirits she sees, she is unwilling to let past evils be forgotten, even as she watches the current bewilderment of the bees. The bees form "a lost constellation," seeing Hogan again and again through "compound eyes" and "in the confusion of a hundred earths/ and rising moons."

Hogan says of the bees, "Desertion's sorrow has not yet touched them," but, like the Osage people, the bees feel the air "growing death cold." Meanwhile, "there is no place to go at dark/ when the air fills up with sirens and suicides" and all the bewildering trappings of modern civilization. This new world is unaware of the spirits, "gray women wavering above the amber heat/ of brushfires/ and a thousand porchlights."

The poem ends with Hogan's wish that she could tell the "noisy bees/ there is a way back home." She adds that "there is nothing more than air between us all," expressing her sorrow and empathy for the landless Osage people. This final line ties the poem in with another of her interests: namely, the existence of boundaries between people or between people and nature, something against which Hogan has struggled all of her life. The presence of this theme is heightened when the poem is read in the context of *Seeing Through the Sun*, where "Bees in Transit: Osage County" appears in a section entitled "Wall Songs."

THE NEW APARTMENT: MINNEAPOLIS

First published: 1988
Type of work: Poem

Hogan describes the features of her new apartment, dwells upon thoughts of the people around her and those who came before her, and returns to her true home.

In "The New Apartment: Minneapolis," Hogan's dislike of the city dominates. The poem begins with Hogan describing her new apartment's unpleasant features: creaking, burn-scarred floorboards, no view of the moon, the way in which the building "wants to fall down/ the universe when earth turns," and the way it "still holds the coughs of old men."

Hogan meditates upon the Indian people who lived in the building before she moved in and recalls "how last spring white merchants hung an elder/ on a meathook and beat him." This beating of an elderly Indian man who was accused of stealing a bottle of disinfectant from a local store makes her feel at war. In one interview, Hogan claimed that Minneapolis was an extremely racist city; she pointed out that the beating became public only because one of the police who investigated it was an Indian.

As the poem continues, Hogan remembers earlier wars "and relocation like putting the moon in prison/ with no food and that moon already a crescent," identifying the Indian peoples with the crescent-thin moon at the time of their forced relocation to inhospitable lands. Hogan, though, warns that they will grow large and strong again, as the moon grows full.

Despite this warning and her anger over the treatment of Native Americans, Hogan does not forget that city society, like all other societies, is made up of individuals, seemingly suspended in air "through the walls of houses": people baking, sleeping, or getting drunk, businessmen hitting their wives, fathers being tender with their children, women crying and joking, children laughing, girls talking on the telephone all night. She talks about the teeming life "inside the walls" where "world changes are planned, bosses overthrown." All this city life, however, cannot hold Hogan, for "beyond walls are lakes and plains,/ canyons and the universe." She compares the features of her city home with her true home: "the stars are the key/ turning in the lock of night./Turn the deadbolt and I am home." Hogan has "opened a door to nights where there are no apartments/ just drumming and singing." In the natural world, the city is forgotten, and no one there "has ever lost the will to go on." With this comment, Hogan points out how city life drains people of their lives and spirits.

"The New Apartment: Minneapolis" ends with Hogan's greeting: "Hello aunt, hello brothers, hello trees/ and deer walking quietly on the soft red earth." Although in the poem Hogan was able to retreat to the natural world, she wrote it in the midst of the city, which lends her final greeting a wistfulness, as if she wanted really to be home.

Summary

Linda Hogan gracefully reconciles her activist obligations with her spiritual outlook. A major device that occurs in nearly all of her work is the identification of herself or her people with aspects of the natural world such as bees, horses, birds, turtles, or the moon. As she stated in one interview, she has "a heart made out of crickets," by which she means that she feels loyalty to all life forms and acts as a spokesperson for the animals. Hogan's work is based upon her strong sense of tribal history and spirit of place, and she uses her words, her wit, and her humor to stand up for those who, like the bees, have no voice in their future.

Bibliography

Allen, Paula Gunn. *The Sacred Hoop: Recovering the Feminine in American Indian Traditions*. Boston: Beacon Press, 1986.

Balassi, William, John F. Crawford, and Annie O. Eysturoy, eds. *This Is About Vision: Interviews with Southwestern Writers*. Albuquerque: University of New Mexico Press, 1990.

Bruchac, Carol, Linda Hogan, and Judith McDaniel, eds. *The Stories We Hold Secret*. Greenfield Center, N.Y.: Greenfield Review Press, 1986.

Bruchac, Joseph. *Survival This Way: Interviews with American Indian Poets*. Tucson: The University of Arizona Press, 1987.

Coltelli, Laura. *Winged Words: American Indian Writers Speak*. Lincoln: University of Nebraska Press, 1990.

Schöler, Bo. "'A Heart Made Out of Crickets': An Interview with Linda Hogan." *Journal of Ethnic Studies* 16 (Spring, 1988): 107-117.

Katherine Socha

GARRETT HONGO

Born: Volcano, Hawaii
May 30, 1951

Principal Literary Achievement
The most prolific and accomplished Asian American poet of his time, Garrett Hongo produces work with striking images and details of place that mark his quests for ethnic and familial identity.

Biography
Garrett Kaoru Hongo was born on May 30, 1951, in Volcano, Hawaii, of Japanese parents. His father, Albert Kazuyoshi, was an electrical technician, and his mother, Louise Tomiko Kubota Hongo, was a personnel analyst. The family left Volcano when Hongo was eight months old and later settled in Gardena, a small city south of Los Angeles. The racially mixed community was bordered on the north by the predominantly black towns of Watts and Compton and on the southwest by the largely white communities of Torrance and Redondo Beach. At the time Hongo lived there, Gardena boasted the largest community of Japanese Americans in the United States outside Honolulu. Growing up in a working-class neighborhood with a variety of ethnic groups early sensitized Hongo to issues of race relations, cultural alienation, and urban street life, which, in turn, influenced his writing of such poems as "Ninety-six Tears."

Hongo was graduated from Pomona College with honors in 1973, studied in Japan for a year under a fellowship, attended graduate school at the University of Michigan in 1974-1975, and earned an M.F.A. from the University of California at Irvine in 1980, where he also completed everything but his dissertation for a doctorate in critical theory. While he was at Michigan, winning the Hopwood Poetry Prize changed the direction of his studies, and soon he was working as a poet-in-residence in Seattle, founding and directing a local theater group called the Asian Exclusion Act. There he staged plays such as Frank Chin's *The Year of the Dragon* (1974) and his own *Nisei Bar and Grill* (1976), among others, and his creative imagination took fire. He became acquainted with Lawson Fusao Inada, a pioneer Japanese American poet, with whom he and Alan Chong Lau collaborated on *The Buddha Bandits Down Highway 99* (1978). In his work and his sensibility, Hongo identifies largely with the West Coast, a mecca for many Asian American writers.

Hongo has taught writing at the University of Washington, the University of

California at Irvine, and the University of Missouri, where he was also poetry editor for *The Missouri Review*. He began to direct the creative writing program at the University of Oregon in 1989, and occasional leaves have allowed him to return to Hawaii periodically.

Two earlier volumes of Hongo's poetry, *Yellow Light* (1982) and *The River of Heaven* (1988), were extremely well received. He won the 1981 Discovery/*The Nation* award for poems later published in *Yellow Light* and National Endowment for the Arts fellowships in 1982 and 1988. In 1987, he received the Lamont Poetry Prize, and *The River of Heaven* garnered a nomination for the 1989 Pulitzer Prize in poetry. In 1990, he received a Guggenheim Fellowship. Hongo credits a six-week residency at an artists' colony and a visit to Hawaii for the final coming together of *The River of Heaven*. In Hawaii, Hongo was inspired by a friend's interest in him and his history to, as he said, "share more of my heart through poetry with the rest of the world."

Hongo, whose name means "homeland" in Hawaiian, is a *yonsei*, a fourth-generation Japanese American. Although his family was not among those sent to relocation camps during World War II, his grandfather, Kubota, was detained by the Federal Bureau of Investigation (FBI) for several days for his leadership in the Japanese American community in Hawaii. In a published essay called "Kubota," Hongo describes his grandfather's story and explains why he feels compelled to speak for the Japanese. In 1982, Hongo married Cynthia Anne Thiessen, a violinist and musicologist who, as Hongo reveals in his poem "Stepchild," is a white woman descended from Mennonites and Quakers. They have two sons, Alexander and Hudson. Biracial issues are thus central to both his work and his private life.

In 1993, Hongo edited and published a groundbreaking anthology of thirty-one poets entitled *The Open Boat: Poems from Asian America*. The volume is important not only because it displays the rich diversity of contemporary Asian American poetry but also because Hongo's twenty-five-page introduction offers an excellent overview of the difficulties and challenges that face a marginalized people as they struggle to produce art and achieve recognition.

Analysis

In an interview, Hongo once said of himself as a poet that "I live on the earth and in the sky." Many issues inform the style and content of his rich writing. Some of his Hawaiian ancestors worked on plantations, cutting sugar cane and stoking vats in the mills; others were professionals. Hongo's own educational background includes a year of study in Japan and graduate school work as a student of Japanese language and literature. He translated his early poems into Japanese, and he has remarked that he sometimes still thinks in Japanese. On the other hand, his experiences growing up in a West Coast multiethnic community and performing poetry with a jazz trio have equally influenced his writing.

Connecting with ancestry is an important venture for Hongo, who uses as one central image in his poetry an old man who eventually turns out to be the poet. The wizened Asian man is mythical and elemental; he seems to hang over Hongo's consciousness as a shadow or an alter ego. He has suffered and is wise, and he is the essence that impels Hongo to live sympathetically and to write well. Some of Hongo's poems contain only vague resonances of the old man; poems such as "What For" seem to speak with the old man's voice, expressing a longing to become "a doctor of pure magic" and heal his father's pain. Another poem, "Roots," identifies more directly the old man, who "hangs over my sleep." Still another, "Something Whispered in the *Shakuhachi*," is a narrative monologue in the persona of the old man that reveals poignant events in his life.

Male relatives are important subjects for Hongo. He shows his father working the swing shift and betting on horses; he recalls his brother playing guitar in the garage when they were younger, "practicing/ for the priesthood, preaching the blues." Several poems and an essay focus on "Kubota," Hongo's maternal grandfather, for whom Hongo, the eldest grandchild, has particular affection. The name "Kubota," Hongo reveals, can mean either "wayside field" or "broken dreams." When Kubota died, a Buddhist priest gave him a name that meant "shining wisdom of the law." A Japanese American born in Hawaii, Kubota ran a general store on the north shore of Oahu before moving with Hongo's family to California. Through Kubota's "talking story," Hongo learned of such events as the bombing of Pearl Harbor and received with the stories Kubota's directive to tell them to others. For Hongo, the obligation to speak is a ritual payment that the young owe their elders. In his poetry, he fulfills that injunction by witnessing and revealing the experiences of Japanese Americans.

Personal memory thus combines in Hongo's poetry with cultural history. Further, Hongo's early experience in the theater is evident in many of his narrative poems that take the form of dramatic monologues. In "*Pinoy* at the Coming World," an anonymous plantation worker who loses everything that matters to him is as sympathetically rendered as if he had been a close relative. "*Jingoku*: On the Glamour of Self-Hate" tells the story of an evacuated soldier in Japan who succeeds for a time at gambling and then is reduced to squalor.

Hongo expresses outrage at the racist treatment he sees Asians experiencing in America. Such expression can be lyrical and sad, as in "Something Whispered in the *Shakuhachi*," which focuses on one lonely man, or searingly painful, as in the depiction of the bombing of Hiroshima and its aftermath in "Stepchild." Though "Stepchild" has been faulted for didacticism and excess, it convincingly exposes the horror that human beings can wreak on other human beings, suggests the biting ways of the dragon and the shark to retaliate, and finally shows outrage as being partially assuaged by healing and hope.

Hongo believes that the impetus of poetry is communion and communication. One poet should not necessarily be compared to others to determine who is superior, he thinks, because such an approach would lead to the institutionalization of poetry, forcing everyone to see the world in the same way. Despite his extensive experience teaching in universities, Hongo describes himself as being basically "anti-institution." He prefers to imagine himself as Matsuo Bashō, the ancient Japanese traveling poet, with a cluster of faithful followers and adheres to the nontraditional style of learning offered in Eugène Ionesco's play *The Student*. He counts as important literary influences on his writing Philip Levine, William Wordsworth, William Styron, and James Agee. He has a great affinity for the sounds of words, for the beauty of language, and for the individuality of different dialects. Hongo's attention to portraying in writing the way people talk is evident in such poems as "Cruisin' 99," in which three friends converse while driving down a stretch of highway.

In his introduction to *The Open Boat*, Hongo explains not only the evolution of Asian American literature but also the motivation behind his own writing. This motivation is partly to fight the stereotypes of Asians in America, he says, and partly to widen the field of what has previously been known as mainstream literature, all the while encouraging "intellectual passion" and "an appreciation of verbal beauty."

YELLOW LIGHT

First published: 1980
Type of work: Poem

An anonymous woman, carrying a parcel of food for supper, gets off a city bus after a day of work and walks to her apartment.

"Yellow Light," the title poem from Hongo's first volume of poetry, uses description to convey personal sympathy and collective resignation. It uses many of the techniques that mark Hongo's best poems and sets the mood for the poems that follow in the collection. These are poems of striking images, full of close details about family members and neighbors, in which the poet examines the roots of his biological and ancestral identity and hones his personal, creative impulses. "Yellow Light" couples exploration with reconciliation, joy and even playfulness with bitterness and class struggle.

The poem begins by closely focusing on an unnamed working-class woman: "One arm hooked around the frayed strap/ of a tar-black patent-leather purse." She is on her way home in a multiethnic community of Los Angeles, a city Hongo knows well. It is early evening, and suppers are beginning to simmer on the stove while tempers start to seethe; adults coming home from work vent their frustrations on their children, and "gangs of schoolboys [are] playing war." Burnt-out ends of days find people worn out and testy.

This is a poem built on contrasts that emphasize have-nots. The poet says he might have written about butterflies and flowering vines had it been spring or summer, but the time is October, and the season's ripeness, rather than being appealing, is congested. The searchlights from uptown theaters and used-car lots are "sticks of light" that "probe the sky." Such brilliant illumination conflicts with the dull patches of light thrown out from kitchen windows, "winking on/ in all the side streets of the Barrio." The poem shows energy being infused into an already crowded and even malcontented community, one devoid of excitement and glamour, seething with routine and dissat-isfaction. In contrast, the uptown lights, signifying where the excitement is, are distant, but "brilliant" even from that distance, while the lights from the barrio apartments and houses are "dim."

The anonymous female worker is poor and tired, and Hongo lets his readers know that her life is not easy and is possibly joyless. From the bus stop, she must walk several blocks uphill and then up two flights of stairs until she reaches her apartment. Her heels are spikes that click "like kitchen knives on a cutting board" as she climbs the steps. She performs routinely dull chores, but Hongo's description of them is anything but routine. In infusing his images with sharpness, he deftly conveys resentment at poverty and anger at an inability to break out of it. The poem's final image is at once uplifting and earthy—perhaps the cycle will be broken, or perhaps something will happen to make it bearable, or perhaps problems will simply be covered up. The image is of the moon, "cruising from behind a screen of eucalyptus," covering everything "in a heavy light like yellow onions." The poem is at once sensuous, poignant, and foreboding.

CRUISING 99

First published: 1978
Type of work: Poem

Three friends, all Asian American poets, drive down Highway 99 in California on a mystical journey in search of truths about individual and cultural identity.

At thirteen pages and with nine sections, "Cruising 99" is the longest poem in Hongo's collection *Yellow Light*. It is also the poem that uses the most variety of line length, meter, stanza, and mood. Though there is a narrative thread to the poem, it is a thin one, broken up with both jazz lyrics and meditative monologue. The many voices Hongo uses in the poem caused one critic to call him "the Rich Little of Asian American writing." His facility is evident, as he stretches readers' minds and limbers his own creative sinews by experimenting with forms and focus. His indebtedness to Beat writers such as Jack Kerouac and Allen Ginsberg is evident, as is his love of music. (Hongo dedicated the volume to his wife, violinist and musicologist Cynthia Thiessen.)

Highway 99 is an old route that connects the inland cities of the West Coast from Mexico to Canada. Hongo's "cruise" along it took him and two friends around Southern California, an area they knew well. In describing rich landscapes of walnut groves, arroyos, and manzanita, Hongo is also obsessively searching for some com-pelling truths about his own origins and identity as the car heads for a town called Paradise. He has remarked that such preoccupations are "more than a nostalgia or even a semi-learned atavism, though these things certainly play their parts. It is rather a way to isolate, and to uphold, cultural and moral value in a confusing time and environment."

As the title suggests, the poem offers an expansive journey that is a search for connectedness and meaning. It is reminiscent of the poetry of Walt Whitman, whom Hongo celebrated in a 1992 essay published in *The Massachusetts Review* and whom Hongo counts as an important influence in developing his own spiritual optimism. Highway 99 is a useful metaphor because so many people have traveled it or live near it. Like elements of Whitman's vision, it is democratic and encompasses many people, each with a different experience, and each with an experience that is changing. Such change creates for Hongo both journey and myth.

The poem was originally published as Hongo's section of *The Buddha Bandits Down Highway 99*, an early collaborative effort with fellow Asian American poets Alan Chong Lau and Lawson Fusao Inada, who are the two friends who accompany him down Highway 99. The poets believe in illuminating cultural history with ethnic connectedness, and they use jazzy rhythms and verbal syncopations to record sensations and to achieve enlightenment. Because Hongo also selected "Cruising 99" for inclusion in *The Open Boat*, it is clearly an important poem to him. It is a tour de force in which Hongo celebrates both the past of his Japanese heritage and the present of his American upbringing.

SOMETHING WHISPERED IN THE *SHAKUHACHI*

First published: 1980
Type of work: Poem

An old Japanese man who makes bamboo flutes is forced to burn them when he is interned in a relocation camp during World War II.

"Something Whispered in the *Shakuhachi*" is an intimate poem, extremely evocative and lyrical. In its focus on one elderly and enfeebled man, Hongo is able to show a personal strength of spirit that can transcend the most challenging and demeaning of conditions. To understand more about how the notion of the old man functions as a seminal concept for Hongo, it is a good idea to also read another of his poems, "Roots." In that poem, Hongo talks about an old man hanging over his sleep whose "signature . . ./ scratches across my unconscious life," a metaphor for his own Japanese origins, which live in his heart. The physical part of his identity, Hongo implies, is a carefree American "girl-watching" in California, and the light in his soul is his Japanese heritage.

The old man of both poems delights in his talent for carving *shakuhachi*, bamboo flutes. His story is made explicit in "Something Whispered in the *Shakuhachi*," in which the old man, interned in a World War II relocation camp, is ordered to leave his home and give up his belongings. Rather than have his precious flutes destroyed, he burns them himself, but even after they are gone, he can hear their "wail like fists of wind/ whistling through the barracks." After the war, when he returns home, the memory of the flutes and their melodies still give him comfort. Whenever times are bad, there is "one thicket/ of memory that calls for me/ to come and sit/ among the tall canes/ and shape full-throated songs/ out of wind, out of bamboo,/ out of a voice/ that only whispers." Although Hongo himself did not experience internment, he speaks on behalf of those who did and, on a broader level, for all victims of social injustice. The poem affirms the power of faith, of will, and of memory to survive hardship and catastrophe.

In *Yellow Light*, the poem closes the book. It is as if Hongo has worked up to baring his soul and, for a finale, offers what is most important to his sensibility and yet most difficult to reveal. The first line of the poem suggests that Hongo will share a "secret" and that the reader who follows carefully will be "enlightened." What is revealed is that the old man is truly enlightened and easily, almost without even being aware of it, still sings his songs with the flutes—a noble, self-possessed, and peaceful role model indeed. He knows what is important in life and lets that clear vision guide him in all that he does.

Summary

Garrett Hongo is an exceptional poet who is accomplished in many forms. He expresses a variety of moods deftly and incisively, and he writes about personal subjects that are important to him as well as about those that affect Japanese Americans in general. Both through his own acclaimed poetry and through his efforts to expose younger Asian American poets to the mainstream reading public, he has broadened the literary palette of America.

Bibliography

Evans, Alice. "A Vicious Kind of Tenderness: An Interview with Garrett Hongo." *Poets and Writers* 20, no. 5 (September/October, 1992): 36-46.

Kaneko, Lonny. "A Journey into Place, Race, and Spirit." *Amerasia Journal* 6, no. 2 (1979): 91-95.

Moffet, Penelope. "Verses Chronicle Tales of Asian-Americans." *Los Angeles Times*, March 19, 1987, p. V1.

Muratori, Fred. Review of *The River of Heaven*, by Garrett Hongo. *Library Journal* 113 (May 1, 1988): 81-82.

Schultz, Robert. "Passionate Virtuosity." *Hudson Review* 42 (Spring, 1992): 149-157.

Jill B. Gidmark

DAVID HENRY HWANG

Born: Los Angeles, California
August 11, 1957

Principal Literary Achievement
A playwright who effectively mixes realism with surrealism to create new conceptions about racial identity and gender politics, Hwang is the first Asian American writer to have achieved international acclaim and success.

Biography

David Henry Hwang was born on August 11, 1957, in San Gabriel, a multiethnic suburb of Los Angeles. His father, Henry Y. Hwang, grew up in Shanghai, China, and in the 1970's founded the Far East National Bank, the first Asian American-owned national bank in the United States. His mother, Dorothy Hwang, born in southeast China and reared in the Philippines, was a talented pianist who encouraged her son to play the violin. Although Hwang's mother and sister became classical musicians, Hwang opted for jazz and played in an all-Asian rock band during college. He even composed an "Oriental riff" for his play *Face Value* (1993).

Educated in an elite preparatory school, Hwang was always interested in words. He was on the school's debate team and was encouraged by his parents to become a lawyer. Hwang's family was actively involved with the "born again" Evangelical Christian Church, a fact bitterly satirized in Hwang's play *Family Devotions* (1981). He grew up feeling that he should date only Chinese girls and for a few years was married to Ophelia Chong, a Chinese Canadian artist. His later plays, such as *M. Butterfly* (1988), *Bondage* (1992), and *Face Value*, use themes of interracial love and rebellion against traditional images and expectations. He has said that there was always a part of him that did things that were not expected of him. In the early 1990's, he began living with Caucasian actress Kathryn Layng in Los Angeles; because so much of his work is produced in New York City, he also keeps an apartment in Manhattan. He promotes in his work the idea of cultures existing harmoniously side by side, and he believes that children of mixed heritages represent the world's future.

At Stanford University, John L'Heurex, a novelist and creative-writing instructor, encouraged Hwang to pursue playwriting. Another of Hwang's early formative influences was the 1978 Padua Hills Playwrights Festival workshop, where he studied under Sam Shepard, an explosive playwright whose work combines human interaction

2497

with mythmaking and to whom Hwang dedicated *Family Devotions*. *FOB* (1978) was staged Off-Broadway and was developed for both the Playwrights' Conference of the O'Neill Theater Center in Waterford, Connecticut, and for the New York Shakespeare Festival. As critic Douglas Street has pointed out, *FOB* is American in style and Asian in its concerns. It explores issues to which Hwang has returned frequently in his writing: the interplay between the insider and the outsider and the exploration of loneliness. The play received rave reviews and garnered many awards, including a 1981 Obie Award as best Off-Broadway production.

The Dance and the Railroad (1981), which Hwang wrote while studying at the Yale School of Drama, focuses exclusively and evocatively on Chinese history. *Family Devotions* is a bizarre Southern California domestic farce about confrontation, alienation, and the loss of ethnic awareness. Feeling that he had exhausted his Chinese American identity as a subject and given the freedom to experiment by a Rockefeller Grant in 1983, Hwang turned to Japanese literature for his ethereally tragic one-acts *The House of Sleeping Beauties* and *Sound of a Voice* (both 1983). Another one-act that also explores the boundary between myth and reality is *As the Crow Flies* (1986), which centers on a black domestic with two identities; Hwang modeled the central character after the woman who cleaned house for his grandmother. *Rich Relations* (1986) was both a critical and a financial flop, but in its attacks on materialism and in its use of an all-white cast—and because its failure liberated Hwang to move beyond the depiction of his relatives—it is an important part of his canon.

A newspaper article about a bizarre French spy trial and the opera music of Giacomo Puccini combine in Hwang's hit Broadway play *M. Butterfly*, which made Hwang the first Asian American to earn the coveted Tony Award and the first U.S. playwright since Edward Albee to become an international phenomenon. (A film version, also written by Hwang, was directed by David Cronenberg and starred Jeremy Irons and John Lone.) After the play opened in New York, Hwang, American composer Philip Glass, and designer Jerome Sirlin mounted the opaquely intellectual monologue *One Thousand Airplanes on the Roof* (1988), a ninety-minute science-fiction music drama that premiered in a hangar at the Vienna International Airport. Hwang and Glass collaborated as well on *The Voyage* (1992), mounted by the Metropolitan Opera to observe the quincentennial of Christopher Columbus' landing in America.

Sexual and racial obsessions surface in *Bondage* (1992), in which an anonymous leather-clad female dominatrix and a submissive male play multiple roles in a series of sexual games. *Face Value* (1993), which centers around the opening of a bogus racist musical called *The Real Manchu*, is a farce on mistaken identities that seeks to fight racial stereotypes by using them. Hwang calls it a "dream fantasy" that employs outrageous caricature to get beyond the issue of race. He has expressed the yearning to abandon grand themes, such as race, and write instead about small, personal details that make up an individual life.

Analysis

The mix of elements in Hwang's work runs the gamut from Chinese opera to television situation comedy. He believes in juxtaposing jarringly diverse features in his plays both for humor and for shock value, to make the reader and viewer self-conscious about the nature of exclusion, to question standards for evaluating what is excluded, and to be responsible for those choices. This is a critical line of thought for a writer of Chinese heritage born in America; Hwang speaks for multitudes of Asian Americans for whom assimilation has not been easy. His strategy for presenting images of exclusion and inclusion is often to pit the realistic against the surrealistic, suggesting the absurdity and damage of racism as the ultimate exclusion.

Broken Promises is the title Hwang gave to the 1983 volume that collected his first four plays. That phrase, in fact, characterizes his later work as well. Beginning with *FOB*, in which a character says, "I'm going to America because of its promises," the theme of promises not kept and dreams shattered recurs in many guises in Hwang's work. The historical prototype, to which all of Hwang's broken promises resonate, is the lure of the "Gold Mountain"—America—for the Chinese immigrants of the mid-nineteenth century. Once the immigrants arrived to build the transcontinental railroad, they discovered harsh working conditions and schemes by American bosses to swindle them out of the little money they did earn. Society offered them not gold in the streets free for the taking, but alienation and racist treatment. Hwang shows how, in striving for success, the "hyphenated" person—the Asian American—experiences along the way a debilitating tension and loss.

Hwang has called his first three plays—*FOB, Family Devotions, The Dance and the Railroad*—his "Chinese trilogy." In them, he explores individual identity, working out the personal ramifications of his own Chinese heritage and American birth. Hwang is very open about the autobiographical elements in both *Family Devotions* and in *Rich Relations*, a play using the privilege and the religion that were a part of his upbringing. His exploration also takes on a more collective resonance and so highlights new cultural heroes. The two characters in *The Dance and the Railroad* are Chinese railroad workers in an 1867 strike who triumph over physical oppression in a psychologically liberating way.

Part of building an identity and claiming a birthright means bridging the distance between men and women. Except in *The Dance and the Railroad*, Hwang uses fully developed female characters that promote gender reconciliation. In *FOB*, for example, both gender and ethnicity achieve a balance. By the end of the play, the mythical warrior woman Fa Mu Lan has taught the warrior god Gwan Gung how to get along in America, and their human transformations, Grace and Steve, have formed a bond of caring friendship.

In a second important direction, Japanese literature and film inspired two hauntingly evocative one-acts by Hwang about tragic love. *The House of Sleeping Beauties* is based on a novella by Pulitzer Prize-winning author Yasunari Kawabata. Hwang has said that this play, which centers on a bizarre and isolated brothel, is a fantasy about how Kawabata came to write. *The Sound of a Voice*, in which a medieval samurai is seduced by a magical crone, was inspired by Japanese legend and ghost stories. In both plays, a mysterious woman harbors a shocking secret that, gradually revealed, leads to an unusual resolution, to love, and to death.

The medium of sound and music drives much of Hwang's work. American pop music is important as symbolic background in *FOB*. *The Dance and the Railroad* uses dancing, singing, and mock-Chinese opera. The melody of the *shakuhachi*, a Japanese bamboo flute, is a critical feature in *The Sound of a Voice*. *M. Butterfly* is at once a parody, a deconstruction, and an elaboration of Puccini's 1904 opera *Madama Butterfly*, freely borrowing from Puccini's music. For two important works, Hwang collaborated with the American minimalist composer Philip Glass. For *One Thousand Airplanes on the Roof*, Hwang wrote a monologue about the "sound" of memory that was voiced over a ninety-minute instrumental piece by Glass. Hwang also wrote the libretto for Glass's opera *The Voyage*, which the Metropolitan Opera commissioned for the Columbus Quincentennial in 1992.

Because Hwang is an experimenter, his works are often on the cutting edge, and not all of them have been equally successful. *M. Butterfly*, however, stands out as a remarkable achievement both in itself, as drama, and for the revolutionary way that it breaks stereotypes and dashes preconceptions about gender, race, public politics, and personal intimacy. As drama, it garnered more mainstream success than any previous work by an Asian American playwright, enjoying an extended run on Broadway, a world tour, the Tony Award for Best Play of the 1987-1988 season, and Drama Desk awards for both Hwang and for B. D. Wong, who initially played the role of Song Liling (also called "Butterfly"). The play was nominated for a Pulitzer Prize and has played to appreciative audiences in two dozen countries. *M. Butterfly* turns the entire notion of tradition and identity inside out and is a landmark for theater and for Asian American literature.

FOB

First produced: 1978 (first published, 1979)
Type of work: Play

Three Chinese Americans grapple with personal rivalries, ethnic identities, the power of myth, and the challenges of assimilation.

The play's title is explained by the character Dale in the first lines: "F-O-B. Fresh Off the Boat. FOB," which are also the play's closing lines. Dale continues his speech by describing the characteristics of FOB's, Asian people who are recent U.S. immigrants. He calls them "clumsy, ugly, greasy" and "loud, stupid, four-eyed." Dale himself is an ABC, an "American Born Chinese," and traditionally the relationship between ABC's and FOB's has been anything but pleasant.

The play, which has only three characters, traces the difficulty of assimilation for Asian newcomers to the United States and the hostility they receive from Americans of Asian descent. There is the added conflict of jealousy when Dale's cousin, Grace, a first-generation Chinese American, shows a friendly interest in Steve, an FOB, but the jealousy is played out in a way that is more comic than tragic. The play delineates a hierarchy of importance and power, self-assurance and self-delusion, within various immigrant groups of Chinese Americans, overlaid with sexual jealousy and identity in flux. Hwang has said that in *FOB*, he is exploring how much of a person's identity is inherited and to what extent a person is shaped by surrounding influences. Because he is himself a person of Chinese descent born in America, Hwang thus uses his characters to explore his personal issues of identity.

There is also a mythological subplot, which Hwang uses to explore the myth that underlies reality. This subplot involves two characters. The first is Fa Mu Lan, a village girl who avenges her people by taking her father's place in battle, a character whom Hwang borrowed from Maxine Hong Kingston's 1976 novel *The Woman Warrior: Memoirs of a Girlhood Among Ghosts*. He also uses Gwan Gung, a Chinese god of warriors, writers, and prostitutes, who appears in Cantonese opera and in the work of Chinese American playwright Frank Chin. Hwang dedicated the play to "the warriors of my family."

FOB takes place entirely in the back room of a small Chinese restaurant in California where American pop music is playing. The plot is fairly uncomplicated, but the innuendoes of dialogue and monologue are richly laden. Steve, a recent immigrant enters the restaurant, which Grace's family owns, and declares that he is Gwan Gung. Grace, in a half-hearted effort to deny her Chineseness, declares that Gwan Gung is dead and that his stories are merely history. Nevertheless, she poses intermittently as Fa Mu Lan. There is an undercurrent of rivalry between Dale, who wants to protect Grace from something he feels is undesirable, and Steve, who wishes to date Grace. They have dinner together at Grace's restaurant, in a scene that includes a macho contest over who can stand more hot sauce, and openly vie for Grace's affection. Grace and Steve eventually go out dancing together. Dale is left on the stage alone; Fa Mu Lan has been avenged, and Gwan Gung has triumphed.

RICH RELATIONS

First produced: 1986 (first published, 1990)
Type of work: Play

A wealthy father and son are pressured and threatened by in-laws who are interested in their money in this darkly humorous farce.

In the introduction to *FOB and Other Plays*, Hwang describes a two-year hiatus from writing that proceeded *Rich Relations* and comments that the play reestablished his commitment to writing. It is about the possibility of resurrection, he asserts, and writing it resurrected his love for work. Elsewhere, he calls the play autobiographical, even though *Rich Relations* is the first play that Hwang wrote that has no specifically

Asian roles. The characters are white because Hwang is testing whether literary segregation implies cultural limitation. As an American author, he believes that he should be able to make his characters whatever ethnicity he chooses.

The play opens with Hinson, a high-tech entrepreneur, showing his son Keith one of his new inventions, a phone hooked up to a television. Hinson calls it "a modern convenience," but Keith calls the device "ridiculous." Hinson uses the invention to telephone his brother-in-law, Fred, who says the connection makes Hinson sound as though he is at the bottom of a sewer. That kind of multiple and contradictory perspective, played for humor, abounds in this play of misunderstood dialogue and misinterpreted gesture. California materialism and Christian mysticism are constant themes what try to unify characters with some common ground, but both are ineffectual.

The characters talk at each other rather than to each other, play for humor the fact of their being related, and bumble into and out of potentially incendiary situations with naïve aplomb. The play's conflict hinges on the attempt of Hinson's sister, Barbara, to force her daughter Marilyn onto Keith for a wife, thinking that such a marriage will make Barbara wealthy. In fact, Keith has brought his girlfriend, Jill, home with him from an East Coast high school, where he coaches debate and where Jill is one of his students. The friendship between Jill and Hinson is sealed when Jill expresses interest in seeing Hinson's spy pens. Purchased from Hong Kong, the pens not only do not work for communicating secret messages but also do not even write.

Because Barbara's pleas to Keith fall on deaf ears, she uses a more drastic measure to communicate, perching on the edge of a high balcony railing in a mock suicide attempt. Jill, whose friendship with Barbara blossoms over a bag of cheese puffs, joins her on the balcony.

Sordid secrets are confessed, but they neither effectively illuminate the listeners, vindicate the speakers, nor move the plot forward in any convincing way. Keith and Hinson aggressively smash inventions and appliances as a symbol of failed energy and thwarted convenience. Marilyn utters the most critical speech of the play, a warning to listen to the "constant voice" which "lurks behind every move we make." Alone, Hinson and Keith crouch, ears to the ground, trying to get past addictive technology by listening for that pure, small voice. As the curtain drops, however, there is no indication that they hear it.

M. BUTTERFLY

First produced: 1988 (first published, 1988)
Type of work: Play

A French diplomat becomes deeply enamored of a Chinese opera singer and is tragically disillusioned when she turns out to be both a spy and a man.

In an intriguing use of "found" material, Hwang used a newspaper article for the basic story line of *M. Butterfly*: A French diplomat falls in love with a Chinese opera singer, and they have a twenty-year love affair before the singer is shockingly exposed as both a spy and a man. The play begins with Rene Gallimard in his prison cell, musing and reflecting about the "perfect woman" as he utters the opening lines, "Butterfly, Butterfly," which give rise to flashbacks that piece together the story. The play closes with Song Liling, Gallimard's "perfect woman," tersely and almost disdainfully questioning, "Butterfly? Butterfly?" after Gallimard has committed *seppuku*, ritual suicide.

Irony and ambiguity saturate the play. Things are not as they seem, and stark reality becomes, for Gallimard, impossible to accept. The title is a direct borrowing from Puccini's opera, which tells the story of Lieutenant Benjamin Franklin Pinkerton, a callous and selfish American naval officer stationed in Japan, who woos and leaves a fifteen-year-old geisha girl named Cio-Cio-San (her name means "butterfly" in Japanese) who bears his son and pines for his return. Three years later, when Pinkerton comes back with his American wife to claim the child, Cio-Cio-San kills herself.

Hwang's protagonist, Gallimard, summarizes at extended length early in the play the plot of Puccini's opera; he says that relaying the synopsis seems to him useful to making sense of his own parallel situation of love and betrayal. In actuality, the Puccini scenario, which relies heavily on racial and sexual stereotypes, is parodied and deconstructed by Hwang's story. While the plot lines in the opera and in the play may be mirror images of each other, the images are garishly reversed. Because of that reversal, themes and identities are shockingly and inexorably confounded. Symbolic of the deceits and transformations, the ambiguous "M." of the play's title signifies "Monsieur" in the male protagonist's language; Hwang thus transforms the gender of Puccini's heroine into its opposite.

When Gallimard first sees Liling, the singer is performing Puccini's opera, which Gallimard, in dazed admiration, proclaims to be his favorite. Liling claims to despise it. As is increasingly obvious throughout the play, Liling repeatedly and completely shatters the mold of shy, subservient Asian woman. Between acts 2 and 3, Liling goes through a costume change onstage and is literally transformed into a man. Liling explains that, even in their most intimate moments, Gallimard never suspected Liling's true sexual identity, primarily because Gallimard chose to believe what he wanted to believe. Gallimard, unmanned, his illusions blown apart, has no choice but to retreat from reality into the "Butterfly" of his imagination, donning Liling's kimono and Butterfly wig. This mutation, however, produces an unnatural creature, and Gallimard must annihilate it by *seppuku*. Liling swaggers above Gallimard's corpse with strength, insouciance, and power, the dominant race and gender, as the play ends.

Summary

In the introduction to *FOB and Other Plays*, the Chinese American novelist Maxine Hong Kingston comments on the authenticity of the idioms that Hwang uses in his plays. She praises him for depicting so well the sounds of "Chinatown English, the language of childhood and the subconscious, the language of emotion, the language of home." Hwang's artistic palette, however, is broader than realism. He uses surrealism, ritual and evocation, and gender manipulation to shock and entertain his audiences as he tears down the walls of racism and creates a new vision of humanity.

Bibliography

Henry, William A. "When East and West Collide." *Time* 124 (August 14, 1984): 62-64.

Hwang, David Henry. "Evolving a Multicultural Tradition." *MELUS* 16 (Fall, 1989-1990): 16-19.

Kim, Elaine H. "Defining Asian American Realities Through Literature." *Cultural Critique* 6 (Spring, 1987): 87-111.

Kondo, Dorinne K. "*M. Butterfly*: Orientalism, Gender, and a Critique of Essentialist Identity." *Cultural Critique* 12 (Fall, 1990): 5-29.

Marx, Robert. "Hwang's World." *Opera News* 57 (October, 1992): 14-17.

Skloot, Robert. "Breaking the Butterfly: The Politics of David Henry Hwang." *Modern Drama* 33 (March, 1990): 59-66.

Smith, Dinitia. "Face Values: The Sexual and Racial Obsessions of Playwright David Henry Hwang." *New York* 26 (January 11, 1993): 40-45.

Street, Douglas. *David Henry Hwang*. Boise, Idaho: Boise State University, 1989.

Jill B. Gidmark

CHARLES JOHNSON

Born: Evanston, Illinois
April 23, 1948

Principal Literary Achievement

Johnson's novels and short stories link African American experience, philosophical topics, and innovative narrative adapted from oral traditions.

Biography

Charles Richard Johnson was born on April 23, 1948, in Evanston, Illinois, to Benjamin Lee and Ruby Elizabeth Johnson. While quite young, Johnson demonstrated a talent for drawing and wished to pursue an artistic career, but his father strongly disapproved of the notion. It was only after the younger Johnson sought and won the support of Lawrence Lariar, an established writer and cartoonist, that his father relented. At the age of seventeen, Johnson began working as a cartoonist, and throughout the years he has contributed his work to publications such as *Ebony, Jet, Black World*, and *Players International*. His cartoons and drawings were also published in book form in *Black Humor* (1970) and *Illustrated Anatomy of Campus Humor* (1971).

As a student attending Southern Illinois University in Carbondale, Johnson was an editorial and comic-strip artist for several college publications. In 1969 and 1970, Johnson worked as a cartoonist and reporter for the *Chicago Tribune* and was a member of the art staff of the *St. Louis Proud* from 1971 through 1972.

While working successfully as a cartoonist and journalist, Johnson also attended to his academic studies. By 1971, he had completed work for his bachelor's degree in journalism at Southern Illinois.

In 1970, Johnson had branched into a new endeavor by creating, coproducing, and hosting a television show on cartooning called *Charlie's Pad*. Fifty-two shows were completed and distributed nationally by the Public Broadcasting System (PBS). Johnson later wrote scripts for other public television series such as *Up and Coming* and *Y.E.S. Inc.*

Johnson's varied interests led him to the study of philosophy, and in 1973 he received a master's degree in that discipline from Southern Illinois. Throughout his writing career, philosophical concerns have remained a dominant theme in his work, and Johnson often combines these with oral narrative formulas and techniques drawn

from black culture, including traditional slave narratives and folktales. In such experimental fusions, Johnson shows the influence of the novelist, poet, short-story writer, and essayist John Gardner, who had a considerable effect on Johnson's formative years as a writer.

At the time, Gardner was teaching creative writing at Southern Illinois, and Johnson sought him out for advice and instruction. It was a wise move, for Gardner, who was one of the most talented of American writers, was also one of the most generous with his time and encouragement. Gardner read and critiqued the six manuscript novels that Johnson had written and helped him to fashion his first published novel, *Faith and the Good Thing* (1974). As might be expected, the novel combines philosophical concerns with subject matter drawn from the black experience in America.

Johnson has credited Gardner with helping him to forge this literary link between the African American experience and philosophical interests. The clear influence of the older writer is evident throughout Johnson's writings, especially in his outstanding novel *Middle Passage* (1990), which is close to Gardner's work in theme, style, and imagery.

Johnson undertook post-graduate work in philosophy at the State University of New York at Stony Brook from 1973 through 1976. His particular areas of interest, appropriately enough, were in literary aesthetics and phenomenology, the study of how external appearances influence internal images of reality. Clearly, this issue is crucial to any writer, but few have studied it as vigorously or as thoroughly as Johnson.

Johnson's academic career continued in 1976, when he became an assistant professor at the University of Washington in Seattle. In 1979, he was promoted to associate professor and in 1982 became a full professor in English at the institution. From 1979 to 1981, he was director of the Associated Writing Programs Awards Series in short fiction.

In June, 1970, Johnson married Joan New, an elementary-school teacher. The couple has two children, Malik and Elizabeth.

Analysis

Four major points distinguish Charles Johnson from other modern American authors. First, as an African American writer, he approaches the traditional themes and concerns of that culture with a new insight while retaining a profound understanding and appreciation of them. Second, he is an intensely philosophical writer, acutely aware of developments in modern thought and able to give those thoughts concrete expression in his fiction. Third, he links this love and understanding of philosophy with a deep respect for moral fiction, a connection also found in the writings of John Gardner, the writer who influenced Johnson greatly and who was, in many ways, his mentor. Fourth, and most important, Johnson has published some of the most innovative and best-written American fiction of his time.

Johnson repeatedly turns to the themes of black history in the United States and the response of black people to slavery, discrimination, and poverty. One of the triumphs of African Americans has been the preservation of a distinct culture and identity even when these were seriously threatened, over long periods of time, by external forces. In novels such as *Faith and the Good Thing* and *Oxherding Tale* (1982), Johnson uses the experience of black life and draws upon the oral forms of African American folk narrative. *Faith and the Good Thing*, for example, strongly relies upon these traditions, with the author pausing frequently to address the reader with the phrase "Listen, Children," exactly as a speaker would summon a listener's attention. *Oxherding Tale* employs these same devices to an even greater and more successful extent. The novel is structured along the lines of a slave narrative, a form of modern parable most successfully developed during the nineteenth century by Frederick Douglass, himself a former slave.

African American culture and literature have traditionally emphasized verbal skill and wordplay, and these are found abundantly in Johnson's work. A master of metaphorical language, Johnson creates scenes that are highly visual and descriptive and that place the reader in the center of the work's action while at the same time commenting upon it. In so doing, Johnson draws from a culture that prizes the apt use of language to control and order a potentially dangerous world.

Another way to establish control and order is through philosophical investigation, and Johnson is one of American literature's most philosophical writers. Yet he links his philosophical investigations to the practical business of writing. In his study of black writing, *Being and Race* (1988), Johnson establishes a careful theoretical foundation that includes a sophisticated reading of the doctrines of philosopher Edmund Husserl. Johnson, however, connects these abstract thoughts to written reality:

> Life is baffling enough for every novelist, and for writers of Afro-American fiction it presents even more artistic and philosophical questions than for writers who are white. Few writers, black or white, bother with such questions, and in the long run they may have importance only to a few people who wonder, as I have for twenty years, about the forms our stories have taken, what they say about the world, and what they don't say. These are not idle questions.

Johnson understands that the enduring questions of philosophy, and the answers that have been advanced, may be difficult but are never idle. He also maintains that all human beings, irrespective of their race or gender, share a profound stake in these questions and answers. This is one reason why Johnson creates characters such as the Swamp Woman in *Faith and the Good Thing*, who may appear to be uneducated, even illiterate, but who can approach the confusion of being and existence with the subtlety of Aristotle or Immanuel Kant—and often quote them as well.

Combining such philosophical concerns with artistic integrity was also a major goal of Gardner, whose own novels, such as *The Resurrection* (1966) and *The Sunlight Dialogues* (1972), often interweave fiction and philosophy. The positive impact of Gardner on Johnson is seen clearly in *Oxherding Tale* and *Middle Passage*, where the philosophical discussions arise naturally from the action and become a part of it.

Finally, Johnson is a talented and original writer who draws upon the African

American experience, the legacy of philosophy, and the teachings of Gardner, but who forges his own fiction and finds his own voice. Even when he handles difficult subjects and complex ideas, he presents them in a clear, almost conversational tone, making such topics come alive with startling comparisons and appropriate examples.

Johnson has a knack for creating vivid, memorable characters who engage the reader's interest and sympathy. Faith Cross in *Faith and the Good Thing*; Andrew Hawkins in *Oxherding Tale*, and Rutherford Calhoun in *Middle Passage* have their own voices, their own presences, and the reader cares about them because of their overwhelming individuality.

Above all, Charles Johnson is a master of language, a writer whose novels and stories are effective because they draw upon all the resources fiction offers. At once thought-provoking and memorable, often intensely humorous and profoundly tragic, Johnson's writings examine all facets of the human condition.

FAITH AND THE GOOD THING

First published: 1974
Type of work: Novel

Faith Cross, a young black woman from rural Georgia, seeks the "good thing" in Chicago.

Faith and the Good Thing works on several levels simultaneously. At times a realistic account of the experiences endured by African Americans moving from the rural South to the urban North, it is also a folk fable concerning mythic figures such as the Swamp Woman, a mixture of philosopher and voodoo priestess. The novel is also, in part, a philosophical inquiry into the nature of physical and spiritual reality and human personality. Finally, it is an adventurous narrative that follows the travels and trials of its title character.

The novel begins when Faith Cross is commanded by her dying mother: "Girl, you get yourself a good thing." Puzzled, Faith consults the Swamp Woman, incredibly ancient and eerie, who orders Faith to go to Chicago but refuses to reveal just what the good thing will be.

In fact, there seems to be little good in Chicago, where Faith quickly sinks into a life of prostitution and drugs, an episode that the novel describes in a surreal combination of reality and illusion. Here, Johnson displays his ability to combine black folk idioms with rich, evocative language.

Faith is rescued, after a fashion, through her marriage to Isaac Maxwell, a young black reporter for a Chicago newspaper. Maxwell, who speaks constantly of the will to power and who fancies himself a dominant personality, is a portrait of the ineffectual black intellectual cut off from his own heritage and not fully accepted by the white culture. Although Faith's material wants are satisfied, Maxwell cannot meet her spiritual needs, and her life remains barren and unfulfilled. When she reveals her past to Maxwell, the marriage disintegrates, and Faith is eventually murdered by a former lover. In the novel's ending, Faith's spirit returns to Georgia, where it exchanges places with the Swamp Woman.

Faith and the Good Thing was Johnson's first published novel, although he had written six others prior to it. He credits John Gardner with providing him with much of the discipline and insight required to construct the work, but the themes, characters, and approach are clearly those of its author.

THE SORCERER'S APPRENTICE

First published: 1986
Type of work: Short stories

A collection of stories that explore the relationship of the individual to the larger world.

An accomplished short-story writer as well as a novelist, Johnson uses the briefer form to explore many of the same themes and concerns touched on in his novels. He is especially interested in the relationship between the individual, particularly the African American male, and the larger world. In the short stories of *The Sorcerer's Apprentice*, this relationship is often expressed in philosophical terms, even though the situations may at first seem to have little connection with philosophy.

In "The Education of Mingo," for example, a young slave in pre-Civil War America is purchased by an elderly farmer, significantly named Moses, who sets out to educate Mingo in the ways of white culture. The result is that Mingo finds his "coherent, consistent, complete" universe replaced with one that is "alien, contradictory, strange." As a result of this re-education, Mingo kills two white people, thinking his actions are expected by his master. Moses recognizes what he has done, and yet he is unable to turn his pupil over to the authorities, who will surely execute him.

The ability of individuals to be remade, sometimes by others, sometimes by themselves, is explored further in "China," which brought Johnson a citation as a Pushcart Prize Outstanding Writer in 1984. Rudolph and Evelyn, a late-middle-aged black couple, have settled into a tedious routine of vaguely dissatisfied married life when Rudolph discovers the lure of martial arts. Soon he is taking lessons in Kung Fu and other Eastern disciplines and exercising seriously to exchange his neglected, flabby body for a disciplined and stronger one. By the story's end, Rudolph has largely re-created himself, to his wife's bewilderment and dismay.

A second theme that runs through this collection concerns recognition and acceptance of one's essential character. In "Alethia," a middle-aged black professor suddenly learns how deeply he has betrayed his native roots. In the science-fiction story "Popper's Disease," a physician ministers to a sick alien in a crashed flying saucer, only to learn that the creature suffers from an incurable and all-too-human malady, the agonizing split between the individual and the outside world.

The title story fuses these themes as it traces the brief, abortive career of Allan Jackson, an apprentice to a black sorcerer, or conjure doctor, in rural South Carolina. Allan has some talent, but not a true gift, and when his failure to cure a sick child makes him realize this, he renounces his career choice. Johnson demonstrates that while such insights can be painful, they are necessary for true maturity and wisdom.

MIDDLE PASSAGE

First published: 1990
Type of work: Novel

A combination of allegory and adventure tale that explores how the individual becomes part of the community.

Middle Passage, Johnson's third published novel, is a complex blend of allegory, adventure story, tall tale, and philosophical meditation. The novel, which won the National Book Award, follows the misadventures of Rutherford Calhoun, the narrator, who is an entertaining liar and consummate rogue. Calhoun, a slave, flees first to New Orleans and then, to escape marriage, to sea. Ironically, he stows away on a slave ship, the *Republic*, and so his adventures begin.

The novel's characters are a motley collection of freaks, misfits, and oddities. Ebenezer Falcon, captain of the *Republic*, is a stunted, twisted dwarf whose brilliant mind and strong will are devoted to his own evil personal ends. Cringle, the first mate, is a well-meaning but ineffectual liberal, able to perceive evils and injustices but incapable of acting to resolve them. Josiah Squibb, the alcoholic, often-married but never-divorced cook, serves as a representative both of humankind's baser instincts and of rough but necessary common sense.

In Africa, the *Republic* takes on a cargo of slaves from the Allmuseri tribe (a group frequently mentioned in Johnson's fiction as a symbol of original African nature and unity. The crew also brings on board an enormous box that contains the Allmuseri's "god," a monstrous shape-shifting creature that drives mad those who listen to it.

On the return voyage, a mutiny and slave revolt, perhaps inspired by the caged god, lead to the destruction of the *Republic* and the death of everyone aboard except Calhoun, Squibb, and three Allmuseri children. Rescued by a passing ship, Calhoun and the others return to New Orleans. Now a changed man, Calhoun finally marries and settles down, having learned that to be fully human requires commitment to others and community.

Johnson clearly modeled his novel on John Gardner's novella *The King's Indian: Stories and Tales* (1974), and there are references to Herman Melville's *Moby Dick: Or, The Whale* (1851) and other classics of American literature. Like these earlier works, *Middle Passage* is focused on the topic of community, specifically the individual's place within and obligations to that community. Calhoun, who begins the story as a self-conscious loner, his hand set against every other man's hand, ends by accepting the necessity of fitting into society. In a similar fashion, the novel implies, the larger, national community (the American republic, perhaps) exists only as the aggregate of individuals linked together. Lacking that unity, the community will sink as surely as a ship in the grip of mutiny and revolt.

Summary

Although Charles Johnson clearly draws upon the African American tradition and its lessons, his work is significantly different from that of many other black American authors, especially as it relates to the role of the individual, of whatever race, in the larger community. In a similar fashion, Johnson's use of philosophy to frame and express his concerns sets him apart from the majority of contemporary American writers of all races and genders.

Johnson's major accomplishments are possible because of his re-creation of traditional oral narrative forms through powerful, metaphorically rich language. This use of language permits Johnson to create characters who can express philosophical dilemmas while remaining intensely and believably human.

Bibliography

Crouch, Stanley. "Charles Johnson, Free at Last." *The Village Voice*, July 19, 1983, 30-31.

Davis, Thadious M., and Trudier Harris, eds. *Afro-American Fiction Writers After 1955*. Vol. 33 in *Dictionary of Literary Biography*. Detroit: Gale Research, 1984.

Johnson, Charles. Interview by Jonathan Little. *Contemporary Literature* 34, no. 2 (Summer, 1993): 159.

May, Hal, ed. *Contemporary Authors*. Vol. 116. Detroit: Gale Research, 1986.

Olderman, Raymond. "American Literature, 1974-1976." *Contemporary Literature* 19 (Autumn, 1978): 497-527.

Page, James A., ed. *Selected Black American Authors*. Boston: G. K. Hall, 1977.

Page, James A., and Jae Min Roh. *Selected Black American, African, and Caribbean Authors*. Littleton, Colo.: Libraries Unlimited, 1985.

Peterson, V. R. "Charles Johnson." *Essence* 21 (April, 1991): 36.

Rushdy, Ashraf H. A. "The Phenomenology of the Allmuseri: Charles Johnson and the Subject of the Narrative of Slavery." *African American Review* 26, no. 3 (Fall, 1992): 373.

Michael Witkoski

ADRIENNE KENNEDY

Born: Pittsburgh, Pennsylvania
September 13, 1931

Principal Literary Achievement

An award-winning avant-garde playwright, Kennedy provocatively and poetically dramatizes the fragmented internal realities inherent in the human condition.

Biography

Adrienne Lita Hawkins Kennedy was born on September 13, 1931, in Pittsburgh, Pennsylvania, to Cornell Wallace Hawkins and Etta Haugabook Hawkins. After Kennedy learned to read at three years of age, she became a voracious reader who had moved alphabetically through the library's shelves before she reached high school.

In 1935, Kennedy's family moved to an integrated, middle-class neighborhood in Cleveland, Ohio. Both parents, college graduates and professionals, influenced Kennedy's writing style: her mother, through humorous stories edged with pathos; her father, a Young Men's Christian Association (YMCA) branch executive director, through nightly recitations of the poetry of Langston Hughes, Paul Laurence Dunbar, and others. Active in the National Association for the Advancement of Colored People (NAACP) and the Urban League, both parents instilled in Kennedy the importance of having a positive impact upon the world.

Throughout her elementary and her high-school years, Kennedy continued to be an all-consuming reader and a superb achiever. In fact, one of her elementary school teachers cautioned her mother that Kennedy could make herself ill from her own high expectations of herself.

Not until she began her freshman year at Ohio State University in 1949 did she experience overt racism that caused her to question her own identity. No longer was she judged on her abilities and her achievements; suddenly, she found herself prejudged on the basis of the color of her skin. The wrenching theme of a personal identity raging in a dissonant universe pervades Kennedy's writings.

With the limited possibilities of education or social work for a major, Kennedy chose education. Although she satisfactorily completed the required course work, she did so without her customary intellectual avidity. In her senior year, however, she attended a course in twentieth century literature in order to fulfill the university's requirements for a bachelor's degree. In that course, Kennedy rediscovered her

need to express herself as a writer.

Three weeks before her graduation, on May 15, 1953, she married Joseph C. Kennedy, a man who strongly supported her desire to write. After Joseph returned from service in Korea, the Kennedy family (now including a son, Joseph, Jr.) moved to New York so that he could attend Columbia University's graduate school in social psychology. From 1954 to 1956, Adrienne cared for their son and took creative writing courses at Columbia University. Later, she also studied at the American Theatre Wing.

A turning point in Kennedy's development as a writer came during a fourteen-month journey through Africa and Europe in 1960 and 1961 during which her husband conducted a research study. Kennedy absorbed the consciousness and the life rhythms of West Africa. Regenerated, she began to integrate the African use of masks and sound into her fragmented dramatic characterizations. In Europe, she assimilated the culture and the history that had fascinated her for years. While overseas, Kennedy completed *Funnyhouse of a Negro* (1962) and gave birth to a second son, Adam Patrice.

Upon returning to the United States, she submitted *Funnyhouse of a Negro* to Edward Albee's Circle-in-the-Square playwriting competition and worked on the drama's subsequent workshop production. Two years later, twelve years after Kennedy had begun writing and submitting manuscripts for publication, *Funnyhouse of a Negro* opened Off-Broadway at the East End Theater; the play won a 1964 Obie Award.

During the next twelve years, Kennedy wrote several one-act plays, including The Owl Answers (1963), *A Rat's Mass* (1966), *A Beast's Story* (1969), *Sun: A Poem for Malcolm X Inspired by His Murder* (1968), *A Lesson in Dead Language* (1968), *An Evening with Dead Essex* (1973), and *A Movie Star Has to Star in Black and White* (1976).

In 1980, under commission of the Juilliard School of Music, Kennedy adapted two Greek plays by Euripedes. *The Alexander Plays* (1992) is a series of four plays featuring the same character, Suzanne Alexander, as the protagonist.

Kennedy has also become known as an innovative autobiographer. *People Who Led to My Plays* (1987) is Kennedy's response to frequently asked questions regarding the influences on her playwriting. This autobiography almost seems like a photo album, a montage of clear and honest snapshots taken from 1936 to 1961. *Deadly Triplets: A Theatre Mystery and Journal* (1990) is written in two parts. The first section, the mystery, interconnects real-life events and people within a British fictional section. The second section, the journal, is a memoir sketching some of the same events and people within the context of Kennedy's Off-Broadway and London theater experiences.

Analysis

Adrienne Kennedy admittedly bases her writing on autobiographical characters and events; however, the autobiographical elements are more profoundly symbolic than simply historic. She is a poet of the theater who purposefully explores the fragmented symbols within her subconscious as her most viable means of survival.

Kennedy's riveting, nonlinear, one-act dramatic style reflects an inner world of discordant realities at war with one another. As such, her plots are rarely chronological, and her characters are frequently more than simply multifaceted. Rather, they are simultaneously characters who are yet other characters who are yet other characters. For example, *Funnyhouse of a Negro*'s cast of characters has as its protagonist "the Negro-Sarah," whose selves are the Duchess of Hapsburg, Queen Victoria Regina, Jesus, and Patrice Lumumba. Lumumba is not only Lumumba, historically a murdered Congolese prime minister considered by many a savior, but also Sarah's dead rapist father, who returns to haunt her until she hangs herself.

Kennedy's surrealistic dramatic style challenges audiences and readers, demanding that they be receptive enough and flexible enough to empathize, to recognize the common elements in their own unconscious perceptions of events. The action takes place in a series of nightmarish sequences and transfigurations that blend into one another through the use of masks, ritual, and repetition. Devastating portrayals of rage and grief demythologize cultural expectations. Wave after wave of piercing imagery bombards the senses, until the separations between characters and spectators are destroyed.

Kennedy is female and black. With the exception of the male role in *Sun*, her dramatic spokespeople are also female and black. Kennedy's world is a world of nonexistence, of alienation and absence. One of her dominant themes is the need for each individual to have a congruent context in which to exist. In *A Lesson in Dead Language*, seven female students in white dresses soiled by menstrual blood ask why they bleed, only to receive an answer from White Dog, their female teacher, that they bleed because they are being punished. With guilt-inducing references to the deaths of Jesus, Mary, Joseph, the Wise Men, and the Shepherd, White Dog infers that the murders of Julius Caesar and Malcolm X are also involved in the girls' menstruation.

As a black female, Kennedy writes of the estrangement of blacks in a white world: blacks such as the Negro-Sarah, who would rather die than be black, in *Funnyhouse of a Negro*; blacks such as the young Suzanne, who wraps her hair so tightly in rollers to straighten it that her scalp bleeds nightly in *The Ohio State Murders* (1992); and blacks such as Clara, who becomes a bystander in her own life in *A Movie Star Has to Star in Black and White*.

Kennedy relentlessly examines the ego destruction inherent in being black and "believing white." Unattainable, romanticized white ideals can lead only to repressed frustration, self-fragmentation, self-loathing, and ego death. With her recurrent imagery of Nazis, murder, multiple personae, infanticide, gnawing rats, and blood, Kennedy provocatively dramatizes the terrors of spiritual suffocation and agitates for the freedom of the individual spirit.

The playwright reveals intimate, unconscious distortions of internalized socially acceptable norms to demonstrate their deadly potential. In *Funnyhouse of a Negro*, blood covers the Negro-Sarah's face, and she carries a clump of her hair that has fallen out. The Duchess of Hapsburg, one of Sarah's selves, hides behind a white mask as she struggles to return her hair from a paper bag to her head. Patrice Lumumba has an ebony mask, because his face has been shattered into unrecognizable fragments. The Mother, bald and insane, refuses to acknowledge that the Negro-Sarah exists.

Religious ideals of the white world are another source of internalized alienation. Clara in *The Owl Answers* becomes not the caged white bird (who is God's dove) of her adopted father, Reverend Passmore, but an owl, a mysterious and magical bird of the darkness. In *Funnyhouse of a Negro*, Jesus is not the tall, slender, charismatic white ideal but a misshapen dwarf who has vowed to murder Lumumba because he has discovered that a black man, not God, is his father. Parodying the incantatory ritual of a Catholic Mass, *A Rat's Mass* concludes with the execution of Brother Rat and Sister Rat by a death squad consisting of Jesus, Mary, Joseph, Wise Men, and a Shepherd; holy Rosemary, in her white communion dress, watches. Clearly, in Kennedy's internal universe, the ideals of white Christianity are toxic to a centered black identity.

In *The Alexander Plays*, the central character in each of four connected plays is the writer Suzanne Alexander, an older version of Kennedy's earlier protagonists. In *She Talks to Beethoven*, Suzanne is visited in Ghana by Ludwig von Beethoven, who keeps her company as she awaits word of her missing husband, David. Suzanne describes herself as having been put together by a new self after exploding into fragments. *The Film Club*, a monologue by Suzanne, and *The Dramatic Circle*, a radio play dramatizing *The Film Club*, concern Suzanne's life in London after David has once again disappeared. In *The Ohio State Murders*, Suzanne, approximately thirty years later, discloses for the first time the events surrounding the deaths of her twin daughters. Also significant is the play's description of the older Suzanne as "Suzanne (Present)." In Kennedy's dramatic world of alienation and absence, this character is fully centered. Suzanne Alexander is a survivor.

Even though Kennedy's dramatic technique is more linear and her characters are less overtly nightmarish in *The Alexander Plays*, the menace is palpable. In these plays, the destructive forces are external, and the dichotomy is a chronological swing between past and present. The dissonance between the controlled narration and the horrifying events accentuates the threatening environment in which Suzanne lives. References to Kennedy's earlier playscripts serve as subtle reminders of the internal dysfunction her characters have experienced.

In *The Film Club*, Suzanne Alexander concludes her monologue with a quotation from the revolutionary black philosopher Frantz Fanon. With this passage, Kennedy reminds everyone that the battle continues to rage and that its ineradicable damage will have to be diligently attended to for many years, lest the wounds putrefy and the war be lost.

A RAT'S MASS

First produced: 1966 (first published, 1968)
Type of work: Play

Brother Rat and Sister Rat seek atonement but are murdered in the midst of a grotesquely shifting, distorted world of holy imagery, Nazi executioners, gnawed sunflower petals, and dead babies.

A Rat's Mass was first produced and directed in Boston by David Wheeler, an avant-garde director for the Theater Company of Boston. In September, 1969, following a successful run in Italy, *A Rat's Mass* was produced by Ellen Stewart for New York audiences at the La Mama Experimental Theatre Club, with Seth Allen directing.

The universe of *A Rat's Mass* is Brother Rat's and Sister Rat's. It is a bizarre maelstrom of terror, oppression, sacrilege, and rage in a malignant conflict to the death. In this universe, Brother Rat has a human body but the head of a rat, and Sister Rat has a human head but a rat's belly. A procession of Two Wise Men, a Shepherd, Joseph, Mary, and Jesus alternately watch and march as Brother Rat (Blake) and Sister Rat (Kay) recall their childhood days of innocence, before their holy home was invaded by screaming worms and gnawing rats in the attic.

Rosemary, an Italian Catholic wearing a communion dress and carrying a catechism book, is a Medusa-like character with worms rather than snakes in her hair. Unlike Blake and Kay, she has a world in which she belongs, a religious heritage, a historic ancestry. Blake and Kay love her as their best friend. They revere her beauty, her holiness, her sense of belonging. At her urging, Brother Rat commits incest with Sister Rat on a playground slide, while Rosemary watches, to prove his love for Rosemary. Then they swear on her catechism book and their father's Bible that they will never tell anyone.

Sister Rat, however, becomes pregnant and has a nervous breakdown. She is taken in an ambulance to a state hospital. Upon her return, Brother Rat and Sister Rat beg Rosemary to help them atone. She refuses and tells them to commit suicide by using their father's shotgun to put bullets through their heads. Brother Rat and Sister Rat beg for the return of innocence.

Finally, the procession deserts Brother Rat and Sister Rat, whose voices and body language are growing more and more ratlike. Brother Rat admits his unwillingness to accept responsibility for his incestuous actions, preferring instead to believe that someone else has impregnated Sister Rat. Brother Rat's central conflict has been his need to protect Sister Rat and his love for Rosemary. The increasingly loud sound of the rats' gnawing and escalating battle sounds accompany the return of the procession, who have become shotgun-bearing Nazis who murder Brother Rat and Sister Rat. Rosemary remains unscathed.

A MOVIE STAR HAS TO STAR IN BLACK AND WHITE

First produced: 1976 (first published, 1984)
Type of work: Play

A struggling writer, Clara, places prominent Hollywood actors from her favorite black-and-white 1950's movies in leading roles to enact her life crises.

A Movie Star Has to Star in Black and White opened at the New York Shakespeare Festival in 1976 as a work in progress. This one-act play is introduced by the Columbia Pictures Lady speaking in Clara's stead. Each scene is first a film set, with the leading roles played by the film's primary actors. Places and people from Clara's life, including Clara, who has only a bit part, appear in parallel supporting roles. In her stage directions, Kennedy describes the supporting actors' attitudes toward the leads as "deadly serious."

Scene 1 includes as characters actors Bette Davis and Paul Henreid in a scene set on an ocean liner from the film *Now, Voyager* (1942); the scene simultaneously occurs in a Cleveland hospital lobby in June and July of 1955. Clara's mother and father, as they were in a 1929 photograph, are on deck. Clara silently joins them, but she isolates herself from the action by writing in a notebook and allowing Bette Davis to speak for her of marital discord, a miscarriage, fears of bleeding to death in labor, and childhood traumas. Clara's dominant response to emotional confrontation is to read passages from *The Owl Answers*, which she has apparently been writing in her notebook. As the scene ends, Clara enters her comatose brother's hospital room and relates what she sees to the film *Viva Zapata!* (1952).

Scene 2, with Jean Peters and Marlon Brando in *Viva Zapata!*, takes place in the hospital room as well as in a wedding-night scene from *Viva Zapata!* and in a *Now, Voyager* stateroom. According to the stage directions, "there is no real separation" between the film scenes and Clara's life at any time during the play. From the hospital/wedding-night bed, Jean Peters speaks for Clara, then rises and falls bleeding onto the bed. Marlon Brando helps her to change the black sheets, leaving the bloodied sheets on the floor. Clara's mother and her father, now in their fifties, divorced and feuding, are present at their son's bedside. Scene 2 ends with Clara observing her parents from the doorway as her mother explains what she knows of her son's automobile accident.

Scene 3, with Shelley Winters and Montgomery Clift from *A Place in the Sun* (1951), is set in Clara's childhood room and cumulatively in every preceding locale. The scene directly reveals Clara: isolated, fearful, standing on the sidelines of her own life, living in the past, bleeding, and uncertain of the truths of her writing. Clara has filled her absence from her own life with romantic film characters she can never become; however, she has recognized that writing is her weapon against her lack of belonging, her means of revealing her repressed, fragmented selves and transforming them into a presence with whom she can "co-exist in a true union." If she does not successfully revolt against her embrace of Hollywood's romanticized ideal and assume a leading role in her life, she, like the character played by Shelley Winters in the film, will drown in silence.

THE OHIO STATE MURDERS

First produced: 1992 (first published, 1992)
Type of work: Play

Successful writer Suzanne Alexander lectures at her alma mater, Ohio State University, only to re-experience the racism of her student years.

The Ohio State Murders was commissioned by the Great Lakes Theater Festival of Cleveland, Ohio, in 1989. It was directed by Gerald Freedman for the Great Lakes Theater Festival's thirtieth anniversary season as a part of the nonprofit company's 1992 Adrienne Kennedy Festival. The play is presented in multiple brief scenes filtered through the memory of the present Suzanne, who acts as narrator. From the stacks of the university library, the writer relives the debasing experiences of Suzanne as a college student from 1949 to 1951.

As a black student, Suzanne is the target of insidious, as well as overt, racism critically destructive to her ego identity. She is told that certain streets are regarded as exclusively white and that an English curriculum is considered too difficult for blacks to declare as a major course of study; in the face of such racism, Suzanne's self-concept deteriorates. She becomes uneasy, anxious, and frightened. Even her white dormitory mates seem to her to be capable of racially motivated murder.

Suzanne's sole source of joy in her freshman year is a required course on the Victorian novel taught by Robert Hampshire, an unemotional white man in his first year of teaching at Ohio State. Fascinated by Thomas Hardy's *Tess of the D'Urbervilles* (1891), Suzanne begins to draw parallels between her life and the successively restrictive, tragic life of Tess. The present Suzanne concludes that Hardy's fictional universe is one in which characters face destruction because its society forces conformity, thereby suppressing the human spirit.

Jarring these reminiscences are the present Suzanne's succinct revelations that someone murdered one of her twin daughters, which were conceived with Robert Hampshire during the school's Christmas break in 1950. Hampshire dismisses the young Suzanne's announcement that she is pregnant as impossible. Soon after, the dormitory director reveals that she has been secretly searching through Suzanne's belongings and has read her diary to the dormitory committee. Consequently, Suzanne is expelled from the dormitory and the university as unsuitable. After the birth of her twins, Suzanne returns to Columbus with her daughters to stay in a boardinghouse run by a family friend.

One of the dominant sources of dramatic tension in *The Ohio State Murders* is the present Suzanne's achronological commentary, which allows the audience to know more than the young Suzanne does. For example, she is unaware that Hampshire has been following her, and she endures the suspicions of the Columbus police for more than a year without knowing that it is Hampshire who has kidnapped and drowned one of her children.

While Suzanne works at her part-time night job in the law library, Hampshire presents himself at the boardinghouse as a graduate researcher. Once inside, he kills his second twin daughter and himself with a kitchen knife. The present Suzanne describes with horrifying simplicity the months she spent willing herself to die while the university and her father covered up the true story of the Ohio State murders. Juxtaposed to these revelations is the present Suzanne's summation that these experiences are the primary source of violent imagery in her writing.

Summary

Adrienne Kennedy counterpoints a polished poetic style with brutal synaesthetic imagery that engulfs those who experience her works. This process generates in her audiences an empathic recognition of the truth inherent in her vision, as well as a hypnotic tension that is further accentuated by her use of rhythm, ritual, repetition, and myth.

Kennedy exorcises her unconscious demons onstage. As such, her plays are a challenge to theater practitioners. Nevertheless, through her writing, she intimately captures and shares the essence of the human spirit's search for self-integration, belongingness, and love.

Bibliography

Betsko, Kathleen, and Rachel Koenig, eds. *Interviews with Contemporary Women Playwrights*. New York: Beech Tree Books, 1987.

Bryant-Jackson, Paul K., and Lois More Overbeck, eds. *Intersecting Boundaries: The Theatre of Adrienne Kennedy*. Minneapolis: University of Minnesota Press, 1992.

Cohn, Ruby. "Black on Black: Baraka, Bullins, Kennedy." In *New American Dramatists, 1960-1980*. New York: Grove Press, 1982.

Harrison, Paul C., ed. *Totem Voices: Plays From the Black World Repertory*. New York: Grove Press, 1988.

Kennedy, Adrienne. *People Who Led to My Plays*. New York: Alfred A. Knopf, 1987.

Kathleen Mills

JAMAICA KINCAID

Born: St. Johns, Antigua, West Indies
May 25, 1949

Principal Literary Achievement

Although Kincaid's poetic, surrealistic short stories have been admired, her partly autobiographical novels concerning the coming of age of a young Antiguan woman mark her most significant achievement.

Biography

Jamaica Kincaid was born Elaine Potter Richardson in St. Johns, Antigua, West Indies, on May 25, 1949. She was her parents' first child and their only daughter. Kincaid's father, a carpenter, provided a good living for his family by local standards, although the family lived without indoor plumbing or electricity. During her early years, Kincaid became aware of the island's powerful tropical beauty, an awareness that was somehow linked with her close and loving relationship with her mother. This picture of her early years forms the setting of her novel *Annie John* (1985).

Kincaid was educated in Antigua's government-sponsored elementary and secondary schools. During her early school years, she became, like her mother, a voracious reader, particularly of British Victorian fiction, with Charlotte's Brontë's *Jane Eyre* (1847) a special favorite. (The British influence on her education resulted from Antigua's history as a dependency of Great Britain until 1967; it became an independent nation in 1981.) Gradually, she became aware that she had an excellent mind, but neither her teachers nor her family seemed to recognize it or to encourage her in academics.

When Kincaid was nine, the birth of the first of her three brothers severed her close attachment to her mother, and she felt increasingly alienated from her family, her schools, even from Antigua itself. By the time she reached adolescence, she saw the island as a place of repressive provincialism and longed to leave.

When she was sixteen, Kincaid found a job as a servant for a well-to-do family in Scarsdale, New York, and left Antigua. After working for the Scarsdale family for a few months, she found another job, this time as an au pair for the well-to-do Manhattan family of writer Michael Arlen (with whom she would one day work at *The New Yorker*). She had hoped to attend college at night and work during the day, but she soon realized that her Antiguan education was inadequate in some areas, and she first

had to obtain an American high-school diploma.

Her work in a photography course at the New School for Social Research won her a scholarship at Franconia College in New Hampshire, but within two years she was back in New York City, having concluded that she would have to educate herself. She briefly held several clerical jobs, but she had few office skills, and that fact, along with her refusal to compromise her strong sense of individuality, probably contributed to her inability to find her right direction. She bleached her hair, cut it very short, and wore brilliant red lipstick and jodhpurs, a look she has called "punk before punk." During this period, Kincaid began to make a serious effort to make a living as a writer by publishing occasional articles in magazines for teenagers.

Also during this period, she became friends with George Trow, who often contributed to *The New Yorker*'s "Talk of the Town" section and sometimes mentioned Kincaid either by her pseudonym or as "our sassy black friend." Through Trow, Kincaid met William Shawn, the editor of *The New Yorker*. He encouraged her in her determination to write, and she renewed her efforts. Soon she was exhilarated to find that her articles were being published ever more frequently.

In 1976, she was hired as a staff writer at *The New Yorker*. In 1978, she wrote her first short story, "Girl," which was published in *The New Yorker* and became the first story in her collection *At the Bottom of the River* (1983). That collection brought her substantial literary attention and established her as a serious writer.

Even more than "Girl," the other stories in the collection depend on poetic language and imagery for their power; they rarely make use of developed characters and are without conventional plot (events occur, but they are reported impressionistically and with a strongly surreal sense). That quality has led to complaints of obscurity, but readers who appreciate her exotic and evocative use of voice and description have defended her work.

In 1979, Kincaid married Allen Shawn (the son of editor William Shawn). Since her marriage and the birth of her two children, her writing has become much more "linear," more dependent on plot and character for its content, a fact Kincaid attributes to the demands that family life makes on her time.

In 1985, Kincaid published *Annie John*, a strongly autobiographical novel about a young girl's coming of age in what seems to be Antigua. A second autobiographical novel, *Lucy*, followed in 1990. Between them, in 1988, Kincaid published *A Small Place*, an essay about Antigua and its heritage after British colonial rule.

Analysis

The power of Jamaica Kincaid's work seems to rise equally from her themes of family relationships and alienation, her use of detail to create exotic settings, and her anger, which is aimed at the world that has betrayed her—that is, at her family (especially her mother) and at the affluent white world, which generally treats Third World people with the same callous disregard that Great Britain brought to bear on Antigua during its rule of the island.

Family relationships are central to Kincaid's work. In "Girl," a story created from one two-page sentence, Kincaid nevertheless manages to evoke the tensions between a young woman and her mother. As the mother instructs the daughter in every level of "right" behavior for a young woman, she is interrupted only twice, and then only briefly, by the protesting daughter.

The tensions of "Girl" are expanded into a major plot element in *Annie John*, a brief novel that begins by describing a child who finds herself in the emotional paradise created by her loving relationship with her mother. Inexplicably, their devotion begins to crumble. No reason is given, and the reader is left to imagine the source of the trouble. Perhaps the mother is distracted by her relationship with her husband. Perhaps it is the inevitable result of Annie John's approaching adolescence and of her simultaneous intellectual and sexual awakening. At the end of the novel, as Annie John leaves her beautiful island to pursue nurse's training in Great Britain, she feels both desolated at the thought of leaving her family and tense with uncertainty and expectation about the future.

In *Lucy*, Kincaid continues her examination of mother-daughter relationships, this time on two levels. Lucy, the novel's central character, seems in many ways to be the continuation of Annie John. As the novel opens, Lucy has just arrived in New York to work as a nurse to the four young daughters of a wealthy family. In the succeeding months, Lucy watches the family, at first assuming it to be idyllic in its happiness. Gradually, she becomes aware of its tensions, and at last those tensions result in the parents' separation and divorce. At the same time, Lucy is carrying out a bitter battle with her own family, especially with her mother. At home, as a child, she had carried out her rebellions secretly, by making friends of whom her mother would not approve and by experimenting sexually (also in secret). She continues this behavior in New York, but she adds to it a refusal even to open her mother's letters. She assumes that such behavior is the only way in which she can free herself from her past. At last, she learns from a family friend that her father has died and that her mother is in desperate need of money. Lucy sends all of her savings to her mother, but she also writes her a bitter letter of rejection and accusation. When she later relents and writes a gentler letter, she includes a false return address, and she knows that her promise to go home soon is a lie.

Kincaid's spare, concrete style is often regarded as a particular characteristic of her narrative skills. Her descriptions of the island (it is never actually named) in *Annie John* and *Lucy* are full of exotic details about foods, plants, animals, and colorful local people. She names the fish that make up every islander's diet—pink mullet, lady doctor fish, angel and kanya fish—and foods such as green figs cooked in coconut milk, plantains, bananas, lemons, limes, almonds, dasheen, and cassavas. She describes the herb-laced baths her mother prepared for her and the stone heap in the yard on which white clothes were dried. She refers to herb and magic doctors (one of them, Ma Jolie, helps Annie John during a dangerous illness) and to people who are possessed by evil spirits. Kincaid's story collection *At the Bottom of the River* is especially rich in this sort of detail.

One critic has noted that Kincaid is uncompromising in presenting these pictures of a world that is quite foreign to most of her readers. She never explains or clarifies details; she never describes the island world in reference to North America. She approaches race in much the same way. She never speaks to the reader as a writer of color; instead, her color becomes the norm. In the same way, she speaks as a representative of the people who have been colonized. In her work, "we" always refers to people of color from colonial countries. The rulers and tourists, like the inhabitants of the middle-class world of the United States, are the outsiders.

Kincaid's anger at the ruins that British colonial rule created in Antigua is the topic of her essay *A Small Place*. She decries the governmental, educational, and administrative shambles that resulted when the British left and complains about the island's inability to govern its own affairs without corruption, waste, and ineptitude. Such problems, she implies, are the natural legacy of slavery and colonial rule.

In *Annie John* and *Lucy*, Kincaid displays the same anger in fictional settings. Annie John, for example, reflects on a new school mate, an English girl, imagining that she must long to be in England, where she would not constantly be reminded of the terrible things her ancestors had done. In the same chapter ("Columbus in Chains"), Annie John writes a satiric caption under a picture of Christopher Columbus in her school book, outraging her teacher. Similarly, Lucy, living in New York, has frequent occasions to make observations about the relationship between wealth and poverty in the world. She notes, for example, that her employers, Mariah and Lewis, often express concern for rain forests and endangered animals without ever reflecting that their own standard of living creates much of the threat to these things. That sort of acerbic observation is as much a part of Kincaid's style as are her references to obeah women and green figs. That she can combine narrative, description, and social commentary into her slender novels is part of her achievement.

GIRL

First published: 1978
Type of work: Short story

In this single-sentence story, a mother instructs her daughter in the ways of womanhood.

Like Kincaid's other short stories, "Girl" is extremely brief and can hardly be said to have a plot, although the reader can easily imagine a dramatic context in which this monologue might be spoken. The central voice is that of the unnamed mother; the reader must assume that the "girl" of the title is her daughter, although the relationship is never stated. Twice the daughter's voice (indicated by italics) interrupts the mother to protest the implications of her instructions, but the mother continues her directions.

The mother is directing her daughter about how to live as an adult woman, and many of her comments are practical advice. From the first clause, when the mother tells her daughter to put freshly washed white clothes on a stone heap and to wash the "color clothes" on Tuesday, the reader recognizes that the story's setting is not the United States. The speaker tells the daughter how to soak salt fish, how to cook pumpkin fritters, how to iron her father's shirt and pants properly, how to grow okra and dasheen, how to sweep the house and yard.

Also early in the story, the reader senses that the daughter is at the edge of sexual maturity. The mother's direction to her daughter to "soak your little cloths" as soon as she takes them off—a reference to menstruation—establishes that fact. Throughout the story, many of the mother's directions are aimed at preventing the girl from becoming the "slut" her mother obviously thinks she longs to be. She directs her not to sing popular music in Sunday School, not to talk to wharf-rat boys for any reason, and not to eat fruit on the street, because it will make flies follow her. This sort of advice is intermingled with commentary about practical matters of cooking and cleaning, but the speaker's primary motivation is to prevent her daughter from becoming a "slut"—or at least from being recognized as one. She also tells her daughter about a medicine for abortion and makes the observation that if her directions about how to love a man do not work, the girl should not regret giving up.

The mother's sexual advice is intermingled with social advice. She tells the girl how to smile at someone she does not like, as well as how to smile at someone she likes very much, and tells her how to avoid evil spirits (what looks like a blackbird, the mother says, may be something else entirely).

The two-and-a-half-page monologue does not actually include the instructions for all these activities; instead, the parallel clauses introduced with "this is how . . ." suggest the ways that adults model behavior for children. Presumably, the daughter is watching and learning. At the same time, the mother's negative tone indicates that she has little hope of her daughter's growing into decent adulthood, so that the daughter's two protests create the story's tension. Nevertheless, the mother has the last word. When the girl asks what to do if the baker will not let her test the bread's freshness by squeezing it, the mother wonders if her daughter will become the "kind of woman the baker won't let near the bread."

ANNIE JOHN

First published: 1985
Type of work: Novel

A young girl comes of age in Antigua and discovers the depth of her anger and rebellion.

Annie John's eight short chapters can be read separately as narrative sketches. Together, however, they trace the course of Annie John's fall from the innocent Eden of her childhood into an angry alienation from her mother and Antigua, which have both nurtured and stifled her. In the first chapter, Annie recalls how, when she was about ten, she began to think about death, realizing that even children can die. She becomes so obsessed with the idea of funerals that she lies to her mother about where she has been in order to attend the funeral of a child she has never even known.

In the second chapter, Annie details her everyday life with her mother, revealing their loving relationship. They shop together; they cook for her father; sometimes they even take herb baths together. She especially loves seeing her own baby clothes, which her mother has saved in a special trunk. Yet Annie also recalls some dark events. At one point, her father tells her the story of the death of his beloved grandmother, and Annie feels an unaccustomed sympathy for him. At the chapter's end her mother announces that they will no longer wear dresses made from the same cloth, because Annie is getting too old. Annie is crushed by this betrayal.

At about this time, Annie begins attending a new school. She is a bright, self-confident student. She writes an autobiographical essay that depicts her relationship with her mother so movingly that some of her classmates weep when she reads it. Annie acknowledges, however, that part of the essay is a lie, created because she cannot bear to confess that the relationship is crumbling. At this time, Annie begins to menstruate; her mother calls the development "coming of age." Annie, though, has mixed feelings about the experience (at school, it makes her faint) and refuses to allow it to draw her close to her mother. It does, however, draw her even closer to her new friend Gwen, to whom she tells everything.

Annie's growing rebellion is shown by her learning to play marbles (an activity forbidden by her mother as too boyish) and by her friendship with the Red Girl, a dirty child who has little home discipline. Annie's mother forbids the association, but to be with the Red Girl, Annie lies to her mother and abandons Gwen.

Soon Annie has trouble with one of her teachers over a satiric caption she has written above a picture of Columbus in her history book. She is coming to see the falsehoods in Great Britain's version of Antigua's history, a history that made slaves of Annie's ancestors. Annie receives no sympathy from her mother for her school troubles.

By the time she is fifteen, Annie is sunk deep in her unhappiness and dreams constantly about leaving the island. Her conflicts with her mother have become worse, and she asks her father to build her a trunk, thus rejecting the special trunk her mother had kept for her. At about this time, Annie becomes sick with a fever that lasts for a long time; when at last she recovers, she finishes school and leaves for England to be trained as a nurse. The last chapter describes her departure. As she and her parents walk to the jetty, they pass countless places of her childhood. As the boat leaves, Annie, feeling strangely empty, waves a red cotton handkerchief at her mother, who has told her in parting that she will be her mother forever and that Antigua will always be her true home.

LUCY

First published: 1990
Type of work: Novel

A young Antiguan woman enters adulthood as she experiences life and work in New York.

Lucy seems to take up where *Annie John* left off, and Lucy herself seems much like a slightly older, angrier Annie. The novel opens with Lucy's arrival in New York, where she will care for the four little daughters of Lewis and Mariah.

From the first, Lucy's affluent new surroundings feel foreign to her. Although she likes the family for whom she works, they call her "the Visitor" because she seems so distant from them. Lucy, though, has divorced herself from her past and has committed herself to her new land and the strange things (such as snow) in it. Mariah promises her that in the spring she will see daffodils, but to Lucy, daffodils are simply the subject of a poem by William Wordsworth that she was once made to memorize in school. The daffodils become an emblem of the British (and American) visions of the world that are irrelevant to an Antiguan.

As time passes, the many differences of race, class, and geography between Lucy and Mariah take on added weight. They will never really understand each other. On the train ride to the family's summer home on the Great Lakes, Lucy sees miles of freshly plowed fields and comments that at least she will not have to do plowing. The remark mystifies Mariah, but Lucy seems to be referring to her awareness of her ancestors in slavery and her consciousness that plowed lands cost someone some hard labor. In fact, although Lucy has come to love Mariah, seeing in her some of her mother, she is also constantly aware that Mariah knows little of the world that produced Lucy.

In her spare time, Lucy has made a friend, Peggy. Mariah does not like Peggy, who smokes, uses slang, and wears cheap, provocative clothes. Peggy and Lucy roam the streets at night, smoking marijuana and considering the sexual possibilities of the men they see in the park, although they never actually approach those men. During the summer at the Great Lakes, Lucy misses her friend; perhaps that is how she enters a love affair with Hugh, the brother of Mariah's friend Dinah. Unlike most of Mariah's associates, Hugh at least knows where the West Indies are; that sensibility earns him Lucy's approval. Lucy recognizes, however, that she wants no lasting attachments, and the affair ends when the family's vacation is over.

Back in New York, Lucy watches her employers' marriage break up. At the same time, Lucy's longstanding conflict with her mother in Antigua comes to a head. For months, Lucy has not opened her mother's letters; now a family friend tells her that her father has died and that her mother badly needs money. Lucy writes her mother an angry letter, blaming her for marrying a man who would not leave even enough money to cover his funeral. She says that she will never come home, but she also sends her some money. When the mother writes back, she says what Annie's mother said: that she would always be Lucy's mother and that Antigua would always be her home.

Lucy writes again, a more conciliatory letter this time, but she includes a false address. Then she quits her job and moves into an apartment with Peggy. She knows that she will not like living with Peggy, and she suspects that her new lover, Paul, is unfaithful. Her meditations as her life changes link her conflicts with her mother and her awareness that she is the product of British colonial rule. As the British had assumed that their black subjects who had once been their slaves could produce nothing worthwhile, so had her mother assumed the same about Lucy, whose anger boils at the recognition. At the novel's end, she takes out a blank journal that Mariah has given her and begins to write her name. Clearly, her future lies in the written word.

Summary

Jamaica Kincaid's work is dominated by the pictures of the beautiful island on which she grew up, by her tortured relationship with her family, especially her mother, and by her consciousness of Antigua's tragic history of colonial rule and its wasted present of corruption and incompetence. In *Annie John* and *Lucy*, Kincaid draws parallels between a government that fails to appreciate and foster its people's abilities and the families of her autobiographical central characters, who also fail their children. The result inevitably is the child's anger and rejection of the place that will always be mother and home.

Bibliography

Als, Hilton. "Don't Worry, Be Happy." Review of *Lucy*, by Jamaica Kincaid. *The Nation* 252 (February 18, 1991): 207-209.

Bemrose, John. "Growing Pains of Girlhood." *Maclean's* 98 (May 20, 1985): 61.

Garis, Leslie. "Through West Indian Eyes." *The New York Times Magazine* 140 (October 7, 1990): 42-44.

Jaggi, Maya. "A Struggle for Independence." *The Times Literary Supplement* (April 26, 1991): 20.

Tyler, Anne. "At the Bottom of the River." *The New Republic* 189 (December 31, 1983): 32-33.

Ann D. Garbett

BARBARA KINGSOLVER

Born: Annapolis, Maryland
April 8, 1955

Principal Literary Achievement
Kingsolver has contributed significantly to contemporary literature by giving cultural, social, and political issues accessibility in her novels and short stories.

Biography
Born in Annapolis, Maryland, on April 8, 1955, Barbara Kingsolver grew up in Kentucky. Her father, Wendell, was a physician, and her mother, Virginia, was a homemaker. Kingsolver, who has kept a journal of personal revelations since the age of eight, learned a sense of community in small-town Kentucky. Community to her meant a place where people "grow their own food and know who they could depend on for help." She writes about community in all of her stories, but she discovered that the reality of community is relatively rare in other parts of the country.

After leaving Kentucky for college, Kingsolver deliberately lost her "hillbilly" accent, which she found was ridiculed wherever she went. "People made terrible fun of me for the way I used to talk, so I gave it up slowly and became something else. It was later in life, about ten years later, that it occurred to me this language was a precious and valuable thing."

Part of her heritage is Cherokee, and many of Kingsolver's stories include American Indian characters, history, and issues. She discovered that the community so important to her is also a fundamental part of most Indians' lives.

Kingsolver earned a B.A. magna cum laude in biology from De Pauw University in 1977 and an M.S. in biology from the University of Arizona in 1981; she has also done additional graduate study. She began her university studies with a piano scholarship, but she switched to biology because it was more practical. Even so, writing is something she has always done, from the journals she has kept since childhood to the scientific and technical writing she did after college. Kingsolver's work has included stints as a research assistant in the department of physiology at the University of Tucson from 1977 to 1979, as a technical writer in the Office of Arid Lands Studies from 1981 to 1985, and as a freelance journalist from 1985 until 1987. It was this later writing that Kingsolver found gratifying, and when she realized that she could make a living doing something she really liked, she began writing fiction.

In her first novel, *The Bean Trees* (1988), a young woman leaves home, adopts a child, and becomes politically enlightened. This first novel achieved both critical and popular success, as did the subsequent *Animal Dreams* (1990), a story of a woman's search for place, and *Pigs in Heaven* (1993), a book about children's rights, loneliness, and poverty. Kingsolver's *Homeland and Other Stories* (1989) consists of twelve short stories. Her first collection of poetry, *Another America/Otra America* (1992), is printed with parallel English and Spanish texts on facing pages. *Holding the Line: Women in the Great Arizona Mine Strike of 1983* (1989) is a nonfiction book that covers a long copper-mine strike that forever changed several mining towns and the lives of the women who lived in them.

The awards and honors Kingsolver has received include a Feature Writing Award from the Arizona Press Club in 1986; American Library Association Awards in 1988 for *The Bean Trees* and again in 1990 for *Homeland and Other Stories*; a Citation of Accomplishment from the United Nations National Council of Women in 1989 for *Animal Dreams*; and both a PEN/Faulkner Award for Fiction and an Edward Abbey Ecofiction award, again for *Animal Dreams*, both in 1991. She has also been nominated several times for ABBY awards.

In the late 1970's, Kingsolver became active in the sanctuary movement to help Central American refugees. She involved herself in a variety of human-rights activities, including writing pamphlets. When she began writing fiction, Kingsolver found her convictions about United States policies in Latin America and other human-rights issues were easy to express in the context of a novel or short story.

The issues Kingsolver chooses to write about come from the heart and from real-life experiences. Her interest in her Native American heritage, her Southern upbringing, her human-rights activities, and her coverage of the Arizona mine strike have all provided material and ideas for her books. Literary and popular critics alike have praised Kingsolver's sensitive portrayals of average people who face everyday victories and losses as well as extraordinary conflicts and crises.

Analysis

Barbara Kingsolver has always been a storyteller with an urgent need to share her deeply felt beliefs. She strives to reach an audience that includes both the well-educated and the less educated, challenging the former without alienating the latter. She uses voices of ordinary middle-class people to tell her stories and incorporates current political and social issues with her awareness of human nature, spunky characters, and colorfully rendered landscapes. The major characters of her novels *The Bean Trees*, *Animal Dreams*, and *Pigs in Heaven* are women struggling to make a place for themselves. They consider every new circumstance and idea with courage and humor, developing a moral sensibility that helps them to progress. These ordinary women draw readers into trials and triumphs, giving them an opportunity to look at the world through a feminist perspective.

Kingsolver lived in the rural South, but it was only after she left home that she realized that the community spirit that had surrounded her there was not easy to find anywhere else. Realizing the importance of having people around for support, culture, and shared values, she brings these elements into her fiction. Having lived around people who care for and need one another lends a deep sense of understanding and insight to Kingsolver's stories. The Indian sense of community is even stronger and more visible than the sense of community she experienced in Kentucky. In spite of her Cherokee great-grandmother, Kingsolver grew up without learning very much about that part of her background, and she has sought to fill that gap; she has also found Indian culture to be fertile ground for her stories. In all of her writing, Kingsolver gives understanding and respect to both Indian and mainstream American cultures, but at the same time, she questions the high value mainstream culture places on the nuclear family. In her view, Indians can give and receive handouts with more ease in their communities, which are generally characterized by extended families, than can other Americans. On the other hand, these other Americans place high value on independence, with few knowing where they came from or belong. For them, the importance of individuality crowds out the reality of dependence on others.

Kingsolver begins writing with a question, rather than a character or story line, then writes her way to a satisfying answer. After *The Bean Trees* was published, she began to look closely at adoption law and discovered the existence of the Indian Child Welfare Act, which states that no Cherokee child can be adopted out of the tribe without tribal consent; this information led her to write *Pigs in Heaven*. In *The Bean Trees*, Turtle is literally given to Taylor, who later devises a way to "adopt" the young Cherokee girl in an effort not to lose her. *Pigs in Heaven* explores the moral and social aspects of the adoption and of Turtle's life with a non-Indian mother.

Holding the Line: Women in the Great Arizona Mine Strike of 1983, Kingsolver's first work of nonfiction, describes labor and feminist issues as well as environmental degradation and the oppressiveness of corporate presence in small mining towns during a long labor strike. The book was an important source of material for *Animal Dreams* and the short story "Why I'm a Danger to the Public," which is included in *Homeland and Other Stories*.

Kingsolver has two degrees in biology, and she uses her scientific knowledge in her stories. In "Covered Bridges," Lena runs a poison hotline and is susceptible herself to deadly bee stings. Hallie Noline puts her skills to better use in *Animal Dreams* by leaving her Tucson houseplant hotline to help repair the depleted soils damaged by poverty and politics in Central America. In *The Bean Trees*, Kingsolver compares the role of bacteria in the survival of wisteria vines in poor soil to the role of underground sanctuary houses in providing safety for refugees in the United States.

Kingsolver is a human-rights activist, and she puts her views into her stories. She believes that by writing about abuses and atrocities in her novels, she can present information and tell the truth in a way sometimes not possible in pamphlets or other media. In *The Bean Trees*, she describes the difficulties Central American expatriots experience in trying to live safely in the United States. In *Animal Dreams*, Hallie Noline travels to Nicaragua to work with the Sandinistas.

In her first collection of poetry, *Another America/Otra America*, Kingsolver describes poverty and danger as well as inner courage and strength; the voices are courageous and familiar. Her poems appear in both English and Spanish, with themes that concern both the United States and Central America. Kingsolver had her poems translated into Spanish to emphasize her strong belief in the importance of multicultural and multinational respect and understanding.

Although she shed her own Southern accent, language is important to Kingsolver, who uses colorful Southern language generously throughout her stories. Language is also a major plot element in Turtle's development. A victim of child abuse before meeting Taylor, she is slow to speak, and her first words are anything but usual: She begins speaking by naming vegetables as though they were a safe topic and only slowly ventures into new topics of conversation.

Typically, each of Kingsolver's novels contains more than one story line. She blends them and gives them life through her vivid characters, dialogue, and descriptions.

THE BEAN TREES

First published: 1988
Type of work: Novel

Although determined to avoid pregnancy and scared of tires, Taylor becomes a mother and a tire-shop employee, sharpening her political and feminist views along the way.

In *The Bean Trees*, Missie Greer begins the first-person account of her youth in rural Kentucky by explaining how she developed a fear of exploding tires after a man overfilled one and was blown to the top of a gas-station sign. Kingsolver presents her storytelling style in this humorous opening scene and keeps it up throughout.

Missie has grown up noticing that many small-town girls experience early motherhood. Her own mother has given her a strong sense of self-sufficiency, and as soon as she can, Missie leaves. She buys a run-down Volkswagen and goes off in search of opportunity and adventure. Missie decides that when she runs out of gas, she will choose a new name to replace the despised "Missie." She runs out of gas in Taylorville, Illinois, and becomes Taylor Greer. Her car breaks down in Oklahoma, where a desperate Cherokee woman shoves a bundled-up child into the car, saying, "Take this baby."

Taylor names the child Turtle because of the way she grabs and holds on to anything within reach. Turtle becomes a pivotal subplot concerning child abuse and survival. Turtle develops slowly and has setbacks, but she is portrayed as an endearing child whose accomplishments give the novel spirit and hope. When Turtle notices that the wisteria blossoms in the neighborhood park have turned to seed pods, she names the bush a "bean tree." The park is one of the places of community that Kingsolver likes to write about, a place where neighbors gather to help and to find help.

Taylor and Turtle arrive in Tucson, Arizona, with a flat tire. Kingsolver also moved to Tucson as a young adult, and her descriptions of the city and the desert landscape have the believable freshness of discovery. Taylor's first business is to get her flat tire fixed; then she needs to find a job and a place to live. This leads her to Mattie, who runs the Jesus Is Lord Used Tire Shop. She meets her roommate when she answers the house-to-share advertisement Lou Ann Ruiz has placed, and her first job is in a fast-food restaurant, a job that lasts only until the strong-minded Taylor blows up at her boss. Mattie then offers her a job repairing tires.

Taylor learns that she is well suited to motherhood, and Lou Ann learns that she is not a helpless loser. Mattie's tire shop is also a sanctuary house for political refugees from Central America. Taylor thus learns about the pain and difficulty endured by people who must flee their countries for political reasons. By the time the story ends, Taylor has also come to terms with issues of custody battles and poverty.

HOMELAND AND OTHER STORIES

First published: 1989
Type of work: Short stories

Twelve short stories revolving around women both young and old.

Homeland and Other Stories, Kingsolver's second book, begins with the touching and poetic title story about a woman attempting to pass along her Cherokee beliefs and values to her great-granddaughter while resigned to a vastly changing world. The last story, "Why I'm a Danger to the Public," is about a young woman fighting for workers' rights in a mine strike, with resignation the furthest thing from her mind.

All of Kingsolver's stories are infused with wisdom and warmth and concern both classic and contemporary issues. "Rose-Johnny" is narrated by a young girl who defends an eccentric outcast in a prejudiced small town. In "Covered Bridges," a husband comes face to face with his wife's mortality while they are in the process of deciding whether to have children.

In "Survival Zones," a middle-aged and very typical farm wife, Roberta, comes to terms with her predictable life. The joke she attempts to tell at the beginning but can never get right finally makes sense by the middle of the story. By the end of the story, she sees that her life, though conventional, is comfortable and fulfilling. She doles out advice to her daughter without interfering, while at the same time she tries to decide whether to keep the warm-climate azalea bush that her mother-in-law planted years ago in cold-climate Indiana. She knows that no one else is concerned about the bush and would hardly notice if it were gone.

The stories have a range of location as well as topic. In "Jump-up Day," an independent-minded girl is forced to live in a convent in the Caribbean; in "Blueprints," a couple moves to the country after ten years of life together in Sacramento only to find their relationship seriously threatened in the new setting.

Characters in the remaining stories include an estranged mother and daughter who are both pregnant, a woman who visits home for Easter and is unexpectedly haunted by the past, and an ex-convict who tries to live a straight life while those around her gossip, meddle, and steal.

Not only do Kingsolver's characters tolerate poverty, despair, disappointment, and injustice, but they also make valiant efforts to understand what has happened to them and to pass that knowledge along. In "Islands on the Moon," Magda tells her resisting daughter:

"We're like islands on the moon."
"There's no water on the moon," says Annemarie.
"That's what I mean. A person could walk from one to the other if they just decided to do it."

Kingsolver seems to have a vast supply of stories at hand, and the energy and freshness of these in her first collection point to a writer who has only begun telling them.

PIGS IN HEAVEN

First published: 1993
Type of work: Novel

Taylor Greer and her adopted Cherokee daughter Turtle go on the run to avoid confronting the validity of Turtle's adoption.

Pigs in Heaven, Kingsolver's third novel, is a sequel to *The Bean Tree*, which ended at the time of Turtle's adoption. *Pigs in Heaven* is set three years after that time.

After a freak accident leading to a heroic rescue, Turtle is pushed into the spotlight with an appearance on a national television talk show. With this exposure, Turtle and her adoptive mother come to the attention of Annawake Fourkiller, an activist attorney for the Cherokee Nation in Oklahoma. Fourkiller, whose own twin brother was adopted out of the tribe and is now in prison, feels strongly that Indian children need to grow up surrounded by their own culture. The Indian Child Welfare Act makes removing children from the tribe illegal without the tribe's consent.

Kingsolver gives both sides of the issue equal time. The Indian culture feels that community and culture are crucial to a child's identity and well-being, while Turtle is clearly well loved by her white mother. The theme of a child's rights versus those of a parent was a timely one in 1993, and Kingsolver's treatment of it is sympathetic. The unique case she describes is thoroughly explored.

Other themes in the story include the high price of helping someone more desperate than yourself; this theme is explored when Taylor befriends Barbie, who is also on the run. Taylor's mother, Alice, claims that it is a family trait of women to be on their own, and this almost proves to be true until the barely believable, but hopeful and happy, ending. Cash Stillwater has credibility as a grieving and sensitive man who happens to be an Indian. His appearance in the story enables it to come full circle: He is Turtle's grandfather, and he falls in love with Alice.

After stops in Western Arizona and Las Vegas, Taylor and Turtle settle temporarily in Seattle. Amazed at the amount of rain, Taylor exclaims, "This isn't a city, it's a carwash!" Kingsolver's heroine has retained her wry and funny view of the world in the face of continued setback and disappointment. The struggles of a single mother's attempt to provide a home for her child are contrasted with the realities of family and neighborly help in the rural Oklahoma Indian community.

Alice's comment to her daughter, "Well, Taylor, you've brought your pigs to a pretty market," comes from a childhood spent on a pig farm, but metaphors such as this are not the book's only source of wisdom or folklore. The title comes from a Cherokee fable concerning boys who, when punished, claim that their mothers have treated them like pigs. The spirits hear them and turn the boys into pigs, and they run to heaven and become a constellation.

Summary

Barbara Kingsolver treats her characters with the respect she would give to a favorite cousin. She draws her rich language and characters from her own background. Not only are they people concerned with ordinary ups and downs but they are also ordinary people: waitresses, mechanics, schoolteachers. Kingsolver gives her characters the spirit, humor, courage and foibles that flavor and tenderize her stories. Then she sets her characters down in familiar places and presents them with issues and predicaments to consider and resolve. Kingsolver's political concerns include the rights of children, workers, women, Indians, and, indeed, all human rights. Her ability to blend humor with social abuses and evocative landscapes with suspense makes her a consummate storyteller.

Bibliography

Cooke, Carolyn. Review of *Animal Dreams*, by Barbara Kingsolver. *The Nation* 25 (November 26, 1990): 653-654.

Mossman, Robert. Review of *The Bean Trees*, by Barbara Kingsolver. *English Journal* 79 (October, 1990): 85.

Newhaus, Denish. Review of *Homeland and Other Stories*, by Barbara Kingsolver. *Times Literary Supplement*, September 7, 1990, 956.

Pence, Amy. "An Interview with Barbara Kingsolver." *Poets and Writers* 21, no. 4 (July, 1993): 14.

Smiley, Jane. Review of *Animal Dreams*, by Barbara Kingsolver. *The New York Times Book Review*, September 2, 1990, 2.

Marilyn Kongslie

JERZY KOSINSKI

Born: Lodz, Poland
June 14, 1933
Died: New York, New York
May 3, 1991

Principal Literary Achievement
Kosinski's novels are powerful and disturbing commentaries on individuality
and the dangers of social conformity.

Biography
Jerzy Kosinski was born in Lodz, Poland, on June 14, 1933, the only child of
Mieczyslaw and Elzbieta Kosinski. His parents were Jewish and educated in Russia;
his father was a teacher of linguistics at the University of Lodz and his mother a concert
pianist trained at the Moscow Conservatory. When Germany invaded Poland in 1939,
Kosinski's parents entrusted their six-year-old son to a friend who took him east,
toward Russia. Caught up in the invasion, Kosinski was abandoned by his guardian
and lived for the duration of the war in eastern Poland, wandering alone from village
to village. The trauma of these years caused him to lose his voice; he did not speak
again until he was fifteen. He was picked up by Soviet troops and placed in an
orphanage, where he was rescued by his parents, who had survived the war. Of the
sixty or so of Kosinski's relatives alive before the war, all were killed except his parents
and himself. In Communist Poland, Kosinski was educated at the University of Lodz,
where he received two master's degrees, one in political science (1953) and one in
history (1955). He was an assistant professor at the Polish Academy of Sciences in
Warsaw and at work on a doctorate in sociology when he defected to the United States
in 1957. He worked at a parking lot in Manhattan and at other odd jobs, eventually
receiving a Ford Foundation grant in 1958 that allowed him to study for a doctorate
in sociology at Columbia University. His area of study was the effect of socialism on
the individual; although he never completed the degree, his experience in Poland and
Russia interviewing officials and ordinary citizens gave him material for what became
his first book, *The Future Is Ours, Comrade*, published by Doubleday in 1960 under
the pen name of Joseph Novak. A version of the book appeared in *Reader's Digest*,
and Kosinski soon had a best-seller. The book was followed by a second, *No Third
Path*, published in 1962, also under the name Joseph Novak. In 1962, moreover,

Kosinski married Mary Hayward Weir, widow of the founder of the Weir steel corporation. He began to work on his first novel, *The Painted Bird*, drawing on his experiences as a child wandering through German-occupied Poland. *The Painted Bird* was published in 1965 to excellent reviews, and his career as a novelist was launched. He was divorced from Weir in 1966. In 1968, he published *Steps*, an experimental novel composed of brief scenes narrated by a nameless man familiar with war-torn Poland, the Holocaust, and the sinister side of New York City. *Steps* won the National Book Award in 1969, and Kosinski became renowned for both his literary accomplishments and his newly achieved celebrity status.

His third novel, *Being There*, was published in 1971. In 1973, he published *The Devil Tree*, a novel that explored rootlessness, corporate greed, and the drug scene of contemporary America. The book seemed to strain for effect and was not well received. It was Kosinski's first literary setback, and he labored to correct it, rewriting the entire novel and issuing the revised version in 1981. In the same year, 1973, Kosinski was elected president of the International Association of Poets, Playwrights, Editors, Essayists, and Novelists (PEN) and served until 1975. In 1975, he published *Cockpit*, narrated by Tarden, an ex-spy on the run from his former organization, living alone in New York and acting out scenarios of vengeance on those whom he feels deserve it. With *Blind Date* (1977), Kosinski established himself as a major writer whose novels charted the dark side of human life—the price of survival for Kosinski's protagonists becomes perpetual aloneness, disguises, the willingness to wreak vengeance on those who would victimize them. Not to be an avenger is to risk being a victim. The grim scenes from his fiction contrasted dramatically with the image of a sociable, witty, and entertaining person he projected on many television talk-show appearances. In 1979 he published *Passion Play*, a novel in which the protagonist, Fabian, a polo player who is definitely not a team player, wanders across America in a motor home complete with two polo ponies. Along with the familiar enemies this Kosinski protagonist must face—conventional morality, deceitful lovers, rival polo players—Fabian confronts his own aging, his recurring fear of the loss of his energy to write, even to live. It is this sense of having lost his creative power that dominates Kosinski's next novel, *Pinball* (1979). Although Kosinski received in this year the Writers Guild of America Best Screenplay Award for the film *Being There*, the reviews of *Pinball* suggested that Kosinski's power as a novelist were indeed declining, as Fabian in *Passion Play* had feared. *Pinball*'s protagonist, Domostroy, is a failed musical composer whose classic works, numbering the same as Kosinski's published novels, are remembered and respected by his fans, but Domostroy cannot write another; his source of inspiration has dried up, and he lives by playing the piano in a rundown ballroom.

In 1982, *The Village Voice* published an article that attacked Kosinski on a number of charges, including having had Central Intelligence Agency (CIA) assistance in publishing the Novak books, having written *The Painted Bird* in Polish and having it translated into English, and having hired editorial assistants to write his novels for him. The charges were never substantiated, and several newspapers and magazines refuted them; but the article so disturbed Kosinski that he devoted his next and longest novel (also his last), *The Hermit of 69th Street* (1988), to the notion that all serious writing incorporates prior writing. The novel's protagonist, Norbert Kosky, is a writer who is falsely accused of not writing his books. This long and rambling book, filled with quotations from other writers, becomes a compendium of the art of writing as well as a kind of vicarious victory over Kosinski's detractors. The book prompted a baffled and negative critical response, and Kosinski began working on a revision of the novel for paperback issue. Kosinski was exhausted by the writing and revision of *The Hermit of 69th Street*. His wife, Katherina von Fraunhofer, whom he had married in 1987 after a long companionship, said that during this time he was writing seven days a week. Depressed and increasingly ill from a chronic heart condition, Kosinski committed suicide in his Manhattan apartment on May 2, 1991.

Analysis

Referring to his earlier life in Communist Poland, Kosinski said that the artist in a police state "has always been trapped in a cage where he can fly as long as he does not touch the wires. The predicament is: how to spread your wings in the cage." Kosinski's notion of flying and cages are metaphors he used to describe his career throughout his life. In Poland, he saw himself imprisoned by a "mad best-selling novelist, Stalin"; he escaped that prison with a flight to America. Writing in America certainly brought freedom to Kosinski; he wrote two best-selling books in an adopted language. Yet there, too, his own writing began to form still another cage. Writing can free; writing can also imprison. He gave up his mother tongue, Polish (and Russian) and wrote in, as he phrased it, his "stepmother tongue," English. In 1971, he said in an interview that "no prison is as impregnable as language," suggesting that it is just as difficult to break into the prison of an alien language, English, as it is to escape the confines of one's mother tongue. The writing of his books formed still new patterns, new cages, which he then attempted to escape. He said in 1980 of *Passion Play* that "because I have written the books that I have written—they form my destiny as it has been lived until now. There is a pattern." The pattern of books forms a cage from which the only escape is new writing. This is Kosinski's dilemma—his writing creates a protagonist (Tarden, Fabian, Domostroy—their names change in the different books, but they confront similar cages) and this protagonist must battle a new confinement. His novels thus confront not only the paradox of the nature of writing but also the paradox of his career as a novelist whose words have both released him from cages and imprisoned him in new ones.

Kosinski's protagonists take on an array of enemies—police-state officials (*Steps*); American corporate greed and mass consumption (*The Devil Tree*); American conformity and passivity, especially in the form of television watching (*Being There* and *Passion Play*); human self-delusion about the predictability of life, whether in the form of a mentality of endless consumerism or socialist state planning (*Cockpit*, *Blind Date*); social conformity concerning sexual behavior (*Steps*, *Passion Play*); and, lastly, the critics and readers who refuse to see the originality of Kosinski's own achievement as a writer (*Passion Play*, *Pinball*, and especially his final, most obsessive book, *The Hermit of 69th Street*). All of his novels portray his protagonists besieged, surrounded by enemies. In the best of them, Kosinski manages to create a convincing and plausible threat as well as a compelling, if often grim, solution—everyone is alone, subject to victimization, whether overt and visible, such as German soldiers herding Jews into boxcars as witnessed by the Boy in *The Painted Bird*, or subtle and invisible, such as the tendency in most people to accept a passive role in the design of their own lives. Survival for the individual relies in taking action to resist victimization, even if becoming a victimizer is the only way. The lessons of his novels are cruel and seem to encourage a survival-of-the-fittest mentality in which the only measure of morality is the triumph of the would-be victim over his victimizer. Yet Kosinski was a survivor both of the Holocaust and a police state; his battles as a writer in America, wings brushing against new wires, he transformed into imaginative narratives that remain disturbing warnings, cruel fables of exploitation and destruction that chart the larger destructions of his time—the Holocaust, the Soviet repression of Eastern Europe, the soulless consumerism and television passivity of contemporary America. Against these forces Kosinski has arranged his books, at least four or five of which remain remarkable testaments of the will of the individual to triumph. Even his carefully planned suicide suggests a refusal to succumb passively to still another design being imposed on him, this time by coronary illness and whatever else he saw gathering to encage him.

THE PAINTED BIRD

First published: 1965
Type of work: Novel

The narrator, an unnamed boy, describes his abandonment as a child in wartime Eastern Europe, his torment by various oppressors, and his ultimate survival.

Although Kosinski published two books before *The Painted Bird*, his achievement as a novelist centers around this book. The unnamed boy of *The Painted Bird* narrates a story that is simultaneously a fable of the Holocaust and an imaginative record of the shaping forces of Kosinski's early life—separation from his parents, wandering through Polish villages hostile to Jews and gypsies, dodging German soldiers, and eventually being rescued by Soviet soldiers and placed in a postwar orphanage. Throughout the years of his abandonment, the boy is bereft of every form of protection except his own initiative, cunning, and duplicity. The novel charts the boy's survival; it also epitomizes Kosinski's values, which he demonstrated in all of his subsequent novels, namely, that the individual is alone, surrounded by systems of persecution and oppression, whether Nazi soldiers rounding up Jews in Poland for extermination or Communist thought police monitoring helpless Polish or Russian citizens. Whatever the source of oppression, *The Painted Bird* (and Kosinski's many novels after it) asserts that the duty of the individual is to seize the necessary power that would turn would-be persecutors into victims. Unless victimization is actively resisted, the individual will succumb and become a victim, and the surest way to avoid victimization is to become an oppressor.

The boy is beaten by Polish peasants, pushed through an ice-covered pond by cruel boys, forced to hang from a beam over a vicious dog, and tossed into an open cesspool and left to drown. His torment renders him a mute; he survives through craft, deception, and the ability to assume the role of victimizer. The boy pulls a murderous peasant into a pit full of starving rats, sets fire to a barn, and sabotages a train full of peasants. The boy at the end of the novel is nearly an adult. He savors his newly restored speech as though it is a prized captive, testing his voice over and over to make sure, as he says, that "it did not intend to escape." The boy's recovery of his voice is also a model of Kosinski's discovery of his own powers as a writer. The boy, taught by Gavrila to read and write (he is still a mute), marvels at his discovery of the power of words: "Books impressed me tremendously. From their simple printed pages one could conjure up a world as real as that grasped by the senses. Furthermore, the world of books, like meat in cans, was somehow richer and more flavorful than the everyday variety." For the boy, literature is like meat in cans—spicier than ordinary life, its flavor always present, sealed away for the reader's special nourishment. So it is with the youthful Kosinski, turning from one kind of writing—the sociological criticism of the Novak books—to the imaginative power of a child narrating an experience so horrifying that he is sometimes unaware of the full horror, only of the grim lessons for survival that are there for the learning. The boy, for example, watches a bird catcher, Lekh, paint a captured bird in gaudy colors and then release it. "We saw soon afterwards how one bird after another would peel off in a fierce attack. . . .When we finally found the painted bird it was usually dead." The boy learns quickly the lesson: Only his own aggressive initiative will prevent him from being turned into a victim, a painted bird pecked to death by his own kind for being different.

The critical response to the novel was overwhelmingly positive, in spite of the painful nature of the narration. The extraordinary power of the boy's narrative, with its combination of childlike awareness and lyric grace, seemed to many critics to signal a new and original voice in American literature. *The Painted Bird* has remained Kosinski's most powerful and popular novel.

STEPS

First published: 1968
Type of work: Novel

The narrator, an unnamed young man, describes his experiences in Eastern Europe and in America, to which he has escaped.

Kosinski's second novel, *Steps*, consists of forty-eight short vignettes narrated by an unnamed young man who moves back and forth between two worlds, Communist Eastern Europe and the West. The first is a claustrophobic environment of peasant villages, compulsory military service, political intrigue at a university, and the endless criticism and surveillance of Party organizations such as the kind Novak described in *The Future Is Ours, Comrade*. The second, the West, especially America, is an equally treacherous environment where the narrator begins as a victim—like the young Kosinski—because he can hardly speak the language. Eventually, the narrator transforms himself from victim to oppressor. He drives fast cars, learns how to use complex eavesdropping devices, and flashes a wallet full of credit cards. *Steps*, then, is the narrator's account, in a voice that is detached, cool, and seemingly impervious to moral insight, of two related transformations of himself from the status of a character plotted against to that of a writer who does the plotting. In both East and West, the narrator begins as an outsider, speaking the language of victimization. In both, he masters the language of his oppressor and then proceeds to work his will on his enemies, first by escaping from the East, second by acquiring the possessions needed in the West to remain independent—income, credit, mobility.

Language and sex in *Steps* can be either sources of power or signs of weakness, depending on how the relationship between the two principals, that is, between speaker and hearer or between sexual partners, establishes itself. The narrator sees both language and sex in terms of the interaction of will. Each activity involves role-playing, and the only roles available are victim and oppressor. The narrator manipulates the words of a woman who thinks he is a deaf mute; the operators of concentration camps control the language of their victims and thus capture and destroy their identity. The novel is full of sexual encounters between the narrator and various partners that seem to test some limit, pass some boundary of restraint. One of his lovers asks of him this question: "Then, all you need from me is to provide a stage on which you can project and view yourself, and see how your discarded experiences become alive again when they affect me. Am I right?" She is. Some scenes in which the narrator deliberately seeks out unpredictable and unconventional sexual ties in order to stimulate a sense of freedom from religious, political, or cultural restraint often end up as sheer exploitation, even sadism. Readers wonder what restraints, if any, the narrator of *Steps* feels obligated to impose on himself in a given encounter.

One scene does reveal the narrator's attitude toward his own impulse to exploit a human relationship. Wandering alone by car through an unfamiliar Eastern European countryside, the narrator discovers a deranged woman kept in a cage inside a barn. Marks on her naked body suggest that she has been sexually abused by the owner of the barn. For a moment, the narrator senses that no one but the woman knows he is present: "It occurred to me that we were alone in the barn and that she was totally defenseless." The situation, he says, is "tempting"; complete dominance over the woman is possible, which he sees as an encounter in which "one could become completely oneself with another human being." What holds him back, he soon realizes, is that the woman, the potential victim, would not recognize how he would be using her. "What I required, however," he reflects, "was the other's recognition of this: the woman in the cage could not acknowledge me." He turns away and reports the incident to the police, who promptly release the woman and arrest the owner of the barn. Yet the narrator's motive is not compassion; he sees only that the woman is useless to provide for him new discoveries of himself.

Although some critics expressed dismay at the seeming lack of moral context for the narrator's voice, *Steps* was admired for its starkness of style, the complex weave of short vignettes (each one a sort of step in the growth of the narrator's self-awareness) that simultaneously seemed elusive and revealing. The novel won the National Book Award in 1969.

BEING THERE

First published: 1971
Type of work: Novel

A naïve man named Chance is expelled from a rich man's estate and quickly assumed by others to be intelligent, distinguished, and powerful.

Kosinki's third novel, *Being There*, is a fable about a perfect language, one that captivates the listener while revealing nothing of the identity of the speaker. The book, Kosinski's shortest, continues his analysis of the embryonic writer testing one new language after another until he discovers the one that both ends his victimization and confers power. Chance, the protagonist, is a simple-minded gardener in a rich man's house. The garden is a refuge: "It was safe and secure in the garden, which was separated from the street by a high, red brick wall." Chance has no self-consciousness and has spent his life watching television. He has no concept of a reality outside his garden and the safe confines of the television tube. Yet he is handsome and well-dressed (with the suits from his now-dead benefactor), and when he is cast out of his garden, he is slightly injured by a limousine carrying a wealthy woman, EE, who befriends him. Assuming that Chance is as intelligent as he is handsome, EE brings him to her home and introduces him to her husband, the industrial magnate Benjamin Rand, who is slowly dying. All Chance can talk of is the world of his garden, but his statements seem somehow incisive—even prophetic—to his eager listeners. Soon he is the guest of the president of the United States and becomes a talk-show celebrity, and at the book's end he is being considered as a vice-presidential candidate. This implausible and amusing satire takes on not only television's ability to limit the human imagination—one of Kosinski's recurring critiques—but also the human propensity to believe what one wants to hear, to be impressed with the new, to escape the burden of ordinariness.

By the end of Kosinski's tale, Soviet computers analyze Chance's vocabulary, syntax, and accents and find that it is impossible to detect Chance's ethnic background or origins in any American community. Thus, for Kosinski, Chance achieves the status that no other of his protagonists reaches—Chance's language is not a mark of identity, vulnerability, or victimization. Language as pure power, divested of its inherent signals of personal origin and past, is the language that the despairing narrators of *The Painted Bird* and *Steps* often imagine speaking. Chance manages to do it just by opening his mouth, and the book ends before anyone is the wiser. Bewildered by all the attention he is receiving, Chance breaks away from still another reception to gaze at a small garden. "Not a thought lifted itself from Chance's brain. Peace filled his chest."

Reviewers of *Being There* saw that the book did not have the depth and complexity of *The Painted Bird*, but most were impressed by the novelty of the plot and by Kosinski's critique of American television and mass dependency on electronic images. A 1979 film version directed by Hal Ashby and starring Peter Sellers and Shirley MacLaine revived interest in Kosinski's slim novel and has kept it in print.

Summary

Within six years, Kosinski had published three novels that marked him as a major force in contemporary American fiction. Of the six subsequent novels he published, two, *Cockpit* and *Blind Date*, further enhanced his reputation as a writer of the dark side of human life whose fictions dwelt on survival, disguise, scenes of violence, and kinky sex. Many of the scenes in both novels resemble events Kosinski experienced in his own life. His lasting achievement, however, centers on his powerful and disturbing voice, which warns of the danger of social conformity (sometimes he resembles a kind of latter-day Ralph Waldo Emerson) while extolling the need for the individual to create his or her own life. The self in resistance, the self in creativity—these are the hallmarks of Kosinski's work that will outlast his extraordinarily troubled and creative life.

Bibliography

Corry, John. "A Case History: Seventeen Years of Ideological Attack on a Cultural Target." *The New York Times*, November 7, 1982, p. B1, 28-29.

Gelb, Barbara. "Being Jerzy Kosinski." *The New York Times Magazine*, February 21, 1982, 42-46, 49, 52-54, 58.

Hicks, Jack. *In the Singer's Temple: Prose Fictions of Barthelme, Gaines, Brautigan, Piercy, Kesey, and Kosinski.* Chapel Hill: University of North Carolina Press, 1981.

Kosinski, Jerzy. Interview by Daniel J. Cahill. *Contemporary Literature* 19 (Spring, 1978): 133-142.

Lavers, Norman. *Jerzy Kosinski.* Boston: Twayne, 1982.

Lilly, Paul R., Jr. "Vision and Violence in the Fiction of Jerzy Kosinski." *The Literary Review* 25 (Spring, 1982): 389-400.

_____. *Words in Search of Victims: The Achievement of Jerzy Kosinski.* Kent, Ohio: Kent State University Press, 1988.

Lupack, Barbara Tepa. *Plays of Passion, Games of Chance: Jerzy Kosinski and His Fiction*. Bristol, Ind.: Wyndham Hall Press, 1988.

Stokes, Geoffrey, and Eliot Fremont-Smith. "Jerzy Kosinski's Tainted Words." *The Village Voice*, June 22, 1982, 1, 41-43.

Taylor, John. "The Haunted Bird: The Death and Life of Jerzy Kosinski." *New York* 24 (July 15, 1991): 24-37.

Paul R. Lilly, Jr.

STANLEY KUNITZ

Born: Worcester, Massachusetts
July 29, 1905

Principal Literary Achievement

A 1959 Pulitzer Prize winner, Kunitz is a poet's poet who has also gained renown as an outstanding editor, translator, teacher, and anthologist.

Biography

The suicide of Solomon Z. Kunitz, a dress manufacturer, before the birth of his third child, Stanley, haunted Stanley Kunitz throughout his life. The widow, Yetta Helen Jasspon, was remarried to Mark Dine when Stanley was eight; Dine died six years later. Yetta tried to expunge the memory of her first husband from her household, igniting Stanley's curiosity about his father. Once when the young boy found a picture of Solomon, Yetta snatched it and slapped him for having it.

In 1922, Kunitz, valedictorian of his class at Worcester Classical High School, won a scholarship to Harvard University. Having been elected to Phi Beta Kappa, he received a bachelor's degree in English, summa cum laude, from Harvard in 1926. He received a master's degree in 1927.

At this point, Kunitz, recipient of the prestigious Lloyd McKim Garrison Medal for Poetry in 1926, hoped to teach at Harvard. The head of Harvard's English department intimated to him, however, that despite Kunitz's outstanding qualifications—which included the appearance of his poems in some of the nation's best literary publications—Harvard undergraduates would resent being taught by a Jew. This disappointment turned Kunitz from the academic world.

Forced to earn a living, Kunitz worked for the *Worcester Telegram* before becoming an editor for the H. W. Wilson Company in 1928; this association lasted for more than forty years. Kunitz was editor of the *Wilson Library Bulletin* from 1928 until 1942, when he left Wilson temporarily to serve in the Air Transport Command of the U.S. Army as a staff sergeant.

Upon his postwar separation from the Army, Kunitz received a Guggenheim Fellowship, giving him a year to write. Two collections of his verse, *Intellectual Things* (1930) and *Passport to the War: A Selection of Poems* (1944), had already won their author recognition in the literary world, although he was equally well known for books he had edited or co-edited in his position at Wilson, among them *Living Authors:*

A Book of Biographies (with Howard Haycraft, 1931); *Authors Today and Yesterday: A Companion Volume to "Living Authors"* (with Haycraft, 1933); *British Authors of the Nineteenth Century* (with Haycraft, 1936); and *Twentieth Century Authors: A Biographical Dictionary of Modern Literature* (with Haycraft, 1942).

Kunitz's marriage to Helen Pearce in 1930 ended in divorce in 1937. Two years later, he married Eleanor Evans, from whom he was divorced in 1958, the year in which he married Elise Asher. His marriage to Evans produced his only offspring, Gretchen.

Fourteen years after the publication of *Passport to the War*, Kunitz's next collection was published. This volume, *Selected Poems: 1928-1958*, earned Kunitz a 1959 Pulitzer Prize. Thirteen years later, his next volume, *The Testing-Tree: Poems* (1971), appeared. In the interim, he had edited a volume of John Keats's poetry, coedited *European Authors, 1000-1900: A Biographical Dictionary of European Literature* (with Vineta Colby, 1967), and served as general editor of the Yale Young Poets' Series, a position he held, concurrently with other posts, from 1969 to 1977. He also was publishing poetry and essays in periodicals and contributing essays and chapters to books.

Kunitz's disenchantment with the academic world had moderated by 1946, when, at the termination of his Guggenheim Fellowship, he became professor of English at Bennington College in Vermont; he continued in that position until 1949. The following year, he taught at Potsdam State Teachers College, where he directed summer workshops in writing from 1949 until 1953. From 1950 to 1958, Kunitz was a lecturer in English at the New School of Social Research in New York City. He left to become director of the poetry workshop sponsored by the Poetry Center of the New York City Young Men's Hebrew Association, where, still employed by H. W. Wilson, he remained until 1962.

In 1963, Kunitz became a lecturer in writing at Columbia University, which in 1967 named him adjunct professor of writing, a position he held until he was eighty. He refused a tenured appointment at Columbia, preferring a looser affiliation with the institution.

Kunitz, whose productivity increased substantially after the publication of *The Testing-Tree*, has been guest lecturer or visiting professor at Yale University, the University of Washington, Princeton University, the University of Rutgers, Vassar College, Brandeis University, and Queens College. Partly as an outcome of his participation in a cultural exchange program with Poland and Russia in 1967, he intensified his translation of poetry from Russian, translating, editing, and publishing works by Anna Akhmatova, Andrei Voznesensky, and Ivan Drach.

During the period following *The Testing-Tree*, Kunitz served a two-year term as poetry consultant to the Library of Congress (1972-1974). He also published a collection of his essays, *A Kind of Order, a Kind of Folly: Essays and Conversations* (1975), as well as four collections of verse: *The Terrible Threshold: Selected Poems* (1974); *The Coat Without a Seam: Sixty Poems, 1930-1972* (1974); *The Poems of Stanley Kunitz: 1928-1978* (1979); and *The Wellfleet Whale and Companion Poems*

(1983). *Next-to-Last Things: New Poems and Essays* appeared in 1985. Kunitz also edited *The Essential Blake* (1987). In 1980, *The Poems of Stanley Kunitz: 1928-1978* brought him the Lenore Marshall Prize for the best poetry volume of the year in the United States.

Analysis

Haunted since early childhood by the murky impressions he had of his dead father, Kunitz often wrote about father-son relationships. Perhaps his most familiar poem is "Father and Son," published originally in *Passport to the War* and frequently anthologized. In the poem, a son quests after his lost father but, after catching up with him, finds him inarticulate. The son tells his father his story of loss and longing. The father, dead, can offer the son nothing, his face a "white ignorant hollow." This is Kunitz's image of his own father, whose fleeting image, as an anonymous face in a photograph, had been ripped from young Stanley's hand by an irate mother.

Kunitz is a careful poet. His poetic production until the early 1970's consisted of only three volumes. The first, *Intellectual Things*, suggested the poet's potential but revealed that he had not yet grasped fully the technique of writing the kind of poetry that is usually adjudged the work of an accomplished artist. The fifty poems in this early collection were, according to Kunitz, attempts on his part to demonstrate that intellect and emotion are too closely interconnected ever to exist independently.

The strongest and most telling poem in *Intellectual Things* is "Vita Nuova," a work influenced by Kunitz's reading of Dante Alighieri. This poem, traditionally formal in its versification, has a first-person narrator who is closely akin to Kunitz himself. The poem depends upon concrete nouns and forceful verbs, eschewing adjectives, adverbs, and qualifiers; its twenty lines, divided into four stanzas of equal length, are in pentameter and have a consistent, if at times stilted, *ababb* rhyme scheme.

In the fourteen years between *Intellectual Things* and *Passport to the War*, Kunitz had matured considerably. Yet this second collection was not large; about half of its poems had appeared originally in his first volume. Many of the new poems, however, were dynamic and had been revised to the point that they were impeccable technically. World War II spurred Kunitz into producing these poems, many of which concern the consequences facing a world that has become mechanized to the point that mass destruction of human beings—indeed, of civilization—is possible, perhaps imminent.

In many of the poems of this second volume, Kunitz is so caught up in the horror of his subject that he sometimes seems to be overreacting. At the time of publication, his work seemed almost hysterical, yet the clarity of his vision has been vindicated by a world that has moved at a dizzying clip toward the looming dangers to which he pointed in the early 1940's. The war poems in this volume use language precisely and effectively, and Kunitz sometimes resorts to distorting his imagery to heighten the impact of his warnings.

In this collection, however, Kunitz's verse is still formal and traditional. He experiments, particularly in the collection's often-cited "Father and Son," with the dream narrative, a poetic form that reflects Kunitz's own hazy glimmerings of a father he was forced from earliest childhood to create in his imagination.

Selected Poems: 1928-1958 contains the poems that appeared in *Passport to the War*, along with two from *Intellectual Things* that had not been reproduced in his 1944 collection. The poems are arranged carefully, lending this volume, like his two earlier ones, an inherent logic.

It is Kunitz the seasoned editor who, after writing the poems, concentrated on arranging them in as effective a format as he could. The volume begins with a love poem (largely concerning emotion) and ends with a poem about poetry (concerning the merging of emotion and intellect, a recurring theme of Kunitz's writing).

In the three volumes to 1958, Kunitz writes in measured cadences, frequently adopting the formalism of the Metaphysical poets, for whom he had considerable appreciation and whose poetically formal ranks he had joined. The public had to wait thirteen years for his next collection, *The Testing-Tree*, which contains twenty-three new poems and seven translations. In this volume, the new Kunitz begins to be evident. Gone is the formality of his first three books of verse. He now uses lines of irregular length—some quite short—and writes in free or blank verse. The tone of his writing is that of one who has, in some curious way, been liberated. The intensity of youth has given way to the mellowness that sometimes comes in middle age.

In this volume, Kunitz appears to have laid to rest some of the ghosts that had haunted him. He suggested as much in the year that *The Testing-Tree* was published. He was invited to his native Worcester to participate in the Worcester Poetry Festival, returning there, quite apprehensively, for the first time since he had left to live in New York. When he returned from that adventure, he wrote "The Testing-Tree," the title poem for his forthcoming volume. In doing so, he perhaps came to grips with many of the demons of his past, thereby freeing himself, in terms of both his emotions and his poetic technique, from much that had earlier constrained him artistically.

The Testing-Tree marked a turning point both in the quantity of Kunitz's output and in his poetic technique. During the next fourteen years, he produced three volumes of poetry, one volume of essays and poems, and one volume of essays, a remarkable advance for someone whose first three books took twenty-eight years to complete. By the time he published *Selected Poems: 1928-1978*, Kunitz had begun to write longer poems. The sixteen new works in this volume are longer than the poems he had previously written, and some, like "The Layers," which consists of forty-four abbreviated lines, are printed as a single stanza.

A KIND OF ORDER, A KIND OF FOLLY: ESSAYS AND CONVERSATIONS

First published: 1975
Type of work: Essays

In these prose pieces, which date as far back as the 1940's, Kunitz analyzes his world, his poetry, and some of his literary colleagues.

Perhaps feeling the pressure of having reached the biblically allotted three score and ten, Kunitz felt the need to provide some organized record of his reflections about the world in which he lives. In 1975, still active in literary circles, teaching regularly, and fulfilling his duties as a consultant in poetry to the Library of Congress, he compiled this collection of his essays, reviews, and conversations. What might have been an incoherent whole, a ragtag gathering of past writing, in this instance is a coherent and cohesive presentation of the intellectual growth of a gifted, intelligent artist. As in the collections of his poems, where Kunitz imposes a controlling framework often without regard to chronology, so in this selection of his prose work has he paid careful attention to the overall arrangement of what he offers his readers.

It is important to note this detail, because if there is one consistent thread in Kunitz's artistic life, it is his concern with ordering information. He has shown himself to be keenly aware of the workings of human intelligence, demonstrating in his critical and biographical writings about such poets as William Blake, John Keats, and William Butler Yeats and of such nonliterary geniuses as Albert Einstein that high levels of imagination do not function in linear, sequential ways. A toss of the intellectual dice leaves ideas scattered and inchoate. It is the work of high intellect to gather disparate snips of information and rearrange them into meaningful form. Such is the task of the highest level of writers and scientists. Knowing facts is not enough; imposing a theoretical framework upon them is what makes them resonate.

This collection has been lauded for the elegance of its style, which, in Kunitz's case, changed quite drastically after 1960, possibly because of his close association with poets Robert Lowell and Theodore Roethke, two of his closest friends. They helped him understand that the Elizabethan, Jacobean, and Metaphysical conventions that had shaped his early poetry could be relaxed. As Kunitz moved toward freer poetic expression in his verse, so did he loosen somewhat the style of his essays.

This volume begins with a consideration of the universe and ends with Kunitz's concerns about art, moving sequentially from the physical to the aesthetic and linking the two immutably. He writes, as in "Sister Arts," about the close connection of all the arts, showing the correlations that exist between painters and wordsmiths.

His appreciative prose portraits of Mark Rothko, Roethke, and Lowell contain shrewd aesthetic judgments, well documented and untinged by personal loyalty. His interview with Lowell remains a major source on that poet. In "The Vice-President of Insurance," a critique of Wallace Stevens' letters, and in his essay on John Berryman, Kunitz reveals another side of his critical disposition, firing sharp but wholly decorous salvos at both poets.

FATHER AND SON

First published: 1942
Type of work: Poem

This largely autobiographical poem is about the dreamlike—sometimes surreal—pursuit of a boy in quest of his dead father.

Perhaps all imaginative writing is autobiographical. The more closely such writing's details conform to verifiable facts in the author's life, the easier it is for readers to see an equivalence between reality and art. Yet such a view contains a hazard to readers of fiction based largely on fact: Writers are at liberty to veer at will from fact to fancy, and when they do, readers may be deceived.

"Father and Son" is Kunitz's best-known and most-anthologized poem. Written as World War II was erupting in Europe, it is the story, which Kunitz says came to him in a dream, about a boy seeking his dead father. Because the poet's father committed suicide before his son's birth, this is not a conventional father-son poem packed with memories of family outings, fishing trips, or ballgames.

Kunitz had to invent his father. Anything he devised was reasonable; the boy had no real knowledge of the specter that had sired him. His mother, a distraught widow who, in the aftermath of her shocking loss, had to struggle to run her husband's manufacturing business and to support her three children, erased the memory of the dead Solomon Z. Kunitz from her household. She could not deny his death, but she could handily deny his having ever existed.

Stanley's sole concrete memory of his father was of a face in a faded photograph, which was torn from his hand by an angry mother who punished him for treading on forbidden ground in his attempt to construct a past for the father he never knew. "Father and son" festered for three decades in Kunitz's subconscious before his eerie dream gave him the stuff of his poem.

"Father and Son" has been variously interpreted. It is a thirty-four-line poem, mostly in iambic pentameter, that blurs time and evokes the misty quality surrounding a pond "down the sandy road/ whiter than bone-dust" past the "curdle of fields, where the plums/ Dropped with their load of ripeness, one by one."

A boy pursues an apparition down that bone-dust road in the first two narrative stanzas, offering it information about where and how he lives. In the third stanza, he implores the father to return, bargaining with him and promising to wipe the mud stains from his clothes. He begs his father to teach him "how to work and keep me kind." The apparition, however, disappoints. It does not—cannot—respond. The boy wants to be "a child to those who mourn/ And brother to the foundlings of the field"; he wants to be a "friend of innocence." His wishes, however, are dashed by the dead father, who can offer only "the white ignorant hollow of his face."

THE POEMS OF STANLEY KUNITZ, 1928-1978

First published: 1979
Type of work: Poems

Marking the fiftieth anniversary of Kunitz's career as a poet, this book contains sixteen new poems and dozens more that had been published previously.

This volume represents the most complete collection of Kunitz's poems to the year 1978. Although only sixteen of the poems are new, this body represents a departure for Kunitz in that some of the new poems are much longer than any of his earlier ones. The last piece in the collection, "The Layers," is a highly reflective poem that, more than any of his earlier verse, seems in tone to be the poet's final message to the world. Like "Father and Son," "The Layers" has about it a dreamlike quality. Unlike many of his other poems, it consists of a single long (forty-four-line) stanza. The author foresees his death, which may overtake him before he is finished with his work.

Recipient of the Lenore Marshall Prize for the best American poetry book of the year, this volume presents new poems that are forthright and unadorned in their language. They make their impact through terse lines and sharp images. In his later poems, Kunitz seems consciously to strive for psychological impact more than he did in his earlier work. He is quite like a painter who has moved from watercolors to acrylics and revels in the freedom the change allows.

Summary

Stanley Kunitz's poetry to 1958 was partly an apprenticeship for what lay ahead. During the first three decades of his literary activity, he wrote meticulously crafted verse, consciously employing the poetic conventions and conceits of classical poetry from the Elizabethans to the Romantics. As he matured, he read and frequently interacted personally with living poets, from William Butler Yeats and T. S. Eliot to Robert Lowell and Theodore Roethke. He finally burst the formal stylistic bonds that had constrained his earlier work and became a modern poet, even though he did not test the experimental extremes of modernism as Eliot and Ezra Pound did.

Bibliography

Busa, Chris. "The Art of Poetry XXIX. Stanley Kunitz." *Paris Review* 24 (Spring, 1982): 204-246.

Hagstrum, Jean H. "The Poetry of Stanley Kunitz: An Introductory Essay." In *Poets in Progress*, edited by Edward B. Hungerford. Evanston, Ill.: Northwestern University Press, 1967.

Hénault, Marie. *Stanley Kunitz*. Boston: Twayne, 1980.

Kunitz, Stanley. "An Interview with Stanley Kunitz." Interview by Cynthia Davis. *Contemporary Literature* 15 (Winter, 1974): 1-14.

——————. Interview by Caroline Sutton. *Publishers Weekly* 228 (December 20, 1985): 67-68.

Martin, Harry. "Warren and Kunitz: Poets in the American Grain." *The Washington Post Book World*, September 30, 1979, 10.

Orr, Gregory. *Stanley Kunitz: An Introduction to the Poetry*. New York: Columbia University Press, 1985.

Ostroff, Anthony J., ed. *The Contemporary Poet as Artist and Critic*. Boston: Little, Brown, 1964.

Shaw, Robert B. "A Book of Changes." *The New York Times Book Review*, July 22, 1979, 1, 20.

R. Baird Shuman

NELLA LARSEN

Born: Chicago, Illinois
April 13, 1891
Died: New York, New York
March 30, 1964

Principal Literary Achievement
A major figure in the Harlem Renaissance, Nella Larsen wrote two novels about middle-class black women dealing with the issue of racial identity.

Biography

Because of Nella Larsen's own reticence, until recently many biographical details were either unknown or cited erroneously. For example, her biographer, Thadious M. Davis, is responsible for establishing Larsen's correct date of birth as April 13, 1891, not 1893, as was previously thought. Nella Larsen was born in Chicago, Illinois, of a Danish mother and a black West Indian father. Nella's father died when she was two, and her mother then married a man of, in Larsen's words, "her own race and nationality." While it is known that Nella did go to a small private elementary school with her white half-sister, evidently her parents found her existence increasingly embarrassing in their society of Germans and Scandinavians. Although Nella had been reared in an all-white world, as an adult she felt herself shut off from it, as well as from her own family. As she told an interviewer many years later, she had little contact with her mother and her half-sister, because her presence would be "awkward" for them.

Nella Larsen first ventured into the black world in 1909 when, after attending secondary school in Chicago, she was sent for a year to the high-school department of Fisk University in Nashville, Tennessee. The following year, she went to Denmark to visit her white relatives. From 1910 to 1912, she audited classes at the University of Copenhagen. When she returned to the United States, Larsen once again enrolled at a black institution, the Lincoln Hospital Training School for Nurses in New York City. After her graduation in 1915, Larsen spent a year as assistant superintendent of nurses at Tuskegee Institute in Alabama. She was not happy there, however, and in 1916 she returned to New York City and to Lincoln Hospital. Two years later, she took a nursing job at the New York City Department of Health.

On May 3, 1919, Nella Larsen was married to the physicist Dr. Elmer S. Imes, to whom she was to dedicate her first novel. She was now a socialite, the wife of a man

who moved in the highest levels of Harlem society. In 1921, Larsen decided to make another change in her life, this time in her career. She became a library assistant at the New York Public Library and, in 1923, after receiving a library-school certificate, she was assigned as a children's librarian to a Harlem branch.

If Nella Larsen was to be a writer, she could not have been at a better place at a better time. Not only was Harlem the center of black society, but black writers and intellectuals were also using it as the base for a new cultural movement, to be known as the Harlem Renaissance. This creative community did more than enable the members of a black intellectual elite, including such writers as Larsen, Jessie Fauset, and Walter White, to meet and exchange ideas; through their contacts in the white publishing establishment, older writers, such as Larsen's close friend, Carl Van Vechten, a white critic and novelist, could help younger ones to get their works published.

Davis points out that Larsen first ventured into print in 1926 with two short stories about white characters. According to Jessie Fauset, however, it was Larsen's reading of *Birthright* (1922), a novel by the white writer T. S. Stribling about an educated mulatto, that inspired her to write her novel *Quicksand* (1928), in order to present a truer picture of what it was like to be the offspring of two different races. Although in *Nigger Heaven* (1926) Carl Van Vechten had glorified the simpler, more primitive existence of uneducated, lower-class blacks, he admired Larsen's book about the prosperous black middle-class and persuaded his own publisher, Alfred A. Knopf, to accept it. The novel won praise from reviewers and a Bronze Medal from the Harmon Foundation. With her second novel, *Passing* (1929), Larsen's reputation was solidly established. In 1930, after becoming the first black female creative writer to win a Guggenheim Fellowship, she began planning a year of research in Spain and France, which would result in a new novel. The projected work was never completed.

It is uncertain why Larsen's career as a writer ended so abruptly. A very private person, Larsen was shaken by accusations of plagiarism made just before her Guggenheim year in Europe, when her short story "Sanctuary" (1930) was said to be similar to an earlier story by Sheila Kaye-Smith. Since they had seen Larsen's rough drafts, however, her editors had no difficulty establishing her innocence. It is also believed that about that time, Larsen discovered that her husband, by then chairman of the physics department at Fisk, was in love with a younger woman. Nevertheless, it is known that Larsen worked on three different novels during her year abroad and that when she returned, she had one of them almost completed. Larsen was still working on novels as late as 1932 and 1933, while she was living in Nashville in an attempt to revive her marriage. It may have been the notoriety that attended her divorce from Dr. Imes in 1933 that drove Larsen into anonymity; it has also been suggested that in the depths of the Great Depression, she felt that there would not be enough income from book sales to make writing worthwhile.

In any case, there were no more novels. Larsen left Harlem and moved to Greenwich Village; eventually, she began to avoid even the new friends she had made there and deliberately isolated herself. In 1941, after her former husband died and her alimony ceased, Larsen went back to nursing. She died in Manhattan on March 30, 1964, at the age of seventy-two.

Analysis

Along with the novels of Jessie Fauset, Walter White, and W. E. B. Du Bois, Nella Larsen's works are often classified as "uplift novels," the purpose of which was to persuade educated white readers that the black middle class was in fact not unlike them and, at the same time, to point out how irrational it was to discriminate against such obviously civilized people. In his pioneering work *The Negro Novel in America* (1958), critic Robert Bone called such writers the "Rear Guard" of the Harlem Renaissance because, in his opinion, they lagged behind the movement. Yet Bone admitted that even though they seemed to advocate the imitation of whites, these writers, if not nationalists or primitivists, were certainly not assimilationists. In their frequent treatments of the phenomenon called "passing," they always made it clear that by rejecting their heritage, black people would lose their identity.

There is, however, considerable disagreement about Larsen's intentions. Some critics believe that, in the "uplift" tradition, she is presenting a favorable picture of the black middle class. Others believe that she means to satirize their affectations, their snobbery, and their hypocrisy. More recently, it has been argued that Larsen's primary concern is black female sexuality, although again there are differences of opinion—for example, as to whether she is a moralist in sexual matters or an opponent of repression. It may be that Larsen's novels reflect her own uncertainties. As a person of mixed parentage, as a member of the aspiring black middle class, and as an intelligent woman in a world dominated by men, Larsen could not have had an easy time sorting out her own identity. It is not surprising that her characters find the task virtually impossible.

Whatever her feelings about the black middle class, Larsen did sensibly restrict her writing to the kinds of people she knew and the types of settings with which she was familiar. In *Quicksand*, Helga Crane is shown first at a black college in the South, then among the harlem elite and in European society, before her unlikely marriage to a preacher and her move to a small Southern town. Significantly, critics feel that the final section of the book lacks Larsen's usual sureness of touch; while they mention problems of characterization, they may also sense the author's unfamiliarity with her setting. When Larsen describes spacious rooms filled with eighteenth century tables and Chinese tea-chests, she is in her own environment; when she turns to washtubs and ironingboards, she is as ill at ease as her heroine. Although some find either deliberate or unintentional satire of the black middle class in *Passing*, citing, for example, the breakfast scene at the beginning of part 2, it is difficult to believe that the fact that her characters use grapefruit spoons and employ servants indicates any satirical intent on Larsen's part. Instead, in her second novel, Larsen is confining her subject matter to her own experience.

The kinds of people that Larsen does attack in her novels are bigoted whites and, even more important, blacks who exhibit contempt for their own race. The unlovely face of bigotry is seen in *Quicksand* in the white preacher who speaks so patronizingly to his audience at a black college and in the white wife of Helga Crane's uncle, who denies any kinship between her husband and his own sister's child. In *Passing*, by his inability to converse about any subject except the black race, John Bellew reveals that he is not only a bigot but also a bore.

Larsen also despises blacks who, in one way or another, betray their own race. In *Quicksand*, her targets range from authoritarian black college administrators who produce subservient graduates to doctrinaire black racists such as Anne Grey, who, while professing their hatred of whites, reject their own rich heritage. It is hardly surprising, then, that Larsen shows Clare Kendry, the black woman in *Passing* who pretends to be white, as a person who deceives her own husband and betrays her best friend, just as she has betrayed her race by denying it. If the selfish, self-centered Clare is meant to represent the kind of person who "passes," it is clear that Larsen carries no brief for assimilation.

Feminist critics also point to the importance of gender issues in Larsen's novels. While they do not have to contend with poverty, socialites such as Irene Redfield in *Passing* are keenly aware of their dependence upon their husbands, who provide their incomes, their positions in society, indeed, their very identities. In the protagonists of her two novels, Larsen shows what seem to be the only two options, other than spinsterhood, for her own gender, which in the 1920's was still so vulnerable in biological, as well as in social terms. On one hand, Irene Redfield, whose husband no longer shares her bed, loses him to another woman; on the other, Helga Crane, whose husband rarely leaves her alone, is completely exhausted by childbearing and child-tending. Given these examples, one can hardly believe that, as has been suggested, the purpose of Larsen's novels was to glorify black female sexuality. Instead, one must conclude that, like so many other women writers of her period, Larsen could show how difficult it was for women to deal with the issues of sexual desire, marriage, and reproduction, but she could not suggest a solution.

What Nella Larsen could do was to urge people to understand one another's problems and to accept one another as human beings. In *Quicksand* and *Passing*, Larsen consistently stresses the importance of loyalty, tolerance, and compassion: loyalty to one's own people, tolerance of others, and compassion for those, like Larsen herself, who find themselves caught between two races and two traditions.

QUICKSAND

First published: 1928
Type of work: Novel

A young woman of mixed ancestry tries to find her place in the world.

Quicksand, Nella Larsen's first novel, is generally considered her best. The work is a superb psychological study of a complicated and appealing woman, Helga Crane, who, like Larsen herself, is the product of a liaison between a black man and a white woman. In one sense, *Quicksand* might be called an odyssey; however, instead of overcoming a series of obstacles and finally arriving at her native land, Larsen's protagonist has a series of adventures, each of which ends in disappointment. Whenever Helga believes that she has found her home, and with it her identity, she eventually comes to realize that she is still just a visitor in someone else's country.

As the novel begins, Helga, the illegitimate daughter of a Danish mother and a West Indian father, is deciding what to do about her job as a teacher at Naxos, a Southern school for blacks, which she now sees as repressive and authoritarian. Despite the urgings of the new, enlightened principal of the college, Dr. Robert Anderson, Helga breaks off her engagement to another teacher, who has become entrenched at Naxos, and leaves the college immediately. After arriving in Chicago, Helga naturally turns for help to her late mother's brother, who has helped with her schooling, but she is sent away by his new white wife. Just when she has reached the point of desperation, Helga gets a job as assistant to a wealthy, prominent black woman, Mrs. Hayes-Rore, who takes her to New York, installs her in the luxurious Harlem home of her young, widowed niece, Anne Grey, and finds her a job with a black insurance company. Instantly popular with the women in Anne's circle, much sought after by eligible young men, Helga seems at last to have found a home.

A year later, however, Helga has become discontented. Tired of being surrounded by blacks, she now begins to think about her mother's people. Just then a letter from her white uncle in Chicago finally reaches her, apologizing for the circumstances that made it necessary for him to break off their relationship but suggesting that she visit her aunt in Denmark. To Helga's delight, he encloses a substantial check to make the trip possible.

Initially, Helga responds to Copenhagen much as she had to Harlem. After being welcomed warmly by her elegant aunt and uncle, she is completely outfitted and presented to Danish society. In Copenhagen, she is treated like an exotic flower, rare and valuable, but totally foreign. When she realizes that even though she is much admired, she will always be an outsider there, she decides to reject a proposal of marriage and to return to Harlem.

Unfortunately, by now Dr. Anderson, the only man who has ever really appealed to Helga, is married to Anne Grey. Although on one occasion Anderson does kiss Helga, he later makes it clear that he does not intend for their relationship to progress any further. Humiliated, Helga slaps him, and she then realizes that she has acted like a fool. Anderson would never give up his place in society for any woman.

It is at this point in her life that Helga makes an even worse mistake. After wandering into a storefront service, she is caught up in a religious ecstasy that leads, almost immediately, to her marrying the Reverend Pleasant Green and moving with him to a small Alabama town. At first, filled with missionary zeal, she is happy. After a particularly difficult childbirth, however, she loses her faith, and with it her reason for living. Now Helga yearns only to escape, to return to the pleasant life she threw away for the sake of a God in whom she no longer believes. Yet she does not want to leave her children. At the end of the book, still weak from her last confinement, Helga is once again pregnant. Evidently she is to spend her life in this alien environment, trapped in poverty and despair.

It is generally agreed that the novel does not prepare adequately for its final chapters, in which, for no compelling reason, the protagonist commits intellectual and emotional suicide. For the most part, however, *Quicksand* rings true. Larsen's psychological study of a young woman caught between two worlds and at home in neither is moving and effective.

PASSING

First published: 1929
Type of work: Novel

A black woman sees her marriage threatened by a friend who is passing as a white.

Passing, Larsen's second and final novel, deals with a topic that fascinated readers of the 1920's, the calculated deception of whites by blacks who decided, for social or economic reasons, to "pass" as members of the other race. Larsen's novel, however, is quite different in approach from works such as James Weldon Johnson's *The Autobiography of an Ex-Coloured Man* (1912) and Jessie Fauset's *Plum Bun* (1929). The protagonist of *Passing* is not the black who chooses to move into the white world but, instead, the old friend whom she seeks out, uses, and finally betrays.

At the beginning of Larsen's novel, Irene Redfield, a socially prominent Harlem woman, opens a letter from the former Clare Kendry, now the wife of John Bellew, a white man who does not know that his wife is black. A childhood friend of Irene, Clare insists that she is lonely, isolated as she is from her own people, and she pleads with Irene to meet her again. With distaste, Irene recalls her encounter with Clare in Chicago two years before, when, invited to tea in Clare's home, she and another light-skinned black woman had been forced to listen to diatribes about blacks delivered by Clare's racist husband. Now, Irene gathers, Clare wants to use her in order to enter Harlem society, where, though still pretending to be white, she can be with her own race.

Because she is both polite and compassionate, Irene finds it difficult to repulse her old friend, even though she knows that this scheme may well endanger Clare's masquerade and her marriage. Irene is well aware of the risks to Clare; what she does not anticipate is the danger Clare poses to her own marriage, which is already on shaky ground, primarily as a result of Irene's refusal to leave New York and follow her husband to Brazil. The moment comes when Irene realizes that her husband, Brian, is having an affair with Clare. In a dramatic final scene, Clare's husband breaks into a party and confronts her with the truth that he has discovered; in the confusion that follows, Clare falls out of a window. Whether Irene actually pushes her or simply wills her death is left for the reader to decide.

Passing is often called "slight," perhaps because, as Cheryl A. Wall suggests, the theme of passing is itself superficial, perhaps because, even before the abrupt ending, Larsen has failed to make her own intentions clear. Because her attitudes toward Irene and Clare can be so variously interpreted, it has been argued that the book has two themes, passing and infidelity; alternatively, it has been suggested that Clare, representing black female sexuality, is a sympathetic character and the real protagonist of the novel. It has even been suggested that the real subject of *Passing* is the desire of Clare and Irene for each other.

Another approach is to see the novel as a work about integrity. Viewed in this way, there is no doubt that the central character in *Passing* is Irene Redfield, and the story is a conventional loss of innocence. As the novel develops, Irene first vaguely senses and then sees clearly that someone who will deny her race will also betray her friends. Seen in this way, *Passing* is as strong an argument against assimilation as any writer of the Harlem Renaissance ever produced.

Summary

Nella Larsen's two novels gained her a place as one of the most important black women writers of her time. When no more works appeared and Larsen disappeared into obscurity, critics became more and more puzzled about the author's intentions.

While it was always clear that Larsen was preoccupied with matters of racial and cultural identity, as viewed from her own middle-class perspective, modern critics have also pointed out her obvious interest in gender issues. Even though Larsen's novels are marred by puzzling ambiguities and flawed conclusions, because of their psychological and social realism, they must be considered masterpieces of the Harlem Renaissance.

Bibliography

Bell, Bernard W. *The Afro-American Novel and Its Tradition.* Amherst: University of Massachusetts Press, 1987.

Bone, Robert. *The Negro Novel in America.* Rev. ed. New Haven, Conn.: Yale University Press, 1965.

Davis, Arthur P. *From the Dark Tower: Afro-American Writers (1900 to 1960).* Washington, D.C.: Howard University Press, 1974.

Davis, Thadious M. "Nella Larsen." In *Afro-American Writers from the Harlem Renaissance to 1940*, edited by Trudier Harris. Vol. 51 in *Dictionary of Literary Biography.* Detroit: Gale Research, 1987.

Gayle, Addison, Jr. *The Way of the New World: The Black Novel in America.* Garden City, N.Y.: Anchor Press, 1975.

McDowell, Deborah E. Introduction to *Quicksand and Passing*, by Nella Larsen. New Brunswick, N.J.: Rutgers University Press, 1986.

Perry, Margaret. *Silence to the Drums: A Survey of the Literature of the Harlem Renaissance*. Westport, Conn.: Greenwood Press, 1976.

Sato, Hiroko. "Under the Harlem Shadow: A Study of Jessie Fauset and Nella Larsen." In *The Harlem Renaissance Remembered*, edited by Arna Bontemps. New York: Dodd, Mead, 1972.

Washington, Mary Helen, ed. *Invented Lives: Narratives of Black Women, 1860-1960*. Garden City, N.Y.: Anchor Press, 1987.

Wintz, Cary D. *Black Culture and the Harlem Renaissance*. Houston: Rice University Press, 1988.

Rosemary M. Canfield Reisman

DAVID LEAVITT

Born: Pittsburgh, Pennsylvania
June 23, 1961

Principal Literary Achievement
A short-story writer and novelist, Leavitt explores the intricacies of human interaction, concentrating on gay relationships and the complexities of family ties.

Biography

David Leavitt was born in Pittsburgh, Pennsylvania, on June 23, 1961, the son of Harold Jack Leavitt and Gloria Rosenthal Leavitt. He grew up in Palo Alto, California, where his father was a professor at the graduate school of business at Stanford University. Being the youngest of three children—his brother, John, and sister, Emily, were nine and ten years older than he—resulted in a self-described precocity, which undoubtedly contributed to his remarkably early literary success. In a 1990 interview he remarked, "I grew up being the child in the room whose presence everyone forgot about. By the time I was 20, therefore, I had absorbed an enormous amount, but I had experienced almost nothing."

One of the pivotal events of his childhood was his mother's long, futile battle with cancer. He explains, "The enormity of that experience cannot be minimalized. It has all gone into my work. Most of what I know about living and dying I learned from my mother." The knowledge gained from his mother's illness and death is reflected particularly in the moving portrayal of Louise Cooper's twenty-year struggle against cancer in *Equal Affections* (1989) and also in the stories "Counting Months" and "Radiation," which appear in *Family Dancing* (1984).

Leavitt left the West Coast to attend Yale University, graduating in 1983. An editor for *The New Yorker* read one of his stories in a student magazine and asked to see more of his work. He obliged by sending her everything he had written to that point, all of which she rejected. She finally accepted the story "Territory," which was published in *The New Yorker* in 1982. His stories and articles subsequently appeared in *Harper's, Esquire,* and *The New York Times Book Review*.

His first book of short stories, *Family Dancing*, was published when he was only twenty-three years old, and much was made of Leavitt's youthful success. The collection was praised by reviewers and was nominated for the PEN/Faulkner Award for Fiction and the Book Critics Circle Award. His first novel, *The Lost Language of*

Cranes (1986), met with considerably less critical success, and *Equal Affections*, which followed, fared a little better, receiving mixed reviews. His work has met with more success in Europe than in the United States; his first three books were best-sellers in Italy and Spain.

In 1989, Leavitt received a Guggenheim Fellowship, and he was appointed foreign writer-in-residence in Barcelona, Spain, at the Institute of Catalan Letters. His European experiences figure in his fourth publication, a collection of short stories entitled *A Place I've Never Been* (1990). The stories "I See London, I See France" and "Roads to Rome," in particular, are reminiscent of the work of Henry James, relating the adventures of young American "innocents" abroad in Italy. In 1993, he published *While England Sleeps*, a novel focusing on the lives of gay men during World War II.

Leavitt remained an East Coast resident after attending Yale, moving to East Hampton, New York. Often criticized for not writing more about the acquired immune deficiency syndrome (AIDS) epidemic in the gay community, Leavitt nevertheless has worked with the activist group AIDS Coalition to Unleash Power (ACT UP). He has said that he feels no obligation to write about AIDS, remarking, "I don't think it's fair to say that writers have an obligation to write about any particular subject. A writer's obligation is to write well." Yet he does write about AIDS in *A Place I've Never Been*, in both "Gravity" and the title story. In the first of these, a son suffers from AIDS, and his mother simultaneously nurses him and resents him for being sick. In "A Place I've Never Been," the protagonist does not suffer from AIDS itself, but rather from its effects on the gay community.

The temptation is great to compare Leavitt's life with his fiction, because his characters' lives often seem to parallel his experience or that of his family. Leavitt, though, claims that such comparison "doesn't lead very far. If a particular character resembles my mother or my sister, so what? It's just gossip, and not even very interesting gossip." Yet the passion and knowledge with which he writes about the homosexual experience, cancer, and family relations obviously spring from an insider's knowledge of the subjects.

Analysis

Although he is known primarily as a "gay writer," David Leavitt actually explores universal themes, and it would do him a great disservice to portray his writing as being of interest to only a limited audience. Although he addresses the problems faced by homosexuals in a heterosexual world, he also explores feelings of alienation common to all people. His work speaks to the human, not just the "homosexual," condition. Leavitt does investigate the ways in which sexual differences isolate the individual, but he also examines other conditions that cause feelings of separation, including mental and physical illness, shame, despair, and physical unattractiveness.

Leavitt often explores this theme of isolation within the milieu of family life. Many of his works describe the precarious balance of family harmony in even the closest families, as he adroitly reveals the turmoil underlying the placid surface of everyday life. Both *The Lost Language of Cranes* and *Equal Affections* present characters shaped by strong family relationships, yet those characters are ultimately defined more by what sets them apart from one another than by what binds them together.

This insight into family relations shapes several of Leavitt's short stories as well, particularly in his first collection, *Family Dancing*. In "The Lost Cottage," a family's futile attempts to re-create their annual summer vacation six months after the parents have separated fails abysmally. The family gamely behaves as if a good time were being had by all, but the charade ends when Lydia, the mother, discovers that her estranged husband has settled his new girlfriend into a nearby motel. Lydia agonizingly declares to her family, "I will always love your father. And he doesn't love me. And never will." The children come to realize the depths of their mother's despair and the fact that they are helpless to assuage her pain.

"Family Dancing" also features a broken family in which the ties, for better or worse, remain strong. Suzanne Kaplan, who has a new marriage, a new figure, and a new life since her first husband, Herb, left her for another woman, throws a large family party to celebrate her "new self" and her son's prep-school graduation. As the party guests admiringly watch a celebratory "family dance" performed by Suzanne and Herb and their son and daughter, the reader, who has been allowed a glimpse beneath the surface, knows that all is not well. Suzanne is still painfully in love with Herb, who no longer loves her; Herb's show of devotion for his ungainly daughter hides his repulsion for her unattractiveness; and their son, Seth, has yet to inform them of his homosexuality.

Leavitt often explores the effect of illness, particularly cancer, on an individual's relation to family. In "Counting Months," the mundane and the unthinkable intermingle as Anna Harrington realizes while reading a magazine advertisement that her doctor had predicted that she would be dead by this day. Later, the unimaginable again invades the everyday as she simultaneously fixes dinner and thinks about how her children will manage when she is dead. Anna's illness makes her feel like an outsider as she feels "the difference . . . growing inside her, through the lymph nodes, exploring her body."

In "Radiation," a mother takes her children to a radiation therapy center while she has her treatments. The staff and patients chat cheerfully about new lawn furniture, children play games and read children's magazines, and patients joke about the hospital gowns they must wear, belying the life-and-death purpose of the center. The mother's life begins to be defined by her illness, as she realizes that the pain, suffering, and humiliation she now accepts as normal would have been unthinkable only a few months earlier. She cries alone in her room, unreachable in her grief, unable to accept sympathy or comfort even from her family.

In "Danny in Transit," Leavitt portrays the ultimate outsider, an unwanted child. Danny's father has left home to explore his newly admitted homosexuality, and his mother gives into her grief, suffering a nervous breakdown. Danny is left to his aunt and uncle, who were reluctant to take him in and now no longer want him because he is not a "normal" boy like their own two sons. As the self-absorbed members of the family meet to decide Danny's fate (he will be shipped off to boarding school), Danny retreats into his own reality, inventing and performing shows on his own imaginary television network.

In "Aliens," an adolescent girl, so unattractive even her own mother finds it difficult to look at her, retreats into an elaborate science-fiction world of her own making in which she is an oracle from the planet Dandril, taking on an "earthly shell" in order to observe Earth. Like Danny, she too has created her own universe, where she has a role to fill and her own "language" with which to explain herself.

TERRITORY

First published: 1982
Type of work: Short story

A son introduces his gay lover to his mother for the first time.

"Territory," the opening story in *Family Dancing*, revolves around the first meeting between the two most important people in Neil Campbell's life: his mother, Barbara, and his lover, Wayne. Although the action revolves around Barbara and Wayne's meeting, the most richly detailed and emotionally powerful relationship in the story, as in much of Leavitt's work, is between mother and son. Barbara has been a devoted mother, PTA member, volunteer at school, and active member of the Coalition of Parents of Lesbians and Gays. Neil's father is "a distant sort," often away on business and emotionally absent even when home, so it is Barbara to whom Neil feels emotionally bound.

Neil is flooded with memories as his lover's arrival forces him to reconcile the boy his mother knew with the man whom Wayne loves. As he nervously awaits the visit, he remembers the day he "came out" to his mother and "felt himself shrunk to an embarrassed adolescent, hating her sympathy, not wanting her to touch him." He also recalls the Gay Pride parade his mother attended to show her support, succeeding only in embarrassing Neil and inflicting pain upon herself.

The story revolves around simple events: Wayne's introduction to Barbara, their first dinner together, and a trip to a theater. The meaning, however, lies not in the events themselves but rather, in Jamesian fashion, in the small moments. When Wayne takes Neil's hand at dinner, Barbara's almost imperceptible reaction speaks volumes about her discomfort in their presence. Later, when Neil puts an arm around both Wayne and his mother at the theater, she responds by stiffening and shrinking away, unwilling to give her son unqualified emotional approval of his sexuality.

As Barbara attempts to cope with the reality of Neil's adult sexuality, Neil also must recognize that his mother's life has gone on "unaffected by his absence." She has "grown thinner, more rigid, harder to hug," and even her dogs are not the dogs of his childhood. He no longer feels a part of her life, a condition he both desires and fears. Barbara, for her part, cannot reconcile the young man Neil has become with the child she remembers. She tells him, "I remember when you were a little boy . . . I remember, and I have to stop remembering." And Neil, who "wept in regret for what he would not be for his mother, for having failed her," knows, as he tells Wayne, that "guilt goes with the territory." As Leavitt so movingly illustrates in this story, the forces that exist between parent and child are, like the power of fate, beyond the reaches of good intentions.

EQUAL AFFECTIONS

First published: 1989
Type of work: Novel

A family faces its children's homosexuality, its father's infidelity, and its mother's cancer and eventual death.

Equal Affections chronicles the history of the Cooper family: Nat and Louise, their children, Danny and April, and Danny's lover, Walter. Although the plot sounds melodramatic—Louise is fighting a twenty-year battle with cancer, Nat is having an affair with an old family friend, and both Danny and April are gay—Leavitt handles his characters and situations with such restraint and understatement that the novel never deteriorates into soap opera. Rather, it presents a subtle study of family dynamics.

The family's history unfolds through a series of flashbacks, arriving at the present as the family is brought together by Louise's final bout with illness. As they watch her die, each character struggles to define a place in the family circle as well as an identity outside it. The temptation to isolate themselves from "messy" human relationships battles with the insistent pull of family ties in each of them.

Danny, the quintessential "good son," has buried himself in a comfortable but stale upper-middle-class existence, surrounded by electronic gadgets. His lover, Walter, has become more involved with his computer sex partners than with Danny, tempted by the possibility of living "without ever having to touch, without ever having to show your face!" April, completely self-absorbed, immerses herself in her career as a lesbian folk singer, fitting her family into her life only when her busy schedule allows.

The characters also struggle between the opposite pulls of domesticity and "wildness." Walter sees parallels between his life and Louise's, noting that they have both sublimated their wild sides to domesticity and conformity. "He saw her as a woman of guileless passion who, for one reason or another, had suppressed that passion and instead steadied her gaze on the dependable horizon of the domestic sphere." Walter also has determined to "incorporate his sexual nature into a life of suburban domesticity, uproot the seed of homosexuality from its natural urban soil and replant it in the pure earth of his green garden."

Nat and April, on the other hand, rather than seeking to tame their "wildness" with domesticity, have summoned it to help them break out of the domestic rut. April, although she possesses strong domestic instincts, demonstrated by her love of baking and desire to have a baby, escapes domestic routine through her career. Nat, a quiet and unassuming man by nature, seeks to subvert domesticity by conducting an illicit affair.

As Louise faces her death, she too comes to terms with her growing sense of "aloneness," as her illness slowly separates her from her family. She realizes that her separateness is the source of her strength as well as her pain, because it allows her to control her own destiny. Conversely, Louise's death brings Walter to the realization that "like it or not, he was inextricably bound with the people who had mattered to him and who mattered to him now, the people whose loves defined him, whose deaths would devastate him. He would never, could never be . . . self-invented, untouchable, a journeyer among the keys. And for this he was glad."

THE LOST LANGUAGE OF CRANES

First published: 1986
Type of work: Novel

The lives of a quiet married couple and their son unravel as the son's revelation of his homosexuality forces his father to face and confess to his own homosexuality.

David Leavitt's first novel, *The Lost Language of Cranes*, is the story of two men of different generations coming to terms with their homosexuality. Like much of Leavitt's work, it is also the story of a family coming apart at the seams.

Rose Benjamin, a copy editor, and her husband, Owen, director of admissions at a private boys' school, lead a tightly structured life, devoting their days to work and their evenings to reading in their twin rocking chairs. Every Sunday, they go their separate ways; Rose reads the paper and works in the apartment, while Owen spends the day at a gay pornographic cinema. Rose has no idea how Owen spends these Sundays and would never dream of asking. When Rose accidently meets Owen on the street one Sunday while taking a walk, she realizes that after twenty-seven years of marriage, she hardly knows him: "She had stumbled into her husband on a strange street corner, running some mysterious errand she knew nothing of, and they had spoken briefly like strangers, parted like strangers."

The first cracks appear on the smooth surface of the Benjamin family life when Rose and Owen learn that their New York City apartment will be going co-op, and they must either buy it or move out. Once their sanctuary from the outside world is threatened, the rest of their carefully structured life begins to crumble as well. Their son Philip, infatuated with a new lover, wants to share his happiness and reveal his homosexuality to his parents, giving little thought to the effect this announcement might have on them. Philip's "coming out" inspires his father to confess to his own long-hidden homosexuality, and Rose is forced to confront the fact that her married life has been based on a lie.

The Lost Language of Cranes also highlights the differences between two generations of gay men. Philip, although initially hesitant to reveal his homosexuality to his parents, has "come out" to the rest of the world. He has a network of friends and a night life in gay bars that his father never had. Owen, aware he was "different" since childhood but believing that his homosexuality was a disease, forced himself to deny this "difference" for years. Finally, when he could no longer suppress his sexuality, he began visiting a pornographic gay theater, engaging in sexual acts with nameless, faceless men but suffering severe guilt when he returned home to Rose.

This novel, like most of Leavitt's work, explores what critic Robert Jones has called "the desire to find a language that describes the isolate worlds we inhabit." The title refers to a case study of a boy abandoned by his mother in an apartment near a construction site. Lacking human contact, the child identified and "bonded" with the cranes he saw operating outside his window, devising his own language based on the noises they made, thus creating a language that had meaning and emotional resonance for him. The Benjamins, as well, struggle to make sense of their own individual "languages" in the context of their family relationship.

Summary

The characters populating David Leavitt's fiction, whether gay men, lesbians, mothers, sisters, or fathers, all strive to overcome a sense of isolation, a sense of being on the outside of life looking in, but they succeed only briefly in making meaningful connections with the rest of the human race. At best, they come to terms with the fact that isolation is part of the human condition rather than a lonely vigil kept only by themselves. In the end, although family ties may always be present, Leavitt sees each individual ultimately making his or her journey alone.

Bibliography

Gorra, Michael. "Fiction Chronicle." *The Hudson Review* 40 (Spring, 1987): 136.

Harvey, Andrew. "The Voice of America: New Fiction from Our Most-Talked About Writers." *Vogue*, September, 1986, 410-411.

Healey, Barth. "Marrying Out of the Clan." *The New York Times Book Review*, October 5, 1986, 3.

Jones, Robert. "The Lost Language of Cranes." *Commonweal* 113 (October 24, 1986): 558-560.

Mars-Jones, Adam. "Gays of Our Lives: The Lost Language of Cranes." *The New Republic* 195 (November 17, 1986): 43-46.

Staggs, Sam. "David Leavitt." *Publishers Weekly* 237 (August 24, 1990): 47-48.

Mary Virginia Davis

ELMORE LEONARD

Born: New Orleans, Louisiana
October 11, 1925

Principal Literary Achievement

Generally acknowledged to be the most accomplished writer working in the genre of the realistic crime novel, Leonard has also earned recognition as an important literary artist.

Biography

Elmore John Leonard, Jr., was born in New Orleans, Louisiana, on October 11, 1925, to Elmore John and Flora Rivé Leonard. His father traveled widely for his job, and the family moved several times before finally settling in Detroit in 1934. Leonard attended the University of Detroit High School, where he earned the nickname "Dutch" as a baseball player (after the Washington Senators pitcher Dutch Leonard). After being rejected by the Marines for his poor vision, he was drafted by the Navy in 1943 and served with the Seabees in New Guinea and the Admiralty Islands. After the war, he enrolled at the University of Michigan, where he majored in English and philosophy. He married Beverly Cline in 1949, was graduated in 1950, and took a job with an advertising agency that same year, first as an office boy and then as an advertising copywriter, specializing in advertisements for Chevrolet trucks.

Leonard had always loved literature, and he began to train himself to be a writer, deciding to begin with Westerns because he enjoyed reading them and believed there was a ready popular market for the genre. He studied Western films, travel magazines, and histories and also the novels of Ernest Hemingway, upon whom he began to model his writing style. He published his first story, "Trail of the Apache," for which he was paid a thousand dollars, in the December, 1951, issue of *Argosy*. Within little more than a year, he had published nine more stories and his first novel, *The Bounty Hunters* (1953). He kept his full-time job during these early years, doing his writing from 5:00 to 7:00 every morning before work. By 1961, he had published more than two dozen short stories and four more novels, all Westerns—*The Law at Randado* (1954), *Escape from Five Shadows* (1956), *Last Stand at Saber River* (1959), and *Hombre* (1961)—and decided to quit his job and become a full-time writer, although he and his wife now had four children. Ironically, the market for Western writing seemed to have dried up at just that moment; Leonard failed to publish another novel for the next eight years,

2576

and he was forced to earn a living as a freelance writer of advertisements and educational films. In 1965, he sold the film rights to *Hombre* for ten thousand dollars and was again able to devote himself to writing fiction full-time. The resulting novel was completed in 1966 and was rejected by eighty-four publishers within three months. After revision, Leonard finally published his first non-Western novel, *The Big Bounce*, in 1969. It was made into a film that same year, and most of his novels since have been sold to Hollywood, though none has resulted in an entirely satisfactory film version. Leonard then began writing screenplays himself, selling a screenplay of his next novel, *The Moonshine War* (1969). He also produced two more Westerns, *Valdez Is Coming* (1970) and *Forty Lashes Less One* (1972).

A turning point in his career came with *Fifty-two Pickup* (1974), the novel that firmly established his direction as a writer of contemporary crime fiction. His personal life took a turn as well; his marriage broke up after twenty-five years, and he joined Alcoholics Anonymous. In 1977, he managed to quit drinking, and in 1979 he married his second wife, Joan Shepard. As his personal life recovered, so did his literary fortunes improve, and in the mid-1970's he rapidly produced a series of novels in which he began to define his own distinctive approach to crime fiction: *Mr. Majestyk* (1974), a novel based on one of his own screenplays; *Swag* (1976); *The Hunted* (1977); and *Unknown Man No. 89* (1977). All five of these works appear regularly on lists of Leonard's best books and constitute a distinct middle period of high-quality output. *The Switch* (1978); his eighth Western, *Gunsights* (1979); and *Gold Coast* (1980), the first of his novels set in Florida, are generally considered to represent a brief decline in his writing during a period of transition that was to lead to his best work.

Leonard's novels had always been notable for their realism, and in 1978 he spent two-and-a-half months observing Detroit police at work in order to research a magazine article. He also hired two research assistants (college friend and private investigator Bill Marshall, who began researching Leonard's Florida novels in 1977, and then Gregg Sutter, beginning in 1981), helping him to produce the more fully developed and detailed worlds that characterize the work of Leonard's latest—and strongest—period, beginning with *City Primeval: High Noon in Detroit* (1980) and continuing through *Split Images* (1981), *Cat Chaser* (1982), *LaBrava* (1983), and *Stick* (1983). Critical recognition finally came with these novels, and *LaBrava* earned the Edgar Allan Poe Award from the Mystery Writers of America as the best novel of the year. Leonard's next novel, *Glitz* (1985), was his first to reach *The New York Times'* best-seller list, and similar national success followed for his subsequent books: *Bandits* (1987), *Touch* (1987; actually written in 1977), *Freaky Deaky* (1988), *Killshot* (1989), *Get Shorty* (1990), *Maximum Bob* (1991), and *Rum Punch* (1992). All but *Bandits* and *Get Shorty* are invariably classed among his finest novels by critics.

Analysis

The oddity of Leonard's finally being "discovered" as a major new writer by critics and a wide reading public only with *Glitz*, his twenty-third novel, has attracted puzzled comments from most reviewers and from Leonard himself, and probably admits of no simple explanation. The novel immediately before *Glitz*, *LaBrava*, had sold only twenty thousand copies by the time that *Glitz* had sold two hundred thousand, yet there seems to be no clear difference in the style, tone, or quality of the two books. While careful students of Leonard's work have noted a greater degree of fine detail and texture in the works of the 1980's and 1990's, the broad similarities between his later books and the best work of the 1970's, beginning with *Fifty-two Pickup*, are far more striking than any minor differences. As the critic Peter Prescott put it, "the margin of difference between Leonard's better and lesser works would admit, with difficulty, a butterfly's wing." Leonard attributes his change of style at the time of *Fifty-two Pickup* to his reading of George V. Higgins' *The Friends of Eddie Coyle* (1972), from which he learned valuable lessons about the use of point of view and dialogue, the handling of which were to become his stylistic trademark.

Part of the explanation for his sudden success with *Glitz* was the publisher's decision to promote the novel more aggressively by spending more money and, perhaps oddly, by saying as little as possible about it in the advertising. Earlier advertising campaigns had made the mistake of comparing Leonard to earlier crime writers who had elevated the genre to the level of serious literature, including Dashiell Hammett, Raymond Chandler, and Ross Macdonald. Readers who expected similar work must have been frequently disappointed, because, apart from the high quality of his work, Leonard has almost nothing in common with these predecessors. In particular, he scrupulously avoided using the sort of colorful metaphors and similes that are typically thought to characterize good writing; as Leonard himself says, "If it sounds like writing, I rewrite it." The great difference between Leonard's style and that of his forebears may be the best explanation for his long wait for success: Readers needed a long time to get used to his unique approach to crime fiction and to accept it on its own terms.

Earlier writers of "hard-boiled" detective fiction had almost universally relied on first-person narratives, related from the point of view of a continuing character who is the protagonist for all the novels in a series. While Hammett, the originator of the hard-boiled genre, switched characters from book to book and sometimes relied on an objective, "camera-eye" point of view, Chandler's Philip Marlowe and Macdonald's Lew Archer always told their own stories through a series of books, establishing a formula followed by innumerable later writers. Leonard, on the other hand, almost never uses a character more than once (two exceptions are Ernest Stickley, featured in *Swag* and *Stick*, and Jack Ryan, in *The Big Bounce* and *Unknown Man No. 89*). The reader's expectations about crime novels are further compounded by Leonard's characteristic practice of relying on multiple points of view, perhaps his most distinctive and original stylistic contribution to the field. Rather than having the protagonist tell the reader the story as a consistent first-person narrative, Leonard typically shifts point of view from one character to another. In many of the novels, the reader is not sure until well into the book who the main character will eventually be, since so many characters' viewpoints are rendered. In *Maximum Bob*, Leonard goes so far as to include a scene written from the point of view of an alligator. Leonard never speaks in his own voice in his later books, delegating all the narrating to one or another of his usually numerous cast of characters. One critic has remarked that "Leonard is a skilled ventriloquist whose own lips never move."

The technique of rapidly shifting points of view seems at first to have more in common with the difficult experimental literature of William Faulkner and Virginia Woolf than with traditional popular fiction, and such an approach could certainly become confusing in the hands of another writer. Leonard, however, always manages to get the reader just the information needed to follow the story. He accomplishes this in part through a heavy reliance on dialogue, always couched in each character's individualized mannerisms of speech and presented in short, dramatic scenes; usually, he ends each scene with a punch line or unexpected twist for closure. He eschews entirely the typical novelist's use of blocks of narrative exposition. Another interesting effect of the use of multiple points of view is that the reader is privy to the thoughts of virtually every character, hero and villain alike, and therefore quickly knows much more about the story than any one of the characters in the book ever could. The result is that Leonard's novels are not, in fact, mysteries in the traditional sense: The reader knows exactly who has committed every crime, and in fact usually witnesses them from the criminals' viewpoints. Leonard's practice of giving the criminal's point of view equal time creates yet another problem for some readers, who can be disturbed by his ability to render the thoughts and feelings of the most depraved characters accurately and even sympathetically. That this intimate association with evil characters never becomes oppressive for the reader results from Leonard's gift of making a sort of deadpan satire come through the realistic dialogue; few of his characters intend to be funny, but the reader finds humor in unexpected places.

CITY PRIMEVAL: HIGH NOON IN DETROIT

First published: 1980
Type of work: Novel

Homicide detective Raymond Cruz relies on both conventional and unorthodox methods to bring psychotic killer Clement Mansell to justice.

City Primeval is widely regarded as the first book of Leonard's strongest period. As the allusion to the classic 1952 Western film *High Noon* in the subtitle suggests, the novel marks a conscious adaptation of the characters and themes of Leonard's earlier Westerns to the contemporary urban settings of his later crime novels. The book's protagonist, Detroit homicide detective Raymond Cruz, is a Texan of Mexican descent who thus has the background appropriate to a Western hero. Cruz's relationship with Clement Mansell, the book's villain, is described in terms of classic Westerns: "No—more like High Noon. Gunfight at the O.K. Corral. You have to go back a hundred years and out west to find an analogy. But there it is." References to Westerns are scattered throughout the book, which opens with a dinner conversation between Cruz and a reporter who accuses him of trying to emulate Wyatt Earp, Clint Eastwood, and John Wayne, and closes appropriately with an old-fashioned show-down between Cruz and Mansell.

This frontier imagery is integrated into a thoroughly realistic context that reveals Leonard's recent in-depth study of the daily operations of the Detroit police depart-ment. Particularly well-handled are a series of interrogation scenes in which the detectives use subtle techniques of misdirection to gain information from uncoopera-tive suspects, who never realize how much they have given away. As in most of Leonard's novels, the difference between the good and bad characters is not strictly a matter of following or breaking the law; the players on both sides operate very near the border between right and wrong, with their ends differing much more than the means used to achieve them. Mansell has in fact found the legal system to be in some ways his best ally; he has been freed from earlier murder charges on legal technicali-ties. Cruz, on the other hand, is forced to work outside the law, tampering with evidence and eventually forcing a confrontation in which he kills Mansell under circumstances that are ethically, and perhaps legally, suspect. As Mansell says to Cruz in the final scene, "Me and you are on different sides, but we're alike in a lot of ways," an observation that typifies the similarity, and even sympathy, that usually exists between antagonist and protagonist in Leonard's work. Mansell's point of view is relied on just as much as that of Cruz or of Sandy Stanton, Mansell's girlfriend, and the reader consequently acquires a degree of familiarity with and understanding of a totally amoral character that is unusual in popular fiction.

GLITZ

First published: 1985
Type of work: Novel

Miami police detective Vincent Mora pursues—and is pursued by—psycho-pathic killer Teddy Magyk from Puerto Rico to Atlantic City and back.

Glitz was Leonard's first best-seller. The book represents an artistic success as well, epitomizing the author's mature style with a complex plot, memorable characters, and crisp dialogue. While most of his earlier crime novels had been set in Detroit, the later novels range more freely, and the action in *Glitz* shifts from Miami to Puerto Rico to Atlantic City, all depicted with his usual meticulous accuracy. Before visiting Atlantic City himself, Leonard had his research assistant, Gregg Sutter, collect a series of interviews with casino employees and police and take 180 photographs in a sequence that would give him views of the entire town.

Miami police detective Vincent Mora is a typical Leonard protagonist, as Atlantic

City casino operator Jackie Garbo describes him: "I said to myself, this guy's got nice easy moves, never pushes, he listens and he learns things." While Leonard's "heroes" are all capable of violent behavior and are as likely to be criminals as lawmen, they prefer a subtle approach to a problem rather than direct confrontation and view violence as a last resort. His amoral antagonists, however, invariably consider violent solutions first. The antagonist in *Glitz* is Teddy Magyk, who had been arrested by Mora for first-degree sexual battery several years earlier and now, after seven and a half years in prison, is intent on revenge. He lures Mora to Atlantic City by killing a friend of his there, and Mora, on leave recovering from an injury, works unofficially with the local police to capture him. This unofficial capacity enables him to work outside the rules, as do all Leonard's main characters. The relatively simple main plot is filled out with a number of subplots involving local mobsters and drug dealers who are loosely affiliated with the city's casino industry.

As in all of Leonard's novels, however, the interest of the book lies not in the plot but in the brilliantly drawn characters and tightly crafted individual scenes. Leonard has remarked that "I'm not a good narrative writer. I put all my energies into my characters and let my characters carry it." Typical of his style is a scene in which Nancy Donovan unexpectedly turns the tables on her husband, Tommy, who owns a casino, and his manager, Jackie Garbo, establishing that she is the one in control of them and their business. Leonard first wrote the scene primarily from her point of view, found that it did not work, and then rewrote it from the viewpoint of Garbo, who can observe, after a careless remark by Tommy, "Mistake. Jackie knew it immediately; he saw Nancy's expression tighten just a little, a hairline crack in the facade." Such an observation would be dramatically impossible for Nancy or Tommy to make, and another writer might have merely included it in third-person authorial narration. Leonard's meticulous attention to such supporting characters and his care to make every detail, every word, fit their personalities makes even his minor characters memorable and fully developed.

KILLSHOT

First published: 1989
Type of work: Novel

A working-class couple become witnesses to an extortion scheme and find themselves the targets of the two killers against whom they are expected to testify.

Leonard continues to work new variations on his own formula in *Killshot*, this time by focusing on a typical working-class married couple, Wayne and Carmen Colson, rather than on his more typical characters who live near the fringes of law enforcement and crime. The book begins with chapters from the points of view of Armand Degas, a professional killer, and then Richie Nix, an armed robber and ex-convict. The reader is thus able to learn about these characters from the inside as they meet and develop a plan to extort money from the Detroit real-estate agency where Carmen works. Wayne drives the men away by force, temporarily disrupting their plan but also turning himself and his wife into eyewitnesses and, therefore, targets to be eliminated by the two criminals.

The genesis of the book, which Leonard had originally planned to revolve around Wayne, exemplifies the way in which his books are driven by the development of his characters rather than by any preconceived ideas about plot or structure. He begins not with a plot but with a set of characters. He decides first on the right names for characters, then works out the details of their background and, especially, the way they talk. Once he has created a set of interesting characters, he improvises a situation that puts them into conflict and lets them dictate the action to him as it goes along, seldom knowing himself what will happen more than a scene or two ahead or how the book will end. This improvisational approach also accounts for the fact that so many of his best characters are minor ones who develop unexpectedly as he writes. As Leonard explained in an interview about *Killshot*, "I started with a husband and wife who get involved in the Federal Witness Protection program. He's an ironworker, and he was going to be the main character—he's a very macho kind of guy. . . . She takes over; she becomes the main character and I was very glad to see it happen."

The Colsons are eventually put in a witness protection program and relocated to Cape Girardeau, Missouri, a location carefully researched and depicted in Leonard's usual manner. Carmen finds herself in nearly as much danger there from Ferris Britton, the deputy marshal in charge of their case, as she had been from Degas and Nix. The couple eventually discover, as do most of Leonard's characters, that the legal system is an inadequate defense against the evil that surrounds them, and they are forced to take matters into their own hands. The book ends in typical fashion with a dramatic armed confrontation between Carmen, Degas, and Nix back in Detroit.

Summary

Leonard has been called a "Dickens from Detroit" because of his remarkable ability to invent a fresh cast of memorable characters for each new book and to depict with realistic detail every nuance of each character's distinctive voice. Critics have increasingly come to recognize that the apparent ease and naturalness of his style is deceptive and that the authenticity and precision of his depictions of contemporary people and places make him an accomplished and important American novelist.

Bibliography

Geherin, David. *Elmore Leonard*. New York: Continuum, 1989.

Hynes, Joseph. "'High Noon in Detroit': Elmore Leonard's Career." *Journal of Popular Culture* 25 (Winter, 1991): 181-187.

Lupica, Mike. "St. Elmore's Fire." *Esquire* 107 (April, 1987): 169-174.

Lyczak, Joel M. "An Interview with Elmore Leonard." *The Armchair Detective* 16 (Summer, 1983): 235-240.

Prescott, Peter. "Making a Killing: With 'Glitz,' Leonard Finally Brings in the Gold." *Newsweek* 227 (April 22, 1985): 62-64, 67.

Sutter, Gregg. "Advance Man: Researching Elmore Leonard's Novels, Part 2." *The Armchair Detective* 19 (Spring, 1986): 160-172.

_____. "Getting It Right: Researching Elmore Leonard's Novels, Part 1." *The Armchair Detective* 19 (Winter, 1986): 4-19.

William Nelles

DENISE LEVERTOV

Born: Ilford, Essex, England
October 24, 1923

Principal Literary Achievement

One of the leading American poets of the second half of the twentieth century, Levertov has had her work widely anthologized, and her poetic theories have been studied by many beginning writers.

Biography

Denise Levertov was born October 24, 1923, in Ilford, Essex, England, the daughter of Paul Philip Levertoff, a Russian Jew who converted to Christianity and became a minister, and Beatrice Spooner-Jones, a Welsh preacher's daughter. Until she was thirteen years old, she and her sister were educated by their parents at home. The environment was rich in books and cultural discussion. Her mother read the great works of nineteenth century literature aloud to the family, and her father wrote in four languages. Her parents had been prisoners of war at Leipzig during World War I, so many refugees came to their home. The religious, social, and ethical discussions that took place profoundly influenced her life and works. She also studied ballet and painted, both of which helped her to develop a sense of rhythm and style.

This background provided a natural environment for learning to write, and at age five, Levertov decided to become a poet. When she was twelve, she sent some of her work to T. S. Eliot, who responded with a letter of advice. At sixteen, she corresponded with the poet and critic Herbert Read and also became acquainted with editor Charles Wrey and author Kenneth Rexroth.

During World War II, she underwent nurse's training and worked for three years at St. Luke's Hospital, where she helped to rehabilitate returning soldiers. During the evenings, she continued to write poetry. At this time, her family was actively engaged in the relocation of Jewish refugees, so the war was a very real part of her life. Yet the war did not directly figure in her first book, *The Double Image*, published in 1946. The poems deal with lost childhood, death, and separation, and Levertov wrote them in the traditional romantic style of the times. She was to develop these themes, along with her social and political ideas, but in a very different style.

In 1947, Levertov married an American soldier, novelist Mitchell Goodman. In 1948, they moved to New York City, where their son, Nikolai, was born the following

year. This move, which engaged Levertov in a new life and culture, radically changed her poetics. Her second book, *Here and Now* (1958), though written in her early style, showed promise of what was to come.

In the United States, Levertov met her mentor, the poet William Carlos Williams, who taught her to focus on things themselves as carriers of emotion and ideas. She also became involved in the life of New York City, its streets and people as well as its artistic movements. She became friends with poets Robert Creely and Robert Duncan, both of whom taught at Black Mountain College and were early publishers of her work in the *Black Mountain Review*. Critics often associate her with the Black Mountain School of poetry. By the time she became associated with New Directions Press in 1959, she had discovered her own voice. The 1960 volume *With Eyes at the Back of Our Heads* illustrates her full involvement with the American literary movements of the times.

In *The Jacob's Ladder* (1961) and in *O Taste and See: New Poems* (1964), Levertov wrote about poetic theory and the imagination. In both of these books, she continued to use the natural world as her subject. More and more, however, she focused on social issues. When the United States got involved in the Vietnam War in the 1960's, Levertov's personal and poetic life reflected her social consciousness. With several other poets, she founded the Writers and Artists Protest Against the War in Vietnam. She participated in antiwar protest marches and was jailed at least once for her involvement. Her poetry and prose of the time reflect these interests. *The Sorrow Dance* (1967) has eight sections that show her increasing involvement in the antiwar movement.

The 1970 collection *Relearning the Alphabet* contains many poems protesting the war, but it also contains poems dealing with other social concerns, such as the Detroit riots and the famine in the African country of Biafra. Levertov's antiwar poetry was collected in the 1971 volume *To Stay Alive*; though well-crafted, these social and political poems did not receive as much critical acclaim as did her other work.

In the 1970's, Levertov continued to produce collections of poetry that show her technical, social, and spiritual development. She was divorced in 1972, and *The Freeing of the Dust* (1975) shows her journey toward a balance and integration in her life and verse.

In addition to her poetry, Levertov has also written essays and short articles, many of which have appeared in anthologies and journals. She has worked as an editor and translator, and she has also taught at Stanford University, the Massachusetts Institute of Technology, the City College of New York, and many other colleges. She has received numerous awards for her writing, including a Guggenheim Foundation Fellowship in 1962, a Lenore Marshall Poetry Prize in 1975, and an Elmer Holmes Bobst Award in 1983.

Analysis

In her collection of essays *The Poet in the World* (1973), Levertov explains the close connection between the poetic and the political: "A sense of history must involve a sense of the present, a vivid awareness of change, a response to crisis, a realization that what was appropriate in this or that situation in the past is inadequate to the demands of the present, that we are living our whole lives in a state of emergency which is unparalleled in all history." The poet cannot stand aside, ignoring these events happening around her, but must address these threats to humanity. Poetry is the appropriate medium to do this, because the poet can personalize these concerns.

In the same book, she discusses her craft. To write poetry is not simply to manipulate words; creating poetry requires the writer to transform personal experience into words by intuiting an order to the experience. The words result from intense perception and immersion in the experience. The action of saying something leads to further perception. Levertov's poems use concrete everyday language in a free verse form that is organic, growing from within the experience that gave rise to the words.

Levertov uses her political experiences as sources for many of her poems. She shies away from very little in the political arena, having written on topics such as pollution, the destruction of the rain forests, the acquired immune deficiency syndrome (AIDS) crisis, animal rights, and many others. In all these poems, Levertov juxtaposes images of life and nature with images of death so that the reader will personalize these events and, as she has done, make the political become personal. In "Silent Spring," from the 1984 volume *Oblique Prayers: New Poems with Fourteen Translations from Jean Joubert* (1984), she uses images of nature, personifying them so that the crisis, the death of the land from the use of poisons and insecticides, becomes transformed by her imagination into the death of all the natural world, including humankind. In "Thinking About El Salvador," from the same book, she finds the outrageous brutality of executions so overwhelming that the only appropriate response is silence. In "Rocky Flats," also from *Oblique Prayers*, she turns her attention to nuclear testing. She emphasizes the self-deception of those who work at carrying out the dangerous experiments and pretend that they are bringing new growth rather than potential destruction. Though critics who feel politics and poetry should remain apart have called her preachy, Levertov disagrees. She believes that people need poetry to help them deal with the changing events that make up history.

Because Levertov is so intensely immersed in these events, she can successfully turn them into poetry. In each poem, language and vision are equally dependent upon each other. Each experience has a form that the poet intuits, an order that perhaps she alone can see. In "Some Notes on Organic Form" (1965), she writes of a poetic process in which a cross-section of several experiences comes together in a moment. The poet is the person who can capture the experiences in words. The form that the resulting poem takes is determined by the experience. In "Carapace," from *Oblique Prayers*, she writes of the desire to retreat into a shell that will protect her from the horrors of people's inhumanity. The poem's stanzas are arranged so that longer lines enclose shorter ones, creating a visual carapace, or shell, in the text itself. In "Snail," from *Rearranging the Alphabet*, the form the poem takes imitates a snail's slow movement. In "A Marigold from North Vietnam," from the same book, the lines are disjointed, with large spaces between the images. The form imitates what was done not only to the country of Vietnam but also to the American spirit by the war. Levertov writes in free verse, but the form is internal. Therefore, there is definitely a form, but it is one that is free in that it is liberated from conventional verse forms.

With this perception of the interrelationship between form and content, the continual dynamics of their interaction, Levertov creates a body of poetry that is accessible to the reader. She uses common language and discusses common experiences such as childhood and the loss of family members as springboards for dealing with larger issues. She makes the political become the personal. In capturing authentic experiences in poetry, she shares her insights in a beautiful way.

THE STRICKEN CHILDREN

First published: 1987
Type of work: Poem

Returning to the scene of her happy childhood, the poet contemplates children who have lost their childhood.

In "The Stricken Children," from the 1987 collection *Breathing the Water*, Denise Levertov recalls her return to the wishing well of her childhood. During that time, the well was a clear bubbling spring less than three feet across, with a bank of rocks protecting it from falling leaves. It was the "smallest of grottoes," holding within it "pebbles of past wishes," some fulfilled, some not. People coming to the well did not throw money but searched "for the right small stone." This well was the place where, year after year, she returned to launch her journeys into the imagination. Like the spring, her childhood imagination could roam uncluttered, and the experiences she encountered nourished her.

When she returns as an adult, however, the wishing well has changed. She had hoped it would be familiar, merely older. Instead, it is "filled to the shallow brim/ with debris of a culture's sickness—/ with bottles, tins, paper, plastic—/ the soiled bandages/ of its aching unconsciousness." She wonders if the spring, so clogged, still flows, and if it was children who deposited the trash, children "who don't dream, or dismiss/ their own desires and/ toss them down, discarded packaging?"

She leaves quickly, for the urgency of her own dreams pushes her onward. She wonders, however, about the children of today, "the stricken children" who cannot find a source of nourishment for their dreams anywhere in the culture of throwaways. The past, the "grandmother wellspring" that gave the stability to dream and to act on dreams, has been, like the well, choked up. Modern culture has strangled the imagination of these children at exactly the time of life when they most need to develop it. More tragically, they have never known the life of the imagination and are unaware of "all they are doing-without."

Like many of Levertov's poems, "The Stricken Children" is easily accessible. She uses images of action, such as throwing pebbles into the well, and of objects, such as trash, to which all readers can relate. These things themselves are the springboards for meaning and ideas. She moves clearly through the three stanzas of the poem, beginning with the concrete physical description of the well and its surroundings, moving to her own personal response to the changes, and finally progressing to the more abstract level of contemplating the fate of all modern children.

This personal awareness of what her own childhood offered in nourishing her life has led Levertov to reexamine childhood itself in the light of the cultural and political climate that produces "stricken children." The world is violent, and this violence enters every life soon after birth. The child does not have time to develop an imagination or a sense of wonder. Levertov's poetry re-creates that wonder at the same time that it warns against the political and social consequences of careless actions.

CARAPACE

First published: 1984
Type of work: Poem

A person needs a protective shell to avoid the tragedies of life but, at the same time, needs to reach out for the experiences life offers.

In "Carapace," from *Oblique Prayers*, Levertov speaks about her response to the world's political tragedies. A carapace is the hard shell of an animal such as a turtle or crab that protects the soft inner part from harm and into which the animal can retreat if attacked. She announces that she herself is growing a shell, even though she regrets the shell-like exteriors of other people that render them insensitive to the world's problems. In the poem, she contemplates children. She begins as though the poet and a child were talking about a situation. The child has seen her own father shot by police; the poet asks the child if she knows what the word "subversive" means. The child replies that "the word means/ people who know their rights"; despite her youth, this child is already an adult, a product of modern inhumanity.

The poet then goes back to contemplating how well her shell is growing, "nicely, not very hard, just/ a thin protection but it's/ better than just skin." Speaking as though she could control the growing of a body part, she remarks that there will be chinks in the armor where the "plates don't quite meet."

Another child enters, this boy only nine years old. When asked how he feels about his missing father, who "has 'disappeared' three weeks now," he replies "with the shrug of a man of sixty." He only says that he is sad. The repeated violence the boy has seen in his short life has rendered him unemotional about even his own father.

The poem ends with the poet urging her shell to grow faster. At the same time, however, the world's problems intrude. Levertov is of two minds: She wants to hide from all the evil that destroys the wonder of the world; at the same time, she realizes that it is impossible to run and hide. If the shell encases her like a suit of armor, she will lose entirely the sensitivity to life and the will to try to change things.

This is clearly the political message of a poet responding not only to the explicit situations of missing persons in Central America but also to all inhumanity. The concrete situations and the dialogue, written in everyday language, paint clear images. A man is shot as he is escaping over a wall, and a young person responds to deep grief with only a shrug. The visual structure of the text itself resembles the subject, a shell. The two scenes with the children are inset, while the comments on the growth of the shell surround them, in the same way that the growing shell covers the vulnerable animal inside. The form and the subject mesh, as the poet arranges these scenes to force the reader to contemplate such inhumanity.

A NEW YEAR'S GARLAND FOR MY STUDENTS/MIT: 1969-70

First published: 1972
Type of work: Poem

Thirteen vignettes of students in a poetry seminar create precise portraits of young people developing into adults.

The thirteen sections of "A New Year's Garland for My Students/MIT: 1969-70," from the collection *Footprints*, were inspired by the students in a poetry seminar during Levertov's year as a visiting professor and poet-in-residence at the Massachusetts Institute of Technology. Each section is dedicated to one student, and each varies in length and line arrangement. Levertov captures the essence of the students by observing telling details and making frequent comparisons with nature.

In "Arthur," she sees a person at a stage in life when nothing seems to be happening. She compares him to the buds of trees and bushes that in winter go unnoticed. Yet the buds are there and are as complex and beautiful as are the "eventual silky leaves in spring." Using the word "silky" indicates her positive attitude toward his development. Silk is a fabric highly valued as well as smooth to the touch; the comparison calls to mind the lowly silkworm that produces the luxurious strands.

In "Bill," Levertov sees a questioner who can disturb the pleasant atmosphere by posing important but dark thoughts. She pictures a garden with a fence around it, but the fence has an open gate. Perhaps she is comparing this garden to the classroom, an enclosure that has an open atmosphere in its encouragement of creativity. The garden is pretty and stable, predictable. Yet in a dark corner lurk the "eyes of some animal" that interject an element of uncertainty into the pleasant surroundings. Like a sharp question that hits a sensitive topic in a discussion, this presence in the garden is disturbing, yet necessary.

Levertov sees herself in another student, "Judy." Because Judy is small and petite, she imagines her to be as light and airy as Greek goddesses or characters in the plays of William Shakespeare. The real Judy, as she sets off bundled up on a winter's evening, reminds the poet of herself at "12 years old,/ trudging home from the library lugging/ too many books, and seeing/ visions in Ilford High Road." As a child, the poet's active imagination turned the commonplace objects on city streets into things of beauty; she imagines Judy to have this same inner quality.

In "Ted," Levertov can see several different people, two clearly. Both are by the sea, but they perceive things differently. A young girl dances with joy and speaks brightly in the sunlight, but an old man, "who sits looking/ into a pit of terror," sees the sea as a horror of unseen terrors, and he is quiet. There are also other voices in Ted, but they must be quiet until the old man issues his "curse or warning." These other voices will wait until this stage in life is over before they rise to be heard.

In nature, a closer look reveals an intricacy unnoticed by the ordinary person and perhaps unrealized itself. In the case of her students, Levertov takes a close look beneath the surface to find their potential for imaginative development. As in her other poetry, Levertov uses experiences as springboards for description that reaches the essence of what is important in humanity. She obviously cares for these people and wants them to develop to their fullest.

Summary

In her 1981 book of essays *Light Up the Cave*, Denise Levertov states that politics are a poetic concern because they are a human concern, an integral part of daily life. A poet who is committed to affirming life is also bound to defend it against political threats of destruction.

The best of Levertov's poems in her more than forty books do just that. She writes in direct language, using organic forms appropriate to the contents of the poems. Throughout her career, Levertov's changing styles and explorations have brought her readers many moments of pleasure and enlightenment.

Bibliography

Gould, Jean. *Modern American Women Poets*. New York: Dodd, Mead, 1985.
Gwynne, R. S., ed. *American Poets Since World War II*. Vol. 5 in *Dictionary of Literary Biography*, edited by Matthew J. Bruccoli. Detroit: Gale Research, 1980.
Mills, Ralph. *Contemporary American Poetry*. New York: Random House, 1965.
Wagner, Linda W. *Denise Levertov*. New York: Twayne, 1967.
——————, ed. *Denise Levertov: In Her Own Province*. New York: New Directions, 1979.
Wilson, Robert A. *A Bibliography of Denise Levertov*. New York: Phoenix, 1972.

Louise M. Stone

CUMULATIVE LIST OF AUTHORS

CUMULATIVE LIST OF AUTHORS

MALAMUD, BERNARD, **4**-1276
MAMET, DAVID, **4**-1291
MARSHALL, PAULE, **8**-2610
MASTERS, EDGAR LEE, **4**-1302
MATTHIESSEN, PETER, **4**-1310
MELVILLE, HERMAN, **4**-1321
MERRILL, JAMES, **4**-1337
MERWIN, W. S., **8**-2619
MICHENER, JAMES A., **4**-1348
MILLAR, KENNETH. *See*
    MACDONALD, ROSS.
MILLER, ARTHUR, **4**-1363
MILLER, HENRY, **4**-1374
MOMADAY, N. SCOTT, **4**-1383
MOORE, BRIAN, **8**-2628
MOORE, MARIANNE, **4**-1394
MORRIS, WRIGHT, **4**-1408
MORRISON, TONI, **4**-1422
MOSLEY, WALTER, **8**-2636
MUKHERJEE, BHARATI, **4**-1435

NABOKOV, VLADIMIR, **4**-1448
NAYLOR, GLORIA, **4**-1463
NIN, ANAÏS, **4**-1473
NORRIS, FRANK, **4**-1485

OATES, JOYCE CAROL, **4**-1497
O'CONNOR, FLANNERY, **4**-1513
O'HARA, FRANK, **8**-2645
O'HARA, JOHN, **4**-1530
OLDS, SHARON, **8**-2654
OLSEN, TILLIE, **5**-1543
OLSON, CHARLES, **5**-1555
O'NEILL, EUGENE, **5**-1567
OPPEN, GEORGE, **8**-2662
OZICK, CYNTHIA, **5**-1583

PALEY, GRACE, **5**-1594
PERCY, WALKER, **5**-1606
PERSONS, TRUMAN STRECKFUS. *See*
    CAPOTE, TRUMAN.
PETRY, ANN, **8**-2670
PHILLIPS, JAYNE ANNE, **5**-1618
PLATH, SYLVIA, **5**-1626
POE, EDGAR ALLAN, **5**-1640
PORTER, KATHERINE ANNE, **5**-1655
PORTIS, CHARLES, **5**-1665
POTOK, CHAIM, **5**-1676

POUND, EZRA, **5**-1688
POWERS, J. F., **5**-1703
POWERS, RICHARD, **8**-2680
PRICE, REYNOLDS, **5**-1715
PYNCHON, THOMAS, **5**-1726

REED, ISHMAEL, **5**-1741
RICH, ADRIENNE, **5**-1753
RICHTER, CONRAD, **5**-1764
ROETHKE, THEODORE, **5**-1772
ROTH, PHILIP, **5**-1783
RUKEYSER, MURIEL, **8**-2689

SALINGER, J. D., **5**-1798
SANDBURG, CARL, **5**-1809
SAROYAN, WILLIAM, **5**-1817
SARTON, MAY, **8**-2698
SEXTON, ANNE, **8**-2707
SHANGE, NTOZAKE, **5**-1829
SHEPARD, SAM, **5**-1841
SILKO, LESLIE MARMON, **5**-1854
SIMON, NEIL, **5**-1862
SMILEY, JANE, **8**-2716
SMITH, LULA CARSON. *See*
    McCULLERS, CARSON.
SNYDER, GARY, **5**-1873
SONG, CATHY, **8**-2726
SOTO, GARY, **8**-2734
STAFFORD, JEAN, **8**-2742
STAFFORD, WILLIAM, **8**-2751
STEGNER, WALLACE, **8**-2760
STEIN, GERTRUDE, **8**-2768
STEINBECK, JOHN, **6**-1885
STEVENS, WALLACE, **6**-1900
STONE, ROBERT, **6**-1914
STOWE, HARRIET BEECHER, **6**-1926
STYRON, WILLIAM, **8**-2780
SWARTHOUT, GLENDON, **6**-1932

TAN, AMY, **8**-2789
THOREAU, HENRY DAVID, **6**-1942
TOOMER, JEAN, **8**-2798
TUROW, SCOTT, **8**-2808
TWAIN, MARK, **6**-1954
TYLER, ANNE, **6**-1972

UPDIKE, JOHN, **6**-1983

CXLI